THE OLDER TESTAMENT

THE OLDER TESTAMENT

The Survival of Themes from the Ancient
Royal Cult in Sectarian Judaism
and Early Christianity

Margaret Barker

Sheffield
Phoenix Press

First published in hardback by SPCK 1987
Reprinted in paperback by Sheffield Phoenix Press 2005

Sheffield Phoenix Press Ltd
Department of Biblical Studies
University of Sheffield
Sheffield S10 2TN

www.sheffieldphoenix.com

British Library Cataloguing in Publication Data

A catalogue record for this book is available from the British Library

Printed by Lightning Source UK Ltd

ISBN 1-905048-19-X

For
Robert Murray SJ

ἀστὴρ ἐν οὐρανῷ ἔλαμψεν
ὑπὲρ πάντας τοὺς ἀστέρας,
καὶ τὸ φῶς αὐτοῦ ἀνεκλάλητον ἦν
καὶ ξενισμὸν παρεῖχεν ἡ καινότης αὐτοῦ,
τὰ δὲ λοιπὰ πάντα ἄστρα
ἅμα ἡλίῳ καὶ σελήνη
χορὸς ἐγένετο τῷ ἀστέρι,
αὐτὸς δὲ ἦν ὑπερβάλλων τὸ φῶς αὐτοῦ ὑπὲρ πάντα ·
ταραχή τε ἦν,
πόθεν ἡ καινότης ἡ ἀνόμοιος αὐτοῖς.
ὅθεν ἐλύετο πᾶσα μαγεία
καὶ πᾶς δεσμὸς ἠφανίζετο κακίας ·
ἄγνοια καθηρεῖτο,
παλαιὰ βασιλεία διεφθείρετο
θεοῦ ἀνθρωπίνως φανερουμένου
εἰς καινότητα ἀϊδίου ζωῆς ·
ἀρχὴν δὲ ἐλάμβανεν τὸ παρὰ θεῷ ἀπηρτισμένον.
ἔνθεν τὰ πάντα συνεκινεῖτο
διὰ τὸ μελετᾶσθαι θανάτου κατάλυσιν.

Ignatius, To the Ephesians, 19

Up in the heavens a star gleamed out,
more brilliant than all the rest;
no words could describe its lustre,
and the strangeness of it left men bewildered.
All the other stars
and the sun and moon
gathered round it in chorus,
but this star outshone them all.
Great was the ensuing perplexity;
where could this newcomer have come from, so unlike its fellows?
Everywhere magic crumbled away before it;
the spells of sorcery were all broken,
and superstition received its deathblow.
The age-old empire of evil was overthrown,
for God was now appearing in human form
to bring in a new order, even life without end.
Now that which had been perfected in the Divine counsels began its work;
and all creation was thrown into a ferment
over this plan for the utter destruction of death.

(Translation by Maxwell Staniforth)

CONTENTS

Late Jewish scholarship was never of a purely linguistic type; its linguistic memories were maintained within the context of religious and legal interpretation, and this in turn may have reacted upon the senses ascribed to words in the biblical texts.

James Barr, *Comparative Philology and the Text of the Old Testament* (Oxford 1968), p. 43.

PREFACE

Having finished this book, I should like to thank those who have helped to make it possible: the University of Nottingham and Heythrop College for permission to use their libraries, and Judith Longman of SPCK for her help and interest. My greatest debt is to Robert Murray who first persuaded me to collect together ideas which had been accumulating in boxes for years. 'Write', he said, and he then read through several versions of an increasingly complicated text. The theme was first outlined in public in a paper to the Society for Old Testament Study in 1977, subsequently published in *JSOT* 15 (1980), and papers developing its implications for New Testament study have been read to Dr Ernst Bammel's seminar in Cambridge, and Prof. E. P. Sanders' in Oxford.

It would be impossible to mention all from whom I have learned, but two teachers from my Cambridge days must be mentioned: Hugh Montefiore and Ernst Bammel who, in their very different ways, taught me to think.

Mine is not a lifestyle which has long vacations and sabbaticals, and so I conclude with thanks to my husband, to my children who have grown up to the sound of a typewriter, and to Messrs Hotpoint, Hoover, Kenwood etc., without whom, in a very real way, this book could not have been written.

Margaret Barker
May 1986

ABBREVIATIONS

AA	Animal Apocalypse
AB	Astronomical Book
AM	Assumption of Moses
Ant.	*Antiquities* (Josephus)
Asc. Isa.	Ascension of Isaiah
ASTI	*Annual of the Swedish Theological Institute* (Jerusalem)
ATANT	Abhandlungen zur Theologie des Alten und Neuen Testaments
AV	Authorized Version
AW	Apocalypse of Weeks
BASOR	*Bulletin of the American Schools of Oriental Research*
BD	Book of Dreams
BDB	*A Hebrew and English Lexicon of the Old Testament*, ed. F. Brown, S. R. Driver, C. A. Briggs (Oxford 1907, 1953)
BETL	Bibliotheca ephemeridum theologicarum Lovaniensium
BH	Biblia Hebraica
B.J.	*Bellum Judaicum* (Josephus)
BJRL	*Bulletin of the John Rylands Library*
BW	Book of Watchers
BZAW	Beihefte zur *Zeitschrift für die alttestamentliche Wissenschaft*
CBQ	*Catholic Biblical Quarterly*
Con B	Coniectanea Biblica
DNB	Dictionary of National Biography
EE	Epistle of Enoch
ET	English Translation
ETL	*Ephemerides Theologicae Lovanienses*
ETR	*Etudes Théologiques et Religieuses*
ExpT	*Expository Times*
HeyJ	*Heythrop Journal*
HTR	*Harvard Theological Review*
HUCA	*Hebrew Union College Annual*
ICC	International Critical Commentaries
IDB	Interpreter's Dictionary of the Bible
JBL	*Journal of Biblical Literature*
JJS	*Journal of Jewish Studies*
JQR	*Jewish Quarterly Review*
JR	*Journal of Religion*
JRAS	*Journal of the Royal Asiatic Society*
JSJ	*Journal for the Study of Judaism*
JSNT	*Journal for the Study of the New Testament*
JSOT	*Journal for the Study of the Old Testament*
JSS	*Journal of Semitic Studies*
JTC	*Journal for Theology and the Church*
JTS	*Journal of Theological Studies*

ABBREVIATIONS

LXX	Septuagint
MT	Masoretic Text
NEB	New English Bible
NS	New Series
NT	*Novum Testamentum*
NTS	*New Testament Studies*
PBA	Proceedings of the British Academy
QE	Qumran Enoch
RB	*Revue Biblique*
RelStRev	*Religious Studies Review*
RQ	*Revue de Qumran*
RSR	*Recherches de Science Religieuse*
RSV	Revised Standard Version
SBL	Society of Biblical Literature
SBT	Studies in Biblical Theology
SJT	*Scottish Journal of Theology*
SOTS	Society for Old Testament Study
SPB	Studia Post-Biblica
SS	Similitudes of Enoch
SVT	Supplements to *Vetus Testamentum*
TEV	Today's English Version
UUA	Uppsala Universitets Årsskrift
VG	Vulgate
VigChr	*Vigiliae Christianae*
VT	*Vetus Testamentum*
WMANT	Wissenschaftliche Monographien zum Alten und Neuen Testament
ZAW	*Zeitschrift für die alttestamentliche Wissenschaft*
ZNW	*Zeitschrift für die neutestamentliche Wissenschaft*

QUMRAN REFERENCES

CD	Damascus Rule
4Q Amram	The Testament of Amram
1QapGen	Genesis Apocryphon
4QDeut	Deuteronomy
4QEn	Qumran Enoch
4QEnAstr	Qumran Enoch Astronomical text
1QH	Hymns (*Hodayoth*)
1QIsa	Isaiah Scroll
1QM	War Scroll
11QMelch	Melchizedek text
4Q Mess ar	Messianic Horoscope
1QS	Community Rule
1QSb	Appendix B (Blessings) to 1QS
4QTLevi	Testament of Levi

INTRODUCTION: THE PROBLEM AND THE METHOD

Biblical scholarship produces two types of study: the detailed monograph or article, which can advance our knowledge in one small area, and the wider survey which has to sacrifice detail in order to draw several strands together. This book falls into neither category, and as such has been difficult to write. I have tried to set out a new point of view. Ideally, this should have been presented in a series of articles, but this was not possible because the arguments used are closely interdependent over a wide range of material, and in isolated articles their significance would not have been clear. I have therefore combined the broad survey and the detailed treatment in one volume, offering a little of each. The result, I am well aware, is an odd mixture. The detailed passages need more detail, and the surveys have been reduced to the barest outline.

There is not space to acknowledge all who have influenced me, nor to refute in detail the positions I find untenable. This does not mean that such operations are not possible. I have not dealt with every aspect of every topic, since there are several aspects of contemporary scholarship which do not touch upon what I am trying to do, and it is pointless to survey in order to dismiss. What I have done is select from a wide range of material sufficient to formulate a theory which brings together many of the problems of this field, and presents them as different aspects of a fundamental misreading of the Old Testament. This misreading is one which has been forced upon us by those who transmitted the texts. Their scholarship was 'within the context of religious and legal interpretation, and this in turn may have reacted upon the senses ascribed to words in the biblical texts'.[1] In other words, the Old Testament texts may originally have had a different meaning from the one which we now suppose. Like Wittgenstein's lion, it speaks, but we cannot understand it – in this case because we have been told what it is saying. Add to this the fact that a high proportion of the opaque texts of the Old Testament seem to be dealing with the same subject matter, namely angels, stars, and the elements which surface in later apocalyptic, and we have grounds for taking a fresh look at the Old Testament and those who transmitted it.

The very complexity of New Testament scholarship tempts me to think that there is a large piece of the puzzle missing. We cannot create new evidence for our inquiries, but it is possible that the missing piece is already at hand, unrecognized because unexpected. The necessary preliminary to the search is the questioning of all expectations, in order to see which of them are based on

1

genuine evidence, and which upon frequently repeated deductions from that evidence. These deductions are necessarily determined by the presuppositions of the scholar in question, and they can become dangerous and distorting assumptions. I have considerable sympathy for the criticism of J. A. T. Robinson when he said that scholarship was under the tyranny of unexamined assumptions, and that several of the situations in the early Church were no more than creations of the critics, or at best highly subjective reconstructions.[2] The same must also be said of the Old Testament. It is introductory questions such as these which must be examined in great detail if scholarship is not to become dangerously unrelated to reality.[3]

There is also the danger of assuming that all the evidence necessary for the reconstruction of Christian origins has survived, or that it has survived in proportion to its original significance in the scheme. The argument from silence is dangerous, but never more so than when it is used to imply that the lost never existed.[4] The best we can do is outline the gaps in our knowledge and leave them clearly defined, rather than attempt to patch the obvious hole with the materials to hand. Subsequent theories can all too easily be built upon such a patch, until it becomes so overlaid with expertise that the dubious foundations are hidden. The heads which rolled after the publication of M. Hengel's *Son of God*, not least that of the gnostic redeemer, are a warning to all. Giants like Bultmann and Bousset, together with all their followers, were accused of repeating an argument *ad nauseam*, without verifying it adequately in the ancient sources. The basis of Hengel's attack was very simple. Was it likely, he asked, that this proposed paganization really took place? He produced a vast amount of evidence and argument to support his case, but it must not be forgotten that he began with the devastatingly simple insight that some things are just unlikely.[5]

In order to define the limits of what could have been possible in New Testament times, we need our background material, and we need to see this as part of a vast whole, rather than as a series of isolated parallels to the material we are examining. It is now several years since J. M. Robinson wrote of the collapse of the traditional categories in New Testament scholarship, and complained that background studies, whether Jewish, Greek or Gnostic, could not be effective when they were simply producing a series of disorganized parallels.[6] The important word is *disorganized*, because the organization of any thought-scheme conveys as much by the shape and arrangement of the component parts as by the parts themselves. If treated as random ideas, a great deal of their import is lost. Perhaps we do not need more information for our background studies, but rather an attempt to see both the texts and their background in a less fragmented way, giving due weight to the relationship between the pieces, and to the spaces between the facts. It is quite possible that our New Testament texts, representing as they do the earliest stages of a new thought-system, may only tell of the parts of that system which differ from the one whence it sprang. Thus the *greater part* of these early Christian beliefs could have been lost, simply because they were too widely accepted to merit any written comment. There would have been scope for disagreement over the new and different parts, and it is important for our reconstructions to bear in mind just how much of the New Testament *was* written to clarify areas of misunderstanding. We must also remember that much of it was written for people outside Palestine, even though the events on which it was based were part of the fabric of Palestinian society. The most pessimistic position could see much of the New Testament as a record of the misunderstandings of those adherents of Christianity who were divorced from the background events which gave significance to the life and death of Jesus, and also from the context of his original teaching.

All but one of the New Testament writers were men of Palestine, in Paul's case an adopted son. The reason for their writing, and for the whole of their mission, was that they believed that something significant had happened in the life and death of Jesus. This belief was not the bald fact of certain events having occurred. An interpretation had been put upon these events, and it was this *interpretation* which prompted the mission.

The Christianity which went out into the gentile world was divorced from its original context, and when we encounter it in its new setting, it may well have shed much of the background which formed the original impact. New methods of teaching and contact will have been adopted. What we do not know is the level at which these adaptations were made. Were the facts of the life and death of Jesus made significant for a new environment, or was it the interpretation put upon those facts which was transferred? If, as we usually assume, it was the *interpretation* of the facts which was preached, i.e. that the life and death of Jesus had been seen by certain people in Palestine as significant, then we have to uncover in the New Testament not one but two layers of interpretation. This point was made in another context by H. Koester, in the preface to his examination of the early pictures of Jesus. These interpretations, these statements of faith from earlier periods *'became substitutes for, rather than expressions of, the substance of the historical revelation in and through Jesus'*.[7] The preaching which went beyond Palestine was the preaching of a Palestinian interpretation, which means that to understand the origin of the earliest Christian imagery, even that which we cannot obviously identify as *Jewish*, we must confine our search to Palestine. The Greek ideas in the New Testament, where they can be identified with certainty, are evidence of a second layer of interpretation, which must not be seen as expressing the work of Jesus in terms of contemporary paganism, but rather as making a less sophisticated equation between something familiar to the new converts, and something present in the existing Palestinian interpretation. This practice of finding pagan parallels had been common amongst Jewish writers for many generations, as can be seen in their surviving writings.[8] It is an extraordinary fact that many of the un-Jewish ideas occur in passages which seem to be quotations of some sort, e.g. the so-called hymns in the Pauline letters. These unfamiliar ideas must have been native to Palestine, if they became the vehicle for the new theology so quickly.

The speed with which the earliest Christian ideas developed is another indication that they were an adaptation of, or a growth upon, an existing system. M. Hengel makes this point in his discussion of Phil. 2.6–8:

> The 'apotheosis of the crucified Jesus' must already have taken place in the forties, and one is tempted to say *that more happened in this period of less than two decades than in the whole of the next seven centuries, up to the time when the doctrine of the early church was completed.* Indeed, one might even ask whether the formation of doctrine in the early church was essentially more than a consistent development and completion of what had already been unfolded in the primal event of the first two decades, but in the language and thought-forms of Greek, which was its necessary setting.[9]

It is not disputed that the language was Greek. What has yet to be proved is that the Greek thought-forms were an original interpretation, and not just a usable parallel to the earlier Palestinian interpretation. Jeremias' excavations through the layers in the parables have shown very clearly that the teachings of Jesus were adapted to the newer needs of the community, and that the original significance of the parables was not infrequently lost in this development. If a similar process affected the teachings about Jesus, and the image chosen to express the original point was retained at the expense of the point itself, this would explain the apparent paganization of Christianity. There was not, in Hengel's words, 'a syncretistic paganization of Christianity among the spiritual leaders ... such as the former scribe and Pharisee Paul'.[10]

My unease about this aspect of New Testament scholarship originated not with Hengel (despite his saying the same thing), but with the reading of Steiner's *Death of Tragedy*, in which he says this, albeit not of New Testament writers:

> When the artist must be the architect of his own mythology, time is against him. He cannot live long enough to impose his special vision *and the symbols he has devised for it* on the habits of language and the feelings in his society ... without an orthodox or public frame to support it ... it does not take root in the common soil ... A mythology crystallizes sediment accumulated over great stretches of time, and gathers into conventional form the primal memories and the historical experiences of the race. Being the speech of the mind when it is in a state of wonder or perception, the great myths are elaborated as slowly as time itself.[11]

Where, then, are we to look for the origin of the New Testament imagery labelled Greek or pagan on the grounds that it is not Jewish? This is the most fundamental of the introductory questions, since, without a knowledge of the frame of reference, there can be no understanding of the points within it. The allusions will escape us, and the signs, parables and works will be interpreted because they are a part of our tradition, and not because they are in themselves significant pointers. Why was the resurrection interpreted in the way that it was? For whom did this manner of expression have significance? It must have been *unexpected*, if the gospel accounts are to be believed, but it cannot have been *inconsistent* with the expected pattern of events, or it would not have been recognized as significant, and in need of interpretation. The first interpretations of the crucifixion provide an invaluable indication of the thought-forms of the first Christians, and yet we are loth to root the supernatural conflict imagery in a Palestinian setting. Similarly, there is the recurring astral and angelic material, present right through the New Testament, and beyond it.[12] It is unlikely that the events of the life and death of Jesus could have found expression at a very early date only in terms of a mythology alien to the setting in which the events occurred. Mythology and interpretation cannot arise simultaneously.

Unless the pre-Easter and post-Easter followers of Jesus were two completely different sets of people, it should be possible to establish, within broad limits, the type of people who made the first interpretation of the death and resurrection. Our eyes must not be dazzled by the Pauline picture, because one of the few things that we do know about Jesus' first followers is that the Pharisees, men of Paul's background, had little but contempt for them and their ideas. The gospel sources make it abundantly clear what sort of people came to hear Jesus, and yet we still spend a great deal of time and energy upon the pursuit of parallels in the thinking of just that group by whom Jesus is known to have been rejected. The thinking of these people has survived in greatest quantity, but this in itself is a warning. What happened to everything else?

A more fruitful approach might be to remove all the recognizably Pharisaic elements from the writings of Paul, and then see what is left. This would very possibly be what Paul found *in* Christianity, the faith to which he was converted on the Damascus road, and which he developed and changed in the light of his own experiences. We have to find something appropriate for a group of Galileans, relevant to their needs and aspirations, but sufficiently coherent (and even recognizable) to draw the hostility of Jerusalem Judaism, as a threat to the Law. We know that his contemporaries put several interpretations upon the ministry of Jesus, and the Gospels record several which were rejected. Is it possible that amongst all those who were attempting to make sense of what they had seen there was none who operated within the same thought scheme as Jesus himself? Jesus and his first followers *must* have operated within the same thought-scheme, if the ministry was seen as a revelation and not as an irrelevance. The single, original insight underlies all the tangled mass of later interpretations, and the diversity comes from transferring the insight to a new environment. Much of the original framework is probably still present in the New Testament, unrecognized because it does not break the surface. Our task is to reconstruct a background *quite independent of New Testament considerations*, appropriate to the world of Jesus' first followers, and *known to exist as a single set of ideas* which threatened the Law. It is pointless to trawl the ancient world for evidence of cosmic powers and redeemer figures if these cannot be seen as an integral part of the scheme whose *strength was the claim to being the true heirs of the ancient Palestinian tradition.*

In order to reconstruct such a background, it is necessary to dig deep, and to work back through the writings of several centuries. I shall begin with the pseudepigraphon known as 1 Enoch (Ethiopic Enoch), and shall then devote the rest of this book to establishing the antecedents of this work, which is known to have been used by the earliest Christians. It is possible that the origins of the New Testament are entirely unrelated to the ultimate origins of 1 Enoch, but the extraordinary parallels which have emerged in the course of this investigation suggest that the theology of 1 Enoch and its complex relationship to that of Jerusalem Judaism are fundamental to our understanding of the New Testament. It is not conventional to establish the relationship between the Old and New Testaments by studying the processes which formed Job, or Deuteronomy, or the symbolism of the Temple; but in order to discover the forces which formed the Jerusalem Judaism of New Testament times, and its reciprocal, the theology of 1 Enoch, we have to go back through five centuries.

The link between Old and New is far more complex than the use of proof texts and the fulfilment of prophecies. These are the tip of an iceberg whose greater part remains invisible. I have tried to reconstruct the invisible mass from its effects which are perceived. Thereby I have left myself open to the charge of going beyond the evidence. The outline offered results from projecting given positions and problems back to the point of their confluence and solution. Whether or not this is an acceptable method remains to be seen.

I was drawn to these extra-canonical writings initially by curiosity, and by an instinctive rejection of the 'chosen people' mentality of the Old Testament. This developed into a bond of sympathy with those whom the establishment chose to reject, and a realization that their mythology was not so alien as its bizarre imagery invites us to suppose, provided that it is allowed to speak for itself, and is not interpreted by the Old Testament norms as we now know them. This mythology underlies the creation theology of Romans 8, the exorcisms and miracles of the Gospels, the heavenly archetypes of Hebrews, and the first Temple imagery of the Fourth Gospel. It is the imagery of Revelation, Jude and the Petrine Epistles, and the song of its angels became the Sanctus of the eucharistic liturgy. Little of this is derived directly from Enoch; the process rather has been one of following the Enochic stream to its source, and seeing what other waters have flowed from it, and were once a part of something much more complex than can be deduced from any one of the writings in which the various parts survive. There is a unity behind the diversity of fringe traditions in both the pre- and post-Christian writings, indicating that the point of reference should *not* be something which shows them as a variety of unrelated oddities. The life and work of Jesus were, and should be, interpreted

6

in the light of something *other* than Jerusalem Judaism. This *other* had its roots in the conflicts of the sixth century BC when the traditions of the monarchy were divided as an inheritance amongst several heirs. It would have been lost but for the accidents of archaeological discovery and the evidence of pre-Christian texts preserved and transmitted *only by Christian hands.*

NOTES

1 Barr (1968), p. 43.
2 Robinson (1976), p. 345.
3 cf. Murray (1982b), p. 195: 'I have become convinced that "early catholicism" is a German Protestant construct, of more use in ecumenical anatomy than in New Testament study.' This article is an excellent outline of the dangers of presupposition in the business of recovering Christian origins.
4 Stanton (1974), p. 5.
5 Hengel (1976), *passim.*
6 Robinson and Koester (1971), p. 13; also Sandmel (1962) on the danger in New Testament studies of collecting parallels to an isolated New Testament, and formulating unreal questions as a result; and Alexander (1983), p. 246: 'Elements must be considered within the system to which they belong and in which they function.' The problem for New Testament scholars is deciding to which system their materials belong. 'There is little to be gained by talking globally about the teachings of early Judaism' (ibid.).
7 Robinson and Koester (1971), p. 203. My italics.
8 Hengel (1974), I, pp. 83ff; Braun (1938).
9 Hengel (1976), p. 2.
10 ibid., p. 18.
11 Steiner (1961), p. 322.
12 Matt. 2; Luke 10.18; Mark 13.24–5; 2 Pet. 1.19; Jude 13; Rev. *passim*; Ignatius, *Ad Eph.* 19. Also Black (1982), which raises the question of the origin of the powers.

1

THE BOOK OF ENOCH

The book we call 1 Enoch is a collection of five Enochic works extant in Ethiopic, and brought to light by Bruce in the early nineteenth century.[1] The five parts are: The Book of Watchers (BW), the Similitudes (SS), the Astronomical Book (AB), the Book of Dreams (BD) which includes the Animal Apocalypse (AA), and the Epistle of Enoch (EE) which incorporates the Apocalypse of Weeks (AW). Much of BW, EE, and a small amount of BD are known in Greek,[2] and there are now the remains of eleven MSS in Aramaic from Qumran, covering all but the SS, as well as some Hebrew fragments of chs. 6—11.[3] An Enochic text named by Milik The Book of Giants was also found, similar to a work known previously from Manichean material. The AB in Aramaic is much longer than the Ethiopic, one of several indications that the later Enochic material was less elaborate than its antecedents, that the Enochic was a declining, rather than a developing, tradition.

Other works are also associated with Enoch: 2 Enoch, which has been preserved in Church Slavonic, is in many respects similar to 1 Enoch; 3 Enoch, the Hebrew Enoch, is one of the Merkabah texts.[4] (All these names are labels given by modern scholars to the texts.) Thus it is clear that the Ethiopic Enoch is neither unique, nor a definitive collection of Enochic material. A comparison of the Qumran and Ethiopic texts shows that the tradition developed and changed; materials were added, others left out. Although I wish to deal here only with 1 Enoch, this cannot be done in isolation from the ongoing and preceding contexts of the tradition.

One of the contexts was early Christianity, which must influence our understanding of both Enoch and early Christianity. It is naive to say that 1 Enoch was an embarrassment to the early Church because it was not canonical and contained some very odd ideas.[5] It has been preserved from the time of Qumran only by Christian hands, which must be significant, and our failure to find a real place for the Enochic tradition in our picture of Christian origins is a good example of blinkered scholarship. The Old Testament is *not* the only ancient authority that New Testament writers recognize or cite, despite what we have been told.[6] 1 Enoch is quoted in Jude as prophecy. The early churches used 1 Enoch as anti-Jewish polemic, even though its symbolism was not fully understood.[7] In the Ethiopian church it became part of the canon, having come in the baggage of the first missionaries, who were monophysite refugees from Syria.[8] Now if it was these Semitic Christians who preserved 1 Enoch, when the European ones by and large did not, the work must have had a particular

8

significance for them. The silence of the Talmuds on the subject of Enoch is doubly interesting.[9]

If we are restricted to using only those portions of Enoch recovered at Qumran, there is little to work on. If, on the other hand, we use the corresponding sections of the Ethiopic Enoch, we have to establish that the later text is a reasonable rendering of the earlier. The Aramaic remains can only be related to less than one fifth of the Ethiopic text, 196 verses out of 1062;[10] but this ratio gives a false impression, because it is not a true comparison. It compares a whole text with fragments. If we make a true comparison, like with like, and compare each Aramaic portion with its Ethiopic counterpart, almost three quarters show a reasonable correspondence. This is a sufficiently high figure for us to use the Ethiopic text when the Aramaic is not extant, provided that we bear in mind the fact that the text was not static. The relationship of the Aramaic, Greek and Ethiopic texts is much debated; comparative studies have shown that the Ethiopic is often periphrastic or confused, and no great structures can be built upon its finer points.[11] Nevertheless, it is a large body of material and is, as Charles said, the most important of the pre-Christian pseudepigrapha.[12]

1 Enoch cannot be isolated from a whole host of related texts. In Jude, for example, there are quotations not only from Enoch but also from the Assumption of Moses (AM). The early Christian writers knew a longer text of AM than is now extant. Ours lacks the passage quoted by Jude in which the devil and Michael dispute possession of the body of Moses.[13] Such of AM as we do have, however, links it beyond any doubt to a widely known and complex tradition about the angels and the last judgement, which is now lost.[14] Jude wrote within this lost tradition, of which Enoch was a part, and we can only assume that this lost tradition was of great importance to the earliest Christians. Until we can make some attempt to reconstruct what is lost, our picture of early Christianity may be sadly astray. I propose to use 1 Enoch as a way into this reconstruction. One could start from many points, but since 1 Enoch is the largest text, and contains some very old material, it provides a broad basis from which to begin.

Ethiopic Enoch divides into five sections, each with a very different character, but all, as I shall show, sharing a common theology.

(i) The Book of Watchers (1–36)[15] tells of the fall of various angels, and the ascent and heavenly travels of Enoch. The oldest fragments of this section have been dated to the first half of the second century, but we cannot assume that they were an original composition at this time.

(ii) The Similitudes (37–71) describe the Son of Man and the great judgement. They have not been found at Qumran. Their place is taken, according to Milik, by the *Book of Giants*. It is unwise to assume that what is not at Qumran did not exist. The Testaments of the Twelve Patriarchs and the Epistle of Barnabas quoted from Enochic material which is not at Qumran,[16] nor in any other known Enochic text.

(iii) The Astronomical Book (72–82) is a treatise on astronomy and the calendar. The four Qumran texts are much fuller than the Ethiopic, and were always on separate scrolls, rather than joined to the other Enochic texts. The earliest MS has been dated at the end of the third century, the latest at the beginning of the Christian era. It was a work of some importance, and is the oldest known Enochic text.

(iv) The Book of Dreams (83–90) tells the history of Israel as a complex animal fable. The earliest material from this section is from the early second century.

(v) The Epistle of Enoch (91–108) consists mainly of prophetic woes upon the wicked, but it contains some older material known as the Apocalypse of Weeks, a history of Israel presented as a series of weeks.

To those brought up in the ways of the Old Testament, 1 Enoch is bizarre and surreal. Parts of it seem familiar, but the context is wrong, and everywhere there are alien forms. Drawn naturally to what is familiar, we have taken the Old Testament as our norm, and attempted to expound 1 Enoch on this basis. The results have not been satisfactory, for although individual elements have been isolated and identified, the overall pattern is still unknown. Some even imply that there is no pattern at all – that 1 Enoch is just a collection of apocryphal traditions, following the style of Daniel.[17] Our own approach to the text may prove to be an insuperable barrier to understanding it, for the processes of modern scholarship are such that those competent to handle and translate these ancient texts are not always those who have a natural affinity with, or even sympathy for, their contents. The modern wise man and his ancient counterpart live in very different worlds. Ancient and modern ideas of knowledge do not coincide, and the ancient processes of perception have little in common with our own. The standards by which these texts are prepared and scrutinized are not those by which they must be absorbed and understood. This has been recognized for some time, although little has changed as a result, as James Barr has illustrated by a series of quotations. F. C. Burkitt's obituary of R. H. Charles in 1931 noted this defect:

> If he came to have any respect for an ancient author he was unwilling to believe that such a person could have entertained conceptions which to Charles' trained mind were 'mutually exclusive', and his favourite explanation was to posit interpolations and a multiplicity of sources, each of which may be supposed to have been written from a single and consistent point of view.

Similarly, T. W. Manson said of Charles that, despite his vast and accurate knowledge (which has yet to be bettered), 'the language of apocalyptic remained a foreign language to him'. There has grown up a dangerous tendency to substitute erudition for insight, and to assume that one's own expertise must be the key to the mystery of the apocalypses:

> The study of apocalyptic literature has been plagued by the tendency of scholars who are specialists in *other* areas to reduce the apocalyptic works to the area of their speciality.

This results in the wildly precise speculations of the German tradition, well exemplified by Barr in his choice of a passage from Jürgen Moltmann:

> While apocalyptic does not conceive its eschatology in cosmological terms, yet that is not the end of eschatology, but the beginning of an eschatological cosmology or eschatological ontology for which being becomes historic and the cosmos opens itself to the apocalyptic process.[18]

– which, says Barr, reminds one of Enoch's place where 'things were chaotic' (1 En. 20.1). Or it can result in the revealing remarks of some American scholars. A recent comprehensive study on Enoch speaks of its authors' interests tending towards '*pseudo*-scientific subjects such as cosmology', and concludes that the *scholars* who produced the earliest Jewish apocalypses '*raided* more sources than just divinatory ones'. A recent study of apocalyptic origins concluded that wisdom was wedded to eschatology in order to improve its image. The visionaries cloaked 'their eschatological message in an aura of eruditeness which helped to establish their authoritativeness'. Again, a major edition of Gnostic material says that 'theological interest is *blurred* by scholarly curiosity in fields such as cosmography, astronomy and meteorology'.[19]

In sharp contrast is a modern writer on alchemy (a tradition in which Enoch is honoured), whose approach can, I think, teach us much about the world view of the apocalypses:

> It involves a quest for knowledge which encompasses the divine as well as the material realm, and, indeed, does not perceive a division between them ... Alchemists aspired to make a perfect elixir of gold which would bring immortality to the soul and supernatural powers to the mind such as the ability to tap the knowledge of the celestial beings ... A person will receive and understand an idea according to his own cultural background, and the age in which he lives.[20]

Or again, from the introduction to a modern work on white magic:

> After a degree of exploration of the inner self ... the development of the awareness of the control of consciousness, the westerner soon realizes that he lacks the vocabulary to identify the various states he attempts to enter and induce, though the experiences are real enough. As a result he turns to words and concepts borrowed from other cultures, or develops new meanings for existing words ... European languages have a poor capacity to handle the more important and deeper levels of the control of consciousness ... The charge that occult rituals are too often a hopeless amalgam of the dubious dross of cultures throughout history, and hence invalid, is

11

easily sustained by the cultural historian or anthropologist, but it misses the point. The test of the ritual is the effect it has on the performer.[21]

Those who write within a similar tradition have a very different view of the situation, and their approach should be taken seriously, because their world is nearer to that of 1 Enoch than is the world of the modern Old Testament scholar.[22] Alchemy, magic or shamanism are relevant to this inquiry, not because there is any direct contact between, for example, the Eskimo shaman and Enoch, but because, at the deeper level, they use the same language, the language which remained foreign to R. H. Charles; they had the same logic, and, as I shall show, their 'knowledge' covered the same fields to a remarkable degree.

Other impediments to our understanding Enoch are that we have assumed its *dependence* upon the Old Testament, and have presumed to define what is the proper content of an apocalypse.[23] Thus we have called Daniel the archetypal apocalypse, *because it is canonical*,[24] but even Daniel has been thought misguided due to its author's ignorance of the true meaning of the Old Testament![25] Having defined apocalyptic in terms of either wisdom or prophecy, each in its turn defined by the Old Testament examples,[26] we find that Daniel cannot be made to fit the picture of apocalyptic. He was famed as a *wise* man, he wrote *histories* in the form of prophecies, which placed him in the Alexandrian canon among the *prophets*, and was then taken as the model *apocalypse*. Features of Enoch which resembled the Old Testament were assumed to be drawn from it.[27] Enoch *interprets* Genesis, Jubilees *adds* to Genesis, an author *fleshes out* the Genesis material, the Similitudes are a *midrash* on Gen. 6 and Isa. 24, the Merkabah texts are *transformations* of what is hinted at in the Old Testament.[28] Closer study of 1 Enoch in recent years has begun to alter these assumptions. An *unexpected* light has been shed on third-century Judaism.[29] Ascent visions and scientific interests had not been part of the received picture of what went on at the time. It is now thought that the apocalyptic writers may have had their own way of reading the Old Testament, their own exegetical tradition.[30] A lost tradition is being recovered from the para-biblical works.[31] No longer can a firm line be drawn between wisdom and prophecy,[32] and so on.

The rediscovery of 1 Enoch, and the beginning of serious study, has forced a reappraisal of the nature of Judaism in the pre-Christian centuries. The classic position was that the apocalyptic works were sectarian because they were not the Judaism of the Pharisees,[33] but now there are fewer certainties about the Pharisees. We cannot be sure that there was a direct link between the Rabbinic tradition and the pre-70 Pharisees. The reconstructions of the period may well be based upon 'massive and sustained anachronisms in the use of Rabbinic sources'.[34] We have insufficient knowledge to retain our old labels with any confidence. Everything has to be reviewed and relabelled with extreme caution.[35]

Although there is general agreement on what are apocalyptic texts, and what not,[36] there is, curiously, no accepted definition of apocalyptic. The various suggestions made have had a Procrustean effect upon 1 Enoch, and parts of the text which did not fit the definition were pruned away to make a better fit. Thus, when apocalyptic was synonymous with eschatology,[37] the wisdom elements were thought to be peripheral,[38] or late additions. If apocalyptic is a genre of revelatory literature,[39] AB in its final form qualifies only with difficulty, and the original not at all.[40] Its archaic and restrained eschatology, dealing only with the great judgement, disqualifies 1 En. 1–5, which stands rather in the tradition of the prophets and the wise men.[41] A detailed investigation of apocalyptic and divination does not deal with Enoch.[42] I wonder if the time has not come when we should abandon the search for definitions, and accept each text on its own terms. The search has served to draw attention to the importance of a phenomenon once deemed peripheral, and we must now reassess everything in the light of the new discoveries. The details of what we call apocalyptic may never be fully known, and we may have to content ourselves with less than precision, if this is the price of keeping these ancient works intact.

We also tend to assume that what has survived is a proportional representation of the ancient system, even though we know that our sources within the canon are carefully edited texts, and that outside it we have only the accidents of history. The light which the Enochic texts threw on the third century was *unexpected*[43] precisely because our expectations had not been formed upon a proper basis. We had assumed the Old Testament to represent everything that there was; an interest in scientific matters, or the ascent visions of the later mystics, were not even considered. Could we but reconstruct the system in which these scientific interests and mystical ascents had their natural setting, we should, I have no doubt, throw unexpected light on even earlier centuries, and discover aspects of the Old Testament we have never before considered.

Our task is to reconstruct a living system from some of its bones. The system can only be seen in its various contexts, but it must be distinguished from them, and indeed, from all the parallels to its component parts.[44] Since we do not know the extent or the content of the Enochic tradition, we must describe it only on its own terms, and not allow our approach to be determined or distorted by unacknowledged assumptions. We do not know for certain that everything legitimate was represented in the Old Testament. We cannot then deduce that what is not rooted in it had its origin elsewhere. By looking at ways in which the Enochic material was used in later times, it may be possible to discern something of its origins, even if these origins cannot be deduced directly from the Old Testament. Again, we cannot be certain that the later emphases were direct and legitimate developments of an earlier tradition, but a pattern does emerge from the later contexts of Enochic material which makes it likely that the tradition originated in the royal cult. The royal cult is something of which the Old Testament tells us very little; we know that there were kings for some four centuries, but the literature which describes that period is curiously silent about several things. We must ask why this is so, since the answer to that question could well answer also the question of apocalyptic origins.

The Manicheans used Enochic material.[45] Their Book of Giants is related to the Book of Giants found at Qumran. They also quoted from an Apocalypse of Enoch which is no longer extant.[46] An extreme dualism such as characterized their tradition was compatible with the Enochic material.

The Western Hermetic tradition also gave an honoured place to Enoch and his angels. There are many points of contact between the Enoch figure and Metatron,[47] and again between the Enoch figure and Hermes.[48] The concern of the very earliest Enochic material is also that of the later alchemists, namely the working of metals and the extraction of juices from plants, by means of a knowledge which encompassed the divine as well as the material worlds.[49] The nature of magic is complex, and ancient magic still imperfectly understood;[50] but the fundamental myth of the Enochic material is that of binding evil angels. This is apotropaic magic of a Mesopotamian type, and raises questions of what else may have been implicit in the Enochic tradition. Angel lists are very important in the texts, because it was knowing the names of the angels which gave power over them. It is unlikely that so developed a demonology as we find in 1 Enoch existed without an associated system of protection and control. The Jews were famed as magicians who worshipped angels, and the name of their God passed into the Mediterranean world as a particularly potent force. Perhaps it was the Jews themselves who were the first to use it thus, and with good effect. Magic must be seen as one of the contexts of Enoch, and we cannot presume to say at what date the Enochic material acquired these associations.[51]

Closely related to magic are the Merkabah texts, one of which, 3 Enoch, is thought to have been edited into its present form in order to remove material used in magical practices and excessive details about the divine throne. Was the cult of the throne associated with magic?[52] Merkabah mysticism was a development within Judaism of the pre-70 apocalyptic, and although the proportions differ, the elements are unmistakable.[53] The oldest Merkabah vision outside the Old Testament is in 1 En. 14, yet 'in the whole of the two Talmuds and the Tannaitic Midrashim, not a single mention of Enoch is to be found'.[54] Merkabah mysticism was known to the Rabbis, and the teaching in the mystical texts is attributed to R. Akiba and R. Ishmael, yet there is a tension between them and the teaching of the Talmuds and Midrashim.[55]

Important in the Merkabah texts is a heavenly figure installed as a great prince and ruler of all princes (3 En. 10.3–6), authorized to act with the authority of God himself. The history of the figure is complex, but royal roots seem likely.[56] A similar heavenly figure appears in the Similitudes, who is identified eventually with Enoch himself, as though the figure was a heavenly reality and Enoch its earthly referent. Fragmentary texts from Qumran identify the heavenly figure as Melchizedek, and invest him with the power which the

Old Testament reserves for Yahweh. Whatever underlies this heavenly figure (and over the centuries there will no doubt have been developments), there seems to be one ideal: the Metatron figure has divine authority, the Melchizedek figure is described by texts which originally referred to Yahweh. If this figure was rooted in a royal cult, it will have been a cult where the king had divine authority, where he was an intermediary figure with more than human status. It is this royal imagery in particular which distinguishes the later Merkabah material from the Gnostic texts with which it is often compared. Scholem described it as 'a Judaised form of cosmocratorial mysticism concerning the divine king', and emphasized the enormous gulf between the system of the Hekhaloth and that of the Gnostics. He described the Merkabah experience as a celestial vision which 'originally proceeded from an attempt to transform what is casually alluded to in the Bible into direct personal experience', but he also pointed out that the oldest mystical writings were almost entirely free of exegesis, and therefore not directly based upon the Bible. Is it then possible that the allusions in the Bible were not *transformed*, but accurately preserved in their original form in the apocalyptic/Enochic tradition?[57]

If the Hermetic and Merkabah contexts were legitimate developments within the Enochic tradition, we should expect to find its roots not only in a royal tradition with a more-than-human king figure, but in a royal tradition where magical powers belonged to the divine agent. Solomon was remembered thus; Josephus describes him as the originator of exorcism in Israel, the composer of beneficial incantations, and a student of properties of the world of nature.[58]

For our purposes, the most significant of the contexts of 1 Enoch was the Christian. Until the tradition is more fully explored and understood, the extent of its use by the early Church will remain obscure. We cannot, however, assume that its bizarre world was as embarrassing to the first Christians as it is to some modern commentators. It is this uneasiness about the Enochic material which has coloured so many approaches, and made it all too easy to attribute the angels and the supernatural figures to foreign sources, whilst assuming that the demands for social justice and the woes upon sinners were the legitimate fruit of the ancient religion of Israel.[59] Similar tendencies have been at work in our reading of the Gospels. If the Enochic tradition was rooted in a royal cult, a great deal of the picture of Jesus begins to fit together very well. He was hailed as a king and a miracle worker, and remembered as a magician with extraordinary powers.[60] The Son of Man figure also occurs in the Christian tradition, but is not necessarily directly related to, or derived from, the Similitudes. The idea that linear dependence is the only possible model assumes that the Son of Man material all derives from one very small and closely knit group. But if, as is apparent in the Similitudes, there was a whole spectrum of such traditions, we have to consider the possibility that all derive from a common source, sufficiently ancient for divergences to have developed, and sufficiently important for the traditions to have persisted in several forms.

At its very broadest, we have to look for a context for the Enochic tradition which could have given rise to a royal/messianic/intermediary figure, magical practices, dualism, mystical ascents and the cult of the throne of God.

Any analysis of 1 Enoch must distinguish between the figure of Enoch itself and the lore and mythology with which he is associated. Both are touched upon briefly in the Old Testament. The figure appears twice in Genesis, and the angel myth explicitly in Gen. 6, Isa. 14 and Ezek. 27, although it underlies a great deal of the Old Testament, as I shall show. *The figure of Enoch is not associated with the mythology in the Old Testament* – suggesting, as does the complexity of the intermediary figure, that Enoch was grafted into another tradition.

The Figure of Enoch

Enoch appears in two genealogies; in the Cainite (J) version of Gen. 4, where he is the third from Adam, and in the Sethite (P) version of Gen. 5, where he is the seventh. It is assumed that P altered the older tradition in order to make Enoch the seventh and therefore the significant patriarch. He became the Emenduranki figure, 'The Jewish literary crystallization of Sumero-Akkadian lore about the seventh antediluvian *king* . . . the founder of a guild of diviners'.[61] This implies that the Enoch of Gen. 4 is the older figure. The tradition which P developed must have had reason for choosing Enoch as the appropriate patriarch to assume the role of the legendary diviner king. Why was someone necessary for this role in Israel? Why were diviner kings not quietly forgotten, especially as diviners are so roundly condemned in the Old Testament?[62] It has been suggested that the P writer saw in the name *Enoch* the idea of *wisdom*, and that this triggered the association.[63] The alternative is that the name was from *ḥnk*, 'dedicate', and that the primary tradition was of a man who built and dedicated a city.[64] Unfortunately, this key characteristic of Enoch does not come easily from the text of Gen. 4. 'Cain knew his wife and she conceived and bore Enoch and he built a city and called the name of the city after his son, Enoch' (v. 17). Apart from the reference in Jub. 4.10–11, this city tradition is not developed elsewhere; Enoch becomes what his legendary counterpart once was, a royal figure of great wisdom. Gen. 4.17 has the possibility of another reading. If the letters *bnh 'yr* are read as *bn h'yr*, the builder of a city becomes an angel child, and we should have reason for Enoch's being chosen to occupy the special place in the genealogy. Noah was also thought to be an angel child,[65] and Gen. 4.1 says that Enoch's father was conceived 'with the help of Yahweh'. If this *was* the reason for the choice of Enoch, we are dealing with traditions which could be very old indeed.

Gen. 5.21–4, the P account, says he walked 'with God' ('*et ha' 'lohim*), but all the later Enochic material read this as 'with the angels', a reference to the heavenly travels. Then he was no more, 'for God took him' (*ki laqaḥ 'oto 'elohim*).

The account of Gen. 5 tallies exactly with the life of Enoch in Jub. 4.16–25. He lived sixty-five years before his son was born, and then had six jubilees of heavenly travel, i.e. three hundred years, before dying at the age of 365. The Book of Enoch was composed with this same biographical framework; the vision of judgement followed by the travels, the return home, the instruction of his children and his last testimony. Given the consistency of this pattern, we cannot simply assume that the later works were an expansion of the Old Testament account. The reverse may be true. 'The ancient aggadic tradition independently attested by Jubilees and Enoch' could also have been known to, and abbreviated by, the writer of Genesis.[66] The important difference between the Genesis account and the later lives of Enoch is that Genesis does not mention his wisdom, or his association with the fallen angels. In Genesis he is a man who *walks with God* (we assume this means that he was a good man); elsewhere he is a *wise man*. The wisdom attributed to Enoch is also absent from the Old Testament, but not, as I shall show, because it was unknown. The wisdom was removed, and has left only traces of itself in our present texts.

When the Enoch figure in the Old Testament is compared to Babylonian parallels, we tend to assume that Israel had no indigenous tradition, and had always to be borrowing. There are various theories as to when these other traditions were absorbed: during the exile, perhaps, as the priestly way of helping people resist the attraction of pagan cults,[67] or at a later date with the spreading influence of the Chaldean sages.[68] Neither of these positions takes seriously the evidence of 1 Enoch itself, that those who returned from the exile were impure and apostate. A Babylonian origin for 1 Enoch, in any meaningful sense of the word, is far from proved, or even likely. More consistent with the stance of the work would be the existence within Israel itself of something akin to the traditions about Emenduranki, which we can recognize only in their Babylonian form because they have not survived elsewhere. Emenduranki was the seventh king of Sippar, the city of Shamash the sun god. He was summoned into the presence of the gods, and there he learned the secrets of creation. Unlike Enoch, he was very long-lived, but Enoch's 365 years are thought to hint at his association with a sun cult. Emenduranki was the founder of the guild of *baru* diviners, who had scientific interests, and he learned divinatory techniques which were later used as the basis of royal claims.[69] Enoch is also compared to one of the *apkallu*, the sage Utu'abzu who was taken up to heaven in the time of Emenduranki, and to the flood hero Utnapishtim who transmitted the antediluvian wisdom. This is a royal wisdom tradition.

Now, interesting though the similarities to the Enoch figure may be, there are problems. Enoch in the Old Testament is not a royal figure (whereas in the Similitudes he is identified with the Son of Man and virtually *becomes* a royal figure), yet the parallel materials concern a royal house and the basis of its claims to power. Nor do Akkadian prophecies presently known have an Enochic view of history; the eschatology is not there. We can no longer claim that eschatology is *the* major and definitive element in apocalyptic, but it is certainly too major a component to be overlooked. The hypothesis of a composite Enoch figure is doubtless correct, as the later accretions show, but the suggested components are not convincing. Did P really 'exercise editorial independence as he drew on foreign traditions'?[70] If there was other Enochic material known to the writer of Genesis, we cannot be certain that this material was foreign. The oldest part of 1 Enoch is the Book of Watchers. It is replete with an eschatology most nearly paralleled in the Old Testament itself, even though the contact text within the Old Testament at Gen. 6 gives no hint of this association. If Gen. 5 was compiled at a time when the traditions of Israel's monarchy were being reworked and relocated after the crisis of 586, could the Enoch figure have absorbed some of the older royal attributes? We know virtually nothing about the ancient kings, which makes any comparison rather difficult, but the most frequent description of the Enoch figure is that he is unique; uniquely prophet and wise man, uniquely combining prophecy and astronomy, uniquely going on heavenly journeys, uniquely combining earthly and heavenly roles. Did all these stem from one source? The uniqueness must warn us that the real origin of the Enoch figure is in *something we do not know*.

The Mythology of Enoch

Separated from the Enoch figure in the Old Testament *and in the Book of the Watchers* is the myth of the angels (1 En. 6—11), which functions as both premise and setting for the heavenly travels and revelations.[71] The myth here is also composite; one strand deals with Semiḥazah and the birth of giants, the other with Asael and the bringing of knowledge. In 1 Enoch as a whole, the combination of the myths implies that it was knowledge brought by Asael which led to the temptation and fall of Semiḥazah and his hosts, i.e. it was the knowledge which came first and was the fundamental element of the myth. Recent study of the text has reached an exactly opposite conclusion, viz that the knowledge element was an addition to the basic Enochic myth.[72] It has been the majority opinion of Old Testament scholars since the time of R. H. Charles that the brief reference to the angel marriages in Gen. 6 was the source of all the later angelic speculation.[73] Now Gen. 6 makes no reference to heavenly knowledge as the cause of the angels' downfall, nor does it mention the birth of the giant offspring who corrupted the earth. Von Rad's analysis of Gen. 6, however, concluded that its text was both dislocated and truncated. Without the giants it lost its point.[74] Could it also have lost its association with wisdom? There is a great deal of mythology implicit in Gen. 1—11 which no longer breaks the surface. The tale of the role and corruption of heavenly wisdom could have been one such loss.[75]

Qumran Enoch uses the marriage myth, the giants and the knowledge. The Similitudes, though mentioning the marriages, have no real emphasis upon them, and develop only the themes of knowledge and judgement. Both Qumran Enoch and the Similitudes record ascents in the context of the angel myth. Either Qumran Enoch and the Similitudes independently amplified the Genesis version with other material to include knowledge, judgement, and heavenly ascents, or the Genesis version was shorn of these elements which the tale had once contained. Since the later *uses* of the myth consistently place the greatest emphasis upon those elements deemed to be accretions by those who favour the priority of the Genesis version, it seems more likely that the 'accretions' were integral to the original myth, and that their *removal* from Gen. 6 caused the dislocation of the text.

There have been several attempts to find parallels to the angel mythology in Greek, Zoroastrian, Egyptian and Canaanite sources,[76] but everywhere there are problems. The eschatology does not fit, the Greek myths do not deal with the superhuman origin of evil, the coming of knowledge is deemed a release, not a curse, or the myth of the divine warrior turns out not to be the foundation myth of 1 Enoch.[77] I wish to explore the possibility that this myth is indigenous to Israel, or adopted at so early a date as to make any alien roots insignificant.

All the components of the angel mythology can be found in the Old Testament. Their coming together in the Enochic tradition may have been due to the creative and imaginative use of previously unrelated material, but we cannot exclude the opposite possibility, that all these scattered texts referred to a lost mythology which the Enochic tradition preserved. In Ezek. 27—8 there is a royal heavenly creature thrown down because he abused his *knowledge*. In Isa. 14 there is a royal figure thrown down because he attempted to set himself higher than Elyon. In Isa. 37 the king of Assyria is defeated before Jerusalem because he came in *pride* against the Holy One of Israel. In each case the reference is political, the judgement of a royal figure. In Ps. 82 there are gods judged who have no *understanding or knowledge*, who walk in darkness and imperil the earth. In Exod. 24.9–11, a very early text, seventy elders ascend to the throne, and *no harm comes to them*. Why say this? Isa. 33 promises a vision of the king in his beauty, and Isa. 24 is so close to the Similitudes that it has been thought their basis. If the roots of all this mythological material do lie in the Old Testament, and what we read in Enoch is a legitimate development, we find new significance in the claim that all who returned from the exile were impure and apostate.

None of these contact texts for the angel mythology has any association with Enoch, strengthening the case for Enoch and the mythology being originally separated. The recurring motif of the angel material is a royal figure; we have already seen that the closest parallels to the Enoch figure are the kings of Mesopotamia. The tradition which Enoch inherited was, I suggest, the royal cult. J. Z. Smith reached the same conclusion, about apocalyptic in general, arguing on an entirely different basis.

19

Apocalyptic is wisdom lacking a royal court and patron, and therefore it surfaces during the period of late antiquity not as a response to religious persecution but as an expression of the trauma of the cessation of native kingship. Apocalypticism is a learned rather than a popular phenomenon ... best understood as part of the inner history of the tradition within which it occurs – rather than as a syncretism with foreign (most usually held to be Iranian) influences.[78]

We are told that Enoch was the product of the stresses of the second century. If this is the case, then its use by the early Church, though interesting, is scarcely of great importance. But if Enoch represents the residue of the old royal cult, then its presence in early Christianity must radically affect our understanding of that messianic movement.

The Tradition in 1 Enoch: (1) The Book of the Watchers

It is important to distinguish as far as possible the system from its application. Eliade was correct when he said

All too often the Occidental allows himself to be impressed by the *manifestation* of an ideology, when he is ignorant of the one thing it is important above all others to know: the ideology itself, that is, the myths ...

In a number of different contexts, – oneiric, ecstatic, ritual, mythological etc. – we find complementary, but structurally indissoluble meanings which fall into a *pattern* ... Furthermore, we do not manage to decipher everything that such a pattern presents, as it were in cryptography, until, after having 'decoded' its particular meanings one by one, each in its own frame of reference, we take the trouble to integrate them all into a whole.[79]

I am inclined to think that this is a more fruitful approach to Enoch than one which tells us that the 'salient facts' are that '1 Enoch is a collection of different apocalypses or apocryphal traditions, following the style of the Daniel archetypal apocalypse'.[80] I shall therefore attempt to recover the mythology of Enoch piecemeal, before trying to form it into a coherent whole.

We must be wary of assuming that the frequency of any feature's relevance to a particular set of circumstances is an indication of its importance in the overall scheme.[81] The setting in which we have seen the earliest apocalypses function, e.g. the troubles of the second century, or the Qumran community, has, until recently, been assumed to be that of their origin. But there is no organic link between the problems of this period and the major *themes or forms* of the literature. These were used only to interpret the problems of the period, they were the established framework within which the world had to be viewed. The ultimate origin of apocalyptic must therefore lie in a setting where ascents to the upper world, the hosts of heaven, astrology, astronomy, and superhuman wisdom were as much at home as those other elements – evil angels, supernatural conflicts mirrored on earth, the visions of history and judgement

20

which were taken up and emphasized for their relevance to the second century. Nor must we be distracted by the Enoch figure itself. The ideas and patterns of 1 Enoch are not unique to that text, even though the Enoch figure is without parallel. He inherited another tradition, and we should not be surprised to find other heirs in Daniel, the Assumption of Moses, Jubilees, the Testaments of the Twelve Patriarchs or the New Testament. The differences between these works show that the tradition was not confined to one group or milieu, but was the basis for an ongoing variety of interpretations. Within 1 Enoch itself there are signs of this growth: 98.4 contradicts the earlier version of the angel myth by saying: 'Sin has not been sent upon the earth, but man of himself has created it'. The earlier version most definitely does see sin as 'sent' into the world. This could present a problem for anyone arguing for the coherence of 1 Enoch, but these different attitudes towards sin are exactly the same as the different attitudes towards knowledge in the same sections. BW condemns the knowledge of the stars and clouds, but AB deals with precisely this subject. We have two distinct constructions, the earlier seeing knowledge as evil, sent into the world as the result of a revolt in heaven, and the later seeing this knowledge as good, but perverted by evil use. The earlier version sees knowledge as an invasion which corrupted the earth; not the expression of a learned group, but rather the fears and suspicions of the unlearned for whom the new age would mean freedom from fear and plenty of food. The later version is more sophisticated, showing that it is not the possession of knowledge which is evil, but its abuse. Thus in AB, Enoch is given knowledge of how the heaven *ought* to work, and is told that calendrical chaos is due to the revolt of the stars. The natural order is perverted by star angels to such an extent that the system will soon become unworkable. Thus the revolt in the heavens is both paradigm and aetiology, if we use the conventional labels; calendrical disorder is both sign and proof of evil acts. Enoch could calculate how long it would be before chaos returned.

BW also shows signs of development. Semiḥazah material has been joined to Asael material. The former tells of two hundred angels who lusted for human wives, and fathered the fearful half-breeds who corrupted the earth. Archangels heard the cries for help and the Most High intervened. Uriel told Noah to prepare his escape from the great judgement, and Michael had to bind Semiḥazah and his earthly helpers. The spirits of the children of the Watchers were condemned to destruction, along with all wickedness. After the judgement, the earth could return to great fertility and peace. The Asael material tells how knowledge was brought from heaven to earth and with this knowledge mankind learned to do evil. Although there are numerous textual problems in 8.2–3, the Syncellus text says that it was the heavenly arts which led the holy ones astray, i.e. it was Asael's instruction which enabled humankind to seduce the hosts of Semiḥazah.[82] The curious Animal Apocalypse agrees with this sequence. The first star to fall was Asael (86.1–2), followed by others who mated with the cows

21

(86.3–4), to produce the elephants, camels and asses. Asael is thus the first mover in the events of the fall. He brings knowledge of metallurgy and cosmetics (8.1–2), of eternal mysteries (9.6), of charms and enchantments, roots and plants. *In its present form* BW is a Semiḥazah myth expanded and explained by insertions of Asael material, but the logic of the sequence makes Asael the original rebel, and the bringing of the heavenly knowledge the original cause of the disaster.

Several attempts have been made to explain the Semiḥazah-Asael conflation. Nickelsburg's analysis has a disappointingly tame conclusion; the Semiḥazah myth grew from Gen. 6, using ideas from Isa. 14, and developed in the light of Hellenistic beliefs of divine descent. The Asael material came from the Prometheus saga, and was to explain the devastation of the world through warfare.[83] Hanson offers a more complex solution, based upon the similarity of Asael and Azazel in Lev. 16, and the materials in Targum Ps.-Jonathan. The original Semiḥazah myth was amplified with atonement motifs from Lev. 16, and the sin of the rebel angel identified with forbidden knowledge.[84] Both suggestions are open to criticism; Nickelsburg thinks that the Enoch material is more primitive than the Targum, and therefore cannot be derived from it as Hanson proposed, whilst his own solution, the unseating of Semiḥazah by an Asael derived from Greek mythology is equally unsatisfactory, since it is the Asael-knowledge myth which dominates elsewhere in the Enochic tradition.[85] Both writers have a problem with the wisdom element. The Asael figure stands for wisdom and its abuse, and it is this myth which is mentioned in the Old Testament, another indication that this is the dominant theme. A veiled figure of that name appears in Zech. 14.5, in a corrupt text dealing with the Day of the Lord and the valley of punishment.[86] There is no hint in the Old Testament that he was the bringer of wisdom, but there is plenty to suggest that the abuse of knowledge was the sin of the angels, e.g. Ps. 82, Ezek. 27—8, Gen. 2—3. In contrast, the correct use of knowledge was important for the king in Jerusalem. Solomon was given wisdom from the Lord (1 Kings 3), and was famed as a great wise man. Isa. 11 promised a great ruler endowed with wisdom, understanding, knowledge and fear of the Lord. This wisdom which the king could possess, but which Asael corrupted, was not the worldly wisdom of accumulated common sense,[87] but was the knowledge of mysteries which enabled man to use and control the creation. It is this wisdom which we meet in Wis. 7.17ff and in Job 38. It was fundamental to apocalyptic, and accounts for its association with magic. It was also fundamental to the prophets' beliefs about the kings and rulers of the world. The Asael-knowledge material is very old, even though it is Semiḥazah who dominates the conflation in 1 Enoch. In this form the combined myth is an attempt to come to terms with the evil rulers of the second and third centuries, and their claim to divine parentage, but the idea of divine descent and the evil sons of God ruling the earth is deep rooted in the Old Testament. In BW the myths are applied to the Seleucid kings, but they did not originate at that period. Their divine parentage and their evil acts were both explicable in terms of older beliefs. Kings had always had wisdom and abused it. That, and the pride which led to this abuse, were the sins of the ancient rulers whom the prophets denounced. The Asael-Semiḥazah material may be newly joined in 1 Enoch as we have it, but the two themes had belonged together for many centuries before the Seleucid crisis.

Within 1 Enoch we see the change from a fear of knowledge as such, and its condemnation, to a belief that knowledge is God-given, and that evil lies in its abuse. In each case, judgement awaits those who bring evil through knowledge. This implies a threefold division: people who were, or had been, hostile to knowledge, people who possessed knowledge which they regarded as good, but felt that others had abused and thus caused evil, and the abusers. The first two groups could express themselves in terms of a common mythology[88] but the third, as I shall demonstrate, used another myth, and deliberately obscured that of their opponents.

The writer of 1 Enoch put the origin of his troubles at the time of the return. Within the Old Testament we read of the beginnings of a bitter division (Isa. 65.15), when the chosen would go one way, and others be remembered as accursed. Could we but identify the groups involved, we could write a history of the period with confidence. But we cannot. Instead we must speculate.[89] It is my belief that the material in 1 Enoch derives from the cult of pre-exilic Jerusalem, and that the myth of post-exilic Jerusalem which has a similar role to the angels myth, namely the myth of Adam and Eve, was offered as a replacement for the older scheme.

In BW we have a form of the myth which condemns knowledge, but implicit in AB is a version akin to that of Jubilees, where the angels are sent with divine knowledge to teach uprightness, and it is only marriage with humankind which leads to the perversion of knowledge. Milik thought that the Jubilees form of the myth was older,[90] but since Jub. 4 uses several details from BW it is likely that the BW version is the older. Irrespective of their relative dates, the versions show that two very different constructions could be put upon the same myth, i.e. that in each case the theology was drawn from the basic myth, and not, as has been suggested, that the myths were devised as vehicles for the theology.[91] There *was* a myth deliberately devised as the vehicle for a particular theology, and this was the myth of Gen. 2—3, whose motifs and concerns show that it was intended to replace an earlier Eden myth. The Genesis version defines the role of knowledge in man's relationship to God. It is forbidden, because it is knowledge which distinguishes man from God. The fruit of the tree, as the serpent promised, would make man like the gods.[92]

The Adam and Eve myth in its present form is not integral to the Old Testament. It has all the signs of being a late addition.

The contents of Gen. ch. 2 and especially ch. 3 are conspicuously isolated in the Old

Testament. No prophet, psalm or narrator makes any recognizable reference to the story of the Fall. One actually does justice to the Yahwist only when one sees him in his isolation, facing the received tradition very freely.[93]

Thus von Rad. Eichrodt has a similar observation:

It is also a theologically significant fact that the profound conception of Gen. 3 not only is never explicitly referred to in the rest of the Old Testament, but only seldom finds even an echo in its thought.

Two pages later, when discussing the characteristics of the post-exilic priestly thinking, Eichrodt says that

the subordination of the whole cultus to the idea of atonement, while it certainly reckons with the universality of sin, yet allows it to remain in the class of momentary transgression of the Law, and says nothing about its origin.
It is all the more remarkable, therefore, that *in the post-exilic community understanding of the Yahwist's concern should be manifestly on the increase.*[94]

I shall devote a chapter to this Eden myth, and the changes which followed the replacing of a royal/angel cult by the era of the Law. Suffice it here to bear in mind that *an* Eden myth emphasizing human transgression was part of that era of the Law, and came later than the prophets' emphasis upon personal responsibility. The earlier cult had had another Eden, the angelic place we find in Ezek. 27—8, which dealt in malevolent heavenly powers, and would have been incompatible with any ideas of responsibility before the Law. It did, however, deal with the *origin* of evil.

The era of the Law began with the return from exile, at the time when the Enochic writer says Jerusalem went astray. We assume too easily that it was the apocalyptists who altered the ancient traditions of Israel, with an influx of foreign ideas; exactly the opposite may be nearer the truth.

When the apocalyptists have a different view of history, we also assume that they were the innovators.

The history of Israel and the nations is abstracted even more strongly [by the apocalyptic writers], and understood as a whole. It was, moreover, no longer judged from the saving present, in the cultus and the Law, but in the light of the imminently expected eschaton.[95]

But if their views were not formed in terms of the saving present in the cultus and Law, do we honestly have sufficient evidence to say that they were *no longer* formed on that basis? When we omit the presuppositions we bring to this literature, is there any reason why our evidence cannot be read as saying that the apocalyptic views of history (indeed of anything) have never been influenced by developments characteristic of exilic and post-exilic thought?[96]

The myth of the angels is one of the major components of BW; the other is the ascent of Enoch and his heavenly travels. It has been said that this myth of ascent and the myth of the angels were originally separate and unconnected, and were brought together for the first time in 1 En. 6—11,[97] but the evidence of the Old Testament suggests otherwise. Ascent to the presence of God and the myth of the angels are both deep-rooted in the Old Testament, and even in the early texts they are closely linked. Enoch's ascent is similar to the prophets' call experiences, and to their claims to have been present in the heavenly council. But the message which the prophets delivered from that heavenly council was couched in terms of the angel mythology. They expected a great judgement, exactly as did Enoch. This use of the angel mythology is seen most clearly in the oracles against foreign nations, but, as I shall show from the Isaiah corpus, the angel mythology of judgement permeates the whole work.

An important feature of Enoch's ascent experience is his own participation in the heavenly events. Enoch himself is a part of the process of judgement (13.1ff; 15.2ff; 16.4), announcing the punishment of the evil ones. He is not simply looking at another world, contemplating the divine throne. He acts within it, and effects something by this means. Such participation is a common feature of practices we call magical, namely that a trained imagination, in conjunction with a rightly directed will, is a potent force within the world we experience as physical.[98] A belief such as this could well underlie the fear of the prophets' words, a belief that the event predicted had already been inaugurated. Enoch not only observed the angels. He was a force among them. But if, as seems likely, Enoch had acquired the role of another, who was it that had previously had such a role in the affairs of heaven?

Enoch's ascent is described in imagery drawn from the first Temple; we cannot appreciate fully the motifs and themes of 1 Enoch because we are almost completely ignorant of what the Babylonians burned, and the reformers of the Jerusalem tradition effectively buried beneath the new ways. I shall show later that the original, angelic, Eden was represented by the old Temple, and that the events of this Eden were the stuff of the cult. It was from this pattern of ideas that many of Enoch's allusions were drawn. He views all history from a high tower, for example 87.3—4, which is the temple (89.50ff). Presumably the Temple was the place of such revelation (cf. Ps. 73). Enoch sees the throne of God in the second house of the heavenly temple (14.15ff), and on the top of a mountain (18.8). The details of the throne are similar to those in Isa. 6, Ezek. 1, Exod. 24 (apart from the crystal, which is not mentioned in the earlier texts), but we cannot assume a simple derivation from the earlier texts. Several allusions indicate that there was more behind the knowledge in 1 Enoch than is present in the Old Testament. We know that the throne of God was in the Temple (Isa. 6, Ps. 11), yet Enoch remembers this as a heavenly mountain. Enoch is a priest in Jub. 4.25, but he is a priest in *Eden*, not in a heavenly temple. Like the High Priest in the sanctuary, Enoch ascends alone (1 En. 14.8ff), to intercede for the fallen angels.[99]

He ascends to see the throne of God, which is not the mobile throne of

25

Ezekiel, but a heavenly fixture. It is suggested that Enoch's is the more developed idea,[100] but I am not sure that we can map Enoch's antecedents with that degree of accuracy. Isa. 6 and Ps. 11, both earlier than Ezekiel, know of a heavenly temple throne, suggesting that a line of development could be drawn between Isaiah and Enoch, seeing Ezekiel's emphasis upon mobility as due to the exceptional circumstances of his ministry to the exiles.[101] A mobile throne was, for him, entirely appropriate, and may even have been of his own devising. We do not know what precipitated the fusion of desert and temple traditions which characterize the Pentateuch. Could it have been the prophet's inspiration to fuse temple throne and mobile ark? We are also directed to the different locations of the throne in Ezekiel and Enoch; Enoch's was in a heavenly temple, whereas Ezekiel's was earthly. Does this necessarily indicate 'a fundamental theological difference between the two authors'?[102] I think not. We may have to take into account such factors as the Temple not being built in the time of the mythical Enoch, or its not being used by the transmitters of this tradition at the time when Enoch was written into its present form; but a more likely explanation is that a distinction between earth and heaven in matters of cult and temple is not appropriate in the pre-exilic period, and therefore the experiences of Ezekiel and of Enoch could well have been similar. Their manner of expression was determined by the historical situation of the two writers, not by their theological framework.[103]

Given that the state of our knowledge relies heavily upon the assumption of Old Testament priority, we cannot with confidence say that Enoch's is a more developed throne vision than Ezekiel's, or that his ascent experience was at the transition period between the prophetic call and the mystical experience.[104] We must never forget that our knowledge of the prophets, Enoch's antecedents, is derived from edited texts, and that we lack any clear statement of editorial policy. If, however, the Deuteronomic school was concerned with the preservation of the prophetic texts, then their manifesto in Deut. 4 must be taken seriously: 'You heard the sound of the words, but you saw no form. There was only a voice.' These words imply that there was some controversy over the vision of God at the time of the giving of the revelation which became the Law. Any record of such an experience in the prophetic writings is not likely to have survived. An argument from silence is dangerous, but we must accept that there was some reason for the Deuteronomic polemic at this point. There were, in all likelihood, those who claimed to have seen God in the context of giving Torah. Many early writings reflect a conflict of this type,[105] and a similar conflict attended the Jewish mystics for centuries. Both Enoch and these later mystics claimed visions of God, and used temple imagery; it was the Deuteronomists who denied this possibility, and they were the self-proclaimed reformers of the temple cult. I should be surprised if this is coincidence.

Before we can place Enoch and his ascents on the map of apocalyptic development, it is essential to abandon the idea that the Old Testament is the norm from which other writers deviated. We have moved sufficiently far to acknowledge the dialogue between canon and apocalyptic.

> It does not fall short of the truth to say that some of the basic attitudes maintained in apocalyptic were formed by some degree of confrontation with some of the prevailing ideas found in scripture[106]

and students of the Deuteronomists have now begun to question whether their viewpoint was so central as we have been led to believe.

> It is usually taken for granted that the work has an official stance, that it represents a proclamation within the mainstream of the ongoing life of the people; so, in more precise terms than are usually used in this connection, it has been presented as the deposit of preaching and teaching activity in the Babylonian synagogue. Some such public and official stance is that normally accepted for the setting of the work of the deuteronomic school. It is perhaps here, however, that the first questions should be raised.[107]

Perhaps it was not apocalyptic which confronted Scripture with different ideas. Perhaps the ideas found in Scripture were developed in the exile and formulated in *confrontation with an older tradition* which survived only in the tradition we recognize as apocalyptic. Enoch claims pre-exilic roots by denouncing post-exilic developments as apostasy, but it does not elaborate. It may be that the difference between Ezra-Judaism and the Enochic tradition was the extent of the apostasy. Enoch's use of temple imagery, and the royal associations, add weight to the claim to be the older tradition.

Closely linked to Enoch's ascent are the heavenly travels, when he goes to the ends of the earth to learn more secrets of creation than any other man (19.3). The geography of these travels has attracted much interest, and points of contact have been found in Babylonian and Greek mythology;[108] but the actual phenomenon of trance travel, as attested in many other cultures, has not yet been fully explored as a means of understanding these texts.[109] Trance travellers report their experiences in terms of their own cultural milieu[110] (hence the recognizable features of Jerusalem and its environs in the Enochic travels and their points of contact with Greek and Babylonian mythology); but the fundamental experience of elevation, transportation and initiation into secrets is universal. The question we must bring to BW is not, 'Was Enoch a magnet for heterogeneous mythological materials?',[111] as though the work had been compiled in the manner of a piece of modern research, but, 'What actual experience does Enoch describe in terms of these materials?' Before there can be any real appreciation of these texts, we have to decide whether Enoch is simply a collection of bizarre mythologies and literary styles, or a record of real experiences which found expression *in the manner traditional to those who cultivated them.* In other cultures the travellers were their shamans and rulers, the wise men and the kings. The present literary form of BW, with Enoch apparently taking over another tradition, begs another question. If Enoch was not the original focus of the ascent and judgement mythology, was it formerly the royal cult of the Temple?

The angel mythology of Enoch is both sophisticated and complex. Its patterns lie beneath several biblical texts, and its characteristic concepts of time, space and reality, when placed in their wider context, can be seen to belong not only to the apocalyptists, but to much of the Old Testament itself. It is a mistake to judge this material by our standards of consistency. There are, it is true, several apparently incompatible versions of the angels myth, but since two of them can appear side by side in Ezek. 28, we are obliged to view them as complementary. (28.5 condemns the prince of Tyre for his pride in claiming to be as wise as a god, 28.16 condemns the king of Tyre for abusing and corrupting his wisdom.) It is possible to construct a whole web of cross-references within 1 Enoch and the Old Testament which equate, or identify – which is even more bizarre to our ways of thinking – stars, angels, and kings. We find stars equated with angels at 1 En. 18.13ff; 87.4; 88.3; 90.20; cf. Job 38.7, which links the morning stars and the sons of God. 1 En. 90.24 links evil stars and the seventy shepherds, the wicked rulers who blur the distinction between earthly and heavenly powers. Texts in the Old Testament also link earthly rulers and stars: Isa. 14 links the day star and the king of Babylon, Num. 24.7 links the rising star with the future ruler of Israel, and even as late as Matthew's Gospel we find a natural association of king and star (Matt. 2.2, 'for we have seen his star . . .'). Enoch describes the punishment of the erring stars as the burning of great mountains (18.13ff); Jer. 51.25 describes the end of Babylon in the same way. The destroying mountain is to be cast down and burned. Thus we can link stars and angels, stars and kings, but Qumran Enoch does not make the third equation explicit; it does not link angels and kings. For this we have to go to the Similitudes, which are based entirely upon this identification. The destruction of the kings and the mighty *is* the punishment of the fallen angels. In Daniel we find the heavenly princes as the counterparts of their nations, a related concept, but in earlier texts we do seem to have a complete identification of king and angelic counterpart. The Lord arouses the *spirit* of the kings of the Medes (Jer. 51.11), the king in Jerusalem is *'el gibbor*, a mighty god (Isa. 9.6), and Solomon and Yahweh are blurred together in the description of the coronation rites (1 Chron. 29). The people worshipped Yahweh and the king (v. 20), and the king sat on the throne of Yahweh (v. 23). At a later date, the system of 1 Enoch was developed for the control of demonic and hostile forces; we do not know when this originated, but something very similar does seem to lie behind several Psalms.[112] We also find a king who is more than a mere mortal (Psalms 2; 79; 82; 110), one who had a role in both worlds, to protect his people from heavenly powers which manifested themselves as foreign rulers and other threats to the wellbeing of his people.

It is hard for us to enter such a world, even harder to determine where such ideas were transmitted during the period of the second Temple. But given the paucity of evidence at our disposal, any points of correspondence must be striking, and a sympathetic and imaginative reading of our materials is more likely to bear fruit than a purely critical analysis.

The Enochic mythology shows that human beings could become angelic, that a transformation of the human condition was believed possible.[113] In the Book of Dreams, both Noah and Moses begin as animals, but become men (89.1, 36), which, in the code of the writer means that they began as men and became angels. The just are also promised that they will shine like stars, have the joy of the angels, and become companions of the heavenly host (104.2ff), a further indication of the stars/angels equation. The elect who inherit the earth will be given *wisdom* (5.8), and sin no more through ungodliness or pride, an interesting choice of sins, given the range that is possible, since these are the sins of the fallen angels. The Old Testament only records the obverse of this belief; those who abuse wisdom lose their angelic status and become mortal (Gen. 3; Ps. 82; Ezek. 28).

If stars were angels, and angels were wise, if sin was pride and the perversion of divine knowledge, a whole spectrum of texts settles into a coherent pattern. The wise who lead many to righteousness will shine like the stars forever (Dan. 12.4); Israel will approach the heaven of the stars (AM 10.9); the righteous are to be made like the light of the stars, the faces of those who practise self-control shall shine more than the stars (4 Ezra 7.97, 125). Nickelsburg's study of these verses, and their points of contact in other works, led him to suggest a lost tradition of angels and judgement.[114] This also dealt with the transcendence of man's physical and mortal state. It is highly significant that one of the contact texts for this tradition in the Old Testament is the Servant Song of Isa. 52—3. If this was associated with the angel mythology, and the Servant Song referred originally to the role of the royal figure, the messianic use by the early Church was not an innovation. Wisdom was a key factor in the apocalyptists' picture of transformation, even though it is not clear whether wisdom effected the change, or was the result of it. The *knowledge* of the Servant was also the key to his role (Isa. 53.11), but this verse has never been satisfactorily explained.[115]

The apocalyptic tradition sees the potential unity of both worlds. Upper and lower, future and present are so often presented as the essence of apocalyptic dualism, but this is seriously to misread their world view. Upper and lower, future and present were not essentially separate, but could only be described and understood in terms of each other. The visible world was described in terms of the invisible, and vice versa. Thus the *māšāl*, the characteristic teaching form of the wise men, can describe the heavenly world to teach about the earth, as in the Similitudes (Num. 24.3, Isa. 14), or the natural world to teach about the heavenly, as in the Gospels. It is a great mistake to read apocalyptic as a dualistic system; nothing could have been more completely integrated.[116]

Wisdom is fundamental to the Enochic scheme, because Enoch is described as a wise man, a scribe (1 En. 12.4, Jub. 4.17). He is also a priest (Jub. 4.25), which immediately gives us a context for this wisdom. But what was it, and how did it relate to the wisdom literature of the Old Testament?[117] No simple map of this process is possible, but the whole area has been considerably muddied by the twin assumptions of Old Testament primacy and Old Testament purity. We do not know what was meant by wisdom in pre-exilic Jerusalem; we have only edited materials at our disposal. Nor can we be sure that these materials give us a representative sample of ancient wisdom, proving beyond reasonable doubt that any other type of wisdom in the apocalyptic writings must have been late and alien to Israel's tradition. I shall argue this case in detail later, and give only a few indications here. For von Rad,[118] the first to take wisdom's role in apocalyptic with any seriousness, prophecy and wisdom, both used in the strictly Old Testament sense, were incompatible because of their differing views of history. In his earlier work he had in mind a wisdom drawn essentially from the wisdom literature, whose scientific concerns were the forerunners of, for example, Enoch's astronomy, but he later dealt with esoteric and mantic wisdom as possible sources for apocalyptic. He saw wisdom *eschatologized* into its apocalyptic form. The practice of predicting auspicious times and the general broadening of intellectual horizons eventually bore fruit in the characteristically apocalyptic view of history and its culmination. M. E. Stone studied the content of the revelation lists in the apocalyptic texts, and concluded that they were 'catalogues of actual subjects of speculative investigation'.[119] Any attempt to define the origin of apocalyptic and its wisdom must, he said, take seriously the fact that the revelations concerned natural phenomena, albeit of a special type, such as the number of the stars and the dimensions of the earth.[120] Mueller[121] rooted apocalyptic wisdom in the arts of the diviner, and in mantic wisdom, which he distinguished from the wisdom of Israel in both its pre-exilic and post-exilic forms. The mantic tradition was always present in Israel, but as an undercurrent, and the crisis of the second century with its Hellenizing rationalism brought it into prominence. A glaring omission in this investigation was the Enoch figure. This was taken up by VanderKam who claimed that Mueller's thesis was decisively confirmed by a study of the Enoch traditions, and their antecedents among the Mesopotamian diviners. The wisdom of the Epistle of Enoch was different, however, and could not be rooted in the mantic tradition, but 'in the more familiar and traditional sort of wisdom that dominate such books as Proverbs, Ben Sira, and to some extent, Job. All of it is, nevertheless transposed into an eschatological key.'[122]

It is in the Similitudes that we see most clearly the gulf between the Enochic tradition and the post-exilic wisdom as exemplified in Ben Sira 24, where wisdom is identified with the Mosaic Law, and dwells in Israel (24.23, 28). This is the position of Deut. 4.6, where the Law is to be the wisdom of the chosen people. In contrast, Enoch sees wisdom as the revelation of heavenly matters to a chosen person; Enoch himself sees the secrets of heaven (41.1), how the kingdoms are divided and the actions of men weighed.[123] The spirit of wisdom is in the Elect One who stands in the presence of God (49.1–3). A component of this wisdom is the *name* of the Son of Man (48.1–7; 69.26), which we have assumed to be the revelation of his identity. It could as easily be read as the revelation of a name, in the magical sense of a power-giving invocation, such as we find in 69.14 as the key to the cosmic oath. A *name* in this sense fits well into a context of heavenly secrets and judgement, and the sense of the passages would then be that this name of the Son of Man was a powerful tool in the process of judging evil. The name was used before the creation (48.3), and it saved the righteous (48.7). At the close of the passage dealing with the power of the cosmic oath, there is great joy because the *name* of the Son of Man is revealed. We cannot be certain that the *name* had these associations, but the devotees of the Enochic wisdom opposed the claims of Ben Sira 24. Wisdom was not Torah. Wisdom had never found a place on earth (1 En. 42), wisdom was forsaken just before the destruction of the first Temple (93.8), and sinners make wisdom evil, and find no place for it (94.5). It would be tempting to see the forsaking of wisdom as a reference to the reform of the temple cult just before its destruction in 586.

If the Enochic wisdom was not Torah, nor heir to the Deuteronomic traditions and the wise men whom they influenced, was abandoned at the end of the monarchy and fell into disrepute, afforded a supernatural dimension to the study of natural phenomena and was possessed by the Elect One before the throne, this wisdom could have been part of the royal cult. The messianic figure in Isa. 11 was endowed with the *spirit of Yahweh* and the *spirit of wisdom*. Even the Deuteronomic account of Solomon (1 Kings 4.5ff) records that he asked God for wisdom, and thus he became wise and ruled. He uttered three thousand proverbs about trees, beasts, birds, reptiles and fish.[124] None of these wise words has survived, unless by stretching the imagination one is prepared to read Proverbs as a treatise on these things. Solomon's wisdom had a scientific component, now lost. He was also remembered as the father of exorcism in Israel, and there is no trace of this in the biblical tradition either. Was this the wisdom abandoned at the end of the monarchy, and transmitted by the Enochic tradition? This wisdom which transforms man into an immortal is akin to that widely claimed by the shamans of other cultures. VanderKam has suggested that the omen texts of the Mesopotamian diviners, a collection of minutely observed phenomena, were 'incipient scientific descriptions because they display that concern to list fully and to classify phenomena which is an essential ingredient of scientific study'.[125] A closer approximation than this is possible from the Old Testament itself. Job 37—8 is the closest parallel to the Enochic lists of revealed phenomena which we possess, but it is not concerned with divination and prediction; it concerns the power to create and to command, and the point of the chapter is to emphasize that Job's wisdom *cannot do this,* because his wisdom is not like God's. This is why such a list has survived in the canon; it serves to refute the claims of the older wisdom.

There are several reports of shamanic experiences which refer to this same power of knowledge to control. The ecstatic experience gives insight into the secrets of nature, and thus gives the initiate power over nature, either to heal with medicines, or to exorcize, or to control the weather.[126] As a result of the experience which revealed the wisdom, the shaman often feels he has endured his own death and lived beyond it;[127] this is reminiscent of the connection between wisdom and the angelic state in apocalyptic. It is clear from 4Q Mess ar that this type of belief was current in Palestine, and therefore evidence for understanding the Enochic materials:

> his wisdom will go forth to all the peoples, and he will know the secrets of all living things. All their calculations against him will come to nought, although the opposition of all living things will be great.[128]

It does not matter who was meant by this 'Elect of God', only that this was actually *believed of anyone* at that time.

Where or how such wisdom was fostered during the period of the second Temple is a mystery. I doubt that its resurgence was a reaction against Hellenistic rationalism. It is more likely that the claims of the Seleucid god-kings had to be met on their own ground, and the oldest traditions of Israel were well equipped for just such a conflict.

The Book of Watchers, more than any other section of 1 Enoch, shows us the *system* of the tradition, but it would be a mistake to consider it either comprehensive or in any way pre-eminent over the other materials of the same tradition. It is only by comparison with these other materials that we can begin to appreciate the richness and complexity of the tradition, and its great age. BW is but one construction on the angel myth. It uses only those elements appropriate to its purpose. It drew from the tradition the myth of Asael and the heavenly knowledge, of Semiḥazah and the angel marriages, of the great judgement and the malevolent supernaturals. Its wisdom could control, create and transform. Its wise men learned secrets whilst travelling in another state, which was structured in the imagery of the old Temple. The second section of 1 Enoch draws different materials from the tradition, to serve a different end.

The Tradition in 1 Enoch (2) : The Similitudes

The Similitudes have not been found at Qumran, which denies us the certainty of a pre-Christian date, but their presence in an Enochic collection means that they must be examined, and their characteristic theology and traditions included in any picture of the Enochic system. How the Similitudes relate to Qumran Enoch (hereafter QE) is not clear; absence from Qumran is not proof of a post-Qumran date, and several parallels to Qumran texts in matters of vocabulary and style suggest that the Similitudes come from the same period, if not from the same community.[129] The various arguments for dating the Similitudes are based upon the application of certain texts to known historical situations,[130] but to date one particular deposit of an Enochic tradition is not to explain its origin. What interests me is the system on which they are based, irrespective of the date at which our particular version achieved the form we know. If the Similitudes and QE represent two streams of the Enochic tradition which were separated by the first century, the differences between them may indicate their respective milieux, but any common ground will point to their origin.

The study of the Similitudes is in its infancy,[131] but such as it is, it suggests that they have a considerable prehistory. They were originally poetry,[132] and they were not associated with the Enoch figure.[133] Since 1 En. 6—11 were originally without the Enoch figure also, we may suppose that both QE and SS took over a non-Enochic tradition which described itself as wisdom.

The three Similitudes are each described as a *māšāl*, and the whole work is a vision of *wisdom* (37.1), crucial words for our understanding of these texts. Wisdom, as we have seen, was the revelation of matters relating to creation and to history, it transformed men into angels, and was closely connected with the royal cult. Here in the Similitudes we find that this wisdom is communicated to the elect by the *māšāl*.

There have been many attempts to define *māšāl*. It refers to a great variety of literary forms, a sure sign that the biblical writers recognized a common denominator which we do not. Each occurrence of the word needs a different English equivalent, *according to our system of identifying and classifying forms*. This suggests that we have failed to discover the essential characteristic of the *māšāl* which distinguished it from other sayings. There are two verbs *māšal*, meaning respectively (1) to represent, be like, and (2) to rule, have dominion. The debate about that noun centres about these two possibilities.[134] There is also the possibility that the meaning of *māšal* has developed over the years,[135] or that the materials which we have in the Old Testament are not truly representative of the genre. Where, for example, are Solomon's three thousand proverbs (1 Kings 4.32) about the world of nature? Josephus implies that he had knowledge of the properties of these forms of nature (*Ant.* viii, 44) and then goes on to describe his powers as an exorcist.

Given the material in Proverbs with which he was specially concerned, McKane was correct to opt for the meaning derived from *māšal*, be like,[136] but the material in Proverbs has passed through many hands, and seen many changes. I am not sure that Suter was wise to adopt McKane's definition as the basis of his discussion of the Similitudes.[137] This is yet another example of the assumption of Old Testament purity and priority, and of the apocalyptists' linear descent from the canonical texts.

If we begin with the Enochic material on its own terms, it is impossible to see the comparisons as merely figurative, or worse, as 'elaborate discourses'.[138] They integrate heaven and earth, the timeless and the historical. They see one pattern both in the created order and in the final justice of God. The nearest that the Old Testament comes to this is in the reply to Job, or the pessimism of Ecclesiastes. Job is told that he does not understand nature; how can he expect to understand justice? We find it hard to relate these two, but those who spoke in the *mᵉšālîm* had as a premise some concept of natural and moral order inherent in the universe. Ecclesiastes finds he can comprehend neither manifestation of this divine plan, because he is not certain of the fundamental belief of the apocalyptists, that the spirit of man goes upward (Eccl. 3.21). The wise men of Enoch's tradition did go up, and they did learn the secrets of the natural and moral order as a result.

There are several longer passages in the Old Testament which are also designated as *mᵉšālîm*, and it is interesting that the expression used is to *lift up* a parable, *nš' mšl* (Num. 23.7, 18; Isa. 14.4; Mic. 2.4; Hab. 2.6) and that the word for a prophetic oracle or utterance is also from this root, *maśśā'*. We find the *māšāl* and judgement at Isa. 14.4; Ezek. 17.2; 20.5; 24.3; Mic. 2.4; Hab. 2.6, as well as in the Balaam oracles throughout, at Job 27, and Ps. 49.13, 21. The judgement theme of Enoch's parables is therefore well rooted in the Old Testament. But what of the cosmic lore? The Similitudes integrate completely the ordering of creation and the ordering of society and history, in a manner akin (but only akin) to the Egyptian concept of Ma-a-t, which saw the life of man and nature in all its aspects as a reflection of the cosmic order.[139] The cosmic order was maintained by the king. In the Old Testament we find this same idea in the few remaining allusions to the cosmic covenant, the Eternal Covenant which bound together God, people and nature in a coherent and stable system centred upon the king.[140] A related idea underlies the prophecies of the Second Isaiah; God orders and creates in the natural world, therefore he can order and create in history. In the Enochic tradition, revolt against God corrupts the entire system, and so we find the evil angels manifested in natural disorder as the erring stars, and in political evil as the kings and mighty who oppress the righteous. The judgement in Enoch destroys the angels' power and restores the natural order to its original state.

We must therefore return to the other possible root of *māšāl* for our understanding of the Similitudes. How does it relate to the ideas of ruling? Was there some concept we cannot fully grasp which bound the essence of wisdom and cosmic order to the king, the ruler?[141] There are some curiously ambiguous examples of the word even in the Old Testament. The sun and moon, whose movements form a major part of the wisdom revealed in Enoch, are set to *rule* the day and night (Gen. 1.16, 18), and the figure in Ps. 8 who is little less than the angels and *crowned* with glory and honour is put to *rule* over all the works of nature.

If we need 'some determination of the life world out of which the Similitudes grew',[142] we need to start from the Similitudes as they are, and not from the supposed antecedents of *māšāl* in the Old Testament. It is quite possible that the highly complex structures of the Similitudes, which far exceed anything in the collections of canonical proverbs, raise questions not only about their own origin, but also about the processes by which certain of their antecedents disappeared.[143]

The same angel mythology is assumed by both QE and SS, but its forms and application are by no means identical. Each has two lists of angel names: the first of the pair (6.7, cf. 69.2) correspond in sequence for fifteen of twenty-one names, but the second (8.1–3; cf. 69.4–12) differs.[144] In QE the second list has names similar to those of the first, but in SS the second list has names which are not known elsewhere in Jewish angelology. Since we know from Josephus[145] that the Essenes had a solemn oath to preserve the books and the names of the angels, the difference between the second list in QE and the second list in SS is significant. It is unlikely that it was a random mutation, and it must, therefore, represent a tradition not preserved elsewhere. The angels of the second lists are the bringers of knowledge, but in QE the process of conflating the two angel myths of the angel marriages and the coming of knowledge has led to a similar conflation of angel names. This suggests that the second list in the SS is older than its QE counterpart. Since these lists almost certainly also antedate the material into which they are now incorporated, and since the part of QE which contains the angel lists is very early, possibly from the third century, the angel lists in SS could be older still. All this is speculation, but given the context, it is not impossible. The angel lists were not just ornament in an oral composition[146] as their function in these texts makes clear. They are part of a magical system whose details we no longer know. In QE the angels of knowledge reveal charms and enchantments, roots, plants, metallurgy, astrology and the knowledge of the weather. The combination suggests that the angels were concerned with what we should call alchemy, medicine, astrology and magic, although in each case we have to remember that these words carry for us certain overtones not necessarily present in the Enochic tradition. In SS the angels teach metal-working and the art of war, the secrets of wisdom, writing, exorcism and abortion techniques, and sorcery and witchcraft (65.6ff; 69.4ff). The angels of the elements are integral to the scheme and must not be seen as alien. It is common magical practice to believe that the fallen spirits must serve the children of light,[147] and that material effects and natural phenomena are produced by the work of evil spirits under the command of the good, because they are bound by an oath. This oath controls them – another feature of the SS – and great destruction results if the spirits regain their freedom. We may easily misread the great lists of natural phenomena in the apocalyptic writings, and mistake their purpose. Power in creation is depicted as power over the forces of nature, and the rulers of the nations appear alongside the elements as *bound*: Ps. 104.7–8; 135.5, 136; 148.6; Job 38.8ff; Ben Sira 43; Prayer of

Manasseh 5; 1QH 1. QE makes much of the fallen angels and their offspring, the giants who corrupt the earth, but these giants have no role in SS. It may be that the different emphasis is due to different concerns; QE deals with the issues of purity, the mingling of divine and human kinds, whereas SS deals with knowledge and heavenly secrets, and with the fate of the kings and the mighty. Two distinct applications of the system show that the underlying tradition was older than both these deposits.

Much of the SS material is closely related to the Old Testament, but we do not know the exact nature of the relationship, nor can we assume one of simple dependence, although this is often done. Nor do we know that originally separate passages in the Old Testament were brought together for the first time by the creator of the SS. Hartmann has shown that the Old Testament texts which correspond to those used in the SS have not been taken out of their natural contexts, nor has their natural meaning been distorted by a strained exegesis.[148] We must therefore view with caution any claim that the apocalyptists transformed and eschatologized the earlier texts. Suter's analysis concludes that SS *brings together* Isa. 24 and Gen. 6, royal hubris and angel revolt, but that conclusion depends entirely upon his premise that they were originally separate and unconnected materials, and *this we do not know*.[149] Gen. 6 is based upon the angel mythology, as is Isa. 24.17, and what we see in the SS is as likely to be a memory of older ways as a new creation based upon the biblical material. In the SS Asael is bound (1 En. 54.67); in the Old Testament we find similar imagery for hostile kings (Ps. 2.3; 149.8–9), and as a description of severe punishment (Lam. 3.6–9; Ps. 107; Job 36.7–12). I shall argue later that there are several other passages which relate to the binding of the angels, and that the Asael imagery in Enoch is similar because it underlies the texts in their original setting. Several other texts recur as parallels to the SS: Isa. 2; 13; 14; 46; 47; 52; 53; 66; Pss. 2; 76; Joel 2; 3; Ezek. 28 and Exod. 14; 15.[150] The majority are from Isaiah, the prophet most closely associated with the cult in Jerusalem. I shall show that these texts also presuppose the lost angel mythology. We should expect to find the roots of the SS in the setting which gave us Isaiah and the Psalms, Ezekiel, Joel and the triumph imagery which underlies Exod. 14—15. We are pointed to the temple cult and the monarchy.

Throughout the SS the angels are parallel to the kings and the mighty. The punishment of the one is the punishment of the other, but the language used is that of the prophetic oracles against the nations. We are told that this is a profound change from the original context of these oracles;[151] but is it? The prophets also used the angel mythology, and, although the more colourful details are not in the Old Testament, there is always the possibility that they have been removed. The Pentateuch was compiled by those who knew and presupposed far more mythology than they saw fit to include; we cannot assume that the prophets escaped untouched. Familiar old titles such as 'Chosen' and 'Elect' appear in the SS in a new guise: the kings and mighty of

36

the earth are the elect and chosen of Asael, the relationship of the old kings to Yahweh. Isa. 43.8ff is another example of Israel and the nations enjoying a similar pattern of relationship with their gods. The other nations have witnesses just as Israel does, and judgement is pronounced against them. We do not know what these witnesses were, but it is clear that Israel and the nations were all integrated into a similar scheme. Thus in SS we find a survival of the older ways, when the kings and the mighty, who are also the angels, are described as the chosen ones of Asael. The importance of this belief in SS explains why the angel marriages are not emphasized as the source of evil. The mingling of human and divine is not condemned, only the abuse of the resulting powers.

The assumption of direct dependence upon the Old Testament has also led to the SS being described as a complex *midrash* upon Isa. 24, devised by an anti-royalist group, but since they are not a commentary upon any particular text, but rather a type of literature otherwise unknown which bears a strong resemblance to some Old Testament texts, the term *midrash* is not the appropriate choice.[152] We have here three parallel compositions based upon memories of the old cult, celebrating the defeat of enemies before the throne of God in Jerusalem, as did Isa. 33 and Ps. 46, two passages replete with the imagery of the old cosmic covenant and well peopled with angelic figures. It was to this throne, once the royal throne in the Temple, that the seer ascended. The ascent is central in each on the Similitudes, to QE and to the later Merkabah texts, an indication of its importance in the underlying tradition. In QE, Enoch sees the outer house and the inner house with the throne (14.8ff). He enters alone, without the accompanying angel of the later texts, and he learns of the impending judgements, before setting out on a heavenly journey to learn the secrets. He sees the throne on a mountain (18.8–9), or on a mountain near a tree (of life?), destined to be transplanted to the Temple (25.3). The various locations may reflect duplicates within the accounts of the journey, but the ascent is located within the mountain–Eden–temple pattern. In the first Similitude, Enoch sees the dwelling of the angels, and the Elect One under the wings of the Lord of Spirits (39.1–4). There is no description of the throne itself, unless the wings are the throne, as they seem to be in several of the Psalms, e.g. 17.8; 36.8; 63.8. We learn only of the heavenly court and the angel song (cf. Isa. 6; Job 1; 1 Kings 22.19). Enoch learns the secrets of heaven in the heavenly court. In the second Similitude he sees the Ancient of Days, the Son of Man, and the judgement (46.1ff), and in the third the throne of judgement surrounded not only by the angels, but also by the righteous who have achieved, we assume, angelic status.

How the SS relate to QE and the Merkabah texts is not clear, although there are clear points of contact between them. QE and SS both emphasize the great judgement before the throne, a memory of the Day of Yahweh which was the original setting of (e.g.) Ps. 73.17; Is. 43.8ff; Amos 1—2. SS and the Merkabah texts, but not QE, give central place to a heavenly mediator figure who is the

Son of Man or the Elect One in SS and Metatron in 3 Enoch. He is a royal figure, and the various threads which meet in and around his person further confirm the links with the old cult. The Enoch figure in QE inherits what was not always his: 6—11, the core of the work, neither features nor needs him. In SS he is also an addition, and it is the editorial framework of the SS which transforms them into an Enochic pseudepigraphon. The original material was orally transmitted, and was 'an account of visions with a midrashic content'.[153] In 71.14, a problem text because it is part of the double ending to the SS, and may be a later addition, Enoch is identified with the Son of Man. This is the first step towards identifying Enoch with other heavenly figures, and the consistency of this pattern of identification and fusion suggests that the framework within which Enoch and the other figures operated was well established, but belonged originally to none of them. Traits emerge in many different sources which, when viewed together, indicate that several figures were inheriting the mantles of another.

Enoch is the great scribe (1 En. 12.3–4; Jub. 4); Targum Ps.-Jonathan at Gen. 5.24 links him to Metatron the Great Scribe. In Ps. 87, a corrupt and impossible text, the heavenly scribe seem to be Yahweh himself. This is one of the threads.

In 3 Enoch, Enoch is identified with Metatron, a heavenly figure with many secret names. There is no agreement on the meaning of his name, but he resembles the archangel Michael as the patron of Israel, and as High Priest of the heavenly temple. Alexander has suggested that Michael was the exoteric and Metatron the esoteric name of the same angel.[154] In 3 Enoch two streams which were originally separate converge on the Enoch figure, and he becomes identified with the guardian of Israel.[155]

The heavenly priesthood recalls the role of Melchizedek, who was associated with the royal cult in Ps. 110, but at Qumran he becomes a powerful heavenly figure playing the role which had been Yahweh's on the day of judgement (11QMelch). We know from Jub. 4.23ff that Enoch was also a priest figure, but in the mountain-top garden of Eden. These are the second thread. Metatron, Michael, Melchizedek; heavenly patron, royal priest and agent of judgement.

Metatron is also called Yahoel (3 En. 48D), and identified in 3 En. 12 with the angel of Yahweh of Exod. 23.20–1. He guides and protects Ishmael on his ascent, just as Jaoel guides and protects Abraham on his (Apoc. Abr. 17). Yahoel and Jaoel are almost certainly variants of the same name, yet in Apoc. Mos. 29 and Apoc. Abr. 17, Jaoel/Jael is used to address God. Thus Metatron is identified with the angel of Yahweh (if that is the correct way to translate these words); he is named with a name of God, and is called the lesser Yahweh (3 En. 12.5). This is the third thread.

Combined, we can construct a mediator figure with all these qualities, and we find that there is a royal, priestly figure whose identity merged with that of Israel's patron angel, and whose role as scribe and judge derived from the most primitive pictures of Yahweh himself. The Metatron figure is installed as God's agent, and described in 3 En. 3.2 as *na'ar*, the servant. 3 En. 4 contradicts this, and explains that the name means 'youth', since Enoch is the youngest of the angels. What was the association of this title, if 'servant' had to be excluded? Greenfield explains this as another sign of two traditions merging in 3 Enoch.[156] The older saw Metatron as an exalted heavenly figure, a Servant enthroned as prince and ruler, wise in heavenly and earthly matters, robed with glory and named the lesser Yahweh. The later one merged this figure with Enoch and began to tone down the more extravagant claims. 'An editor has subjected the materials he received to an orthodox redaction.'[157] In the later text Metatron is humbled, and any speculation about the actual appearance of God on the throne is avoided. If this theory of editing is correct, we have to take into our account of the Enoch tradition this further evidence that it became less, and not more, exotic with the passing of time. (The extensive additions to the astronomy sections of Enoch which have been found at Qumran, in comparison with the Ethiopic version, are the most obvious example of the traditions decreasing over the years.) The most colourful and apparently alien elements could be the oldest, and the attributes of Metatron those of an even earlier figure.

Metatron and the Son of Man are the same figure (1 En. 46, cf. 3 En. 48C.9; 1 En. 61.8–9, cf. 3 En. 10.4–5; 3 En. 48C.8) even though the descriptions of Metatron are much fuller, and by the time of 3 Enoch the figure is no longer messianic, possibly in reaction to the Christian use of the messianic tradition.[158] QE, SS and 3 Enoch suggest that the Enoch figure was grafted into an existing messianic tradition, which shed certain elements in the later stages of its development. Enoch was identified either with the key *role* of that tradition, as in QE which has no heavenly figure, but does record that Enoch tried to mediate for the fallen angels, or with the key *figure*, the Son of Man/Metatron. The tradition which Enoch inherited knew Yahweh as an angel figure, the patron of Israel, manifested in the earthly king.[159] The king was a priest, the agent of God on earth; the ideal was incarnated in a succession of ancient kings, and subsequently attached to other figures; Moses was one, Enoch another, Jesus another.

There is still no agreement about the 'Son of Man' in the SS, about the origin of the figure, or its relevance to the Gospels. The whole issue is complicated by the possibility of Christian influence on the present form of the SS. No part of them has been found at Qumran to prove pre-Christian origins, but we cannot assume that the Qumran library had a copy of every known text. Nor is there any quotation from the SS in early Christian writings,[160] but since interest in the Son of Man Christology 'died out with the composition of the Gospels' this cannot help us. Nor can their transmission by Christian hands be made to prove anything since they contain the (for Christians) extraordinary identification of Enoch with the Son of Man (71.14ff). Given the present state of our knowledge, the Son of Man problem can have no certain solution; a more fruitful exercise might be to look for possible antecedents in older texts.

The Son of Man passages in the SS have affinities with several texts. Nickelsburg has shown that 1 En. 62—3 is related to Isa. 14; 52 and 53, as well as to several other non-biblical texts which suggest that all are part of a lost tradition about the last judgement, a great angel who is both warrior and priest, exaltation and ascension. Theisohn sees the Son of Man in the SS as an interpretation of Dan. 7 in the light of Isa. 11 and Ps. 110, royal texts, but using also the Servant Songs and Proverbs 8. Suter finds the links to be with Exod. 14—15 and Isa. 13.7–8. Hartmann cites many sources texts from Isaiah and the Psalms in his study of 1 En. 46, and concludes thus:

> In the relatively broad description of the divine ruler which we have encountered in this pericope, the author has accordingly applied to the Daniel Son of Man epithets which in the Old Testament are applied to David, the Davidic Messiah, the righteous Branch, and the Servant of Yahweh. From this we may reasonably suppose that he started from a biblical interpretation which identified these figures with one another.[161]

It is here that our questions about the Son of Man figure must begin. Do we find in the SS a creation essentially alien to the Old Testament texts it most resembles, or do we see a picture of a heavenly ruler and the great judgement which also lies behind – i.e. is presupposed by – the royal texts of the Old Testament *and several other texts which we have not recognized as royal*? Theories about the Son of Man figure in the SS begin to cohere if they are related to the old royal cult. Many fit very well. First we have in Enoch a human figure who acquires the Son of Man status. Second, we have the theory that the Son of Man is a representative deity, like those of the other nations.[162] Until we know exactly how Elyon, Yahweh and the king were related, the possibility that the Davidic kings were both the representation and the representative of Yahweh cannot be dismissed. Third, we have the role of the Son of Man in the great judgement. We know that a Day of Yahweh was expected during the period of the first Temple, and that the Temple was its setting. What we do not know is the role of the king in this process, but Pss. 2 and 110 give us some idea.

Within the SS are several strands of material, which must affect our understanding of the Son of Man/Elect One since the figure is not confined to any one of them. In several passages he is called the Elect One, evidence perhaps of a separate source, but there can be no doubt that the figures are identical.[163] They have many attributes in common. The two Son of Man passages in 1 En. 46 and 1 En. 62—3 are also thought to be variants upon a common tradition,[164] implying that it was broadly based, yet touching upon the same Old Testament materials and dealing with the same themes of judgement and the heavenly figure. Suter has described the SS as a *midrash* on Isa. 24.17–23 which was independent of 1 En. 6—11, even though producing a broadly similar picture. This points to a common origin for both QE and SS. Both were separately dependent upon a traditional interpretation of the Isaiah passage. What we do not know is the *date* at which this traditional interpretation began. Nor do we know that this traditional interpretation of the text was not the original meaning of it. We cannot say, with Suter,

> Although the traditions dealing with fallen angels represent the thought of Judaism in the Hellenistic age, they would have been perceived as related to specific passages of scripture. The determination of the exegetical background of a complex of traditions is therefore of primary importance in understanding the history of these traditions

and imply that traditional interpretation and extenuating circumstances altered the original meaning of the texts.[165]

In the Similitudes, the Son of Man/Elect One is a heavenly figure, but since we know that the SS functioned simultaneously on two levels (the heavenly phenomena *are* the righteous on earth, 43.4; the evil host *are* the kings), we should expect the Son of Man figure to have an earthly referent also. The question we ask should not be, 'Why was Enoch identified with the Son of Man?', but 'With whom was the Son of Man identified before he was identified with Enoch?'. Enoch came late to the tradition.[166] Before his time there are several hints in the Old Testament that it was the king who enjoyed the divine-human status: Isa. 9.6–7; Isa. 11; 1 Chron. 29.20–2; Ps. 2; 11; 21.8; 45.6; 75; 89; 110; and the very setting of the SS indicates a royal figure as the earlier referent of the Son of Man. In the main body of the SS the referent is the community by whom and for whom the SS were composed. Implicit in 62.1, for example, is the idea that the kings and the mighty will recognize in the Elect One those whom they have ill-treated. Nickelsburg has traced the recognition of the heavenly figure from its root in Isa. 52—3, where the Servant is exalted before kings, through Wisdom, where it is the wise and righteous man who is exalted and recognized, to Matt. 25.40 where the last judgement condemns those who did not recognize the great king in his people.[167] To these must be added Acts 9.5, the conversion experience of Saul, 'I am Jesus whom you are persecuting'. The SS certainly have corporate reference, but the tradition in which they stand is that of a single figure, the Servant who eventually comes to represent the whole people.[168]

The last major feature of the Similitudes is the cosmic oath. In the first Similitude, Enoch sees the great angels, then the secrets of heaven, the weathers, the sun and moon, and the stars. He sees how they keep their appointed roles because they are bound by an oath. No other angel has the power to impede this process. In the third Similitude, the oath is associated with the lists of the fallen angels. 1 En. 69 gives the two angel lists side by side, the first having only names, but the second with both the names and the details of the angels' sins. An obscure passage follows, which describes how Kasebel wanted to learn the oath and the name, presumably for evil ends. Suter has made an excellent suggestion for another reading at this point.[169] Kasebel, he says, was not a fallen angel, but joined forces with Michael to restore the cosmic order by means of the oath and the name. The oath is the means of creating order; the sea and the depths are made fast, the sun and moon keep their courses, the winds and weathers obey, and all glorify the Lord of Spirits. This great oath can only be understood in the light of the magical tradition which it most closely resembles, where the oath is the means of binding the fallen spirits who operate through natural phenomena, in order to make them serve a higher purpose.[170] To be initiated into the oath gives great power; knowing the angelic names enables the initiate to summon and bind the spirits in his service, by means of the even greater name whose authority he uses.[171] There are plenty of examples of such magical practices, but for our purposes one of the most interesting must be a magical text described as the 'Hebrew Logos' in the great Paris Magical Papyrus. The magic formula is derived from this passage in 1 Enoch.

> It is evident that the author of this magical formula in the Greek papyrus had access to the Book of Enoch ... It is not impossible that the author of the Book of Enoch, as well as the author of the conjuration might have had access to a much older text, which each of them adapted according to his own special requirements, as it looks almost like an interpolation in Enoch ... The connection between magical papyri and the Jewish pseudo-epigraphical literature, notably mystical literature, must have been much closer than has hitherto been anticipated.[172]

In 3 En. 13.1 and 41.1ff the oath functions as a spell to control the forces of creation. Such later examples only show us that the cosmic oath *became* part of a magical tradition. It is more important for our purposes to see if there is any possibility that this cosmic oath had earlier associations with magical practices, or, at the very least, to define the area within which it originated.

A possible link is to the eternal covenant which we find at several points in the Old Testament. It is a covenant which assures the stability and prosperity of the natural order, and it has to be pieced together from several sources such as the earliest account of the creation, or the royal psalms. In Ps. 89 the king is the centre of the natural as well as the political and moral orders. He manifests on earth the power of Yahweh in heaven. Job 38 describes the creation as a series of bindings; the sea is shut in, the stars are bound, the floods receive their orders. The commands which govern the creation are equated with *wisdom* (39.26), and Job acknowledges the power of this wisdom. The Prayer of Manasseh 2–4 describes how, at the creation, the deeps were sealed with the name of God. It was wisdom in creation such as this which the fallen angels brought. The arts which they revealed all concerned the use and control of the natural order. The archangels sought to counteract the effects of their knowledge with their great oath. If the great oath was broken, the system began to collapse. Hence the joy in 1 En. 69.26ff when, having described the sin of the angels and the power of the great oath, the righteous rejoice when the *name* of the Son of Man is revealed to them.[173] That *name* was the most powerful means of restoring order to a broken world.

There are several early passages where breaking the eternal covenant brings disaster and punishment. The themes of the SS are prominent. Isa. 24.4ff tells of a broken covenant, and the withering of the creation. Judgement follows, when the kings of the earth and the host of heaven are imprisoned, and the Lord of Hosts eventually reigns in triumph. Isa. 33.7ff tells of broken covenants, angels despised,[174] a mourning creation and the beginning of the great judgement. The enemies of Zion acknowledge the might of Yahweh and those who are righteous are promised a *vision* of the *king* in his beauty. Isa. 24 is so close to the SS that it has been suggested as their basis, and indeed the whole chapter is so similar to the later apocalypses that it has been thought a later insertion into its present context. But there is nothing in this chapter which marks it off from the rest of Isaiah, as I shall show, and its apocalyptic world is that of the prophet himself, i.e. the old royal cult. Isa. 33 has the same picture of a broken covenant, and revolt of political and natural evils against the Lord of Hosts and his city, but the themes and vocabulary of this chapter link it to Ps. 46. Both are related to the Priestly flood story of Gen. 9, and the cosmic charter which follows the deluge.[175] This charter was not the invention of the Priestly writer, but a memory of the more ancient eternal covenant which dealt with both the threat of evil and the ordering of creation.

> It is the recent preoccupation with political covenant models which has blinded scholars to this ancient and profound aspect of covenant thought. Not that the cosmic covenant is without political connexion, for the king is at the heart of it.[176]

It is against such a background that we must read Hos. 2.17, which looks forward to the end of an evil domination, that of Baal and his names, and to the restoration of the covenant of harmony and peace; Jer. 33.19–26, which links the future of the Davidic house to a covenant with the day and night; and Ezek. 34.25, which promises a future David and a covenant of harmony and peace to follow once Yahweh has released his people from their enslavers.

Central to this system of covenant control was the king figure, endowed with the Spirit of the Lord as judge, whose reign brought harmony back to the created order (Isa. 11). Ps. 72 is similar, Ps. 89 is clearest of all. The royal throne is part of the natural order, the everlasting covenant fundamental to the royal theology of Jerusalem. The SS derive from it, as do several features of the New Testament. The commissioning of Peter (Matt. 16.13ff) has been compared to the commissioning of Enoch, and there is no doubt that the Enoch and Peter figures were later associated.[177] Peter is given a specific power to bind and to loose on earth and in heaven. Whatever may have been the later understanding of this verse, the original relates to the magical materials of the Enochic tradition, and to the powers which Enoch's antecedent had over the evil forces in creation.[178]

In the SS we find one aspect only of the Enochic tradition. For all its strangeness, it exhibits a logic which enables us to piece the components together into a system. Upper and lower worlds are inseparable, even identical. Heavenly figures are earthly realities. The creation has been corrupted by wisdom used for evil ends, but has been restored by the power of the great oath, the great name. The evil are judged, the righteous attain wisdom and the angelic state. Central to all is the royal figure, the Son of Man. Despite their absence from Qumran, the SS point clearly to their own milieu. The first Christians knew a similar tradition about a heavenly figure with an earthly referent. They also knew that creation was waiting for its *release* when the sons of God appeared (Rom. 8). They performed and expected miracles. Egyptian magicians also used the tradition and recognized the power of the angelic oath. Merkabah mystics accomplished extraordinary feats as the direct heirs of this tradition. Is it likely that so powerful and widely used a tradition grew as the result of the creative exegesis of promising but originally unrelated biblical texts on the part of a small minority of dissidents? I think not.

Conventional readings of these biblical texts have led us to the reconstruction of their world in a particular way, and then to the assumption that the different interpretations of the Enochic tradition are in some way forced, or produced by current fashion. The patterns of association behind the SS are too consistent for that; it is imperative that the texts which have been labelled non-royal be re-examined, not only for the understanding of the Jerusalem monarchy, but also for that of the real roots of the Christian messianic texts.

The Tradition in 1 Enoch (3) : The Astronomy Book

The third section of Ethiopic Enoch is devoted primarily to astronomy, but the text is clearly the remains of something much longer. The section finishes abruptly, after dealing only with the ruling stars of spring and summer, although 4QEnAstr[d] has a section on winter which may be a part of the missing material. 73.1—74.9 is a resumé of a much longer text known from 4QEnAstr[ab], which synchronizes the movements of sun and moon.[179] 74.10–17 is a 'badly bungled attempt' to relate the lunar and solar calendars over an eight-year cycle.[180] There have also been dislocations, and several chapters seem to repeat earlier material. Finally, 80—81 have been added in order to point out the relevance of calendrical chaos to the days of the sinners. There are four MSS from Qumran; 4QEnAstr[a] is the oldest, from about 200 BC, and deals only with the synchronizing of sun and moon, but since 4QEnAstr[b] contains this material and parts of chs. 76, 78, 79, 82, there can be no doubt that the additional material was once attached to the AB.[181]

The whole treatise is a revelation to Enoch. The angel Uriel shows him the laws which govern the movements of the heavenly bodies. 72 describes the movements of the sun through twelve gates, riding in a chariot driven by the wind (cf. 18.4), and how this affects the lengths of day and night throughout the year. The day is divided into eighteen parts: nine light and nine dark at the equinoxes, twelve light and six dark at midsummer, and twelve dark and six light at midwinter. The light of the sun is seven times that of the moon, and the equinoxes are noted.

73—4 describes the phases of the moon, which also travels in a chariot driven by the winds. The whole calculation is based on sevenths and multiples thereof.

75 describes the intercalary days at the end of each quarter (ignored by some people, 75.2), which ensure a year of 364 days. Sun, moon and stars travel the heavens in chariots, with their serving creatures. There is some confusion in the chapter: warmth comes from doors in the sun chariot, but also from windows on either side of the gates on the horizon (vv. 4, 7).

76 describes the winds and their gates in a purely schematic way, which bears no resemblance to real climatic conditions. The winds from the cardinal points bring rain, dew and blessing. Those from the intermediate points bring drought, devastation, locusts and other disasters. This change from astronomy to meteorology has led some commentators to wonder if the passage is misplaced in a text which calls itself the Book of the Course of the Heavenly Lights. VanderKam has tried to explain this with reference to Akkadian astronomical material, which shows that the world regions could be denoted by their winds, a usage appearing in the post-exilic (i.e. post-Babylonian) books of the Old Testament – Ezek. 42.20; Zech. 2.10; 6.5; Dan. 7.2; 8.8; 11.4 – suggesting a Babylonian influence also on the AB.[182] I wonder about this; although the winds in the next chapter clearly do denote the four quarters of the earth, the material in this chapter, for all its confusion, deals not with astronomy but with the weather, a very natural context for a list of winds as winds. The winds of heaven are also a part of Enoch's revelation in 33—36, and the system is the same. Winds from the cardinal points bring good, and the others harm. Here too the list of winds is a part of Uriel's revelation of the names and orbits of the heavenly bodies. No matter how disjointed the present text of AB may be, its contents are similar to other parts of 1 Enoch; both the BW (33—36) and the SS (41, 60) have the same materials. The stars and weather also appear together in the first of the Qumran hymns. The *wisdom* of God created everything; the spirits and the law for their works, the mighty winds ... the heavenly lights, the stars ... the thunderbolts and lightnings ... all their mysteries.

77 deals with geography, but the Ethiopic differs from the Aramaic and is shorter. 4QEnAstr^bc together show that the earth is divided into four quarters but also into parts. The number of these parts is not clear. The Ethiopic has only the northern quarter divided into three parts, which may be a memory of

a threefold division of the earth, but it is possible that the Aramaic described only a twofold division.[183] Milik, on the basis of a disputed reading, has found in this chapter a view of the world corresponding to a Babylonian world map of 600 BC, but this must remain uncertain.[184]

78 has much which duplicates earlier sections, with further emphasis on the 1:7 ratio of moon to sun. We are given for the first time the two names of the sun, perhaps describing its appearance at two different times of the year, and four names of the moon. The names of the sun, Oryares and Tomases, are thought to come from *'or ḥeres* and *ḥammah*, diminished light and heat, and those of the moon, Asonya, Ebla, Benase and Era'e are even less certain. The second and fourth may come from *lᵉbānah*, pale, and *yārēᵃḥ*, moon.[185]

79 summarizes the information given by Uriel to Enoch, and transmitted to Methuselah (cf. 76.4).

80—81 are an addition, pointing out the relevance of the astronomical chaos to the evil actions of the sinners, presumably those who have altered the calendar and set the heavens out of phase.

82 warns Methuselah to preserve the teachings, and to pass on the wisdom to his children. Men will err in matters of the calendar, and omit the quarterly intercalary days. Then follows a list of the angels who lead the months, and their leaders who separate the seasons. The text is not complete; only spring and summer are described, although 4QEnAstr^d has a description of winter which probably belongs here.

The Astronomy Book is very different in character from the other sections of 1 Enoch, but this is due to its emphases, and not to any fundamental discrepancies. AB is a detailed scientific treatise, and fills out one or two elements in the list of secrets revealed to Enoch (chs. 41, 43, 60). We must assume that other such works existed, which dealt with the foundation of the heaven, the regulation of the thunder and lightning, and so forth. These lists were central to the revelations of the seers,[186] and were related to the activities of the fallen angels, who also taught astrology, constellations, clouds, signs of the earth, signs of the sun, and the course of the moon. Although the fallen angels are not mentioned by name in the AB, their presence is implied. The laws are given which they must obey, and we are told that the heavens are in chaos. We must understand this in the light of BW where, on his first journey, Enoch sees the stars, the thunder and lightning, the great rivers and mountains, the treasuries of the winds which move the stars in their orbits, the pillars of earth and heaven, and *the place of punishment for the stars who did not come up at their proper time* (18.14ff). Immediately Uriel shows Enoch the angels who took human wives and led mankind astray. In the second heavenly journey Enoch also sees the places of punishment for the erring stars and the fallen angels. The places are separate, but erring stars and fallen angels stand side by side in Enoch's scheme of things. The AB gives the true wisdom regarding the laws of heaven, and the application of this wisdom enables the wise to detect the presence of erring angels in the distortions of the calendar. Hence 80—81, which link calendrical chaos to the days of sinners. All nature is distorted because the true order of the stars is not known to sinners (80.7). Enoch, in contrast, had read the heavenly tablets, and passed the information to his son.

Two major questions arise from this section: how old is the material in it, and why did the solar calendar represented in this text become part of a theological dispute? What was at issue?[187]

The Jews were known as astronomers in the fourth century BC, and the early date for AB is confirmed by Ps-Eupolemus, who links Enoch with astrology.[188] We have, however, had reason to believe that the Enochic material was not always associated with that figure. VanderKam's arguments for a Babylonian origin for both the astronomical material and the Enoch figure may not be the only ones possible. The question I wish to put to the AB is not 'How old is it?' because clearly we have insufficient evidence to draw any conclusions, but, 'Is it possible that this material also comes from the time of the monarchy, and is as old as the other Enochic traditions?'

Several pieces of evidence suggest that the solar calendar which AB depicts was *abandoned* during the exile, implying that the solar calendar was very ancient, and associated with those who did not accept the exilic innovations. This is quite consistent with what the people who transmitted 1 Enoch tell us about themselves. Jub. 1.13–14 implies that Israel left the divinely revealed solar calendar before the return to Jerusalem. CD III, 13–14 says that after the destruction, the remnant learned the 'hidden things' in which Israel had erred, and that these were calendrical.[189] The Qumran community, which strictly observed the solar calendar, never accuses its Jerusalem enemies of deliberate deviation in calendrical matters. 'We can only deduce that there was a calendrical difference, not that the difference created the sect.[190] The solar calendar is presupposed by many of the priestly writings of the Old Testament, and influenced the final form of several post-exilic texts.[191] A good case has also been made for the antiquity of the Jubilees calendar by tracing the pentecontad elements to a primitive agricultural calendar in Canaan, and the solar elements to the royal cult in Jerusalem which was dominated by solar imagery.[192]

Given the small amount of Aramaic material which has survived, and the relative state of the Ethiopic text, certainty must be out of the question, but there are other factors compatible with an early date. We know, for example, that the naming, binding and numbering of the stars were signs of the power and wisdom of God (Ps. 147.4–5; Isa. 40.26; Job 9.9; 38.31), exactly as in the cosmic oath passages of the SS. There is also the possibility that the names of the sun and moon derive from Hebrew rather than Aramaic, although the evidence here is slender and should not be pressed. Further, the form of the solar calculations in the AB is very primitive, the twelve gates of the sun are not to be equated with the Zodiac, as earlier writers thought, nor is there any explicit reference to zodiacal motion of sun or moon.[193] The gates of the sun in the east are determined by dividing into six the arc of the horizon between sunrise at midwinter and sunrise at midsummer, and the gates in the west by a similar process for the sunsets. The horizon is thus the only system of reference known to the writer, and Neugebauer concludes:

> We are dealing with an extremely primitive level of astronomy, which shows no relation to the sophisticated Babylonian astronomy of the Seleucid period, nor to its Hellenistic Greek sequel. Of course no chronological conclusion should be based on such negative evidence, for procedures which might well be of *local Palestinian origin*, uninfluenced by contemporary scientific achievements elsewhere.[194]

The stars have no real significance in the scheme, functioning simply as the guardians of the solar determined months and seasons. The distribution of intercalary days is unique, no parallel for it is known,[195] yet the pattern fits well with, and was probably determined by, the seven-day pattern of the Jewish week. The resulting scheme of months gives four quarters, each of exactly thirteen weeks, so that the festivals would fall on the same day of the week every year. The 7:1 ratio of sun to moon is mentioned in Isa. 30.26, a passage which also tells of a mysterious teacher to be revealed, and Isa. 59.19 tells of winds which drive a shining heavenly body, Yahweh rising on his city.[196]

Even though there was great controversy surrounding the calendar in the second century, there is no polemic in this treatise, except in the inserted chapters which tell of calendrical errors in the times of sinners. The error which the writer warns against is not the lunar calendar, but the omission of the intercalary days, a dispute of which we now know nothing. It must antedate the fierce polemic of Jubilees, and come from a time when the calendar was not caught up in a theological dispute. The AB does not mention any of the festivals. It cannot have been cultic in the narrow sense of the word, yet it is a theology in the sense that the whole scheme is depicted as the law of God for the guidance of the angels, revealed by an angel to a seer, for the benefit of the elect. If the solar calendar *was* abandoned during the exile, this material in AB, like so much else in the Enochic tradition, could be a fragment of something pre-exilic.

The methods of reckoning time in the Old Testament are not easy to determine, and must remain something of a mystery. We have several dates of the type 'the ... day of the ... month', and the procedures for fixing the festivals in relation to each other, e.g. Lev. 23, Deut. 16; but nowhere is there any detail of how the calendar was established. This was a matter of great cultural importance, and such an omission is surprising. The calendar may have been the concern of the king: 1 Kings 12.32ff describes how Jeroboam altered the appointed date for a feast, and celebrated it 'in a month he had devised of his own heart'. Or it may have been the concern of the priests; later Samaritan tradition records that the calculation for the calendar was not derived from Torah, but was separately revealed to the High Priests, and handed down by them. The means of calculation were engraved upon the High Priest's staff.[197] We should, then, expect the calendar to be associated with the Temple.

Two curious pieces of evidence point to a major calendrical change at the end of the monarchy. In the early period, days were reckoned from sunrise, but in the later, from the evening. The change occurred 'between the end of the monarchy and the time of Nehemias'.[198] Similarly, sometime after the reign of Josiah, the ordering of the year was altered. The Babylonian system was adopted, with Babylonian names or simply numbers to designate the months, and a spring new year.[199]

Now days counted from sunrise *could* indicate a solar reckoning,[200] such as was abandoned during the exile, and the reordered calendar, beginning in the spring, would have shifted the emphasis of the new year festival from the older cult's celebration of the kingship of Yahweh and his triumph over hostile forces, to the Deuteronomic reformers' Passover and Exodus from Egypt.[201] Was there, I wonder, any connection between the adoption of a foreign calendar in the wake of a great reform to purify Israel of foreign ways, and the statement that the paraphernalia of sun worship was removed from the Temple as a part of the same reform? Was a foreign calendar the only alternative to the tainted sun cult? Both pieces of evidence are consistent with the claims of Jubilees and CD that the old solar calendar was abandoned, but a connection with the reforms of the Deuteronomists would give us a reason why the solar calendar became a *theological* issue. It was those who objected to the new ways of the apostate and impure generation who kept to the older reckoning.

Josephus' description of the Essenes' morning ritual, praying to the sun with traditional prayers,[202] must have had some basis in fact, and yet it seems incredible in a group dedicated to the purity of the faith, unless their practice was related to the sun worship reported in Ezekiel's time (Ezek. 8.16), another eastward facing ritual. We assume that this was a pagan rite, but those who worshipped thus may have thought otherwise. 1QH12, 4–9 says that the laws governing the days and hours and seasons are the laws of the Great Light of Heaven. Does this refer to the sun and the solar calendar, or does it refer to God? We cannot tell, but there is comparable imagery in the Old Testament. Yahweh is the sun and shield (Ps. 84.12); his light rises over Jerusalem as the sign of her deliverance (Isa. 60), coming as a shining heavenly creature driven by the wind, as in the AB. The coming of the morning is the time of deliverance (Isa. 17.14; 33.2; Ps. 46.6). Perhaps we should take this imagery more seriously. The material of the AB could be very old indeed.[203]

The Tradition in 1 Enoch (4) : The Book of Dreams

The fourth section of 1 Enoch is the Book of Dreams (BD). Fragments of four MSS have been found, 4QEn[cdef], the oldest of which, [f], dates from the late second century. Unlike the other parts of Enoch, it is not a composite work; its author wrote within the Enochic tradition, and shows us how this was used to give the Maccabean revolt a context within the divine plan for history. Daniel, written at the same time, uses the same framework, although the BD and Daniel emphasize different parts of the overall theological system. BD has nothing to correspond with the Son of Man, whereas Daniel has no detail of the great judgement, even though the SS have both together. Both Daniel and the BD describe the history of Israel in terms of good and evil angels, although again the detail is different in each. Both describe the period since the exile as one of domination by a succession of four powers destined for destruction before the advent of the kingdom. Both Daniel and Enoch are also wise men, who deal in visions and dreams. The pattern of history was just as much their business as the pattern of nature and the pattern of the stars. Insight into the natural order and into history are both gifts from God. Dan. 2.20–3 shows how the changing times and seasons, the rise and fall of kings, and the deep and hidden things of God are all entrusted to the wise man. The first of the Qumran hymns is similar; it links the ordering of creation and the destinies of men: 'These things I know by the wisdom which comes from thee.' The whole argument of the Second Isaiah for the new beginning of Israel after the exile is derived from this association of wisdom and history. The wise, says the prophet, *cannot* predict what will happen, and thus their claims are groundless. Only the God of Israel knows the future, because he creates both the natural order and the pattern of history. There was to be a new creation and a new history. The wise would be discredited. The wise were not, however, discredited in the circles which produced both Daniel and Enoch. We must ask why this was, and why the tradition most closely associated with that of the restored community, that of the Second Isaiah, differs on this point.

The BD has two parts. The first is a short dream about the destruction of the earth, the second a complex history of Israel in the form of an animal fable. Both dreams come to Enoch before his marriage, and both were told to Enoch's son Methuselah. The BD is important for several reasons. We have here a history which covers the same period as the canonical texts, although in much less detail and with different emphases. The history is *joined* to the myth of the angels, just as we have seen Enoch *joined* to the story of the Watchers. As in Daniel, the post-exilic history is told with animal symbols; but unlike Daniel, the BD uses a scheme which culminates in the great angelic judgement. We also see that the enemies in this section are not evil men within the community, fellow-Israelites who persecute the righteous, as in the epistle of Enoch, but Gentile rulers and those whom they have influenced; they are called the shepherds and the blinded sheep.

The history begins with Adam and Eve, Cain, Abel and Seth. There is no reference to the events of Gen. 3. A single star falls from heaven to disturb the primeval peace, but unfortunately the Ethiopic text is not clear at this point, and the effects of his coming are not clear. But it is clear that a single star precedes the many who come later to take human wives. The single angel was probably the Asael figure, the teacher of forbidden knowledge. The children of the angel marriages are three distinct types of giants, here described as elephants, camels and asses, but in 1 En. 7.2 as giants, nephilim and Eliud.[204] A similar list appears in Jub. 7.21–2, and the curious variety of names for the giants in Gen. 6 has led some to think that the three types of giants were known when Genesis was written.[205] The sequence of angelic arrivals here shows that the single Asael figure precedes Semiḥazah in the scheme, that knowledge corrupted the earth before the angel marriages, and that the angel who brings this knowledge comes in the time of Adam and Eve, a possible contact with Gen. 3, where the unexplained serpent is at hand to corrupt mankind with knowledge which will make them like the *elohim*.[206] This period before the flood is described in great detail, little of which can be derived from the Old Testament. Even 1 En. 6—11 is not a direct source, since the roles of Semiḥazah and Asael are different. Stories about the evil which preceded the flood are also thought, on other grounds, to be *missing* from the priestly stratum of Genesis, which has no account of human rebellion in Gen. 1—11, or any trace of an Eden story. F. M. Cross observes: 'P's summary statement referring to violence and corruption (in the Noah story) must presume a knowledge of concrete and colorful narratives of the corruption of creation.'[207] Have we here another example of material about angels being removed from the tradition? (Compare von Rad's remarks about Gen. 6.)[208]

Enoch then sees seven archangels, described as white men, leaving heaven. Four begin the judgement, and three take Enoch up to his place of vision, a high tower. It is important at this point to notice two things: the angels are described as men, in contrast to the human race who are described as animals, and the high tower from which Enoch sees his vision of the future is the Temple (cf. 89.66). Daniel has a similar way of describing earthly and heavenly figures; the kings are rams and goats (8.3ff) and the angels are men, or sons of men (10.5ff; 10.16; 12.6); but we are not told the setting of Daniel's vision of the Son of Man. The throne and the judgement make it likely that this too had a temple setting. As early as the time of Ps. 73 the Temple was associated with visions of the judgement. The psalmist describes the ways of the wicked on earth, how they taunt Elyon and say he has no *knowledge*. Their end is seen in the sanctuary of God. At the end of his vision from the high tower, Enoch sees the punishment of the angels exactly as it is described in 1 En. 10.4–6; this is the earliest material, and possibly the source used by the writer of the BD. Was this early material also set in, or associated with, the Temple? Enoch sees one angel bind Asael, another punishes the angels who have taken human wives, and a third stirs up strife among their offspring. Unlike the account in the BW, there is no emphasis here upon Semiḥazah.

Noah is born a white bull and is instructed in a secret. He becomes a *man*. After the flood, new animals appear to attack Israel: lions, tigers, wolves and others appear. The saga of the patriarchs, who are white bulls, alters with the birth of Jacob, who is the first white sheep. Moses and the Egyptians are sheep and wolves, and the Lord of the sheep comes down from his lofty house in order to rescue his flock. The Lord of the sheep accompanies the flock, terrifies the pursuing wolves and they flee. He appears to the leading sheep on a summit of rock, and that sheep also becomes a *man*, who builds a house for the Lord. The period of the Judges is one of occasional blindness, culminating in the choice of a ram, Saul, and another ram, David. A great broad house is built for the sheep, and a tower on which the Lord of the sheep stands. The era of the monarchy is not emphasized. Chosen sheep, the prophets, are rejected and killed. One of them, Elijah, is rescued and brought up to join Enoch on the tower. Those who forsake the house and the tower become blind, and the Lord of the sheep permits their slaughter. He leaves his house and tower, and gives the flock over to other shepherds, seventy shepherds, whose deeds are to be recorded in heaven (89.61–2). They raise 'the most vexed question in Enoch'.[209] The shepherds all exist together, they are commissioned together (89.59; 90.21). They cannot be human, for they are represented as *men*, not as animals. They are subordinate angels, left in charge of the sheep. All their deeds are recorded by 'another' in books to be sealed and produced at the great judgement where the shepherds are condemned along with the fallen stars, the angels who have taken human wives. This dual existence of the angels is another of the apocalyptists' characteristics; they exist simultaneously, yet act in succession in the seventy epochs. This view of time and mythology cannot be described simply in terms of paradigm and aetiology: this is too modern and too Western a way of thinking. It obscures the apocalyptists' use of events in another dimension (even this is not a good word, since events happen in time), in order to structure and understand what they perceive. The other dimension constantly penetrates the world of experience, and its effects have to be perceived in time, in history, even though the causes of these events are not temporally prior to them. This other dimension lies afresh and in its entirety beneath each new epoch of history and can be used to interpret each new crisis. It transforms the confusion of life by giving it a context. The angel mythology here represented by the seventy shepherds can be accommodated to our ways of thinking by the use of labels such as paradigm or eschatology, but these labels are something of our own devising, tools to enable *us* to translate from the one to the other. They do not represent anything actually present in the ancient apocalypses or their use. Here in the BD we have seventy angels, spirits of history, lords of nations who exist simultaneously outside time, but who appear in a series within history, because humankind lives and thinks within the dimension of time. The same pattern of angelic lords appears in Zech. 2, although here we find the number four, as in the pattern of Daniel's four great empires, rather than the seventy pattern we find in Enoch. Four horns scatter Judah, Jerusalem and Israel. These horns are not *smiths* (Zech. 2.3), but angelic creatures, of whom we now know nothing. The root *ḥrš* appears in several ambiguous texts, especially in Isaiah,[210] and should be understood in the light of (*ḥereš*) 'magic', satirized by Isaiah as (*ḥārēš*) 'dumb', when he mocks the ancient gods. Daniel 7.5 describes the four beasts coming out of the sea, apparently together, even though they are the four world empires who dominate Israel in succession.

The animal apocalypse (AA) sets out to explain the suffering of Israel in a manner related to that of the Deuteronomic histories. Both attribute the sufferings of Jerusalem to the disobedience of its rulers, but the emphasis is different. The Deuteronomic history deals with the pre-exilic period, and defines obedience in terms of the Mosaic Law, and the one sanctuary, whereas the AA deals with the post-exilic period and defines obedience as ruling within the limits prescribed by God. The sufferings of Jerusalem are seen as sign and proof of the evil of its rulers, and not as punishment on the city. The rulers are in revolt against God's plan, but we are not told why God permits the evil state of affairs to continue. The seventy-based scheme of the AA is related to the expectation of 1 En. 10.12, that seventy generations would pass before the judgement of the angels.[211]

The idea that nations are ruled by their patron angels, their shepherds, is quite common in the Old Testament, although the shepherd imagery associated with the royal texts has been attributed to the pastoral origins of the royal line. This obscures an important aspect of the royal mythology which links it to that of other nations, and to the AA. Angels were appointed by Elyon, each to his nation (Deut. 32.8), and Yahweh was the angel allotted to Israel. The shepherd rulers could be envisaged in their heavenly aspect, as in Ps. 80, the shepherd of Israel enthroned on the cherubim, or their earthly, as in Ezek. 37.24. The two could merge, as in Isa. 40.11, where the divine shepherd carries the flock, or in Micah 5.1ff, where the divinely appointed shepherd appears after a time of suffering. The shepherds ruled other nations than Israel; thus 'Cyrus my shepherd shall fulfil my purpose' (Isa. 44.28), and they could be destroyed by the divine wrath, as at Jer. 49.19 and 50.44, 'What shepherd can stand before me?', the theme of the oracles against Edom and Babylon. The shepherds and their flocks could be foreign armies attacking Jerusalem (Jer. 6.3) but most frequently in the Old Testament the shepherds are the evil rulers of Jerusalem, as in the BD. Isa. 56.11 describes shepherds with *no understanding* (cf. Ps. 82, where this is the charge against the evil rulers who are the gods of the heavenly council). Jer. 25.34 describes judgement on the shepherds, the lords of the flock, a passage thought to underlie the judgement scene in the BD.[212] Zech. 11 describes the rule of the shepherds, the rule of kings, as a punishment from God (11.6). The prophet himself is called to be a shepherd, but the text is confused. Ezek. 34 promises judgement on the shepherds who have failed Israel. The Lord himself will be the shepherd. In the BD the shepherds are angelic; most of the references in the Old Testament need not be. They could refer simply to earthly rulers. I shall argue later that the political philosophy of pre-exilic Jerusalem requires that these shepherds also be thought of as angelic, or having an angelic aspect. The history of Jerusalem was seen in the context of warring angels in revolt against God long before the scheme of the seventy shepherds was penned to explain the crisis in the time of the Maccabees.

The seventy angels are also seventy periods. The first ends with the return from Babylon (89.72), when the shepherds have pastured the sheep for *twelve* hours. The second ends with the coming of the Greeks (90.1), by which time thirty-five shepherds have completed their allotted periods. The third ends after another twenty-three have served (90.15) and the fourth begins with the birth of new lambs into the flock of Israel, lambs with open eyes, who cry out to the blinded sheep. This fourth period is described in great detail: it is the writer's own time, the era of the last twelve angels before the judgement. A similar scheme of history, according to the allotted periods of the angels, has been reconstructed from the two Hebrew fragments listed as 4Q180 and 181, but there is insufficient text to draw any real parallel with the BD.[213]

The history in the BD divides into four eras with each change of dominion; the first period is the rule of Babylon, the second Persia, the third Egypt, and the fourth Syria. A similar scheme occurs in Daniel, although the BD does not use Daniel's symbols of a statue and the monstrous beasts to depict the fourfold scheme.[214]

The epoch of the last twelve angels ends with the great judgement. The throne is set up and the books are opened. The seventy shepherds are judged, together with the fallen angels and the blinded sheep. The books of judgement and the heavenly scribe are another ancient theme which we find in the prophets and the Psalms long before the time of the BD. Ps. 87, a corrupted text, describes Yahweh writing down the names of the citizens of Jerusalem. Ps. 69.29 prays that sinners may be blotted from the book of the living (cf. Ps. 56.8). The book of Yahweh lists both righteous and sinners (Exod. 32.32–3) and Isa. 4.2, another unclear text, tells of the people written down for life. Isa. 30.8 is a judgement against rebellious sons, and the prophet is told to record this in a book. Isa. 34.16 refers the reader to the book of Yahweh for details of the coming judgement. Dan. 12.1 promises deliverance for those written in the book. Mal. 3.16 refers to a book containing the names of those to be spared at the judgement, Isa. 65.6 refers to those written down for destruction. The apocalyptists knew of several types of heavenly books. There were the registers of the righteous and the books of judgement, which may have been identical, since both seem to have had a part to play in the great judgement. We find these throughout Enoch (81.4; 89 *passim*; 90.17, 20; 104.7). There were also the tablets of history on which everything was inscribed, and from which the seers drew their knowledge of what was to come (Ps. 139.16; Dan. 10.21; 1 En. 81.1–2; 93.1–3; 103.2; 106.19; 107.1; Jubilees *passim*); heavenly tablets which described and prescribed what ought to happen, either in matters of the calendar (e.g. Jub. 6.29ff) or laws and festivals (Jub. 6.17–18; 16.16–29; 18.18–

19), and many more, perhaps including the tablets of the ten commandments; also heavenly blueprints for the building of the Temple (Exod. 25.9, 40; 26.30).[215] As with all the cases where there is a similar usage in the Old Testament, we have to ask if the apocalyptists were deliberately reusing something because it was in the Old Testament, or simply using something because this was a part of their tradition. If they were reusing sacred texts, it is strange that they are not quoted.

After the great judgement, Enoch sees the new Jerusalem, and the ingathering of all the sheep with their eyes opened. A white bull, a human Messiah figure appears, and eventually all those in the kingdom are transformed into white bulls, i.e. they return to the state of Adam.

The AA is written so as to focus interest on the fourth period, the time of the last twelve shepherds which leads up to the great judgement. The key passage for dating the work is 90.6–16, which describes the events leading up to the early triumphs of the Maccabean revolt. The great horned sheep is Judas who fights against foreign armies and is not defeated. The text of the crucial verses (vv. 13–16) is not clear. It describes the battles of the great horned sheep. Charles rearranged the text so as to give vv. 13–15 and vv. 16–18 as doublets, with v. 19 belonging to each, but more recently Milik has read vv. 13–15 as an account of the battle at Bethsur, v. 14 referring to the appearance of the angelic horseman to help Judas' army (2 Macc. 11.8). The last reference to earthly battles is in v. 16, with Judas still alive and victorious. The great judgement begins in v. 17, when the prediction style of the vision ceases to be a description of past events, and starts to be genuine prediction. The great sword is given to the sheep to destroy their enemies, a detail thought to derive from the prophecy against the shepherds in Jer. 25.34ff. Thus the writer of the BD saw in the uprising the beginning of the End. He must have been writing during the early years, before the death of Judas in 160.[216]

There can be no doubt that the BD is a development of the tradition of the BW, applied to a particular crisis. Both works use the myth of the fallen angels, albeit with different emphases, suggesting that the relationship was not one of narrow, linear dependence, but rather of interpreting within a broader tradition. Both expect the judgement as the prelude to the kingdom, both anticipate a fiery abyss for the place of punishment (10.6; 18.11; 90.24), and both look forward to the conversion of the Gentiles (10.21; 90.30 – if this is how we are to understand this verse). In other respects the differences between them – and they are slight – are consistent with the BW coming from a period when Israel still used a royal mythology which involved the hope of fertility and prosperity, and when Jerusalem and its Temple were not thought impure. Thus the setting for the new age in the BD is a *new* Jerusalem, whereas in the BW it is the present earth, purified and restored to the happy state it enjoyed before the coming of the angels. In the BW the life of the new age is finite but happy (10.17; 25.6), but in the BD there is a vague picture of euphoria, with all transformed into white bulls, restored to the paradisal state of Adam. In the BW the conflict is between God and the fallen angels; the earth merely cries out to heaven in its suffering and the judgement begins, but in the BD there is great emphasis upon the struggle and the time of the sword, as there is in the eighth week of the Apocalypse of Weeks (91.12). The people participate in the struggle. In the BW the divine throne is set up on the highest of the seven heavenly mountains (18.8; 25.13); but in the BD the picture is less colourful, and the throne is simply in a pleasant spot (90.20), near enough to Jerusalem to supervise the dismantling of the old city and the erection of the new.

These developments are consistent with the BD being the application of the earlier tradition of the BW to the Maccabean crisis, just as Daniel applied other elements of the old tradition in the vision of the Son of Man. Where these traditions were preserved and transmitted we do not know, but it is significant that the BD, like the AW, sees the second Temple as an impure place.

The Tradition in Enoch (5) : The Epistle of Enoch

The fifth section of Ethiopic Enoch, the Epistle of Enoch, is known from two Qumran MSS dated towards the end of the first century BC. Of these, 4QEn^g contained only material from the epistle, whereas 4QEn^c had the epistle, the BW, the BD and the Book of Giants. The Ethiopic form of the text suggested long ago that there had been dislocation in the early chapters of the epistle, and the Aramaic has confirmed this, even though the exact nature of the dislocation, and its significance, is still debated.[217] The epistle has none of the colourful heavenly visions of the BW or the SS, and, upon a first reading, seems to be a very different type of text. No angel is mentioned by name, and no punishment is dwelt upon in graphic detail, except at 103.7. The bulk of the epistle resembles the prophetic books, with their woes against evildoers and their exhortations to the faithful. It is concerned with the affairs of this earth. Embedded in the epistle is a cryptic account of Israel's past and future known as the Apocalypse of Weeks because it divides all history into ten 'weeks'.

Closer comparison of the BW and the EE, however, shows that they have much in common, and that the difference between them, as between the BW and the AB, is one of emphasis and application. Both name God as the Great Holy One (10.1; 14.1; 25.3; cf. 92.2; 97.6; 98.6) and the Great Glory (14.20; cf. 102.3). Both compare the regular pattern of nature to the deviation of man (2.1—5.4; cf. 101). Both refer to Israel as a 'plant of righteousness' (10.16; cf. 93.2, 5, 10). Both promise the wicked no peace.[218] Both look forward to the last judgement (100.4; 102.3; 103.6ff). Both know of Enoch's ascent to heaven, and both know a scheme of history based upon the number seventy; there are seventy generations until the judgement of the angels in 10.12, and the judgement of the angels is in the seventh part of the tenth week in 91.15. Both know a heavenly wisdom which is the secrets of creation. What is revealed to

Enoch on his heavenly journey in BW and the wisdom revealed in the seventh week are very similar: the voice of the Holy One (14.24), the works of heaven, the breadth and length of the earth, the foundations of heaven and the resting places of the stars (17.1ff; cf. 91.11–14).

Differences do exist between the BW and the EE, but these must be seen as variations within a common scheme, applications of an underlying tradition. The Apocalypse of Weeks, for example, reckons its ten weeks from the time of Adam, but the BW reckons seventy generations from the fall of the angels. We seem to be dealing with two different histories both written to a scheme of seventy, rather than different versions of the same history. The two versions are fused together in the BD. Although both expect a messianic kingdom, there are different ideas about its coming: 10.12 envisages a plant of righteousness appearing at the end of seventy generations, as the onset of the messianic kingdom, whereas 91.15 sees the kingdom beginning with the victorious resurgence of the righteous in the eighth week. The BW has no place for a new temple in the future kingdom, whereas the AW sees a new temple as part of the messianic age. The BW envisages an earthly resurrection (5.9; 10.17; 25.6) with the righteous enjoying a prosperous old age. The EE sees the final end of the righteous among the hosts of heaven (104.2ff). The BW solves the problem of suffering with the promise of renewed earthly life, whereas the EE is more sophisticated. The righteous will enjoy earthly prosperity during the eighth to tenth weeks, and the righteous dead will be raised as members of the heavenly host after the great judgement. The BW sees evil as the work of fallen angels on earth; the EE says it is caused by evil men, even though the great judgement is upon the angels.

Both the BW and the EE look for a pattern in history, and expect a messianic kingdom with a chosen group called the plant of righteousness appearing in the last days. Both expect a last judgement. The EE, however, has developed its ideas beyond those of the BW. In the AW an earthly struggle is to bring in the kingdom, not just divine intervention, implying a politicization of the struggle, rather than a simple conflict against evil in all its forms, the manifestation of the fallen angels. The BW has no criticism of the Temple because it antedates the corruption, whereas the EE hopes for a new temple. The BW has no place in the heavenly host for the common man, whereas the EE foresees eternal life for the righteous, shining among the stars. Above all, the EE makes men, not angels, the agents of evil. The EE is a development within the Enochic tradition after certain events have taken place. The history of Israel has been written and is known in the form familiar to us in the Pentateuch and the former prophets, the Temple has become in need of renewal, access to the heavenly host has become possible for ordinary mortals, not just kings and wise men, and the older ideas of angelic responsibility for evil have been modified by an emphasis upon human responsibility, perhaps, as we see in the BD, in the form of co-operating with the evil ones.

The oldest section of the EE is the Apocalypse of Weeks, a cryptic history of Israel in seven 'weeks', from the first patriarchs to the last judgement. Schemes based upon multiples of seven like this, e.g. 70 or 49, were common during the post-exilic period, but it is not possible to trace their origin with any certainty. It has been suggested that they derive from the seventy-year prophecy of Jeremiah,[219] but I think it more likely that in Jeremiah's time seventy was already a significant figure to describe a period of distress which would end with the intervention of God. The second Isaiah, without mentioning the 'seventy', sees the exile as ended by judgement upon the angels who had ruled the old order; i.e. he sees that period as one which ended with what he understood as the judgement and the new creation.[220] In the post-exilic period we find great diversity, the common elements being the seven-based scheme, and the idea that all history is predetermined (a fundamental difference from the scheme of the Deuteronomists), moving towards the judgement and the establishment of the chosen people. Thus we find seventy years, seventy generations, seventy angels, seventy weeks of years and their equivalent, ten jubilees. We find the seven linked to the sabbath rest, the last jubilee to the Day of Atonement, and the end of the seventh week to the New age, the jubilee.[221] The histories are reckoned from primeval times, from the fall of the Temple, from the fall of the angels, from the establishment of the priesthood. All agree that seventy denotes a time of wickedness; for Jeremiah or his editors it is the exile after which the punishment of the people will be over, but Jeremiah is conspicuously isolated in this view. The other histories view the seventy period as one of evil domination, of evil inflicted upon the people. God's intervention would bring release.

1 En. 10.12 promises seventy generations from the fall of the angels until their final judgement.

Dan. 9.24–27 has Gabriel explain that seventy weeks of years are decreed to bring an end to the present wickedness, although this passage is now thought to depend upon the theme of Jeremiah, but not his actual words.[222]

1 En. 89.68ff has seventy shepherds ruling history from the destruction of the Temple until their judgement.

T Levi 16.1ff predicts seventy weeks of priestly error, making void the Law and polluting the sacrifices. 17.1ff is a history of the priesthood in jubilees; in the seventh, the evil of the priests leads to captivity. Appended is a scheme of weeks, with the return from Babylon in the fifth week, and another decline of the priesthood in the seventh.[223]

From Qumran have come several indications of similar schemes:

11QMelch has a jubilee-based scheme, culminating in the Day of Judgement at the end of the tenth jubilee, when Melchizedek brings judgement upon Satan and his host.

4Q180, 181 describe the activities and periods of various angels, which are engraved on the heavenly tablets.

4Q384–9, attributed to Ezekiel, contain a series of weeks and jubilees.
4Q390 has a scheme of ten jubilees reckoned from the fall of Judah.

The different histories vary in their view of when the time of evil began.[224] The earliest, the BW, links it to the fall of the angels, but the later ones link it to the fall of the first Temple. As a result they see the exile, the period of evil, continuing into their own time. They are still waiting for the judgement and release which were proclaimed by the second Isaiah as a *thing of the past*. For one group only, the people for whom the Second Isaiah wrote, the exile ended after seventy years, and was seen as a punishment for disobeying God's law. For the others, it lasted for a period which had to be related to the number seventy, the time of wickedness and evil rulers, which would end with the great judgement of the sinners and the release of the faithful. Given the sharp division between those who believed the exile to have ended, and those who believed that it had not, is it likely that the latter would have adopted and adapted a prophecy of the former? It is more reasonable to suppose that both groups derived their seventy-based scheme from a common heritage, from something which belonged to all Israel before the divisions precipitated by the return from Babylon.

The AW is a mixture of a jubilee-based scheme, and a seventy-based scheme. The Ethiopic text has a seven-week scheme separated from weeks eight to ten, and although the Qumran material now shows that the ten-week scheme was the original, the climax of the seventh week remains the focal point of the history as it would have been in a jubilee-based scheme. In its ten-week form the apocalypse has a chiastic structure, with judgements in weeks two and nine, the beginning of righteous judgement and its execution in weeks three and eight, the wonders of Sinai and its covenant in week four with its counterpart in week seven, the revelation of sevenfold wisdom to the elect, which must have been seen as another covenant.[225] Weeks five and six, the central weeks, deal with the building and destruction of the temple. The significant events of weeks 3–8 each happen at the close of the week; at the end of the seventh week there is the most significant event of all, the jubilee bringing release. This represents the author's own time, after which weeks eight, nine and ten see the triumph of righteousness, the rebuilding of the Temple, the great judgement upon the angels and the creation of a new heaven with new powers.

If the symmetrical construction is significant, the correspondences should tell us something of the people who composed and transmitted this apocalypse. For them, the turning-point in history was during the sixth week, when those who lived in the Temple became blind and forsook wisdom. A man (Elijah) was taken up to heaven. The giving of the covenant in week four is accompanied by 'visions of the holy and righteous', not the account of Sinai with which we are familiar, except perhaps in the truncated fossil of Exod. 24.9–11. The counterpart in the seventh week reveals sevenfold wisdom about the creation to the elect. In the Ethiopic form of the text, this seventh week is followed by a summary of the heavenly secrets, suggesting that these secrets *were* the sevenfold wisdom concerning the creation. Such wisdom was not possible for all, but only for the chosen. It marked the beginning of the new era. 93.10 has a striking resemblance to two other texts, CD I and 1QS8. The former summarizes post-exilic history: God remembered the covenant and he caused a *plant* to spring up. Before correct teaching was given, the penitents were *blind*. The latter describes the chosen community as an eternal *planting*, the elect who repay the wicked.[226] It is possible that all three passages derive from a common tradition about the end-time, the seventh week of the AW, but the AW does not imply, as does CD, that it was a change of heart which brought the penitents back to the true path. The setting of the AW within the EE implies rather that those who transmitted and interpreted this apocalypse were the original aggrieved party, the guardians to whom the others should, and did, return.

The dislocations of the apocalypse have been seen as evidence of interpretation of the AW in the manner of a Targum. Elements of 91.11 appear several times in 91.1–11, not just as random fragments, but as an expanded commentary upon the 'roots of violence' and the 'structure of falsehood'. The passage following 91.17 in the Aramaic, but absent from the Ethiopic, is thought to underlie both Eth. 91.17 and Eth. 92.3, 5, and to set the resurrection of the righteous as the climax to the expanded version of the AW. Such a reconstruction must, of course, be tentative; but if the AW was one of the materials from which Qumran Enoch was composed, it is very early evidence for an interpretation of history which differs radically from anything in the Old Testament.

The AW also differs in several respects from the Book of Dreams. The BD deals with hostile Gentiles and apostates, the AW simply with sinners. The BD envisages a new Temple after the judgement, the AW before it. The BD envisages a time of struggle before the final judgement, the AW before the messianic kingdom which then culminates in the judgement. On some matters the texts are not clear; the nature of the kingdom which follows the judgement in the AW may, or may not, differ from the ideas in the BD. The exact nature of the resurrection hope in each section cannot be established.[227]

On the major issues, however, the two agree *against the Old Testament*. Both expect the angelic judgement as the goal of history, both see the post-exilic period as one of uncleanness and apostasy, both look forward to a new Temple, both recognize the importance of three major figures who were believed to have achieved angelic status. In the BD there are three figures who begin as animals and end as *men*, i.e. in the code of the apocalyptists they start as mortals and become angelic; Noah (89.1) became a *man*, Moses (89.36) became a *man*, and Elijah (89.52) was caught up to heaven. In the AW these same three, and no others, are referred to as *men* (93.4, 5, 8). In other words, we see in each of these histories the essentials of the apocalyptists' scheme: judgement, renewal, post-exilic deviation, and the possibility of angelic existence for mortals.

The AW must not be divorced from its context in the EE. Of the sections of 1 Enoch this seems the least promising if we are trying to piece together the world of the apocalyptists as something bizarre and unrelated to the Old Testament as we know it. The BW gives us the mythology of the angels and the heavenly travels. The AB gives us the scientific interests. The BD gives a view of contemporary history in the form of an animal fable, and a distinctly nationalistic interpretation of the last judgement. The EE is different. It is disappointingly like the prophetic books of the Old Testament, and serves to remind us that the prophets may also have had a context like that of this epistle. The epistle gives us a valuable picture of the people who transmitted the Enochic tradition, and lived by its precepts and hopes. We see the debates of their time. We see their enemies. We see their aspirations. Unfortunately we have insufficient evidence to determine when this time was, or who were the enemies. All we can do is let the EE speak for itself, and not insist that it be read in the light of our existing ideas.

The people of the EE (I avoid the fashionable word 'community', since this implies a defined minority group) used and interpreted the AW for their own time. They are therefore to be numbered with those who were heirs to the traditions of Israel, but who believed that the exile did not end with the return from Babylon. They claimed direct revelation (91.1; 98.8; 103.1ff, 104.8) and, by implication, claimed to be the true upholders of the eternal covenant (99.2), since their enemies were those who had perverted it. Enoch, like Balaam, spoke to them in *parables* (Num. 23.7, 18; 24.3, 15; cf. 4QEn^g at 93.1, 3 – different in Eth., which has no reference to parables). They were also the upholders of wisdom. The seventh week of the AW promised that the elect would learn the secrets of creation as the preliminary to the new age, and the EE links the accepting of this wisdom to salvation (98.9, 14). Wisdom is a body of teaching, not just a pattern for good living; the sinners actually try to annul it. No place will be found for wisdom in their evil times (94.5).

These emphases upon wisdom and keeping the eternal covenant in the face of those who would pervert and annul them, raise again the question of what was meant by each of these terms. The form of week seven, and the insertion which follows it, show that wisdom was a part of the new covenant, and involved a knowledge of cosmic processes and the power to restore harmony to the created order. The 'sinners' had rejected this.

The form and nature of this dispute also sheds light upon our people. The debate is over injustice in this life, and whether or not there is any other life in which sinners will receive their just rewards. The sequence of the argument is seen most clearly in the climax of the epistle (102–4).[228] 'This life is short', say the sinners; 'eat, drink and get rich by any means; death is the same for all men, no matter how they have lived.' The revelation entrusted to the righteous is that there is more to life, and that everything is recorded in the heavenly books (103.1ff). The righteous spirits will live and rejoice, whereas sinners will be punished in Sheol. This is an implicit condemnation of Deuteronomic theology; prosperity is not the reward for good works. In fact, prosperity only adds to the self-deceit of the sinners, since they take it as proof of God's favour (96.4). The repeated thrust of the argument in the epistle is that there is to be a great judgement, something the sinners deny. All deeds are recorded in heaven (98.7ff; 103.2ff; 104.1ff). The angels remind God about the state of affairs on earth (99.3). The righteous will one day judge the sinners (95.3; 96.1); and they will enjoy angelic status as lights in heaven (104.2ff).

Although the details are not present, perhaps because they are assumed, it is the mythology of the BW which provides the framework for this argument. Exactly as in the EE, suffering humanity begs the angels to intercede and ask for the judgement (9.3; cf. 15.2 where the fallen angels are told that it is they who should intercede for man.) The deeds of the evil doers are recorded (12.3ff), although this is clearer in Jub. 4.18ff. After seventy generations the angels will be punished (10.12). The EE has some details not in the BW; the angelic status of the righteous after death, for example, and the righteous as the judges of the persecutors.

Nickelsburg has compared this argument against sinners to that of Wisd. 2, and has shown that both 1 En. and Wisd. use the same pattern.[229] The sinners argue for a short, sweet life with no fear of judgement, and the righteous claim knowledge of mysteries, resurrection and judgement. Both argue against the Deuteronomic belief in rewards in this life. He finds in both 1 En. and Wisd. evidence for an older belief in the last judgement which underlies also Dan. 12; Ass. Mos. 10; Jub. 23; and T Jud. 25, although the form in 1 En. 104 has certain differences, for example, in not using the language of Isa. 52—3. What is most important is that this belief is not the *conclusion* of the argument of the epistle, but its premise. The assertions of the sinners are contradicted *on the basis of this established belief.* It is unlikely that these beliefs arose as a response to the crises of the second century.

We must therefore conclude that denying wisdom, espousing a Deuteronomic-based belief in rewards, denying the last judgement and perverting the eternal covenant were in some way related, and that they characterized those who opposed the Enochic tradition. Those who preserved this tradition could question, as did Job, why it was that they, the righteous, should suffer the curses of breaking the covenant; 103.9ff is a 'pastiche of words and phrases from Deut. 28'.[230] The epistle depicts a divided society. It does not deal with pagan or gentile oppressors, as does the BD, but with those who have been altering the received tradition. The sinners are described as idolaters and blasphemers (99.7; 104.9; 94.9; 96.7), who can, nevertheless, reckon themselves the blessed of God. This should warn us against taking the accusations of idolatry and blasphemy too literally. Throughout the epistle we have a picture of social injustice alongside religious disputes. The people of the epistle were the victims of oppression and injustice, and the boundaries of privilege corresponded with a different interpretation of the covenant. The closest parallel I can find to this situation is in Third Isaiah. Comparison with such an early text may cause alarm, but I shall show in my treatment of Isa. 56—66 that those chapters also describe a divided society where religious differences and social deprivation coincided, where there was dispute over the true meaning of the covenant, where the practices of the wicked were described as idolatry, where the sinners espoused the arguments of Deuteronomy, and where the righteous did not agree that the exile had ended. They still looked forward to a time of judgement and restoration.

It is no coincidence that the literary forms of the epistle are those of the prophets. The writer of the epistle claims knowledge of the heavens just as the prophets did of the divine council. He brings woes upon sinners with a promise of future judgement, and exhortations to the righteous that they should not fear, but rather look forward to judging their enemies, and to shining in the heavens when their tribulations have ended. The exhortation of 95.3 bears a strong resemblance to the old holy war oracles (Num. 21.34; Deut. 3.2), as do the promises of 91.12; 96.1 and 98.12.[231] Given that we have no means of dating the original of the epistle, is it wise to imply that the prophetic forms used are a *conscious imitation* of the older oracles, or that the judgement scene so fundamental to the whole argument is 'creatively reused' in 104? What we find in the EE are prophetic forms closely associated with wisdom forms, claims to direct revelation, and access to the affairs of heaven. We find arguments for divine justice, and a pattern of Israel's history based upon belief in the great judgement, angels and a holy war ideology.

Grelot has suggested that there is Essene eschatology in the EE,[232] and, although Nickelsburg does not accept that there is decisive evidence for this view, he also thinks that the EE could be pre-Essene, and thus evidence for the beliefs of a fairly early period. What is important for my argument is that we have in this epistle clear evidence of prophetic and wisdom forms used together within the framework of the angel mythology, in conflict with the Deuteronomic ideology, and indicating a deep-rooted dispute among the heirs to the traditions of Israel.

The Application of the Tradition

It is not easy to date the Enochic material in any meaningful sense of the word. The MSS from Qumran can, of course be dated with varying degrees of accuracy, but unless we can prove that any particular deposit of the material is an original composition without significant sources, and is in its turn the source of all references to similar themes, dating the material must remain impossible. We must content ourselves with surveying material associated with the Enoch figure, and how it is applied. We cannot, for example, use a supposed reference to the second or third century AD as evidence for anything but the date of one part of a complex and composite text. We do not date the biblical texts on the basis either of their actual MS remains, or of the latest redaction or allusion discernible within them. Such a procedure would be recognized as ludicrous, yet it is the one scholars employ to decide the date of the Enochic material. Nor can we conclude that the myths in the Enochic materials were composed during the late Hellenistic period on the grounds that they are unlike what we read in the Old Testament but similar to certain Greek myths.[233] It is wiser to look only for *applications*, not dates, since this constantly acknowledges a substratum older than any particular deposit.[234] Further, the great variety of applications which we can see even within the texts of 1 Enoch, and the period of time over which these applications were made, suggests that the tradition in this work was not only deep-rooted, but also broadly based, and in a state of good health for many centuries. Two factors must always be borne in mind when deciding whether or not a suggestion is reasonable: the people who wrote this literature regarded themselves as the purists over against the corrupted establishment in Jerusalem and enemies from abroad, and the arguments which they use *assume* certain myths as an accepted basis from which to proceed with their theology.

The BW emphasizes the sins of the angel marriages; other sections of 1 Enoch do not. We should therefore expect this marriage/purity issue to have been uppermost in the minds of those who composed the BW. A good case can be made for the BW having been prompted by debates about the purity of the priests in Jerusalem,[235] especially as there are other texts which link writings of Enoch to this dispute. T Levi 14.1 refers to a writing of Enoch which predicts that the priests will go astray in the last days. Their major sin is impure marriage. A similar association has been found in 4QTLevi,[236] and the theme of priestly purity is also prominent in the Damascus Document which lists all those who fell through 'whoredom', beginning with the Watchers, and culminating with the priests (CD II). It is interesting that a passage so closely related to the SS, Isa. 24.17, is also interpreted in CD IV, 14–18 in terms of the sins of the priests. Thus a link between the fallen angels and the priests is clearly established,[237] and we may regard the dispute over priestly purity as one in which the angel mythology was not only deemed relevant, but was of sufficient status to be presented as the *basis* for criticizing the religious establishment of the time. In the present form of the BW the myth of the heavenly knowledge has been joined to the marriage myth, and the priests were also accused of false teaching (T Levi 14.4–6; CD I, 19; IV, 16–17). But this false teaching is wrong interpretation of the Law, and not the more exotic revelations of the fallen angels; this shows that the myth was originally intended to deal with another situation, and that the condemnation of the priests and their teaching was a secondary application.

Several attempts to find the milieu of the BW link it to criticism of the

Temple; the Asael material was polemic against the Day of Atonement teaching.[238] 1 En. 12—16 was written by a Galilean group opposed to the contemporary Jerusalem priesthood.[239] We know from the Blessing of the Priests found at Qumran that an ideal of the priesthood in this period was to be like angels in the heavenly sanctuary,[240] so that to describe the sins of the priests as the fall of the angels is a natural application of the myth, even though this cannot have been the original setting, nor the priests the original referent. They were not superhuman giants corrupting the earth, nor was their knowledge the secrets of creation. Many elements of the myth are redundant in this application, further evidence that it originated elsewhere.

The history of the priesthood during the period of the second Temple is complex and defies summary, but several difficulties and discrepancies warn against treating any one view of the period as the objective truth. Concern for purity was characteristic of the restoration period, yet this condemnation of the impure priests in the BW is couched in that very angelic mythology which there is good reason to believe the reformers tried to suppress. This implies that accusations of impurity were made by both sides in the dispute, and that the ideas of the reformers were not the only ones on purity at this time. Further, details which can be deduced about the priestly marriages of the period from non-biblical material call into question the real motives of the reformers[241] when they expelled certain members of the High Priest's family. There are several hints that the Jerusalem priesthood was not acceptable in all quarters even at that early date; the association of Enoch with the impurity of the priests may not be a second-century phenomenon. Both the historical surveys in 1 Enoch condemn the cult of the restored community, and even within the Old Testament there is striking evidence that the purity of the restoration priesthood was in doubt. Satan challenges the purity of Joshua in the setting of the heavenly court (Zech. 3), and in language reminiscent of Deuteronomy we find that the Lord who has chosen Jerusalem also chooses to purify Joshua and give him the right of access to the heavenly court, the sanctuary. Malachi deals at length with the corruption and false teaching of the priesthood, and promises a future judgement when the Lord will appear in his temple. It is significant that the condemnations of both Zechariah and Malachi presuppose the angelic court and the temple judgement theophany which are central themes in 1 Enoch. The original text of Isa. 61.5ff shows that this prophet also knew of priests who were not recognized. He was addressing a group over against his own, who aspired to such recognition.[242] Ezra is presented as the legitimate son not of his father but of the last officiating High Priest of the pre-exilic Temple (Ezra 7.1ff). He is also furnished with a complex genealogy unique in the Old Testament, and one wonders if this was necessary because his claims were disputed.[243] We shall probably never know what really happened, but the uncertainties at least make it possible that the priestly impurity with which the Enochic writings were linked was not that of the second century. The dispute could have arisen in the time of the restoration, whose cult was condemned by both the BD and the AW.

Other attempts to locate the BW have suggested that it was not religious but political comment,[244] and that the problem addressed was not corruption within the priesthood, but Israel over against her enemies. Some of the key evidence for the priestly application has to be dismissed as being a minor motif before this case can be made[245] but it is none the less an interesting suggestion. It gives due weight to an element of the myth which the priestly interpretation left redundant. The superhuman giants who terrorize the earth and destroy it through their evil knowledge are, it is suggested, a reference to the evil rulers who terrorize Israel. The wars of the Diadochi (323–02), and the struggles of Egypt and Syria for the control of Palestine (217–198), have both been offered as possible settings for the Semiḥazah myth, which was inspired by an exegesis of Gen. 6 in the light of certain Greek myths.[246] Perhaps this attributes too much ingenuity to the author of the BW, and does not take sufficiently into account the claims of this tradition to represent something which was not a deviation from the ancient ways. There was, after all, a complex of political philosophy within Israel's own tradition designed to cope with the claims of kings who thought themselves divine, and it is unlikely that any myth and its interpretation would have been composed simultaneously. Nevertheless, the relevance of the Enochic myth to the crises of foreign domination cannot be disputed, and just as Enoch is cited elsewhere as condemning the impurity of the priests, so too another aspect of this mythology emerges in a text whose concern with evil foreign rulers is not in question.

Dan. 8 describes the horn which exalts itself against the Prince of the Host[247] and his sanctuary. The concern of this chapter is with rulers not priests, but the fact that the arrogance is directed against the sanctuary shows that religious and political considerations were inseparable. Both Daniel and Enoch describe an ascent to the throne for the judgement of evil rulers, either by the Son of Man, or by Enoch, who in the SS is eventually identified with the Son of Man and has the same role. It is possible that we should read the BW as applicable to the impure priests and also to the evil rulers, although perhaps these applications were not made at the same time. Both interpretations accord with the evidence of other texts, but neither does justice to all the elements within the mythology. This implies that neither was the original application nor the original setting, but that both political and religious interpretations were recognized as legitimate uses of the older material.

Like the BW, the SS has many levels of application, but again, none uses all the elements of the tradition. None can be used as evidence for the one true meaning of the SS, nor of the one date at which they were written. All we have is evidence for various dates at which the Enochic tradition was the basis of a living theology. In the SS, for example, we find the wisdom elements of the tradition listed, but there is no attempt to interpret them or to apply them.

They are a part of the hope of the chosen. The angel marriages are also mentioned, but nothing is built upon them. What we can detect, however, is a dispute about religious matters which has caused division. A great judgement awaits those who deny the Lord of Spirits or the Son of Man (38.2; 48.10; 54.2; 63.7), but it is not clear whether these sinners are pagan foreigners or apostates who have left the tradition which 1 Enoch represents. It would be tempting to read this text in the light of the protests in Third Isaiah,[248] because in both cases there is also a social division. The righteous are oppressed by sinners, who do not fear that there will be a great judgement upon their wickedness. In addition, the myth of the angelic judgement is applied in the SS to rulers condemned not for oppression but for immorality. The hot springs of the rift valley were favoured by Herod the Great, and he is thought to have inspired 67.4ff, which observes that even the presence of waters heated by burning angels had failed to impress upon the king the fate which awaited him.[249] Such a passing reference can hardly be considered a major application of the tradition, but the very fact that something so trivial is also expressed in terms of the angel mythology shows how far the mythology permeated the thought-world of the time. The forbidding landscape around the Dead Sea had, as we shall see,[250] been associated with the last judgement for a long time. Another interpretation within the SS mentions the Parthians and Medes (54.5ff), for whom several dates have been suggested in attempts to locate the SS;[251] but here again, the fact that the movements of foreign armies can be interpreted in terms of the angels is probably more important than the precise identification of the enemies in question. Thus in this one section of 1 Enoch we find the mythology, complete with several redundant motifs, used to describe and explain religious division at home, crises abroad, evil native rulers and their fate, and the geological phenomena of the Dead Sea valley.

The AB shows how another element of the material was used. Of all the secrets of heaven revealed to the seers, we have detailed information only about the stars and the weather. 75.2 shows that this material had at some stage been applied to a dispute about intercalary days of which we know nothing, but 80.2ff is the clearest example in the whole corpus of how various facets of the tradition were applied to the contemporary situation. The chapter presupposes a calendrical dispute caused by sinners, and the tradition is applied thus: the stars and the months are out of order, the seasons and the phases of the moon are distorted. A picture emerges like those of the creation when the eternal covenant has been broken. This is evidence that the *stars* have rebelled, that evil is at work. The new calendar is presumably the sign of the evil, because it is not cited as its source. The sinners are punished by being denied access to the truth about the stars,[252] unlike Enoch who is confident in his heavenly knowledge from Uriel. Sinners even regard the stars as gods. Once again, it would be unwise to suggest a date for this dispute. We can only note yet another aspect of life for which the mythology provided a natural and accepted framework.

Of all the sections of 1 Enoch, the BD is probably the only one we should attempt to date. It is not a composite work, and its references are so specific that it would be hard to argue for a date other than in the heyday of Judas Maccabaeus.[253] Here the tradition of the angels is applied to the whole history of Israel. We find the familiar material of the Pentateuch and the former prophets permeated by unfamiliar angels[254] and punctuated by different emphases. The past is not prelude to the present, but to the future. The angels of the apocalyptists' last judgement are shown to have had a role throughout Israel's history, but the greatest emphasis is placed upon the post-exilic period. The evil time of the seventy angels is that of the second Temple, and the writer's own time is the beginning of the expected end. There is no distinction between the heavenly dimension and the earthly.

The EE, like the SS, addresses sinners who doubt the beliefs of the Enochic tradition, and live as though there would be no great judgement. As with the Parthians and Medes in the SS, so here there have been several attempts to identify these righteous and their enemies, the sinners, but there is insufficient evidence in the text for any certainty.[255] More important than the identity of these parties is the manner in which the condemnations are made. The EE makes it clear that its enemies are those who espouse the theology we associate with the Deuteronomists,[256] and the teaching of the reformers is scorned on the basis of beliefs derived from the angel mythology. This tells us nothing about the date of the dispute, but it does show that it could have been much earlier than the second or first century. The EE has been thought to be the work of Pharisees, to be Essene, or even pre-Essene;[257] but none of these identifications is as important as the possibility that this text actually opposes a particular stance within the Old Testament, especially as it is the stance associated with those who proclaimed themselves as *reformers* of the cult of Jerusalem. The EE also contains the AW, recognized as a distinct, older text. The AW in its turn is both based upon an older system of sevens and tens, and also expounded by a later writer to make it relevant to a new situation.[258] It does not mention the desecration of the Temple, even though it shows great concern for the affairs of the Temple, but it does seem to describe the rise of a distinct group within the seventh week.[259] It would be tempting to date the AW in the years before the Maccabean revolt, but again, we find that the complexity and variety within the Enochic tradition to which this historical survey testifies, is more important than the date of its composition. There are within 1 Enoch two different accounts of Israel's history, the AW and the BD. Both are based upon the same numerical scheme, but each uses it in a different way, suggesting an established pattern of history writing which antedates both. Each refers to the same three people achieving angelic status. This is hardly coincidence, but shows that beneath each account lay a belief exactly similar to the apocalyptists' hope for the transcendence of death. This is not the only example of differences within the Enochic scheme. There are two distinct attitudes to the heavenly knowledge.

In the BW and the SS it is evil, but in the AB it is entrusted to Enoch, and in the EE it is the reward and the sign of the chosen. No source, however, doubts that there is such knowledge, or that it is associated with the angels. Despite this evidence of diversity within 1 Enoch, everything coheres if it is read as an application of, or a dispute conducted within the framework of, the basic mythology.[260] As in any religious tradition, the applications were open to debate and negotiation, but the fundamentals were not. The myth of the angels was fundamental.

I believe that 1 Enoch is of far greater importance than has hitherto been realized, not only for our understanding of the inter-testamental period,[261] but also for our understanding of the Old Testament itself. It has proved possible to trace the roots and antecedents of its mythology into the very earliest stratum of the Old Testament. I do not, however, think that this early mythology fell into disuse and was then rediscovered and revived by the prophets of the restoration. It was in continuous use in some circles, but was officially abandoned by certain elements who exercised a disproportionate influence upon the present form of the Old Testament text. The mythology was that of the royal cult, but it outlived the kings whilst retaining the patterns of thought which had once centred upon them.[262] Much of the ancient cult was diffused. We find some traces of it in the metaphors and assumptions of the Old Testament texts,[263] and others in the later legends which attached themselves to biblical materials and biblical figures. Much of the ancient cult was deliberately suppressed, and we then find its traces in the otherwise inexplicable polemic of certain texts, or certain curious silences we cannot fail to hear. Many of our texts were, I believe, not the ancestors or sources of the Enochic tradition, but were written over against it. Some even record the disputes and divisions which marked the parting of the ways. How far the two traditions were separated in the minds of ordinary folk we cannot know, but there is no mistaking a polemical thrust in much of the Old Testament and in most of the apocalypses. Can we be sure that the enemies in each case were not enemies within?

I shall devote the rest of this volume to exploring this possibility. In order to range widely, I have had to be brief on several points, and offer only the bones of an argument. I do not pretend to offer a comprehensive answer to anything. My aim is more modest. I wish to establish, on as broad a base as possible, the validity of the question I am raising. The working out of any new approach to Old Testament studies is far from easy, and involves a considerable amount both of cross reference and complex argument. Were it possible to read all the chapters simultaneously, the force of my argument would be more clearly perceived. Such a manner of reading is, however, not possible. I therefore offer a series of studies which interrelate, rather than a conventional sequence of chapters in which each builds upon its predecessor. The whole must be read in the light of the New Testament, whose problems this study sets out to illuminate.

NOTES

1 Details of the recovery in Knibb (1978), vol. 2, Introduction.
2 Black (1970).
3 Milik (1976). For details of earlier scroll discoveries in the third and ninth centuries see Nardi (1960), summarized by Bamfylde (1984), p. 31.
4 Alexander (1977).
5 Rowston (1975); E. P. Sanders (1985), p. 143 shows how there has been a similar tendency in the treatment of gospel materials.
6 *Contra* J. A. Sanders (1972), p. xiv.
7 Milik (1976), pp. 46, 73.
8 Metzger (1977), p. 22.
9 Alexander (1977), p. 156.
10 Knibb (1978); also Greenfield and Stone (1977), p. 61.
11 Milik (1976), p. 88.
12 Charles (1913), p. 163.
13 But it was known to Clement of Alexandria, Origen, Didymus the Blind and Gelasius of Cyzicus; see Rowston (1975), p. 557.
14 Nickelsburg (1972), p. 39.
15 A name first used by Syncellus in his preface to 1 En. 6 (Black [1970], p. 21).
16 Black (1970), p. 13.
17 Black (1970), p. 5.
18 Barr (1975), pp. 31–2; Burkitt in PBA xvii (1931), p. 443; Manson in DNB 1931–40, p. 170; Moltmann, *A Theology of Hope* (ET 1967), p. 137; cf. Collins (1978); Koch (1972), p. 125: 'The difference between what man was in ancient times and what he is in essence today grows in proportion to the progress of historical research. It is no wonder that theological exegesis is becoming more and more colourless and anaemic.'
19 The Americans are VanderKam (1984a), pp. 139, 190, and Hanson (1975), p. 9. The last quotation is from Milik (1976), p. 35. The italics are my own.
20 Gilchrist (1984), pp. 19, 33, 38.
21 Chevalier (1976), pp. xii, xx. cf. Halifax (1979), p. 144, a conversation with a south American Amahuaca shaman: 'You must realise, my friends, that the deeper we go into this, both written and spoken words of formal language become less and less adequate as a medium of expression. If I could arrange it, we would have a session of visions ourselves, and then you would understand. But that would take time. Meanwhile we will continue with indifferent words, and inflexible modes of expression.'
22 Barr (1975), p. 33, observes that in all currents of study of apocalyptic 'there is no strong religious cultural tradition connecting us through the centuries with these books'. True. We must turn elsewhere.
23 Gruenwald (1979), p. 4, talks of the natural tendency we have to take the OT as the norm; Koch (1972) is better described by its original German title *Ratlos vor der Apocalyptik*; cf. Collins (1979).
24 Black (1970), p. 5, but for a more constructive debate, see Stone (1980b), p. 42; Davies (1980); Collins (1981).
25 Fohrer (1970), p. 479.
26 Koch (1972) and VanderKam (1984a), ch. 1, summarize well the approach from wisdom; Hanson (1975) exemplifies the approach from prophecy. Also Rowland (1982), esp. Pt 3.

27 A few examples are: Nickelsburg (1977a), p. 318, 'imitation'; (1977b), p. 387, 'imports'; ibid. p. 404, 'elaborates'; (1981), p. 581, 'drawn from'; VanderKam (1984a), p. 8, 'expanded Gen. 5'; p. 115, 'borrows'; p. 119, 'his biblical models'; Hanson (1977), p. 232, 'goes far beyond the biblical text'. Perhaps we still assume that a biblical basis is the hallmark of theological respectability, cf. Collins (1978); Koch (1972), p. 124: 'The weakness of present biblical scholarship becomes evident. The non-biblical material which is used is employed in a purely illustrative way; its exegetical application seems superficial and a matter of chance; the material is not fitted together with the biblical statements into one overall context of life, since it is not understood as being the product of one and the same history.'

28 Respectively Dimant (1983), pp. 21, 23; Nickelsburg (1978); Suter (1979a); Scholem (1965), p. 46; all the italics are mine.

29 Stone (1980a), p. 35.

30 Dimant (1983).

31 Nickelsburg (1972).

32 Nickelsburg (1977a), p. 327.

33 Schechter (1910), pp. xxvi ff.

34 Alexander (1983), p. 244; York (1984); Kaufman (1985).

35 Murray (1982b).

36 Collins (1981), p. 83: 'There is a remarkable degree of agreement on a core group of apocalyptic texts and their general characteristics', with the dangerous explanatory note, 'The significant point is that the *agreed* core texts provide criteria by which the relevance of disputed works can be assessed', form a classic circular argument. *We* define apocalyptic by consensus, and then sit in judgement upon the ancient texts.

37 Often the case where the NT is the starting point, e.g. Käsemann (1969); Hennecke (1963), vol. ii, Introduction; Schmithals (1975), p. 130.

38 Hanson (1975), p. 9.

39 Collins (1979); Rowland (1982).

40 VanderKam (1984a), pp. 107ff.

41 VanderKam (1984a), p. 119.

42 Mueller (1972).

43 Stone (1980a).

44 Alexander (1983), p. 246.

45 Milik (1976); Greenfield and Stone (1977).

46 Cologne Mani Codex 58.1–60.12 (ed. and tr. Cameron and Dewey 1979).

47 Alexander (1977), pp. 165ff.

48 For bibliography see Hengel (1974), vol. i, p. 215; vol. ii, p. 141 nn 677–80.

49 Enoch's association with this tradition can be traced for centuries, e.g. French (1972); Laycock (1979), a systematization of the curious language which the magi attributed to the Enochic angels.

50 There is a good introduction and bibliography in Hull (1974), showing clearly the refusal of NT scholars to consider evidence other than of their own choosing.

51 Neither of these characteristics, nor their association with astronomy, is ever stressed. It is even denied. Beckwith (1981): 'the Jews do not appear to have practised astronomy themselves', despite Theophrastus, *de Pietate*, in Stern (1976), vol. i. 'The Jews converse with each other about the deity, and at night time they make observations of the stars, gazing at them and calling on God in prayer'. For magic see Strabo, *Geographies*, xvi. 2: 'The people are sorcerers and pretend to use incantations'; Justin, *Trypho* 85.3, the name of the God of Abraham used by Gentile exorcists; Origen, *c. Celsum* 1.26, 'They worship angels and are addicted to sorcery'; the Prayer of Nabonidus, published by Milik (1956); the Jewish exorcist who healed the king's ulcer, Gaster (1901); Morton Smith (1978), pp. 69ff on the widespread use of the name YHWH in magic.

52 Alexander (1977), p. 178.
53 Alexander (1984).
54 Alexander (1977), p. 176; Scholem (1965), pp. 75ff. Jehudah the Saint who edited the Mishnah was a rationalist who tried to exclude references to the Merkabah.
55 Alexander (1977), p. 176; Neusner (1966), vol. ii, pp. 180ff.
56 Odeberg (1973); Alexander (1977).
57 Scholem (1965), pp. 55, 46, 45 respectively; Gruenwald (1979), p. 29, argues that although mystical visions had biblical roots, apocalyptic had a *new* mood. Or should we just say a *different* mood, until we know more about the editorial processes which produced the OT?
58 *Anti.* viii, 45; cf. Porta (1658): 'A certain Frenchman in his book called *Daemonomania*, Tearms me a magician, a conjuror ... whereas I never writ here or elsewhere what is not contained within the bounds of nature.' See also 2 Kings 5.11, the expectation that the king of Israel can cure (*'sp*) Naaman's leprosy. *'sp* here may be from Akk *ašapu*, to practise exorcism, as suggested by J. Gray (1970²), p. 505, and MacLaurin (1975).
59 Collins (1978) emphasizes that a biblical basis is synonymous with theological respectability.
60 Hull (1974), Introduction; Morton Smith (1978).
61 VanderKam (1984a), p. 8.
62 VanderKam (1984a), p. 41 n61 draws attention to a possible corruption of *bârım*, 'diviners', to *baddım*, 'liars', at several places. Such corruption of texts is, as I shall show, very common when the material concerns the older cult. Isa. 44.25 associates *hars*, diviners, wise men, and knowledge; Jer. 50.36 curses princes, wise men, diviners and warriors of Babylon. Most significant of all is Hos. 11.6, where there are several suspect words: 'cities' could be 'watchers', *'ryw*; 'gates' could be 'diviners', *bdyw/ bryw*. There follow *counsels* of wise men and a line which can no longer be read at all.
63 Grelot (1958b) suggested this on the basis of Arabic and Ethiopic cognates.
64 VanderKam (1984a), p. 29.
65 1 QapGen, col. 2.1–16; Fitzmyer (1971), pp. 50–3, 80–1.
66 Dimant (1983).
67 Grelot (1958b).
68 Jansen (1939), summarized by VanderKam (1984a), pp. 13ff.
69 VanderKam (1984a), pp. 38–51.
70 VanderKam (1984a), p. 50.
71 Dimant (1978): 1 En. 6—11 were extracted from an independent source to give background to the Enochic texts. 'Such an assumption may explain the existence of Hebrew (and not Aramaic as the rest of the Enochic writings) fragments in Qumran of this particular text.' Collins (1978) challenges this conclusion.
72 See below, pp. 21ff.
73 Charles (1912), p. 14.
74 Von Rad (1963 rev. edn), p. 111.
75 Cross (1975), esp. pp. 306ff. Also the later debates as to what was meant by the *sons of God* in Gen. 6, in Alexander (1972).
76 Glasson (1961); Nickelsburg (1977b); Bousset (1902); Betz (1969); Gray (1957); Hanson (1975).
77 Against, respectively, Gray, Nickelsburg, Betz, Hanson.
78 J. Z. Smith (1983).
79 Eliade (1960), pp. 70 and 119.
80 Black (1970), p. 5.
81 Collins (1978). We cannot go behind Enoch. Traditions exist only in particular formulations. Meaning and function differ from one to another.
82 Although attributed to Semiḥazah's angels, possibly through conflation. The angel lists and their interrelationship are complex. Suter (1979) explores this problem in the SS.

83 Nickelsburg (1977b).
84 Hanson (1977); Dimant (1978) includes the teaching of the angels with the Semiḥazah tradition. Asael was a late addition; the Semiḥazah tradition was contaminated with the instruction motif very early (pp. 329ff).
85 See Dimant (1978), p. 336, for a strong criticism of Hanson's article.
86 See Chapter 3.
87 This is the wisdom of McKane (1965).
88 Moltmann (1974), p. 74: 'In the crises of history, inquiry was made for that which is everywhere, and always from all time true, and a common mind about a common origin had more weight put upon it than a will to a common future.'
89 We find here the same characteristic division as we find in both Qumran Enoch and the SS: the *chosen* over against those who will be cursed. The divisions in the Third Isaiah's community are extremely important for understanding the milieu of Apocalyptic.
90 Milik (1971).
91 Nickelsburg (1977b); see rather Steiner (1961), p. 322: 'When the artist must be the architect of his own mythology, time is against him. He cannot live long enough to impose his own special vision and the symbols which he has devised for it, on the habits of language, and the feelings of his society. Without an orthodox and public frame to support it, it does not take root in the common soil.'
92 This same theme appears in another form in the Enoch tradition; knowledge is characteristic of the angelic state, and the gift of wisdom marks the beginning of the new age.
93 Von Rad (1963 rev. edn), p. 98.
94 Eichrodt (1967), vol. ii, pp. 408ff.
95 Hengel (1974), p. 194.
96 Roessler (1960), of which Koch (1972), p. 42, says, with certain qualifications: 'Roessler has succeeded in bringing out the independence of apocalyptic ideas on law and history, compared with what *later* counted as Jewish.'
97 Nickelsburg (1981), p. 575.
98 Parunak (1980), pp. 66, Ezekiel's participation at the centre of the vision; Nidditch (1980), Enoch is like a shaman because he is a visionary intercessor; Weiss (1973), Shaman and priest are not different functions; priests are the offspring of shamans. A slight shift in how the participants interpret what they are doing could transform an essentially shamanistic seance into a priestly ritual (p. 46); Wilson (1978), p. 243ff, quotes F. King and S. Skinner, *Techniques of High Magic* (1976), on the four basic assumptions of magic:
    (i) That the physical universe is only part of total reality;
    (ii) That human will-power is a real force, capable of being trained and concentrated, and that the disciplined will is capable of changing its environment and producing paranormal effects;
    (iii) That this will-power must be directed by the imagination;
    (iv) That the universe is not a mixture of chance factors and influences, but an *ordered system of correspondences, and the understanding of the pattern of correspondences enables the occultist to use them for his own purposes, good or evil.* See also Gruenwald (1979), p. 96. Priests had special experiences in the Holy of Holies: Simon encountered an old man in white, cf. Dan. 7.9; Yishma 'el ben Elisha' saw God on his throne; Yoḥannan heard a voice; Zacharias the father of John the Baptist saw an angel. 'If the experiences recorded in the Tannaitic sources, and which referred to *temple life* really occurred, Judaism of that period must have been prepared for the mystical experiences of the kind we find in the Hekhaloth writings in a manner seriously misrepresented by the scepticism of some of the scholars who have discussed the phenomenon.'
99 Gruenwald (1979), pp. 36ff: 1 En. differs from the Merkabah texts in this respect, because in the later texts there is an angelic guide.

100 Nickelsburg (1981); Rowland (1979), but is it not prejudging the issue to describe Ezekiel and Isaiah as *ingredients* of Enoch's vision (p. 140)?

101 See also Mettinger (1982), p. 99.

102 Nickelsburg (1981), p. 581.

103 Parunak (1980): three visions in Ezekiel are specially identified as visions of God, *mar'ot 'elohim*, 1.1; 8.3; 40.2. Ezekiel is *lifted up* by the spirit. The first vision is the call theophany. The second is set in the Temple after Ezekiel's heavenly journey to the Temple, and it is the lawsuit against Israel and the sentence. The spirit *leaves*: cf. Gen. 6 where the spirit leaves man as punishment for the sins of the angels. The third is the visionary trip around the new temple. Ezekiel sees the ideal temple: cf. Moses in Exod. 25—31. The link between the subject matter of these particular visions and the apocalyptic tradition is striking. The new sanctuary theme does not occur in Enoch, but it does appear elsewhere. See M. Stone (1976), esp. p. 415 and p. 445 n3, the tradition of the heavenly pattern of Zion.

104 Nickelsburg (1981), p. 581; see rather Childs (1960).

105 Rowland (1982), p. 53, notes that Daniel, 2 Baruch and 4 Ezra have neither heavenly travel nor vision of God; see Gruenwald (1979) for an account of the later disputes; Rowland (1979), pp. 152ff; Chernus (1982a).

106 Gruenwald 1979, p. 19.

107 Mayes (1983), p. 137.

108 VanderKam (1984a), pp. 137ff.

109 Rowland (1982) mentions shamanism, pp. 450 n3; 481 n34. Carley (1975) recognizes the importance of the phenomenon.

110 Eliade (1964), pp. 266ff. Shamans interiorize their own mythology and cosmology which then becomes the map of ecstatic journeys. Halifax (1979), p. 18:

> In the experience of initiation through which the shaman passes, the mythic images woven into a society's fabric suddenly become not only apparent but often enacted and made boldly visible and relevant to all. The initiatory crises of death and resurrection, then, do not represent a rending of the individual from his or her own social ground. Rather they are a deepening of the patterns that compose the sacred ahistorical territory that supports the more superficial and transient aspects of human culture.

111 VanderKam (1984a), p. 140, 'In the BW Enoch plays the part of a magnet that attracts heterogeneous mythological materials apparently from a variety of sources including the Bible.'

112 MacLaurin (1975).

113 Charlesworth (1980). Adam was an angel before the fall; Jacob/Israel were the angel and the earthly referent. 'This phenomenon seems to have been widespread' (p. 146). Perhaps we should assume, then, that what we see of angels at Qumran was part of a wider heritage. cf. Origen, *On First Principles* (tr. G. W. Butterworth [London 1936]), pp. 47–51, 212-13, implying that bodily transformation is possible. See Gross (1938) on early Christian ideas of divinization. Longenecker (1970): Christ as an angel. Collins (1974); J. Z. Smith (1970); Wilson (1978): the widely attested phenomenon of another existence parallel to that of our own consciousness. This belief is crucial for our understanding of the role of apocalyptic ideas in the formation of early Christian belief. It is almost totally neglected by writers on the subject. See, for example, Koch (1972) (p. 43), on von Rad's neglect of this vital aspect.

114 Nickelsburg (1972), p. 39.

115 This may underlie the ambiguity of knowledge/humility in Isa. 53. cf. Winton Thomas (1968). It may not be necessary to choose between the two.

116 cf. Collins (1974).

117 It would be hard to argue, against this evidence alone, for wisdom or the Asael-knowledge material being a late addition to the tradition.

118 Von Rad (1965), vol. ii, pp. 303, 309; (1972), esp. ch. 14; Koch (1972), pp. 42ff, offers a devastating criticism of von Rad's views on apocalyptic in the context of the German scholarly tradition.
119 Stone (1976), p. 436.
120 Job 38, which I shall discuss later, shows that these wisdom lists were deep rooted in the wisdom tradition, and used in Job as part of a debate as to the role and limits of that wisdom.
121 Mueller (1972).
122 VanderKam (1984a), p. 172.
123 Compare the lost tradition reconstructed in Nickelsburg (1972) and the analysis of the patterns of the SS in Suter (1979), pp. 142-3. They are very similar.
124 Does this lie behind the 'rule' (mšl) of the king figure in Ps. 8?
125 VanderKam (1984a), p. 55.
126 Halifax (1979), pp. 140ff, on the training and practices of a south American shaman.
127 Halifax (1979), pp. 5ff; Eliade (1964), pp. 63ff.
128 Fitzmyer (1965).
129 Greenfield and Stone (1977), p. 56.
130 See, for example, Charles (1912), pp. liv, 67, 72ff; Black (1976); Milik (1976); Greenfield and Stone (1977); Knibb (1979).
131 An excellent survey in Suter (1981a).
132 Suter 1979a, p. 139.
133 ibid., p. 130.
134 McKane (1970), pp. 23ff.
135 Mowry, 'Parable', in IDB 3.651.
136 McKane (1970), p. 25.
137 Suter (1981b).
138 Charles (1912), p. 70.
139 Bleeker (1967), pp. 6-7: 'It can be said without any exaggeration that Ma-a-t constitutes the fundamental idea of ancient Egyptian religion. For Ma-a-t expresses the typically ancient view whereby the various fields of nature and culture ... cosmic life, state policy, the cult, science, art, ethics and the private life of the individual ... still form a unity ... In Pharaoh's government policy he follows the example of the Sun-god who established Ma-a-t at the time of the creation. Thus the structure of the polity is not the product of the human brain, but a reflection of cosmic order.' Also Broadie and Macdonald (1978): the human and divine aspects of Ma-a-t, the king as the centre of the dispensing of Ma-a-t, and the difficulty of western-oriented scholars in grasping a totally different attitude to the cosmos. 'Have we any right to translate Ma-a-t as justice, truth or righteousness, instead of order, regularity or conformity?' This is relevant to our understanding of the debate in Job 38, and hence of the whole concept of wisdom.
140 Murray (1982a).
141 The discussion of the likeness/rule debate in McKane (1970) here goes sadly astray. He suggests that the link lies in the fact that the ruling men are model or representative figures.
142 Suter (1981), p. 218.
143 Perhaps again the magical association is important. The closest parallels seem to be there. See e.g. Wilson (1978), p. 280. The simplest form of magic is based upon the saying attributed to Hermes Trismegistos, 'As above, so below.' The laws of the heavens were reflected in man himself, p. 473: 'There are other realms of being that run parallel with our own, and the nodal points ... can create some kind of bridge between the two realms.'
144 Suter (1979a), ch. 4; also Knibb (1978), pp. 76, 159. 1 En. 96.2 is copied from the Ethiopic version of 1 En 6.7.
145 *B.J.* II. 142.
146 Suter (1979a), p. 93.

147 Chevalier (1976), p. xiv.
148 Hartmann (1966), p. 126.
149 Suter (1979a), pp. 91ff.
150 ibid., pp. 107ff.
151 ibid., p. 39.
152 Nickelsburg (1978). Luke 1—2 has also been described erroneously as *midrash*.
153 Suter (1979a), p. 132.
154 Alexander (1977), p. 162.
155 ibid., p. 159.
156 Greenfield and Stone (1977).
157 Alexander (1977), p. 178; Chernus (1982ab); for a discussion of the whole area, Segal (1978).
158 Odeberg (1973), Introduction; Stone (1975) seems to describe a similar movement within the tradition.
159 Chernus (1982ab), p. 145. The later Merkabah mystics did not distinguish between God and the visible manifestations of God. Riesenfeld (1947), p. 50: Yahweh and the Israelite king were identified with each other.
160 Thus Knibb (1979); Milik (1976); Black (1976) all emphasize the absence of references to the SS in patristic texts; but see rather Schultz (1978), where he lists Irenaeus' accounts of the teachings of the evil angels as 'the bonds of witchcraft, sorcery and idolatry' (*Epideixis* 18), which list he mistakenly attributes to 1 En. 69. It actually refers *in order* to 1 En. 65.6: 'magic arts, the power of enchantments, the power of those who cast molten images'. This is the description of the angelic knowledge in the SS, and not in the BW. How much of Enoch, then, did Irenaeus know? Charles (1913, pp. 174–5) says Origen and Tertullian knew the SS.
161 Nickelsburg (1972), p. 75; Theisohn (1975); Suter (1979a), p. 118; Suter (1978); Hartmann (1966), pp. 119–20.
162 Survey in Collins (1984), pp. 147ff; see also Morton Smith (1978), pp. 114ff. Only Jewish magical texts use historical figures in the manner of gods. Was this a memory of divinized figures?
163 Charles (1912), pp. 64ff.
164 Nickelsburg (1972), p. 75.
165 Suter (1979a), p. 101.
166 Hooker (1967), pp. 36ff, asks how anyone was able to make the identification of Enoch and the Son of Man. Collins (1980) says that the balance of probability inclines to the view that the identification of Enoch with the Son of Man is a secondary addition; also Collins (1984).
167 Nickelsburg (1972), ch. 2.
168 Collins (1980), p. 125: 'The SS are evidently closer to Paul's pattern of religion than to any ... which E. P. Sanders finds to be typical of Palestinian Judaism' (in Sanders 1977) – a highly significant remark.
169 Suter (1979a), p. 21.
170 Chevalier (1976), Introduction.
171 Hull (1974), esp. pp. 42ff; J. Z. Smith (1970): Origen's commentary on John quotes from the Prayer of Joseph, in which Jacob wrestled with Uriel and told him his *name*. Morton Smith (1978), p. 35.
172 Gaster (1901), pp. 116ff. Other treatments, e.g. Deissmann (1927), Betz (1986), do not make the link to 1 En.
173 Collins (1980) for discussion of pre-existence, and whether or not it is implied here. Compare the tradition in Tol'doth Jesu that Jesus' miraculous powers were due to his knowing the Divine Name.
174 For this sense see Dahood (1966); Murray (1982a), pp. 212ff; (1984), p. 312.

175 Dimant (1978) shows how the Noachian commandments are specifically related to the sins of the fallen angels, confirmation from another angle that the cosmic charter and the fall of the angels are related. Sperber (1966) shows from widely differing sources (the Babylonian and Jerusalem Talmuds, the Odes of Solomon, a Coptic Baptismal Office, the Prayer of Manasseh, later speculations in the Midrash) that they shared a common theme, 'namely that of the sealing up of the abysses with the name (=seal) of the Lord. The nature of the differences between these various sources is such as to assure us that they do not derive from one another. (They are) dependent upon some earlier creation cycle, apocryphal no doubt.' (p. 171).

176 Murray (1982a), pp. 209–10.

177 Nickelsburg (1981); also Milik (1976), pp. 70ff. The most important text of Greek Enoch was found in a Coptic cemetery bound together with the Apocalypse of Peter and the Gospel of Peter.

178 Emerton (1962), p. 326, 'Their use in a magical sense is probably irrelevant to these passages in the NT'! I disagree. See rather Murray (1985), p. 271.

179 Milik (1976), p. 275.

180 Neugebauer (1981), p. 17.

181 VanderKam (1984a), pp. 76–8; Knibb 1978, pp. 12–3.

182 VanderKam (1984a), pp. 98ff.

183 VanderKam (1983); Knibb (1978), p. 180.

184 Milik (1976), p. 289, following Grelot (1958a), pp. 34ff, 67ff.

185 Charles (1912), p. 167.

186 Stone (1976).

187 Davies (1983b), p. 88: 'The origin of the calendrical discrepancy as a theological issue certainly requires further investigation, and we need a plausible hypothesis. I also share the belief that the ultimate origins of the Qumran community are closely bound up with this issue. But the second century BC is not the setting for either of these; almost certainly *they both go back very much earlier*.'

188 Theophrastus, *de Pietate*, in Stern (1976); Pseudo-Eupolemus in Eusebius, *Praep. Ev.* IX, 17, 2–9, in Black (1970).

189 Davies (1983a), pp. 84ff; Davies (1983b).

190 Davies (1983b).

191 Jaubert (1953); (1957); VanderKam (1979), discussed by Davies (1983). The dispute now centres not on the antiquity of the calendar, but on the date when it was abandoned.

192 Morgenstern (1939, 1955, 1964), and many more.

193 Charles (1912), p. 151, thought the gates were the signs of the Zodiac, but Neugebauer (1964) argued for their being the six segments of the horizon. See Hengel (1974), vol. ii, p. 160 n834, for notes and bibliography on the early zodiac, which originated in Babylon *c.*400 BC. Neugebauer (1957), pp. 102, 140, 170.

194 Neugebauer (1964), p. 58; in Black (1985), p. 386 he says the AB 'reflects faithfully the simple concepts that prevailed in the communities which produced the Enochian literature ... (which contains) a conglomerate of closely related versions made by generations of scribes'.

195 Neugebauer (1981), p. 8.

196 I shall argue for this translation of Isa. 59.19 in Chapter 8.

197 MacDonald (1964), pp. 319ff; Bowman (1977), pp. 39ff, quoting the introduction to the Samaritan Chronicle *Tolidah*.

198 De Vaux (1965), pp. 180ff.

199 ibid., p. 183.

200 Driver (1965), p. 328: '*Sons of Light* would be a suitable appellation for a party who held that the day began with the daylight, just as *sons of darkness* would be for a rival party who

held that it began with the onset of darkness. Thus a double entente such as the covenanters loved would underlie the names which they bestowed respectively upon themselves and their opponents.' A nice idea.

201 See also Mettinger (1982), pp. 67ff. I disagree with his reconstruction of the reason for the change, but the *fact* of that change is clear enough. Such a change might explain how the triumph songs of the earlier festival were adapted to the new one, e.g. the changes apparent in Exod. 15, which *now* belongs to the Exodus cycle, but did not originate there.

202 In the Appendix to *B.J.*

203 But see Neugebauer (1964), p. 60: 'The learned speculations of modern scholars about an early form of the Hebrew calendar ... completely misunderstand the purely schematic character of our text.' In Black (1985), p. 388, apparently at variance with p. 386 (see n194 above), he says, 'Enoch is not an old Semitic calendar ... Enochic astronomy is an *ad hoc* construction, and not the result of a common Semitic tradition.'

204 For details of the variants and textual confusion here see Knibb (1978), p. 78.

205 Sons of God, nephilim, mighty men, men of renown. Charles (1912), *ad loc.*, says the three names in the later texts arose from the set of names in Gen. 6.4, in keeping with his theory that the whole of the angel mythology arose from this passage in Genesis. Black (1985), pp. 14, 126, 154, says that the three names of the giants are unconnected with the three types of animals in the AA.

206 In 4Q'Amram[b]. The figure (probably a 'Watcher') in 'Amram's vision is described as a snake in dark garments: Fitzmyer and Harrington (1978), pp. 92–3.

207 Cross (1973), pp. 306ff.

208 Von Rad ([2]1963), p. 110.

209 Charles (1912).

210 I shall suggest in Chapter 6 that this is one of several words used to conceal lost angel figures.

211 I shall elaborate upon this number system below, when dealing with the Apocalypse of Weeks.

212 VanderKam (1984a), p. 166.

213 Milik (1976), p. 251.

214 Collins (1975a); Hasel (1979); Hengel (1974), vol. i, pp. 181ff; Lacocque (1979), pp. 122ff.

215 Charles (1912), pp. 91ff; Stone (1976).

216 Charles (1912); Milik (1976), pp. 44ff; VanderKam (1984a), pp. 161f for full notes and bibliography.

217 Black (1978); Milik (1976), pp. 248ff; VanderKam (1984b).

218 Charles (1912), p. 219.

219 Knibb (1976).

220 As I shall show in Chapter 6.

221 Knibb (1976); Ackroyd (1968), pp. 240ff.

222 Knibb (1976), p. 254.

223 Milik (1976), pp. 252ff.

224 For a complete bibliography of the discussion of 'seventy' see Ackroyd (1968), p. 240. I think it more likely that we shall explain the seventy-then-judgement pattern if we concentrate equally upon the seventy and the judgement. I suspect that the origin is to be found in the festival calendar. It is well known that the festivals of the barley and wheat harvests became associated with the Exodus and Covenant making; see de Vaux (1965), ch. 17. It is not hard to imagine a schematized pattern of history based upon the agricultural festivals. The system of Jubilees, which uses the same solar calendar as Enoch, is built upon just such a seven-based scheme, and is thought to derive ultimately from a pre-Israelite agricultural calendar (Morgenstern [1955]). If the yearly cycle of the old solar calendar began and ended in the autumn, we should expect the autumn festival to represent both

the climax and the renewal of history. In the apocalyptic scheme this appears as the last judgement followed by the new creation, a theme which can be traced as early as Isaiah of Jerusalem, and which continues through into 1 Enoch. Were the schematized histories based upon the calendar, the judgement would correspond to the autumn festival, and the seventy would have had to correspond to the period leading up to that festival. The present double scheme of the AW here affords a clue; the history climaxes at week seven, with the revelation of wisdom, and also at week ten with the judgement. There is exactly this pattern of seven-plus-three weeks at the end of the year if we reconstruct the calendar from the account of the festivals in the Temple Scroll. From the New Barley to the New Wheat was seven weeks; seven weeks later was the New Wine, seven weeks after that the New Oil, and then after *three* more weeks, the Day of Atonement. See Caquot (1978); VanderKam (1979); Yadin (1985), Part III, pp. 84–111. 11QMelch actually relates the end of the tenth jubilee to the Day of Atonement: 'And the Day of Atonement is the end of the tenth jubilee, when all the sons of (light) ... will be atoned for.' The details of the calendar are complex and require considerable expert knowledge; but the correspondences between these two schemes of calendar and history writing are, to say the least, striking, especially in view of the evidence of 11QMelch.

225 VanderKam (1984b) begins to explore this chiastic structure; I have built upon his foundation.

226 Nickelsburg (1982).

227 Charles (1912) draws too much from the text. See Nickelsburg (1972), pp. 112ff, for a full discussion.

228 Nickelsburg (1977a).

229 Nickelsburg (1972), esp. ch. 4; also Nickelsburg (1977a).

230 Nickelsburg (1977a), p. 322.

231 ibid.

232 Grelot (1958c).

233 Nickelsburg (1977b).

234 Collins (1978).

235 Suter (1979b).

236 Milik 1976 pp. 23–4, but VanderKam 1984a, p. 113 disputes because the reading is not clear.

237 This is perhaps reflected in the later name given to the child of an impure priestly union. He was *ḥll*, the name also given to the angel figures who became mortal. See Jeremias (1969), pp. 317ff, and my treatment of Ezek. 28 in Chapter 10.

238 Hanson (1977), pp. 218ff.

239 Nickelsburg (1981). Nickelsburg and Suter (1979b) both reach similar conclusions from very different arguments and evidence, strengthening the possibility that they are correct.

240 1QSb iv, The Blessing of the Priests: 'May you be as an angel of the presence...'

241 See ch. 7.

242 See ch. 8. The differences between Third Isaiah and 1 Enoch are not so great as has been suggested, and are as likely to be due to emphasis as to any fundamental difference. cf. Nickelsburg (1977b).

243 Koch (1974), pp. 190ff.

244 Bartelmus (1979); Nickelsburg (1977b).

245 Nickelsburg (1977b), p. 390.

246 ibid.

247 Lacocque (1979), pp. 159ff, details the problems of the chapter, but his own suggestion is more complex than is necessary if we understand the chapter in the light of the Enochic mythology.

248 The Third Isaiah was, as I shall show in Chapter 8, working within the pre-exilic scheme

of mythology, and had not been influenced directly by the destructive developments of the exile.

249 Charles (1912), p. 134; Bampfylde (1984), pp. 28ff.

250 See below, ch. 11.

251 Bampfylde (1984), 50 BC; Greenfield and Stone (1977), 40 BC; Sjöberg (discussed by Hindley), before 70 AD; Knibb (1979), end of the first century AD; Hindley (1967), after 113 AD; Milik (1976), followed by Black (1976), 270 AD. For full notes see Knibb (1979), p. 345; Mearns (1979), p. 360.

252 This argument is similar to that in the call vision of Isaiah; the sinners are punished by being denied access to what could help them.

253 See note 216.

254 The Genesis Apocryphon is, of course, another example of the angelic version of familiar tales.

255 e.g. Charles (1912): Pharisees and Sadducees; VanderKam (1984): Hellenizers.

256 Nickelsburg (1977a).

257 Respectively: Charles (1912); Grelot (1958c), Nickelsburg (1977a).

258 Black (1978).

259 Thorndike (1961) sees the whole of the AW as a history of the sect, but this seems to distort the evidence too much.

260 The fact that the SS has not been found at Qumran, even though it has much in common with the Qumran texts, could also indicate a division amongst those who preserved the Enochic tradition; Greenfield and Stone (1977) suggest, *inter alia*, that there may have been a calendar difference involving the status of the moon.

261 Should we continue to call it the *inter*-testamental period, if we cannot be sure of the dates of the so-called *inter*-testamental writings?

262 J. Z. Smith (1975).

263 Lakoff and Johnson (1980) is a very thought-provoking book, and its insights applied to the Old Testament texts could bring very interesting results.

2

WISDOM

The study of wisdom is now an important part of New Testament scholarship. There is a wisdom Christology, and discussion of the role of wisdom in the infant churches and the development of early Christian thought. But what was wisdom? It is customary to make comparisons with material drawn from a very wide area,[1] and the most cautious of the conclusions is that wisdom represented 'a way of speaking about God in creation, revelation and redemption without actually speaking about God'.[2] Wisdom brought with it into the Christian tradition the idea of Jesus' pre-existence, and the development of this can be traced through the Gospels' picture of Jesus.[3]

It is unfortunate that this definition of wisdom brings with it several problems. The wise man and the wisdom of this world can be seen as *hostile* to the gospel (1 Cor. 1.19ff), and the activities of God in creation and redemption can be described as the very opposite of wisdom (1 Cor. 1.27). Knowledge, a closely related matter, is destructive (1 Cor. 8.1), and so on. Many of the passages where a wisdom theme is detected have an important element in common, the supernatural powers. The wisdom of the rulers of this age is contrasted with the hidden wisdom of God (1 Cor. 2.7); the affirmation in 1 Cor. 8 is made in the context of the other gods. The manifold wisdom of God is made known to principalities and powers in heavenly places (Eph. 3.10); there are principalities and authorities in Col. 1.15–17, a passage frequently cited as evidence of the wisdom influence, and the wisdom passage at the beginning of Hebrews continues with a discussion of the relative status of Jesus and the angels (Heb. 1.1–3).

When faced with such diversity, we can either attempt to relate these passages to other known usages of the term wisdom, or we can construct something which must have been the case if these passages are to be read as a consistent pattern of reference to one underlying idea of wisdom. If we adopt the latter course, we shall construct a wisdom which is neutral, i.e. can be used by the gospel or by the world, which is linked to the heavenly powers, and entails conflict with them at certain points, and which is bound up with the processes of creation.

In studying the pre-Christian Jewish concepts of wisdom, I have never encountered one based upon the evidence of the Enochic literature. This is surprising, since 1 Enoch is quoted in the New Testament, and was used by the Qumran community during the period of Jesus' ministry. It is here, I believe, that we must begin to look for the concept of wisdom which influenced the development of early Christian ideas.

Enoch the seer is a scribe and a wise man (Jub. 4.17). Wisdom in 1 Enoch is heavenly secrets, given to men through the pride and corruption of fallen angels who, by fathering human children, were able to perpetuate a regime of evil and decay upon the earth. Enoch's wisdom was, as we have seen, associated with maintaining the correct order of creation, the eternal covenant, and many of its applications were magical. Wisdom was no personification of God's immanence, but was rather a body of knowledge and practices which gave power over creation when used in conjunction with supernatural forces. It was the essence of all that had been corrupted through pride and rebellion. One of the problems faced by New Testament scholars is how wisdom and pre-existence can relate to the idea of the virgin birth;[4] but read in the light of the Enochic wisdom, this is no problem at all. The birth of a son of God would have marked the beginning of a new era, when the old decay and corruption were reversed, and wisdom in an uncorrupted form brought into creation. Thus sonship and obedience belong naturally together, since the agents of the first corruption were rebel sons of God. The evil spirits which they left to torment the earth were those which Jesus encountered in the miracles, who feared that they were being destroyed *before the time* (Matt. 8.29). It is these demons who recognized Jesus as the Son of God, and they knew that this affected them.

At first sight the Enochic picture of angelic wisdom seems to meet many of the requirements of the New Testament wisdom concept, but the description of wisdom in 1 Enoch raises enormous problems, since it is so very different from the wisdom legacy which we find in the canonical texts. Wisdom, like apocalyptic, has suffered from definitions devised by scholars on the basis of canonical texts. Both terms are overdue for redefinition as a result. Even within the canon we find problems: Daniel is a wise man, and we might expect his book to be a wisdom book. But it is not. We label it 'apocalyptic', but the Alexandrian canon put it among the prophets. Even the material which is generally accepted as wisdom is known to have reached its present form only after extensive editing and transformation. All attempts to reconstruct the earlier form of wisdom on the basis of the canonical texts run into great difficulties; massive inconsistencies are all too obvious, and we are obliged to assume that something is seriously amiss in the approach.

Two major studies of wisdom[5] have demonstrated the changes which occurred in the course of its development. W. McKane says that

> In the late pre-exilic period the wise men, who stood in an international tradition of wisdom, were beginning to come to terms with Yahwism, wisdom had begun to make its bow to distinctively Israelite biblical traditions and the wise men were in the way of becoming biblical scholars, devoted to sacred learning.[6]

Such a summary, which is not untypical, conceals several very interesting gaps.

The distinctively Israelite tradition to which the wise men were accommodating themselves was, in fact, a fairly recent arrival in Jerusalem. The centrality of the Law, and the characteristic theologies of history which became so important in the post-exilic community, were not distinctively pre-exilic Israelite – or, at any rate, not distinctive of pre-exilic Jerusalem. The whole question of the nature and status of the Law in pre-exilic Jerusalem is wide open, and the Moses figure is a shadowy one at this time.[7] Since these Moses/Deuteronomic traditions were only recently come to prominence in Jerusalem, and the pre-exilic wise men began to conform to *this* tradition, we have to ask what was meant by Deut. 4.6, which seems to be saying that the Law was to function as the wisdom of the chosen people. Does this mean that the central role of the Torah was formerly the role of wisdom? Deuteronomy, which is not noted for its toleration of foreign ways, is here finding a central place for something which we assume to have been foreign. Perhaps their precious Torah was being offered as a substitute for something in the older cult whose legitimacy they could not deny. Wisdom was an older form of communication between God and his people. Wisdom was something which the Deuteronomists reformed.[8] This possibility is crucial for my argument.

Astral cults, or whatever is meant in Deut. 4.19 by the sun, moon, and host of heaven, were also permitted on certain terms. Von Rad comments upon this unusual toleration of idol worship,[9] but the text at this point is *not* dealing with idols. The attitude of Deuteronomy implies that an astral cult, like wisdom, could not simply be denounced. Yahweh of Hosts was an ancient title, linking Yahweh to these hosts of heaven,[10] but Deuteronomy did not want this to continue for the chosen people. This implies that there were Yahweh-worshippers, not regarded by the Deuteronomists as chosen, for whom the hosts continued to be their form of religion. The longer reading of the LXX at Hos. 13.4 is a memory of this separation between the people of the heavenly hosts, and the people whose myth was the memory of a sojourn in Egypt:

> I am the Lord your God, the creator of heaven and earth, whose hands formed all the host of heaven, and I did not show you how to follow them, and I led you from the land of Egypt and you knew no God but me.

Deuteronomy has a curious relationship to both the elements which we later encounter as the fundamentals of the apocalyptists: the hosts, and wisdom. There must have been some reason for this limited tolerance, and even if we can say no more, we know for certain that these elements were sufficiently prominent in the system over against which Deuteronomy defined itself to merit a special attention.[11]

We know that wisdom changed considerably in the era of the Law, but the people who cherished both the mythology of the heavenly host and the unbiblical wisdom which we find in the apocalypses, looked back to the time of the restoration as one of apostasy, when the returning exiles went astray. What might we conclude?

Whybray and McKane have both demonstrated that some of the post-exilic wise men became students of the Law, but their reconstructions have only enabled us to see the later stages of the wisdom process. Great discrepancies still exist between these and the other major attempts to reconstruct the ancient wisdom.[12] This invites us to continue the search in the light of what is known of wisdom from 1 Enoch and the other non-canonical sources.

A major problem in this reconstruction is how we actually understand certain texts. It is all too easy to read what is not there, or to do one's best in the interests of what seems *to us* to be sense. For example, in Prov. 9.10, and 30.3, wisdom is defined as knowledge of the *holy ones*, and could refer to the knowledge which Enoch's angels possessed. But we translate this as a plural of majesty, and assume that the Holy One is what was intended by the writer, because a plural would have made no sense.[13] McKane's treatment of 2 Sam. 16.23, and 14.20 is similar.[14] The texts compare human wisdom to that of God or an angel, and in both cases he explains that this is a contrast between two totally separate systems of wisdom. Now there is nothing in the text to say this, even though we usually do read it in that way. One is also impatient to know what is missing from the text at certain points. Prov. 30.1ff[15] is completely mutilated, and I shall not attempt to translate it, but the LXX of v. 4 reads the plural, *sons*. Given the general theme of the passage, namely ascent to heaven and power over creation, this plural form reminds one immediately of the sons of God in the Enochic mythology. It is these *sons* who have also disappeared from the Hebrew of Deut. 32, suggesting that the opacity of Prov. 30 may not be accidental. Various solutions have been offered for the problems of each of these verses, but it is interesting that we invariably read the difficult texts, and reconstruct the mutilated ones, on the assumption that wisdom and angels were not part of the ancient system. We read in a Deuteronomic manner.

Reconstructions of the earliest wisdom use two sources: the basic stratum of Proverbs and the allusions in the prophets. The former has clearly been altered several times, and scholars generally admit that the original readings may have been very different from the ones we now read, or read into, the text. Thus von Rad says we must remain open to the possibility that the sentences have changed in the course of their transmission, and that their total intellectual and religious consciousness could have changed.[16] The old sentence wisdom in Proverbs was separated by an enormous gulf from piety of the post-exilic type, and there is not a trace of serious theological motivation in terms of the specific acts of inspiration involved in the acquisition of knowledge. A less scholarly approach to these chapters could be forgiven for seeing them as a hotchpotch of trivia, some witty, others just banal. What possible need or motivation could there have been for these secular ideas to have been subsumed under the Law?

Why, we may ask, should the Deuteronomists have compared their precious Law to the harmless chatter of old men?

The wisdom sentences say nothing about history and nothing about Law. As they now stand they represent neither threat nor contradiction to the Deuteronomic position. Nor could their original secularity have been the reason for any alterations, since Deuteronomy itself is a fairly secular book. The only theology in these sayings, if there is any theology at all, is a theology of the divine in creation, and natural justice.

The reasons for the changes to wisdom must lie elsewhere, perhaps in those very aspects of wisdom which are no longer extant in the biblical texts as a result of the alterations. Our present biblical collections, edited and modified by the later wise men, will have been modified towards the later legalism. It is these modifications which will indicate the difference between the older and the later wisdom, and the fact that there is no theology discernible in the present form of the sayings suggests that it was this theology upon which no compromise was possible. The alternative – and this is what we are usually offered – is that an untheological wisdom tradition, alien to the traditions of Yahwism, was drawn into it by a group of ardent nationalists and cultic reformers whose hostility to foreign ways is without parallel elsewhere in the Old Testament. This is unlikely. Judaism came to terms in later times with Hellenism, and formulated a *modus vivendi*, because it posed a threat to the fundamentals of its way of life. What was the threat of wisdom to the reformed ways of the Deuteronomists?

The weak link in scholarly reconstruction of Israel's ancient wisdom is inconsistency. We find wise men in court or school settings elsewhere in the ancient world, and assume these as the context for Israel's wisdom. But we do not also assume that the manner of operation of the other wise men might have been similar to that of Israel's. Having given the wise men their setting, we then credit them with only the edited texts as evidence for what they were actually about. Thus we fill the courts and schools of Israel with muddled platitudes, which is all that remains of Israel's wisdom, and have then to invent a secular rationalism to explain the prophet's wrath, and an incursion of foreign magicians to explain the rise of apocalyptic.

McKane has made many important contributions to the business of defining ancient wisdom, and he is convinced that Proverbs is a reworking of older material.[17] Texts which had once dealt with the education of the individual were reworked as Yahwistic piety. Although others have argued that the piety was early, and that it was in later phases that wisdom became a secular pursuit, McKane rejects the idea that ancient wisdom was in general religious, in favour of evidence which can be drawn from the text of the Old Testament itself. This favours the later date for the Yahwistic sayings. At this point we must examine his assumptions. The later Yahwistic sayings are, he says, characterized by the assertion that God enforces a moral order in relation to individuals by rewarding the righteous man and punishing the wicked.

> Where this doctrine of theodicy obtrudes itself in the wisdom sentence the limits which old wisdom set itself are exceeded, and far reaching assumptions about the structure of human life in relation to the will of Yahweh which transcend the range of careful empiricism of old wisdom are made.[18]

Are we in a position to say what was the nature of the old wisdom? Unless there is positive evidence from outside the Book of Proverbs as to the nature of the old wisdom, there can be no basis for his argument. It is circular. All that can be said, as the result of his careful analyses, is that there are several different layers apparent in the book. The order in which they were laid down must be determined entirely by external evidence. An opposite conclusion, which could be drawn from the evidence of the layers, is that they all existed simultaneously, evidence of the many facets of the ancient wisdom. Were this the case, we should still have no good reason for Deuteronomy wishing to make Torah the wisdom of the chosen people, since there would have been a compatible tradition of piety to be recommended rather than subsumed. We are obliged to turn outside Proverbs to find the nature of the older wisdom.

Another of McKane's major contributions is his *Prophets and Wise Men*,[19] which shows the older wisdom operating in the sphere of politics, and coming into conflict with the prophets over priorities, and the correct source of guidance for the politics of the chosen people. The older wise men, he says, had a strictly non-religious attitude towards politics. They based their decisions upon experience and delicacy of judgement, and were the intellectual élite of their time, at home in the high places of the court. Conflict came when this secular wisdom, with its ethical neutrality, differed from the prophet's demand that Israel accept only the guidance of the Lord.[20] The prophets took over the vocabulary of the wise men, and reused it for their own message.[21] In Egypt and Babylon the scribes were both politicians and wise men; in Israel they were the same, and yet they were not the same, for the wise men of Egypt claimed descent from ancient kings, a tradition reflected in Ezek. 28. The esoteric wisdom of the foreign courts was strictly separated from the politics of Judah. It did exist (cf. Isa. 3.2–3), but in its Babylonian form it drew the scorn of the Second Isaiah. Secret lore and dreams were worlds apart from the open-minded statesmanship of Judah's native wise men. Strangely, though, it was the esoteric strand of wisdom which reappeared in apocalyptic, a literature far removed from the writings of the prophets. The older wisdom of the statesman was transformed; Jer. 8.8–9 shows the turning-point. The wise men began to nationalize their international tradition, and began to present the Law as true wisdom. Late passages in the Old Testament described wisdom as an endowment of the Spirit. The picture of the ideal king as a wise man, Isa. 11, is thus late, an exilic composition. McKane depicts the time of the monarchy as one in which level-headed politicians involved in the international power game were confronted by prophetic idealists. The clash was between secular wisdom and divine rule. The reconstruction of the old wisdom is meticulous, but the contortions needed to arrive at his conclusion – two unrelated streams of wisdom – must make one wary.

Von Rad's reconstruction of the ancient wisdom is very different. It was, he said, the teaching of the wise men, and he recognized, but did not explore, the fact that Proverbs represents only one aspect of the ancient wisdom. The diversity of the later wisdom was thought to be of later origin, *something missing from*, rather than unknown to, the writers of Proverbs as we know it.[22] The silence over these other aspects of wisdom must be taken as a question concerning their exclusion, rather than as confirmation that they did not exist. The diversity in Proverbs, he said, points to a *Sitz im Leben* outside court circles, perhaps amongst the middle classes and small landowners, as implied by the dialogues of Job. The adjective *ḥākām*, 'wise', has a variety of applications. It could be used of craftsmen and rakes, and 'unwise' could describe a stillborn child.[23] In parts of Proverbs which von Rad thought pre-exilic, wise men were no more than the opposite of fools.[24] Only later are there details of wise men as teachers in Israel. The wise men were not scribes; their duty was the study of ancient lore and prophecies.[25] Wisdom as God's gift is a late idea, and the earlier sentence wisdom of Proverbs has no trace of what we would call serious theological motivation. Modern scholars read tension into the ancient texts, whereas the ancients did not distinguish between rational and religious perceptions.[26] Both presupposed a reliable system sustained by God, which thus made investigation possible. 'Fear of the Lord' was an integral part of the older system, and this phrase was not evidence of a later assimilation to Yahwism. Von Rad suggested that the abruptness and frequency of the phrase might indicate that some polemic was involved.[27] The older wisdom lacked any underlying myth. It had no framework for its rules, and no discussion of good and evil.[28] Much suggests that the small part of the wisdom tradition which found its way into the Old Testament was that which appealed to a general circle of readers. The more specialist knowledge simply did not survive.[29] We have only hints of a world more mysterious than that of the historians of Israel, who give no indication of the inexplicable vastnesses beyond their tidy world. What, asked von Rad, was the common point between them? 'Is not the late Deuteronomic history comparable to the later wisdom in that it was *obliged* to present history once again from quite new aspects?'[30] He warned that wisdom was not natural to our ways of thought. For ancient Israel, wisdom was a gift of God, an intellectual power freed from the chain of mythical powers. There was no evil power, no division of the world into two spheres ruled by good and evil.[31] This only appears in the Wisdom of Solomon. The wise men did not talk of the divine spark, nor of man in the image of God. There was no ideal for man beyond mere survival. All life's disorders came from man himself.

A third and very different picture of the older wisdom is that of R. N. Whybray.[32] He is cautious about development theories derived from the form of Proverbs.[33] Wisdom literature, he said, occupies an entirely unique place in the Old Testament, in that whereas all other literature is rooted in the religious tradition of Israel, the wisdom books say nothing about Israel or its election, history, cult, laws, priesthood, or prophets. The books are a constant reminder that there was more to Israel than the other Old Testament books *permit us to see*. Wisdom dealt with practical matters, the stuff of survival in this life. Israel borrowed from abroad in the time of the monarchy, as the result of the traffic of diplomats and scribes.[34] Although there was a widespread tradition of Solomon as the patron of wisdom which cannot be ignored, the would-be reconstructor of this pre-exilic material faces enormous problems, because the whole development of wisdom is shrouded in mystery. There is little evidence of how wisdom was regarded by those outside wisdom circles. Isaiah and Jeremiah show wisdom and prophecy as two distinct options for Israel. Even though the literature that we have is directed mainly to the individual, we know that its principles were applied to the running of the state. Hence the conflict with the prophets, who maintained that the only basis for political decisions was divine guidance. The prophets could use wisdom vocabulary, and even seek a *modus vivendi* with wisdom.[35] The view of God is distinctive. He is the remote and sovereign judge who does not interfere with the lives of men. Nor is there any attempt to base ethical demands upon the holiness of Yahweh, or upon the notion of covenant. In the pre-exilic period the two traditions were far apart, even though the seeds of whatever brought them together may have been present. The *process*, however, cannot be deduced from Proverbs. The destruction of Jerusalem in 587/6 had a great effect upon the wisdom tradition, for the élite found themselves in Babylon. By the time of Ezra, the Judaizing of wisdom was completed, for Ezra 7.25 describes the Law as 'the wisdom of thy God'. Although the pressures of life in Babylon will have provided the impetus for unifying or drawing together the two traditions in the interest of survival, the details of the process are now lost to us. 'Wherever we turn we are merely presented with a *fait accompli*.'[36]

In his later work, *The Intellectual Tradition of the Old Testament*, Whybray adds to the picture and to the mystery. There was, he said, no professional class of wise men, only a wisdom tradition. The dialogue of Job is between prosperous and educated farmers, and not men of the court circle. There is no mention in Proverbs of dreams as a means of communication even though this is recorded in Job 4.12ff; 33.14ff, and though there are dream tales associated with both Daniel and Joseph. How representative, then, is Proverbs, and of what?[37]

The great differences between the three reconstructions show that the older wisdom is still largely an unknown quantity. It should be possible, however, to take certain of the insights, and by examining their implications in the light of other evidence, such as that of the Enochic writings, to draw one or two new conclusions.

The whole business of reconstruction is riddled with contradictions, all of which point in one direction. The prophets, for example, attack the wise men as politicians, and yet the early material we have is not obviously relevant to politics. Has the political element of early wisdom disappeared? Was there, for want of a better word, a political philosophy of which we know nothing? Then there is the interest in the natural sciences and esoterica which is apparent in the later writings such as the Wisdom of Solomon. Solomon himself was credited with an interest in natural science, and yet in the middle period, when the books we use to define wisdom were written down, we have none of this material.[38] Has this element also disappeared from our canonical sources? The prophets condemned the wise men and their teachings; the Deuteronomists were far from happy with them. Can we assume that these condemned ideas were transmitted accurately, and in their original form? Have we made our reconstructions from the wrong materials? The ancient wise men of Egypt and Tyre were certainly at home in politics, as was the wise woman of 2 Sam. 16, yet these were not cool-headed rationalists. Theirs was a more violent and colourful world of dark sayings and divinations, the wisdom whose offspring we meet in the apocalypses. Again we note the gap between the oldest and the latest which seem to correspond, and the centre period which has none of these things.[39] All that we can so certainly identify in our picture of ancient Israel – law, cult, prophets, history – is missing from wisdom.

Everything points to a development during the exile which radically altered wisdom, but which did not succeed in destroying it. The older tradition reappeared in the later works. How this happened we do not know. That it happened is a reasonable construction upon the evidence. Wisdom as we know it in the canonical texts was born in the community which Enoch, a later wise man, condemns as impure and apostate. The crucial mid-point of the Apocalypse of Weeks says that the generation just before the fall of the first Temple had turned away from wisdom. This explains the peculiar wisdom which we find in the middle period. Enoch *has*, perhaps we may say *has preserved*, a political philosophy, an interest in natural phenomena, and its own characteristic account of the history of Israel. It has no obvious concern for Law, for cult, or for the Deuteronomists' account of history. Now McKane believes that the wisdom of the political advisers was subjugated to the Law after the advent of Deuteronomy in Jerusalem. This is crucial, for if he is correct, the present subject-matter of Proverbs may be no more than confirmation of the work of the subjugators. Great weight is placed upon this book as evidence for early wisdom, some seeing it as evidence for progression towards humanism, and others the opposite, but I have never found anyone who asked why such a book should have been preserved at all. Could it be the remains of something older? Von Rad thought the early wisdom to have been without theology, yet McKane described the conflicts of wise men and prophets. Would there have been conflict if no theology was involved? Or was the basis of the conflict some theology which is no longer extant? For all the expertise of McKane's arguments, I cannot imagine anyone wanting to fulminate against the purveyors of the harmless platitudes which now form the Book of Proverbs.

Let us suppose with von Rad that the ancient wise men had more to say than is apparent in their surviving sayings,[40] and that these represent the writings of a widely condemned group. If we see their wisdom as a secular force opposed to divine rule, we may only be reading what the later reformers want us to read. Von Rad makes much of the fact that the specialized scientific knowledge of ancient Israel has not survived, and all that the wise men have left us is the feeling that their world was more mysterious than the tidy world of the historians. This world of mystery is not the world of McKane's wise men, with their rational processes as the gentlemen scholars of the ancient foreign office. The world which he reconstructs is far removed from one where decisions were made with arrows, teraphim, and livers. One can understand why the Deuteronomists objected to that type of wisdom. The weak point in McKane's reconstruction is, as I have said above, that he takes the prophets' picture of the *function* of wisdom, but not their picture of its content. 'The counsel of the wise was not acceptable because . . .' – and then we have a reconstruction based upon Proverbs. One of his key verses is 2 Sam. 16.23, which deals with the counsel of Ahithophel, and the *dabar* of God. 'The counsel which Ahithophel gave was as if one asked for the word of the *elohim*' (my translation). This is interpreted to mean that there were two 'parallel and unconnected systems of reliable guidance in matters of state'[41] and that the advice offered by Ahithophel was 'a purely human product, the fruit of empirical sagacity'. This is assumption.[42] Similar treatment is given to David, even though we are told he was like an angel of God (2 Sam. 19.28; 14.17, 20), and the royal prophecies of Isaiah promise the king wisdom from the Lord. The writer of 2 Samuel probably meant what he wrote, that the king was wise in the manner of an angel. He was not alluding to two totally unrelated systems of policy making.[43] This line of distinction does not inspire confidence. The prophets' conflict with the wise men must be an important factor for understanding the older wisdom. Unfortunately, we cannot be sure that our picture of the prophets is any more authentic than that of the wisdom in Proverbs, for both have been edited. Despite these limitations, the prophetic texts can yield certain clues, but the investigation can be hampered by too rigid an approach. Unquestioned certainties can create serious distortions.

It is possible to read the wisdom passages in the prophets in another way, and thus to meet some of von Rad's observations. Isa. 5.19–24, for example, might indicate not the ethical neutrality of the wise men, but their perversion.[44] It was what the wise men *did* with their wisdom which caused the conflict with the prophets. Wisdom was not in itself a bad thing, but if misused it was the source of much evil. 'The fear of the Lord is the beginning of wisdom' occurs many times, and reminds us that there was some conflict, now lost to us, which involved wisdom and the attitude to the Lord. One of the strands in the intertestamental literature reflects a similar position; wisdom was not inherently evil, but became so through misuse.[45] The theme of pride and the misuse of wisdom is vitally important to the understanding of Isaiah, and is the basis of Ezek. 28, which describes the fate of the Prince of Tyre when he abused his wisdom. Now if the profession of scribes and statesmen can be illuminated by reference to Egypt and elsewhere, should not the content of this wisdom also be relevant?[46] The wisdom of the other nations *as depicted in the Old Testament* points us to a world of magic and mythology, and it may be that the prophet's conflict was with those who abused these gifts. Our natural inclination is to make the wise men of the Bible as much like ourselves as possible, and this leads us to blot out the esoteric aspects of wisdom. It is, as we have been warned,[47] a blanket term of *our own devising*, coined to cover what we can reassemble from a far from representative collection of texts.

If wisdom is represented in terms of a certain set of words, and the investigation is confined to these areas, the conclusion will inevitably be found to lie within it, and we have a neat, but circular, argument. The reinterpretation of wisdom vocabulary is another area where there are hidden assumptions in our arguments. We can see by simple inspection whether or not certain words are used; but, just as we cannot know for certain the extent of the wisdom vocabulary, so too we are unable to determine the original meaning of the words. How then can we know the manner of their *reuse*? If the change was the result of events of which we also know nothing, our reconstructions are doubly hazardous. It is an extension of this wisdom-vocabulary-and-reconstruction-from-Proverbs approach which has so distorted our assessment of the place of esoteric lore. We reason thus: the esoteric material is not in Proverbs therefore it cannot have been Judah's native wisdom, but since it is fundamental to apocalyptic, the latter must have been infiltrated by foreign influences. Now the only control we can offer for this reasoning is the setting of the earliest *non-canonical* apocalyptic literature, which shows that its devotees were nationalists concerned for the purity of Israel's traditions. It is not likely that they would have cherished a wisdom which was foreign and pagan.

Until we can extricate ourselves from these webs of assumption, we shall learn nothing which we have not concealed in our own premises. The problem with Daniel is one of our own making. Cited as *the* Old Testament apocalypse by many modern scholars, the text itself claims to be about a *wise man* who predicts the future, interprets dreams and functions at court. Josephus regarded him as a prophet (*Ant.* x, 267). How typical a wise man was Daniel? Joseph, our only other canonical model, is very similar; he functions at court, interprets dreams and predicts the future. The court role fits well with what we can deduce from the prophetic texts, but our *wisdom* texts have none of this. It seems as though our wisdom characters are speaking the wrong lines when they

91

take them from Proverbs. Daniel is sufficiently Judaized to observe the food laws, but how are we to explain his dealings with heavenly beings, and his use of an inexplicable mythology? The elaborate structures of the book suggest that it was using a known framework, and not constructing imagery as it went along, but there is no hint of such imagery in Proverbs, *except in passages where the text is now corrupt*. This suggests that the wisdom elements in the non-canonical apocalypses which have no obvious roots in the Old Testament may not be foreign accretions, but elements of an older wisdom which reformers have purged. It is important for our knowledge of esoteric wisdom, such as prediction and divination, that in Daniel they flourish in a clearly nationalistic setting, even though they had been condemned by the Second Isaiah as incompatible with *his* theology of the restoration.[48] Again we find the pattern: early and late resemble each other, but the writings of the early second temple period are different.

Daniel also points us to a lost tradition underlying many apocalyptic texts which is rooted in the older strata of the Old Testament. Dan. 12.1–3 has been studied in detail by Nickelsburg,[49] and shown to have contacts with material in Ass. Mos. 10; Jub. 23; T Jud. 20 and T Jud. 25. Between them these texts have complex links to Deut. 33, Isa. 14 and Isa. 52—3. The relationship is not a simple continuum from older to later texts, but shows rather that Daniel and the non-canonical materials depend upon a tradition other than the Old Testament, although related to it. This was a mythology of angels and of scenes of a great judgement.

If we pursue just one of these texts, Ass. Mos. 10, we find affinities with Deut. 33, but also non-Deuteronomic elements such as a great angel, the destruction of Satan, and Israel's exaltation to the stars. Now Deut. 33 in its present form is a very obscure text: it is a theophany passage with seventy per cent of its words in dispute. One wonders why a contact text for a 'lost' tradition behind the apocalypses should be in this state of preservation. The elements of Ass.Mos. 10 which are not in Deuteronomy appear in Daniel in a muted form. The exaltation to the stars appears as the wise who turn many to righteousness shining like the stars for ever, and the Old Testament contact text for this seems to be the 'Servant Song' of Isa. 52—3. Wisdom tales have a similar pattern; the exaltation of the wise man is a common motif. Certain significant words point us to the original setting of the exaltation and judgement language of the 'lost' tradition which has disappeared from the Old Testament. The wise man has *knowledge* of God, is a child/servant of the Lord, has God as his father and, as God's son, will receive help (Wisd. 2.12ff). At the great judgement he will be exalted and take his place with the sons of God, the Holy Ones (Wisd. 5.1ff). In 1 Enoch this pattern is applied to the Son of Man, the Elect One, or to the community of the righteous elect ones (1 En. 46.62–3; 104). Both Wisdom and 1 Enoch have details in common with Isa. 13—14. Nickelsburg's treatment of the texts is brilliant, and he uncovers a complex web of allusions, but I wonder if his conclusion is the only one possible. Did civil persecution of the Jewish leaders in the period of the second Temple lead to reinterpretation of the Servant Song using Isa. 13—14 for extra detail because it dealt with an arrogant foreign king figure? The common patterns in the later exaltation texts could also be explained if the star myth of Isa. 14, the Servant Song of Isa. 52—3 and the celebration of Yahweh's kingship in Deut. 33 all existed as parts of a single tradition, and were therefore originally interdependent and legitimately read in that way. The sons of God, the Holy Ones and the knowledge of God will also have belonged in this tradition which shaped the wisdom tales. The pattern of the 'lost' tradition therefore included, as well as the angels and the great judgement, the stars and the foreign kings, the kingship of Yahweh, the Holy Ones, exaltation, sonship and wisdom.

Wisdom lists in the apocalypses also point to an element missing from the canonical sources.[50] These lists occur at the climax of the seer's visions, indicating their importance in the original tradition, and showing an aspect of it hitherto unsuspected. Such revelation is entrusted to Moses on Sinai (2 Bar. 59) and to Enoch (1 En. 41 ; 43 ; 60.11ff). In Enoch's list the revelation concerns the lightning, thunder, secrets of the winds, clouds, dew, hail and mist, the movements of the sun, moon and stars, the secrets of the heavens and the duties of the various angels. It is associated with the cosmic covenant, not with the Mosaic. Similar lists occur in Job 38—9 and 4 Ezra 4, but in these cases they function to *deny* that man can have such knowledge. It belongs only to God. Job's question about suffering is met with this catalogue of God's creative powers which Job cannot share, but must observe and accept. Implicit in this wisdom list, as in the cosmic covenant material in the Similitudes, is the idea that right wisdom gives power to *create*. Ezra's question about suffering receives a similar answer, suggesting that the writers of Job and 4 Ezra are opposed to this idea of wisdom which is now found only in the apocalyptic tradition. Now Job is a relatively early text, and the use of a wisdom list in polemic at this period raises questions as to what upheavals were taking place in the concept of wisdom at this time. The purpose of Job seems to be to deny the possibility of the apocalyptists' wisdom. 4 Ezra not only denies this wisdom, but opposes the Enochic tradition in other ways also; it denies that man can ascend to the heavenly world (4 Ez. 4.8), and that he can contemplate and describe the heavenly throne (4 Ez. 8.21). Nor does 4 Ezra attribute the origin of evil to supernatural beings. Although resembling the apocalypses, 4 Ezra in fact uses the vision pattern merely as a literary form,[51] in order to give a view of the heavenly truths.

Stone (1976, p. 437) pointed out that magical, medical and demonological knowledge occur only at Wisd. 7.20, and that the wisdom lists do not contain any of the forbidden sciences revealed to the Watchers according to 1 En. 7—8 and Jub. 8.3ff. The knowledge of 1 En. 69.8ff – writing, exorcism and medicine – has contacts with Jub. 4.17ff, where Enoch learns writing, knowledge, wisdom and calendrical calculations, and with Jub. 10.1–15, where the demons are bound, and the unfallen angels teach Noah the medicine necessary to counteract the ills of the fallen angels. A distinction must therefore be drawn, he says, between these two bodies of learning, that revealed by the fallen angels, and that revealed to the seers. I am not sure that this distinction can be maintained. In Jub. 4.17, for example, Enoch learns the forbidden art of writing *and* the calendrical calculations which 1 Enoch includes amongst the revealed secrets of heaven. The fallen angels had also taught signs of the stars, sun, moon and earth (4QEnAstr^a, 4QEnAstr^b), and it would be very difficult to distinguish these from the astronomical knowledge revealed in 1 En. 41 and 43. There was, I believe, a body of lore known to the seers, of which the AB preserves but a few fragments, which was the key to their great power. To possess such knowledge was believed to be a sign of, or to confer, angelic status, but the fallen angels stood as a warning of what could happen when the knowledge was used in the spirit of rebellion. A similar distinction is made between the practice of good, (white) magic, and evil, (black) magic, even though the lore and techniques are similar.

As with the lost tradition of the *angelic* judgement, so here we find in the apocalypses a wisdom tradition revealed by *angels*, which has no clear antecedents in the Hebrew Bible, but can be used in it in a polemical setting as early as Job. It involves several assumptions to say, with Stone (1976, p. 438),

> What appears to be clear is that in the wisdom literature which antedates the apocalypses we do not find anything which helps us directly to explain the more curious and less obvious objects of apocalyptic speculation. It seems most probable that part of the speculative concern of the apocalyptic lists derived from wisdom sources, although the lines of connection may prove difficult to trace. It is impossible, however, to see the wisdom tradition as the only source from which the interest in these subjects sprang.

Until we can date the AB of Enoch, we cannot say for certain that the wisdom literature of the Hebrew Bible antedates it. Until we know that our definition of wisdom (devised by ourselves, it must be remembered, from the canonical texts) is an accurate description of Israel's ancient wisdom *as it was*, can we be sure that the lists in the apocalypses derive from *more* than a wisdom tradition? In these two clear cases, the tradition of the angelic judgement, and the tradition of revealed wisdom, the wisdom tradition as we define it exhibits a curious hiatus.

This is what I propose as a working model. There existed in Israel as elsewhere, wise men whose interests and skills covered all those listed in Wisd. 7.17ff and implied by Job 28. This wisdom was the knowledge which the angels brought from heaven to corrupt the earth in the Enochic account. To possess this wisdom made one as wise as an angel (2 Sam. 14), like a son of God. Unlawful use of this wisdom corrupted the earth and aligned the wise men with the fallen ones destined for judgement. These were the 'blinded' of the Apocalypse of Weeks, who left true wisdom in the period before the fall of Jerusalem, and were destined for the judgement described in the Book of Dreams. Those who acted evilly did not have true knowledge (Ps. 82; Jer. 23.11); but the ideal king (or the ideal of kingship) was wise, and his wisdom effected justice and harmony on earth (Isa. 11). Wisdom was the secrets of creation, learned in heaven and brought to earth, the recurring theme of the apocalypses. There must have been some way in which the king, and the wise men, 'went' to heaven like the prophets in order to learn these secrets by listening in the council of God (Job 15.8; Prov. 30.1–4); cf. Deut. 30.11–14 which compares the commandments favourably to something else, unspecified, which had to be brought from heaven by someone else. Wisdom included medicine, taught to Noah (Jub. 10.10) and to Tobit (Tob. 6.6) by angels, and brought by the rebels in 1 Enoch 8, where they taught the cutting of roots. In the Old Testament the art of healing belongs to God (Exod. 15.26; Deut. 32.39; Job 5.18) and the gift of healing was given to prophets (1 Kings 17; Isa. 39). We know virtually nothing of the medicines. There are details in Lev. 14 for the control of infectious diseases, quarantine, and conditions for readmission to public life, but no medicine as such. Closely linked to medicine was exorcism, and it has been suggested that *Joseph*, the wise man, was in fact an exorcist. The psalms of *Asaph* were for exorcism.[52] The king also had this power to heal; the king of Israel was asked to cure (*'sp*) leprosy (2 Kings 5.6), and replied that only God had this power. Solomon was also believed to have left methods of exorcism for the benefit of his people.[53]

Another of the angelic arts was metal-working, and we find wisdom attributed to a variety of craftsmen in the Old Testament: smiths, masons and weavers (2 Chron. 2.12ff; Exod. 28.3; 35.25; 36.4; Isa. 40.20; Jer. 10.9). 1 En. 8 links this skill to the arts of war, and in Isa. 10.13 we do find that the king of Assyria's military prowess is called wisdom. Job 28 implies that wisdom extended to the techniques of mining, damming and irrigation. Ezekiel 27.8–9 says that the navigators and shipwrights were also wise. The knowledge of mathematics required for these skills is also presupposed by the later astronomical material in 1 Enoch, and by the calendrical calculations which proved the erring ways of Jerusalem at that time.

Wise men who could predict the movements of the stars and the seasons could also predict the future, and this implies a deterministic view of the world. Von Rad's discussion of the doctrine of the proper time understates the case: 'The knowledge about the right time rested ... on the quite simple experience of specific orders and limits of which one could be aware.'[54] This can only be true if we have concrete evidence that the ancient wise men were the cool rationalists we have been told they were. The prediction of auspicious times is a widely attested activity of those entrusted with esoteric lore, and it is possible that the knowledge of the future which the wise men claimed was based upon something more exotic than the accumulated common sense of the time. The two wise men of whom we know anything in detail, Joseph and Daniel, did have the ability to predict the future. Both interpreted dreams, and Daniel had visions, yet the Book of Proverbs has little to say on the subject of future times. If wisdom was radically modified during the exile, we should have an explanation for this silence, since the whole thrust of the Second Isaiah's argument is that there is a group who claim to predict the future, but in reality can do no such thing. If the determinism implicit in the ancient wisdom had remained credible, that prophet's message would have fallen upon deaf ears, because he based everything upon the belief that there was to be a whole new plan, a new creation into which they had no insight. In other words, *the determinism which made the world of the wise men a possibility was the very thing which the Second Isaiah had to overthrow before he could present his theology of the new people of God.* This point is crucial for understanding the theology of the exile, and for understanding the differences between the views of history in the canon and in 1 Enoch.

The selection of auspicious times is closely bound up with the business of divination, and it is this which shows us as clearly as anything the difference between pre- and post-Deuteronomic religion. Deut. 18 prohibits the use of all divination in no uncertain way, and regards such practices as the reason for rejecting the ways of Canaan. They are represented as the very opposite of the ways of Moses, who was the only legitimate source of instruction for the chosen people. Outlawing all but the authority of the Deuteronomic law is the characteristic stance of the book: its statutes and commandments were to replace wisdom for the chosen people. This does not mean that we should now equate divination with the arts of the wise man, but such practices are quite consistent with the ways of Daniel and Joseph, and enable us to see from another angle that there was polemic beneath the surface of Deuteronomy. It is clear from the accounts of the restoration that the people of the land who had not experienced the exile were described as Canaanites, and their ways as abominations (Ezra 9.1), even though they worshipped Yahweh. There is ample evidence from the prophets that diviners had been part of the established worship of Yahweh in Jerusalem. Were these also the ancient wise men? Isa. 3.2ff lists diviners, magicians and enchanters (if that is what these words mean) as a part of the Jerusalem establishment. Jer. 27.9 says that they predicted prosperity for the city, Jer. 29.8 that they prophesied, divined and read dreams (an interesting combination) *in the name of the Lord.* Mic. 3.5ff links seers, diviners and prophets, and says that they will all be disgraced, in contrast to himself, who will be filled with the spirit of God. Ezek. 13 has the clearest picture of all, where we see all that the prophet abhorred performed in the name of the Lord. There are foolish prophets who follow their own spirit, and give lying divinations which include peace for the city. There are women who practise magic and hold people in their power. Ezekiel tells us that the defeat of such people will be a sign of the power of the Lord (13.23), a hope to be expressed again in 1 Enoch where it says that the power of the evil ones lay in the knowledge whereby they corrupted the earth and terrorized its inhabitants (1 En. 8.4); their power was to be overthrown by the great Holy One (1 En. 10.1ff). This is parallel to Ezekiel's conclusion, 'then you will know that I am the Lord' (13.23; cf. Phil. 2.11, 'every tongue shall confess that *Jesus is the Lord*'). We have no concrete evidence that these magicians were associated with the wise men, but their presence in Jerusalem must be remembered, and also the fact that these rites were performed in the name of Yahweh, if Jeremiah is to be believed. The cults of Canaan may not have been so foreign to the cult of Yahweh as our post-Deuteronomic sources would like us to think. We have to find a place within Israel's tradition for a tree-oracle (2 Sam. 5.24), for Urim and Thummim (Num. 27.21, Deut. 33.8) and for the belief that the outcome of any lot was determined by the Lord (Prov. 16.33). Daniel and Joseph both give God the credit for their skills as diviners (Gen. 41.6; Dan. 2.27). These accounts could reflect a later acceptable face of wisdom; or, as von Rad believes, they could show us the older wisdom which was dependent upon Yahweh and part of the religious tradition. It is significant for our understanding of Qumran Enoch that when Daniel was written for the comfort of a people of uncertain future, it was written as the work of a wise man. Prediction of the future, even at that late date, was the domain of the wise.

When there were no longer kings in Jerusalem, the wise men lost their patron and their figurehead.[55] Later descriptions of the wise men draw their imagery from the royal cult, and the texts which we label as either apocalyptic or wisdom are joint heirs to that tradition of learning. The original apocalyptic was revelation of wisdom in all its facets,[56] and it was the crisis of the exile and the subsequent realignments which identified wisdom with the Law. The Second Isaiah had mocked the old wisdom and its angels, whom he saw as defeated gods, because it conflicted with his message of a new beginning which no one had predicted. Deuteronomy replaced the old wisdom and its angels with the Law and the emphasis upon One God.

Many traces of the old wisdom remain. We identify wisdom sayings as those based on observation of the natural order, even though we have *texts* which link wisdom to the Law, and theories which link it to the business of government. We read that David was wise like the *elohim*, a compliment in those days, but that Adam was expelled from Eden because he took steps to acquire that wisdom. Between these two accounts *something must have happened to the status of the elohim and their wisdom.* By the time of Ben Sira (38.24ff), the old wisdom of the craftsman was still remembered as necessary for a civilized life, but it was inferior to the wisdom of the scribe. In the era of the older wisdom, the control of the creation had been a special skill, based upon observation and prediction, but also upon techniques which we would call magical. The spirit of God which gave this skill was the spirit of wisdom, counsel, understanding and might (Isa. 11.2). It was part of the ideal of kingship, but not restricted to the ancient kings.

After the demise of the monarchy, and with it the older wisdom, the stewardship of creation passed to everyman, and we read in Gen. 1 that Adam, not the king (cf. Ps. 8), was to subdue the earth *by obedience* to the command of God, and not by godlike wisdom. Ecclesiastes and Job, the two major wisdom texts of the Old Testament, both show wisdom in crisis. Ecclesiastes shows man coming to terms with the created order which was fixed, and over which *man had no control*, the vital element of the older wisdom. What, it asked, gave man his special place and made him superior to the beasts? How could man know that his spirit went up (Eccles. 3.18), a crucial part of the wise man's claim? Job claimed to challenge the *wisdom of God*. In the old wisdom, this was the original sin. In Job the arguments of the old wisdom are used to explain its own destruction. Job can observe the power and works of God, but he cannot create. His wisdom is not one of power, but only of delusion.

It is possible that we do not have sufficient evidence to reconstruct the ancient wisdom of Israel, but the greatest barrier to our understanding such evidence as we have remains our own presuppositions due to the difference between the ancient wise men and their modern commentators. (I had thought at this point to write 'counterparts', but the modern biblical scholar is in no way the counterpart of the ancient wise man; rather he is the counterpart of the ancient scribes who later tried to domesticate the ancient wisdom.) The skills needed to handle and translate these texts are not those most conducive to a sympathetic reading of them. It is necessary to stand back, well back, and to see the wise men in their wider context, a context which has been obliterated from the Old Testament for reasons apparent in both Deuteronomy and the Second Isaiah, texts which are fundamental to our understanding of the Old Testament, but also texts which have a very negative view of wisdom and the wise men. We must recognize the affinities of the ancient wise men with the shamans and magicians of other cultures, and not be overly influenced by our own post-enlightenment conditioning.

In a recent review, W. McKane wrote:

> Old Testament scholarship suffers from the burden of too many received critical assumptions hung about the necks of its practitioners like Coleridge's albatross. It needs the transfusion of a kind of scholarship which is not a further development of critical positions accepted as premises but is rather an *ab initio* investigation, unburdened by too many bibliographical cares, and concentrating a fresh eye on the Hebrew Bible.

This reminds me of Jung's comments on the *I Ching*:

> The irrational fulness of life has taught me never to discard anything even when it goes against all our theories, so short lived at best, or otherwise admits of no immediate explanation. Of course it is disquieting, but security, certitude and peace do not lead to discoveries.[57]

I began this chapter by outlining the type of wisdom demanded by the various references in the New Testament, a wisdom neutral in itself, but able to be used for good or ill, a wisdom involved with the heavenly powers and their conflicts, a wisdom linked to the created order. The ancient wisdom of Israel, with all its bizarre history, does meet these requirements, and the presence of 1 Enoch amongst the writings used by the first Christians shows that a work in this ancient tradition was known to them. Where that tradition was perpetuated in the centuries between the demise of the monarchy and the founding of the Qumran settlement is not known; but now that new work on the period of the second Temple is revealing a type of Judaism wholly unexpected, in that it was concerned with mystical ascents and revelations of heavenly secrets, we must not be too certain that we know what can, and cannot, have been the case. E. P. Sanders, after an exhaustive survey, concluded that Paul 'represents an essentially different type of religiousness from any found in Palestinian Jewish literature'.[58] He said that Paul's attitude to the Law was unparalleled in Judaism, that he had a different concept of sin, and worked with a system of the lordship and rule of heavenly powers. He assumed that Paul was a coherent thinker, working out something in terms of a pattern which *we no longer know*, and he emphasized Schweitzer's famous observation, that a theme cannot be central which does not *explain* anything else.[59] The central theme in Paul is still unknown. Sanders needs two systems to explain his thought, but thinks that the two were not distinct in Paul's mind. To elaborate further would anticipate my conclusions, but the traumatic rejection of the older wisdom and its traditions by the newer ways of Torah Judaism might well explain the New Testament's attitude to the Law. *The simplest, and most likely idea of wisdom to underlie the New Testament is that of the Enoch tradition.*

NOTES

1 Dunn (1980), pp. 168–76.
2 Dunn (1977), p. 221: 'Wisdom, like the Name of God, the Spirit of God, the Logos, etc., denotes the *immanent* activity of God, without detracting from God's wholly other transcendence. For pre-Christian Judaism, Wisdom was neither an inferior heavenly being, (one of the heavenly council) nor a divine hypostasis (as in the later Trinitarian conception of God)... Wisdom in fact is no more than *a personification of God's immanence.*'
3 Dunn (1980) pp. 204–6; Dunn (1977), p. 225: 'The thought of pre-existence first came in through a wisdom Christology ... in the Fourth Gospel the concept of a personal pre-existence of Jesus himself begins to emerge.'
4 Dunn (1977), p. 225.
5 McKane (1965); Whybray (1965).
6 McKane (1970), p. 19.
7 Widengren (1970).
8 Stone (1976).
9 Von Rad (1966b), p. 50.
10 Compare two parallel accounts: Isa. 37.16 and 2 Kings 19.15. In the Deuteronomic account

the title *Lord of Hosts* is missing from Hezekiah's prayer. For a detailed account of the change see Mettinger (1982).

11 Skehan (1954). The Qumran text of Deut. 32.8 differs from the MT, reading *sons of God* for *sons of Israel*. The LXX is similar to the Qumran text, suggesting that the Song of Moses with its 'ancient and unfamiliar conceptions' (von Rad) describes a time when Israel was chosen and allocated to Yahweh in the context of a polytheism now lost to us. The links between the Song of Moses and the materials of Deut. 4 can only be established by means of the Enochic tradition, which has retained the association of the stars, the heavenly powers, and the rulers of the nations.

12 McKane (1965), p. 49, describes the wise man as one of intellectual rigour and probity, refusing to take one step beyond the evidence, applying a sharp and disciplined mind to every facet of any situation ... Deuteronomy would have had nothing to fear from such a man, but he seems to me to have come from the senior common room of an ancient university, and not from the webs of magic and omens which were the stuff of ancient statesmanship. Von Rad's wise man, not surprisingly, is a German Protestant scholar: 'In wisdom two things were joined; that manly confidence in appropriating life, and, at the same time, that knowledge of the boundaries set, and the readiness to make shipwreck with all wisdom before God.'

13 In both passages, the Hebrew has a plural, knowledge of the *Holy Ones*, but it is assumed to refer to a single being because *Elohim* often does so though grammatically plural. This is an invalid assumption, because the title 'Holy One' existed in a singular form as a title for God, e.g. Isa. 5.19; 'the holy ones', plural, are the angels who appear throughout the Enochic literature under the rule of the great Holy One, e.g. 1 En. 1.3, as in 4QEn².

14 There is no ground for seeing two systems here. If they did exist, they cannot be deduced from this verse. David's wisdom and that of the angel are said to be parallel systems of thought, 'equal in respect of luminosity and utter dependability'. Where does all this come from? Not from the text! See McKane (1965), p. 59. All we know is that David was like an angel in respect of his wisdom, in much the same way as Isa. 11 promises wisdom from the Lord for the Davidic king. All this text tells us is that the angels were wise, and that their wisdom was in some way attributed to/shared by the king.

15 McKane (1970), p. 644: 'In such a verse, where there is hardly a glimmer of light, one feels powerless to make even the first move towards its elucidation.' Others have felt a similar sense of defeat. Torrey suspected that the obscurity is no accident. McKane comments (ibid.): 'It can only be explained as a deliberate process of mystification, in which case one has to look for a motive. Why should such a riddle be constructed? There seems nothing objectionable or dangerous about either of the conjectural reconstructions which would make it appear expedient *in the interests of orthodoxy* [my italics] to conceal them. If, then, we are to think in terms of deliberate mystification, we should look for an original which has the appearance of being theologically scandalous.' Since these verses deal with understanding, wisdom, ascent to heaven, creation, the name and the name of the son, one 'theologically scandalous' context immediately suggests itself. It is possible that we have here a wisdom ascent text from a very early period. Deut. 30.11–14 is clearly a denial of this verse, as is noted by J. Ashton (1986). As elsewhere in Deuteronomy, the Law replaced an earlier wisdom, cf. Deut. 4.6. The original of Prov. 30.1 must be guessed from what follows.

30.2 '*For* I am more brutish than man, I have not the discernment of man', is the explanation of 30.1. 'Brutish', *ba'ar*, is a word with interesting associations. It seems to be (i) a technical term used by the wise to describe those without wisdom (Ps. 73.22; 92.7; 94.8; Prov. 12.1; Ezek. 21.36), where the unwise are also the destroyers, and (ii) a term used to mock the claims of the wise (Jer. 10.8, 14, 21; 51.17; Isa. 19.11; Ps. 49.11, 19). The accompanying themes are mockery of idols, creation, and judgement. Prov. 30.2 has one who claims to be too brutish to be a man and to lack discernment, but the texts then diverge.

LXX has, 'God taught me wisdom and I have learned the knowledge of the *holy ones*', implying the reading *w'l lmd 'ty ḥkmh*. MT has, 'I have not learned wisdom and I have learned the knowledge of the holy ones', reading *wl' lmdty ḥkmh*. The point at issue must have been the *source of wisdom*. 30.4 asks who has ascended and ordered the elements of creation, discovered the name and the name of the son (LXX 'sons'). This must be read in the light of the Similitudes, where ascent and knowledge of the names give power to restore the order of creation. This is wisdom. The presence of the angel mythology explains the corruption of the text; cf. Deut. 32.8 where it is the *sons of God* who have disappeared from the MT. What, then underlies 30.1? Several readings have been suggested, but none is 'theologically scandalous'. See McKane (1970), p. 644:

lā'ītī 'ēl lā'ītī 'ēl w'ēkel	I am weary O God, and exhausted.
lū 'ittī 'ēl lū 'ittī 'ēl	O that God were with me.
lō'e 'ēt hā'ēl wayyūkāl	He who has exerted himself much with God and triumphed.
lō' 'ānōkī 'ēl w'ūkāl	I am not a god that I should have power.

We need something to explain the obscurity of the text. I suggest that we read from *'ātāh*, 'come', and from either *kūl*, 'comprehend, endure', or *yākōl*, 'have power, endure'. *kūl* is used in Isa. 40.12 of measuring the creation, in 1 Kings 8.27 the heavens cannot contain (?) Yahweh; Amos 7.10, the land cannot endure the prophetic word; Jer. 10.10 and Joel 2.11, nations cannot endure Yahweh's wrath. The clearest parallel would seem to be in Job 31.23, where *'ūkal* is read from *yākōl*, the evil man cannot 'endure' the majesty of God. If we read the consonants of 30.1 as *l' 'tyty l'l l' 'tyty l'l w'kl*, we should understand 'I have not come to God, I have not come to God and endured (his presence) (or – with Torrey – that I should have power) for I am a brute and not a man, and I do not have knowledge.' Since 'man' in this context implies one who does have knowledge, we have here an example of 'man' used in the sense of the apocalyptic histories in 1 Enoch. In the Apocalypse of Weeks and in the Book of Dreams, a 'man' is one who has knowledge and is taken up to God, whereas other mortals are depicted as animals, brutes.

16 Von Rad (1972), p. 33.
17 McKane (1970), p. 21.
18 McKane (1970), p. 421.
19 McKane (1965).
20 The argument is based upon the *locus classicus* for the definition of *'eṣah*, 'counsel' (2 Sam. 16.23), but there is no ground for seeing two separate systems in this verse. The comparison says that they were *like*, not unlike See McKane (1965), pp. 55ff.
21 ibid., pp. 86ff. The prophets took over wisdom vocabulary to show that true knowledge was knowledge of the history of Israel in God's hands. Now the reinterpretation of wisdom vocabulary undoubtedly did take place, but I cannot find any basis for this in the texts cited, Hos. 4.6 and 14.10, for example, suggest that lack of knowledge is due to failure on the part of the priests which will result in a natural wasting away like that of Jer. 4.22, where the foolish who do not know God are the preface to a natural (or is it a supernatural?) disaster. There is no threat of exile or specific punishment; the context demands a creation theology bound up with the knowledge of good and evil, and the use of that knowledge (cf. Isa. 11). The cosmic covenant is the more likely setting for this piece.
22 Von Rad (1972), p. 16. cf. Hanson (1975), p. 9. Wisdom was adopted by the apocalyptists to give their predictions an air of learning. This makes the ancient wise man too like a modern scholar.
23 Exod. 28.3; 2 Sam. 13.3; 2 Chron. 2.12; Hos. 13.13.
24 Von Rad (1972), p. 20.
25 ibid., commenting on Ben Sira 39.1-11.

26 ibid., pp. 57, 61. The world was 'apperceived by a perceptual apparatus in which rational perceptions and religious perceptions were not differentiated'.

27 ibid., p. 76. The object of the polemic is not known, but must have been a knowledge which was wrong because it began with a wrong attitude to God. Thus the older wisdom began with the right attitude to God, and the later wisdom held that knowledge itself came from God.

28 ibid., p. 88: 'It is quite impossible to describe the decalogue as the ethical norm from which the teachers of the sentences began.' It was formerly assumed that the decalogue was implicit in the older wisdom, but when that assumption is removed, it is quite a revelation to examine what is left. If the theophany at Sinai, *pace* von Rad, was only linked to the decalogue at a later stage, we are left with a very spectacular context for . . . what? The wisdom sentences rely upon a type of revelation totally different from that of the decalogue, and there are other traditions about what was revealed on the mountain (cf. Stone 1976), or what took place there (cf. Meeks 1970).

29 Von Rad (1972), p. 287. This is his weak spot. It is far too modern a view of the book trade! The knowledge which was excluded did survive, at least in fragments in 1 Enoch and Wisdom.

30 One would like to know what these new aspects were.

31 He says that even in Job there is no hint of an evil power outside God. I disagree.

32 Whybray (1965). I say *a* third, because there is a vast amount of material in this field, and I have space only for three examples of contributors.

33 He does argue for a development discernible in passages which deal with the personification of wisdom.

34 In Jeremiah's time there were three influential groups: the priests with their *torah*, the prophets with their *dabar*, and the wise with their *'eṣah*. In the earlier chapters of Proverbs, Whybray observes, the mere use of the name Yahweh and the absence of references to Egyptian beliefs incompatible with Yahwism show that any material that might have been borrowed was adapted in the process. He questions how far the religious element in Proverbs may be called the religion of Israel (i.e. what *we* think of as the religion of Israel). None of the writers denies that Proverbs has features not found elsewhere in the Yahwistic tradition, assuming that this is coterminous with the Old Testament.

35 Wisdom was one of the qualities to be given to the ideal king, but was not one of the qualities enjoined by the Deuteronomic historians. Like Adam, the king had to be obedient.

36 Whybray (1965), p. 29.

37 Wisdom vocabulary is commonest in Isa. 1—39, Jeremiah, Daniel, and Deut. 1—4. The word wisdom occurs in the Joseph tales in Genesis, in describing the craftsmen who made the tabernacle in Exodus, and in the framework of the Deuteronomic code where three of the seven examples equate wisdom with obedience to the Law. In the Deuteronomic histories it occurs mostly in what used to be called the succession narrative, but not in the evaluation of kings or events. The Chronicler uses the word to expand the Solomon passages, Ezra and Nehemiah refer to wisdom as the Law of God. In Daniel it occurs in the narrative sections, in Ezekiel in the taunt against Tyre, in Isaiah to show the opposition of human wisdom and divine, in Jeremiah that the law misused was not wisdom (Jer. 8.8).

38 Stone (1976).

39 cf. Murray (1984), p. 303.

40 If he is correct in saying that popular appeal ensured their survival, then there is no question of a censorship theory. But do we know for certain how the Hebrew Bible was preserved and finally assembled? A popular referendum seems unlikely. Canonical criticism has emphasized the role of the community in transmitting texts, but we must ask *which* community, and at what period. The divisions in Palestine would have fostered different ideas and different developments. The whole notion of community tradition changing texts derives from

modern notions of lay involvement in religious matters, and does not give sufficient weight to the undoubted power of élites in any religious system to mould the tradition as they wish and to transmit it as orthodoxy. See also Barr (1968), pp. 42–3: Hebrew may have changed its meanings as the result of the conscious efforts of those who transmitted the religious tradition. Mayes (1983), p. 138: do we know that the Deuteronomic view was the mainstream of Israel's thought as is usually assumed? For the other side of the question of wisdom and its popular role, see Nickelsburg (1982): the Epistle of Enoch, a work with strong but (on our present terms) inexplicable wisdom elements, may have been a pre-Essene composition, and be evidence that apocalyptic literature was *not the product of closed conventicles.*

41 McKane (1965), p. 55.
42 It comes from reading into the text, and not from anything the texts actually say. He even admits that the rest of the book says nothing about the crucial distinction (p. 61).
43 It is important to note the connection between angel figures, wisdom and the royal figure. The association may only be proverbial, but that in itself is highly significant.
44 McKane (1965), p. 55.
45 The account in Jubilees implies this.
46 No consideration is given to the all important *pride* motif in Isaiah which occurs in wisdom contexts, and is cited by McKane only when dealing with the wise men of Egypt who claimed descent from ancient kings. Note again the royal connection. Ezekiel's Prince of Tyre also thought himself as wise as a god, with access to secrets, but for his pride he was thrown down from the mountain of God.
47 Von Rad (1972), p. 7: (The term wisdom) ... 'first emerged in the scholarly world and has since become established. It belongs, therefore, to the fairly extensive number of biblical-theological collective terms whose validity and content are not once for all established and which have to be re-examined from time to time from the point of view of whether they are being correctly used.' Also Lambert (1960), p. 1. To attempt to define wisdom in terms of what has survived is dangerous on several counts. The category itself is quite arbitrary, the evidence is known to have been edited but with what criteria we do not know, and the lack of outside control upon them makes all our arguments circular.
48 I shall show from the Second Isaiah that there were certain heavenly beings who opposed Yahweh's plans for Israel with the claim that they could predict the future. The prophet argues that these beings have no power to predict the future; they do not even exist. This suggests that the Second Isaiah was caught up in the demise of the older wisdom. The link between the First Isaiah and the Second would be that the first recorded the conflicts with the ancient wisdom and its political philosophy, whereas the Second moved beyond this to a whole new world of monotheism and Judaism without the ancient wisdom and all its associations.
49 Nickelsburg (1972).
50 Stone (1976).
51 Rowland (1982), p. 53.
52 MacLaurin (1975).
53 Josephus, *Ant.* viii, 45.
54 Von Rad (1972), p. 143.
55 J. Z. Smith (1975).
56 Stone (1976).
57 McKane (1978), p. 381; Jung (1972), § 1000.
58 E. P. Sanders (1977), p. 543.
59 ibid., p. 441.

3

THE NAMES OF GOD:
(1) THE HOLY ONE

A perennial New Testament problem is the significance of various titles given to Jesus. The first chapters of Mark, for example, are full of them, and yet commentators can offer little more than the supposition that they were a contemporary Jewish usage. Jesus is described as the Holy One of God (1.24), Son of God (3.11), Son of God Most High (i.e. of Elyon, 5.7). Each time it is an evil spirit who recognizes Jesus. The titles used by the evil spirits are described as 'presumably Messianic, though there is no evidence that the term was so used by the Jews' (of 1.24); 'The evangelist attached great importance to it (the title Son of God) ... but it is not possible to know exactly how he understood it ... it is as Son of God rather than as teacher or prophet that Mark represents Our Lord' (of 3.11), or the problem is ignored (of 5.7). These examples are taken from one standard commentary,[1] yet each of these titles and its context needs no further explanation if read in the light of the Enochic mythology.

Luke's annunciation narrative also has a collection of titles which we have no reason to believe are an unnatural association of disparate elements. The child was to be a son of Elyon, and to be given the throne of his father David by the Lord God. He was to be called Holy, a son of God. In context, we may assume that these were royal titles, yet they are the same titles as appear in Mark in the context of the exorcisms. We must therefore explore the relationship between the angel myth and the messianic titles, to see how it was that the royal figure was associated with the expulsion of demons. Evidence for this association has already emerged in the study of 1 Enoch.

It is well known that certain strata of the Old Testament have a preference for particular names and titles for God. 'The Lord your God who brought you out of the land of Egypt' immediately associates the text with the Deuteronomists, and patterns of names in the Pentateuch led to a whole new development in study of that field. In 1 Enoch we find a preference for the titles Most High, Great Holy One and Lord of Spirits. The Genesis Apocryphon also favours the titles Great Holy One, and Most High; it too has an angel mythology. Noah was such a remarkable child that his father was thought to have been a Watcher, or a Holy One, or a son of Heaven.[2] This is similar to Luke's annunciation narrative, and shows that children of heavenly origin were not unexpected in New Testament times. Of the titles favoured by 1 Enoch, the most problematic is Elyon, and for this reason I shall not deal with it until there is more evidence to hand. Another title appears at 39.12, where the angels sing the Trisagion of Isa. 6, but Isaiah's *Lord of Hosts* becomes in Enoch the *Lord of Spirits*, a title which also occurs at 57.4. Evidence which emerged from the 'wisdom' inquiry suggests that the Hosts were viewed with disfavour by some of the post-exilic community, but here in 1 Enoch we discover an equivalent to the title Lord of Hosts which is entirely consistent with the theology of the book. *The Lord of Spirits* may be a link between the earliest parts of Isaiah and the Enochic tradition, between the angels of Isaiah's vision in the Temple, and the setting of the Similitudes.[3]

1 Enoch's most characteristic picture of God is as the Great Holy One, ruling the angelic world, and my main concern in this chapter is this title. Isaiah uses the title Holy One, and since he also uses the title King, we can establish that the prophet uses all the titles characteristic of the later works which used an angel mythology. Lord of Hosts is the most favoured of Isaiah's titles, but this title also occurs elsewhere. The same is not true of the title Holy One, which is hardly used at all outside Isaiah, and may therefore have had a special significance in his theology. If I am to establish links between Isaiah and 1 Enoch, this cannot be done simply by comparing the two works. I shall therefore establish a possible set of associations for the title Holy One, using material from other sources to provide a control and prevent circular argument. If any picture emerges from texts associated with the title Holy One, these should provide the context of Isaiah's and 1 Enoch's usage *if the occurrence of the title is significant.*

Habakkuk. In Hab. 1.1, *my Holy One* is an expression of confidence in the face of enemies. The context is the international activities of Israel's God, and we also find the title *Rock* whose meaning is unknown, but which appears elsewhere in association with *Holy One.* There is extensive and violent creation imagery, very different from the ordered calm of Gen. 1. Hab. 2.2 has a vision written upon tablets, and a time of waiting for revelation to be realized. There is the title *Lord of Hosts*, and hope that the whole earth will be filled with his knowledge. Hab. 2.17ff is obscure, but a favoured reading finds here Behemoth and Leviathan. Hab. 2.20 has Yahweh in his Temple, and the whole earth silent before him. Hab. 3.3ff is a theophany where the text is obscure. The Holy One comes from Mount Paran accompanied by two beings, possibly the demons of plague and pestilence. The central passage is now unreadable. There are the sun and moon, but their role is not clear. The Holy One brings salvation for his people and for his anointed. How this is effected we can no longer read, but a great number of variants and difficulties in a passage often indicates that angels are, or were, the problem. The least impenetrable parts of this passage *do* deal with heavenly figures.[4] In Habakkuk the *Holy One* is associated with creation imagery, visions, tablets, knowledge, judgement in the Temple, theophany and salvation for the anointed one. Of these elements, most are present in 1 Enoch, namely the mysteries of the created order, visions, tablets, knowledge, and salvation in time of trouble. Two elements, the Temple and the royal figure, are not obviously present in 1 Enoch, but they are there, I think, in another form. Enoch's heaven, the place of the judgement, is modelled on the Temple,[5] and the anointed one (e.g. in 1 En. 48.10) is clearly a royal figure with supernatural powers. The correspondence is striking.

Jeremiah. Jer. 50.29 equates the *Holy One* with the *Lord of Hosts*. Babylon will be punished for its pride. Jer. 51 (*passim*) deals with the *Holy One*, and looks forward to the fall of Babylon at the hands of strange creatures. The passage deals with creation, with wisdom, and with something very like Enoch's picture of the angelic judgement.[6]

The Psalms. Ps. 22.3 addresses the Lord as Holy, or as a Holy One, enthroned upon the praises of Israel. The enemies of the one who trusts in God are depicted as fearful beasts, or as the encircling powers of death. This is a royal psalm, and the king claims a special relationship to God.[7] Ps. 71.22 is another royal psalm, praising the *Holy One* of Israel. It expresses confidence in time of trouble, and uses the title *Rock*. As in Ps. 22, the psalmist recalls his dependence upon God from birth, and he prays not to be forsaken in his old age. Ps. 78 has a whole cluster of significant titles: *Holy One* in 78.41; *Elyon* in 78.17, 35, 36; *Rock* in 78.35. The original intention of the psalm is clear. Repeated rebellions by Jacob, Israel, Ephraim and Joseph are contrasted with Judah, Zion and David. Written in the style of a wisdom poem, it claims to tell dark secrets from ancient times. It is little more than a recital of national prejudice, reflecting upon the history of the early period, but mentioning nothing after the fall of Shiloh (78.60). The ideas of the Deuteronomists are dismissed (78.55) in favour of a theory of Israel's rejection due to constant rebellion.[8] Ps. 89 expresses confidence in the *Holy One*, and recounts the promises to the Davidic dynasty, guaranteed by the great power of the Holy One in creation. David his servant is both crowned and anointed. There is a clear pattern of parallelism in the two first sections of the psalm. The supremacy of the Holy One in the heavens is the supremacy of his Davidic king on earth. Like God himself, the Davidic king has power over waters (89.25), and his security is like that of the sun and moon, perhaps a reference to the eternal covenant. Again we find the title *Rock*.[9]

In these examples there is a pattern clearly associated with the title *Holy One*. Many of its elements are those of the later apocalypses, such as visions, heavenly tablets, theophany and angelic judgement, but the royal figure is also prominent, dependent for his power upon the might of the Holy One. The royal figure faces threats and enemies, but, we assume, overcomes them. Judgement upon foreign nations is also part of the pattern, and there are associations with the Temple.

In 1 Enoch the Great Holy One is the ruler of the angels, the *Holy Ones*, and since it is unlikely that the Great Holy One was totally different from those Holy Ones over whom he ruled, texts which deal with these angel figures should also fill out the picture. There are several passages where these figures appear, but many are very difficult to read. This seems to be the result of

106

deliberate attempts to rework or obscure the text, since a comparable number of difficulties does not accompany any other set of ideas.

Deuteronomy 33.2–3 mentions the Holy Ones. The passage is very obscure, but it describes a theophany in which Yahweh became King, 33.5, rising and shining upon his people. The crucial lines are 2cd and 3abcd, seventeen words of which fourteen are disputed.

2c	wᵉ'ātāh mēribᵉbōt qōdeš	2d	mīymīynō 'ešdāt lāmō
3a	'ap ḥōbēb 'ammīm	3b	*kol* qᵉdōšāyw bᵉyādekā
3c	*wᵉhēm* tukkū lᵉraglekā	3d	yiśśa' middabbᵉrōteykā

The words in italics are not in dispute.

33.2cd in the LXX is σὺν μυριάσιν Καδής, ἐκ δεξιῶν αὐτοῦ ἄγγελοι μετ' αὐτοῦ, reading *qōdeš* as the place name. The Hebrew has the right hand, but no angels, unless they are in the unknown *'ešdāt*, which surely cannot mean 'a fire of law'.[10] T. Onkelos found angels here, 'myriads of holy ones', and T. Jonathan 'myriads of holy angels'.

33.3b reads 'all his Holy Ones in your hand' (perhaps better 'his hand'). The Syriac, confusing daleth and resh, reads *bydk* as *barrek*, 'he blessed': could this originally have been some form of *bdd* 'separate'?

33.3c reads 'and they ... at your feet' (inserting a yod to give the plural 'feet'). The LXX has οὗτοι ὑπὸ σέ εἰσιν, implying submission, a nuance missing from the RSV 'follow in thy steps'. Massive emendations are suggested for the whole line; the verb *tukku* is especially difficult. In Isa. 1.5 these same consonants are understood as 'be smitten', and the context is rebellion against God. If this is the meaning here, 33.3bc would be describing the separation of the Holy Ones at the time of the judgement, and their being smitten at the feet of the Lord.[11] If 33.3 has a chiastic structure (and 33.3bc suggest that it does), then we should expect to find this also in 33.ad.

33.3a. Is it likely that *ḥobeb 'ammim* means 'he loved his people' (RSV, following the LXX ἐφείσατο τοῦ λαοῦ αὐτοῦ)? The verb *ḥbb* is not attested elsewhere in the Hebrew Bible. Rather than make *'ammim* singular, I suggest (with Kittel BH 2) reading *ḥrb* III 'attack, smite down': this is what God does to the peoples.

33.3d. The LXX has καὶ ἐδέξατο ἀπὸ τῶν λόγων αὐτοῦ, understanding *middabbᵉrōteykā* as from *dābār*, word. The form of this plural is difficult; all suggestions run into difficulties. I wonder whether this comes not from *dābār*, word, but from *dᵉbīr*, sanctuary. The proud creature of Ezek. 28 is thrown from his sanctuary in the judgement.[12] Ps. 73.17 perceives the end of the wicked in the sanctuary. The verb is also difficult; 'lift, carry' is hardly sense. BH 2 cites the Samaritan as having a form from *šā'āh*, 'crash in ruins', a good parallel to *ḥārāb*, 'smite down', in 33.3a, and associated elsewhere with the theme of judgement (Isa. 6.11; 17; 12; 37.26).

It is possible (and only possible) that we have here solar imagery: the rising and shining god, the mountain of the Lawgiving (Sinai), the scene of the great judgement, a temple setting for both, a theophany which makes Yahweh the King, and a judgement scene involving the angels. Even if we can deduce no details, and all my suggestions are rejected, there still remains the problem of a passage dealing with theophany, kingship and angels which has become unreadable. Why is this text so corrupt?

Holy Ones appear in Zech. 14, which describes the Day of Yahweh and the great battle near Jerusalem. This text is also corrupt. Like Deut. 33.5 it describes the day when Yahweh becomes king. The passage is thought, as a result, to be based upon the pattern of the pre-exilic autumn festival, in which the kingship of Yahweh and his Chosen One was linked to the control of waters and hostile powers.[13] Before the theophany there are earth movements and the mountains split (14.4). Obscurity then descends upon both the Hebrew and Greek until the end of 14.5, when Yahweh appears with the Holy Ones. 14.6 also has problems. While all the versions support 'there will be no light', this contradicts 14.7 which speaks of continuous light. In v. 6 the versions read 'cold and frost' after 'light', apparently reading *'ōr w^eqārōt w^eqippā'ōn*. But did 14.6 refer to other lights? It has been suggested that *y^eqārōt y^eqippā'ōn* be read 'the glorious ones (i.e. the stars) shall dwindle'.[14] This is a common element in descriptions of the theophany of the last judgement, and would not be out of place in this passage. But the real problem lies in 14.5a: *w^enastem gēy' hāray kī yaggiya' gēy hārīm 'el 'aṣal*. The LXX has [ἐμ]φραχθήσεται, reading *wnstm* as a niph'al of *sātam*, 'shut up, block'[15] and giving 'the valley of my mountain shall be blocked' (or 'the valley of the mountain of Yahweh shall be blocked', *hr yhwh* for *hry*) 'because ...' At this point the versions and translations diverge. The LXX has 'the gully of the mountain shall be joined to Iasod'; the RSV and NEB both take *nāga'* in its commonest sense of 'touch, reach, strike', giving respectively 'the valley of the mountains shall touch the side of it' and 'new valley between them will reach as far as Asal'.

None of these is satisfactory. At Eccles. 8.14, however, we find *naga' 'el* used to describe what is *allotted to* a man as his fate. In the context of a judgement theophany, such a meaning would be appropriate at Zech. 14.5. The valley was to be blocked as in the days of the earthquake, for it was to be the lot of *'aṣal*. The LXX renders this by Ἰασοδ or by Ἀσαηλ. A similar name appears in the Greek of 1 En. 8.1, Ἀζαηλ, and the present state of Zech. 14.5 may be due to this name.[16] The theophany would bring judgement upon Asael who was to be imprisoned in a valley near Jerusalem (cf. 1 En. 10.6; 21.7–10; 54.6; 90.24), the final punishment of the angels in a valley of fire to the south of Jerusalem, to be distinguished from the interim punishment of imprisonment whilst awaiting judgement (1 En. 10.5; 54.5).

Excursus I   Upon the word *'aṣal*

In Exod. 24.11 we read: 'And he did not lay his hand on the *chief men* of Israel; they beheld God and ate and drank.' The chief men are *'aṣīlē b^enē* *yisrā'ēl.* The whole chapter is beset with problems.[17] It is thought that the covenant ratification passage 24.3–8 was introduced by the compiler, who thus obscured the original context of these verses, which neither knew, nor implied, a covenant between Israel and its God. The older passage was a remnant of a theophany tradition 'unique among and independent of ... other theophany traditions contained elsewhere in the Sinai narrative'.[18] Moses was not the key figure, and probably did not appear at all in the original version. Who, then, were these pre-Mosaic 'chief men' of Israel?

Even so thorough a treatment as that of Nicholson has several points at which the presuppositions of scholarship break the surface. The most important of these concerns the nature of the *'asīlē bᵉnē yisrā'ēl.* The translation 'elders' is by no means without difficulties. He lists various possibilities – e.g. 'lay aside', 'side or corner', 'deeply rooted', 'of superior origin' – and opts for the idea of nobility and ancient origin. The LXX renders the word ἐπιλέκτων, 'the chosen ones': not an exact translation, but another characteristic of these figures which can be deduced from other texts may explain that choice.

Isa. 41.9 has *'āṣal* in parallel to *qᵉṣōt hā'āreṣ,* 'I took from the ends of the earth and called from its *farthest corners*'. It is possible that *qṣh* will reveal something of the meaning of *'ṣl.*

The root *qṣh* has at least two meanings: (i) '*cut off*', whence the words from extremities and far corners, and (ii) 'judge or ruler', whence *qaṣiyn,* 'ruler, chief'. It is clear that both *'ṣl* and *qṣh* have the same apparently unrelated sets of meanings. If the consonants of Exod. 24.11 and Isa. 41.9 are read in the same way, as 'rulers', the Isaiah text takes on a very different aspect, and begins to look like the account of Israel's origins which we read in Deut. 32.8ff; we should have to read 'Israel my servant ... whom I took from the *qᵉṣōt hā'āreṣ,* from its *elders/rulers*'. The rulers of Deut. 32.8ff, however, were the heavenly rulers, at home on the mountain of God. If this is what underlies Exod. 24.11, it explains the curious statement that the elders were not punished, even though they were on the mountain of God. We have to read this as a special privilege granted to Israel, but not to other nations, whose rulers were cast off from the mountain of God. There are several examples in the Old Testament of ruling figures ascending the mountain and being cast off: Isa. 14 and Ezek. 28 both describe such royal figures being hurled from the mountain of El, and Jer. 51.25 describes a destroying mountain (cf. 1 En. 18.13: this was a way of describing the angels) rolled down because the Lord stretched out his hand against it. The Exodus account emphasizes that this was *not* the fate of the rulers of Israel. The LXX also says that none of the chosen of Israel was in disagreement, an element entirely lacking in the Hebrew. Was the LXX translator aware of the discord described in the ancient myth?

It is possible that the *'asīlē bᵉnē yiśrā'ēl* were the heavenly rulers of ancient

Israel, embodied in their earthly counterparts. Enoch does fuse the earthly and heavenly rulers of the nations, but we do not know how old this tradition is. Ps. 89, which has the roles of Yahweh and king in parallel, suggests that the idea was very old, as does the curious reference in 1 Chron. 29.20, 23.

The number *seventy* is another detail unlikely to have originated in a twelve-tribe system. Seventy elders (although here not '*ṣlm*) shared the leadership with Moses (Num. 11.24–5), received some of the Spirit which had been his, prophesied *wᵉlō' yspw*. This was read by the Targums and Vulgate as *lō' yāsūpū*, 'they were not *destroyed*', cf. Isa. 66.17, 'they shall *come to an end*'. Is this a memory of the same myth as underlies Exod. 24.9–11? 1 En. 89.59 has seventy shepherds, angelic figures with charge over Israel who are judged with the fallen angels.

None of this is conclusive, but I doubt if it is coincidence. The theophany of Exod. 24.9–11 antedates the Mosaic tradition, and agrees with the Enochic, and with several other otherwise inexplicable Old Testament texts:

(i) The LXX of Exod. 24 reflects the discord which led to the downfall of the other heavenly beings;

(ii) Ps. 15 applies this to the Temple, which was the Holy Mountain of God: 'Who shall dwell in your Holy hill?... He who does these things will never be moved.'

(iii) Isa. 33.14 may even refer to the fire which the later mystics associated with the ascent: 'Who among us can dwell with the devouring fire? He who walks righteously will dwell on the heights ... your eyes will see *the king* in his beauty.'

Isa. 41.8–9 describes Israel/Jacob as the servant and the chosen one (the old royal titles), who was not *cast off*.[19]

For confirmation of this meaning of '*ṣl* we turn to the other entity in Isa. 41.9, the *qᵉṣōt hā'āreṣ*, which appear parallel to the '*ᵃṣīylīm*.

Excursus II   Upon the words *qᵉṣōt hā'āreṣ*

Isa. 40.26 has *qᵉṣōt* parallel to '*īyyīm*, usually rendered 'coastlands',[20] but '*iyyim* in Zeph. 2.11 is parallel to 'gods of the earth' and in Isa. 59.18 to the 'enemies of God'. Isa. 49.1 makes better sense if '*iyyīm* is a heavenly figure of some sort; Isa. 42.4 and 51.5 could be read this way, though these latter do not demand another reading. Isa. 41.1 could also be read of a heavenly figure, which brings us back to the immediate context of Isa. 41.5, where the '*ṣlm*, 'rulers' and '*iyyim* are in parallel. We must look for a meaning for both terms in the context of gods of the earth and enemies of God.

There is thus ground for thinking that '*aṣal* was associated with the cult of the Hosts; Zech. 14.5 is obscured for this reason. The problem with this text is to determine the significance of the name at that period, given that it is a relatively late text, and that the names and roles of the supernaturals altered over the centuries. If the name 'aṣal had once designated an angelic function, as did the name Satan, it too might have become a proper name in the course of time. The Day of Atonement prescriptions in Lev. 16 have a creature of similar name, *Azazel*. Both he and Yahweh receive goats during this ritual, and later traditions link the desert places of the Azazel ritual to Enoch's site for the imprisonment of Asael.[21] Whatever the origin of these associations, Azazel must have been an important figure, since he is the only supernatural apart from Yahweh for whom offerings were prescribed.

The Holy Ones occur in Ps. 89, a royal psalm. They are the sons of the gods who sit in council. Yahweh is feared in this council, and acknowledged as its ruler. This is very different from the picture in Job 1, where Yahweh is one among equals, challenged by his peers to test his servant Job. The major theme of Ps. 89 is the royal covenant; the supremacy of Yahweh over the other heavenly beings is balanced by the supremacy of David over the kings of the earth. David is the firstborn, the Elyon of the kings of the earth. Here we have the myth of Exod. 24 modified to serve the cult of the single monarch. As Robertson Smith observed, 'What is often described as a natural tendency of Semitic religions towards ethical monotheism is in the main nothing more than a consequence of the alliance of religion and monarchy.'[22] The older group rule is replaced by that of a single figure, whose supremacy is guaranteed by the supremacy of Yahweh in the heavenly council. The Holy One of Israel, i.e. the patron angel, has a son, says the psalm, the earthly ruler of his people and his mouthpiece. The king's power over the rulers of the earth is linked to his triumph over the rivers and the sea (89.25, 27), although we cannot penetrate the system sufficiently to be able to elaborate upon the nature of this link. (At this point reference is often made to the very similar Ugaritic tale of the struggle with Yam/Nahar, but equally relevant is the gospel tradition of stilling the storm as a sign of the messianic king.)

When a single king became pre-eminent there was a heavenly counterpart to the earthly event. The angels became the rulers of the other nations, as in Deut. 32.8, and Jacob became the special concern of Yahweh, the angel of Israel. The ideas in this Psalm bear a striking resemblance to those of the Prayer of Joseph, a work of unknown date quoted by Origen. Attention has been drawn to this important text by J. Z. Smith.[23] The material it contains is unique, and therefore difficult to fit into any context. Jacob is described as the earthly counterpart of a heavenly figure, Israel, an *angel* whose name means the *man seeing God*. He is the firstborn (cf. Ps. 89.27), and the chief angel of the power of Yahweh. There are several indications, small but consistent, that the original context of the ideas which surface in the Prayer of Joseph was that of the roots of 1 Enoch, i.e. the royal cult. A Merkabah text from Nag Hammadi describes a 'firstborn whose name is Israel, the man who sees God' standing near the throne during the heavenly liturgy, and a discussion of Jacob's ladder attributed to two first-century Amoraim in Palestine describes the two separate aspects of Jacob/Israel. His image is on high, whilst his earthly part sleeps below, just as one may ascend to see a king sitting in judgement and descend to find him sleeping in his room. Many of the titles attributed to Jacob/Israel 'are applied by Philo to the Logos, by rabbinic literature to Michael, by Jewish mystical literature to Metatron and by Jewish Christianity to Jesus. This suggests, without arguing direct literary dependence, *a community and continuity of tradition*' (my italics). Smith at this point suggests Hellenistic mystical Judaism as the milieu for these materials, and he is doubtless correct in saying that they flourished there. But did they originate there? I think not. 'What distinguishes the PJ from other ascent literature is the paradigmatic figure of Jacob-Israel, for, within Hebrew and Aramaic Merkabah texts, the patriarchs play no normative role.' It is *this* which points us in the direction of a source other than the patriarchal sagas, and I suspect that we find here in the Jacob/Israel figure a startling confirmation of the older pattern of belief associated with the king figure. Later debates within the apocalyptic tradition and amongst its heirs, as we have seen, centred around the ascent and the vision of God. Here in the Prayer of Joseph we find an angel figure who ascends, sees God, who has an earthly counterpart, but who, in his *heavenly aspect* is described as a man.

The most important elements in this setting for the Holy Ones are the creation and covenant motifs. The royal covenant in Ps. 89 is clearly the dividing line between the rule of the chosen king and the rule of the sons of the gods and the evils they represent. It is easy to see in this psalm a remote ancestor of the Similitudes' hope for the revelation of one who was to bring about the restoration and transformation of creation, and the defeat of the evil ones. Cross has discussed this psalm in detail,[24] since it is the only one specifically to link the themes of covenant and sonship. He suggests a fusion from two sources: the covenant from the old tribal league, and the sonship from the old Jerusalem monarchy. There is no need for this distinction, since there was a covenant associated with the monarchy. Its details have been largely overlaid in the Old Testament by the Deuteronomic account of the royal covenant in 2 Sam. 7, and by the preoccupation of modern scholarship with political covenant models. Both the psalms and the prophets show that there was a royal covenant closely linked to the stability of the natural order, which has survived in the occasional fragmentary references to an eternal covenant.[25] When Cross discusses the possible meanings for the word *b^erīt*, covenant, he does not emphasize these important associations with the power to create. The linking of covenant with creation is almost certainly more than an association of similar sounding words. The verb *bara'*, 'create', is used exclusively of God's act of creating, and the association of *b^erīt* with binding has long been recognized. What is not emphasized is that in the tradition we encounter as apocalyptic, the process of creation *is* a process of binding. In the Similitudes the creation is restored, and by implication the eternal covenant renewed, with the power of the name of the Son of Man, the ancient method of binding evil forces.

The creation imagery in Ps. 89 describes the power of the king; the royal mythology set the king figure at the centre of the natural order. Ps. 72 associates justice and fertility with the role of the king; Isa. 11 describes a ruler who brings knowledge and justice, and the harmony of all creation. In Ps. 89 the royal figure has to control the evil forces in the political, the natural and the social order (89.23, 25, 30ff). Similarly, in 1 Enoch, we find that these are the spheres in which the evil ones operate. They corrupt nature, they are the evil rulers, and their agents bring social injustice and break God's laws. Daniel also has this ancient triumph imagery; the man figure triumphs over the beasts from the sea (Dan. 7), and the angel of Israel fights against the heavenly princes (Dan. 10). These must not be read as aberrant growths due to foreign influences. They are echoes of the older cult.

Finally, we must note that the characteristic relationship of earth and heaven which we find in 1 Enoch also underlies the thought of Ps. 89. The heavenly reality has/is its earthly counterpart. The angels are the evil forces and rulers of the earth; Yahweh must, in some way, have been the king. 1 Chron. 29.23 reminds us that the king sat on the throne of Yahweh, and there are many passages in the Psalms (e.g. 21.8ff; 45; 63) where the distinction is not clearly drawn. Perhaps none was intended.

Job mentions the Holy Ones twice by name, but the mythology surfaces several times. In 5.1 Eliphaz asks if Job can turn to any of the Holy Ones for an answer to his problem. Job cannot be pure when even the Holy Ones cannot be trusted and have been accused of error. Man, he says, is destined to die *without wisdom*, and there is then an allusion to the Genesis Eden myth. Affliction does not come from the ground, as did the thorns and thistles of Adam's curse; man gives birth to trouble (Dhorme's pointing) as the sons of Resheph fly upwards. Leaving aside the finer points of detail, we can see that Eliphaz argues in terms of angels, holy ones, demons, evil born from human kind, and other features of the old mythology now familiar. God does not trust the Holy Ones (15.15), there is a heavenly council (15.8), wisdom is important (15.18) and it is a crime to stretch out one's hand against God (15.25). The introduction to Job depicts the heavenly court, with Yahweh one among many and challenged by the other gods to test the loyalty of his servant. This may be a glimpse of Israel's beliefs before the exile, and may throw some light on the sufferings which the king had to endure in order to prove his faith and loyalty.

Hosea has one reference to the Holy Ones, a muddled text which we are accustomed to emend before translating. Hos. 12.1 (11.12) contrasts Judah and Ephraim, and praises Judah for remaining faithful to the *Holy Ones*, plural. This is usually translated as a singular, although there is no reason why this should be done.

Proverbs 9.10 defines insight as 'knowledge of the holy ones', indicating the knowledge which wise men sought to possess. The tree of knowledge in Eden, (which was forbidden to Adam!) and references in 1 Enoch, e.g. 9.7, show that there was a long tradition of men wanting to acquire the knowledge of the Holy Ones, but it is not clear if this is to be understood as a subjective or an objective genitive. We do not know if it was knowledge *about* the Holy Ones which was desired, such as their names which were so important in later writings, or knowledge which the Holy Ones themselves possessed. Proverbs 30.1–4, which I have discussed in the context of wisdom, has that obscured reference to the Holy Ones and their travel between earth and heaven, their knowledge, their links to a theology of creation and an association with sonship. The passage as it has survived is virtually unreadable.

The final source of information about the Holy Ones is Daniel. Here we see them at their most developed *within the canon*. This qualification is important, because Daniel was written later than some parts of the Enochic material which has far more emphasis upon angels. What we find in Daniel may not be evidence of accretions from foreign sources, but an ancient tradition surfacing in this text, but surviving in fuller form in 1 Enoch. Dan. 4.5 (Eng. 8) says Daniel has the spirit of the Holy Gods (*'elāhīn*), enabling him to read dreams and foretell the future. This is not necessarily a simple statement that Daniel was inspired by God. It could represent what a pagan king thought about a wise man; he was inspired by the *'elohim*. Dan. 4.10 (Eng. 13) describes a Holy One coming from heaven. The creature is called a 'watcher' (*'ir*), the name given to them in the intertestamental literature, and the name which enables us to uncover a great deal of information about them in the Old Testament itself, since there are many passages where these consonants are read in other ways, or where a set of allusions to them is no longer recognized: e.g. Isa. 14.21, where the earth might be filled with hostile *cities*; 2 Kings 10.25, where the guards go to the *city* of the house of Baal; Lam. 4.14, where *blind* (LXX ἐγρήγοροι, 'watchers') are defiled after the sack of Jerusalem. Dan. 4.14 (Eng. 17) shows how these beings functioned in the heavenly order. By their decrees they show that Elyon rules the politics of the earth and disposes the kingdoms of men. Apart from showing us that the Holy Ones inspired the wise men and were the agents of Elyon's rule, these three examples in Daniel give us three equivalent names for the heavenly creatures, by which we are able to identify them in yet more Old Testament contexts. They were the *'elohim*, the Holy Ones and the Watchers. Since the activities of Daniel's Holy Ones are exactly like those found in the earlier Old Testament texts, we must not assume that the character they have in Daniel, or their other roles, is late or alien to Israel's traditions. The pattern does not change; they deal with politics, with heavenly decrees from Elyon, they communicate through visions and work through the wise men who advise the king.

Dan. 8.11–13 is said to be the most obscure passage in the book; two holy ones discuss the fate of the Jerusalem sanctuary in terms of the angel myth. The little horn grows great to the host of heaven, and casts down some of the stars. It makes itself as great as the prince of the host, whose sanctuary and offerings are taken away.[26] The Hebrew at this point is unreadable; Theodotion and the LXX differ completely. The obscurities disappear if the prince of the host is the Jerusalem deity, and the little horn seen as yet another aggressor against the holy city. His end is depicted in terms of the fallen angel rulers, just as the aggressors of old were depicted by Isaiah, Jeremiah and Ezekiel. The Holy Ones, both here and in the older cult, would have known what was planned for the affairs of men.[27] Everything was ordained, and at an appointed time, there would be a day of judgement as described in Psalms 58 and 82, or 1 Enoch. Given that these chapters come from a time when Antiochus, a foreign ruler, had claimed divinity for himself, and was threatening the city and people of Jerusalem, it is hardly surprising to find the angel myth employed. It dealt with just that problem: foreign rulers who had claimed to be divine, and set themselves up against God and against his holy mountain (cf. Isa. 14; 37.21ff; Lam. 4.12; Ps. 2). The Holy Ones in Dan. 8 can only be understood in this context, and the question raised by their presence there is not where they came from in the second-century *mélange* of oriental religious ideas, but where their cult had been perpetuated during the centuries since the demise of the monarchy.

There remains the most problematic of all the texts which mention the Holy Ones. In Dan. 7 they are closely linked to Elyon, and promised the kingdom forever, after the defeat of the fourth beast. The horn of the fourth beast made war on the Holy Ones and gained power over them until the Ancient of Days intervened on their behalf with a great judgement. In 7.27 we meet a 'people' of the Holy Ones who receive dominion and glory. The structure of the chapter suggests that the Son of Man figure in the first part of the vision corresponds to the 'people' in the second. This is the heart of the problem. How can one figure be the people of the Holy Ones? So much has been written on this that even the briefest of summaries is an enormous task. I shall confine myself to views which have most rapport with the text as it stands. To say, for example, that there is no mention of angels in the chapter is hardly reasonable, and arguments derived from such a position must be suspect.[28] The passage almost certainly contains older materials, but to say that these are drawn from several sources begs several questions, and should only be considered when one source has been shown to be quite inappropriate. Speculation about the Son of Man figure originating elsewhere in the ancient Near East should also be used as a last resort. What we have in Dan. 7 is a prophet or wise man speaking to his endangered city. The religion and existence of his people is at stake; their monotheism has been mocked and their sanctuary desecrated. *Is it likely that the message would be cast in anything but the most traditional of materials?* I used the same argument with the Enochic histories; could their feelings of outrage at the developments during and after the exile have been expressed in terms of a mythology which was itself alien to their traditions?

The vision of Dan. 7 concerns the fate of Jerusalem and the promise of her future power and glory. The ancient monarchy had also concerned itself with these things, as can be seen from the triumphalism of the Psalms. This ancient cult is the most obvious place to look for the roots of the vision. Any reconstruction of the affairs of the ancient Temple must be made with caution, but if my proposed reconstruction is compatible with the evidence, even though not derived directly from it, it needs to be considered, because what evidence we have is only chance survival, and by no means a representative selection of texts and ideas.

Daniel 7 begins with beasts from the sea. It has been suggested that these were originally a separate vision, joined to the Son of Man material, but this should not be taken as our first option. The interpretation in the text says they were foreign rulers oppressing the people of God, and fighting against the Holy Ones. Later parts of Daniel describe the battles of Michael, the Prince of God's people, against heavenly princes who are the patrons of foreign nations. The beasts and the princes therefore represent the same thing. Any attempt to root this vision in a single source must find a place for these beasts in the ancient cult, and for their hostility to a figure who could have been the Son of Man.[29] Now the Psalms do have several references to hostile beasts, and even if they became no more than figures of speech, they are unlikely to have originated thus. There are bulls with mouths like lions, dogs and wild oxen (Ps. 22); lions (Ps. 35.17); beasts with teeth of spears and arrows, and with tongues like swords (Ps. 57.4); the fallen gods are serpents and young lions (Ps. 58.6); howling dogs (Ps. 59); water beasts and bulls (Ps. 68). These are enemies of the royal figure. Since the writers of apocalyptic also had a code whereby the rulers of foreign nations were animals, we cannot be certain that this originated in the manner of Aesop's fables and not in the beast terrors of the ancient cult. At a much later date we find that all the evangelists interpret the death of the King of the Jews in terms of Ps. 22, which is full of beast enemies. It is possible that they knew something of the ancient context of this Psalm which we no longer do, that the enemies were the terrors which assailed the king in his time of trial. Daniel's beasts were at home in this tradition. Their rising from the water should also then be explicable in terms of the ancient cult, and again, this is not impossible. The Psalms often refer to water as the place of danger from which God rescues his people, yet this is strange in a people whose land had little water, and which was not subject to flooding. One can understand the fear of drowning in the imagery of a seagoing people, but for the cult of Jerusalem, there is no obvious source for this fear unless the waters be the primeval deeps of the creation mythology. The danger of waters can be personified (Ps. 18.16), and rescue described as deliverance from those who were too strong, and hated the sufferer. Deliverance from enemies is rescue from waters in Ps. 32.6–7; 40.2; 42.7ff;

enemy heads are shattered and the faithful brought back from the depths of the sea (Ps. 68.22); those who hate the psalmist are deep waters (Ps. 69.1–4); enemies who might have triumphed and floods which might have overwhelmed appear together (Ps. 124). These are but a few examples, to make the point that water was the image of defeat, evil and despair. From it, God rescued his people. The Exodus pattern springs to mind as an obvious source of this imagery, but the fact that the Second Isaiah depicts the Exodus in terms of the defeat of a sea monster, and that the Song of the Sea in Exod. 15 is based on an older pattern of defeat of enemies in terms of the hostile waters, points us behind the Exodus story as we know it to an older myth of watery monsters and enemies which was later used to give form to the events of Israel's history such as the escape from Egypt, or the return from Babylon. Thus waters, beasts and angel rulers all describe the enemies of the king and his city, and it is not impossible that these elements of the vision in Dan. 7 originated in the older cult. How these various elements functioned we can only guess. There was a bronze 'sea' built for Solomon's Temple which was a major feature, occupying half the width of the Temple. It must have had some place in the rituals, even though we have no description of its being used except to wash the sacred personnel (2 Chron. 4.6).[30] If the liturgies enacted what is described in the Psalms, this 'sea' would have been integral to the royal cult. At a much later date we do find rising from the waters associated with the recognition of divine sonship (Luke 3.20), and with the ancient coronation psalm (Ps. 2). Was this a Christian innovation? It is apparent that there is a great deal of the older royal imagery in the gospel accounts, and the more that is reconstructed from intertestamental sources, the more the evangelists' allusions fall into place. In 4 Ezra 13 a man figure, similar to Daniel's, comes up from *the sea* with the clouds of heaven. The tortuous explanations given by the writer indicate that he was interpreting older material and applying it to his own situation. We find here the triumph of the people of God, and the massing of enemies against the man figure who goes up to heaven. Both Daniel and 4 Ezra confronted similar situations, Daniel under the Seleucids and 4 Ezra under the Romans. Both saw Jerusalem in danger, and both, I think, used the triumphalist imagery of the royal cult and employed a figure who had once been the king. Daniel does not reveal whence the man figure came, but if he was the king, he probably came from the sea and then ascended. The differences between the visions may point to two different traditions, but the underlying similarity of both content and context favours the view that the two were drawn from one tradition, which must be reconstructed by taking elements from each vision to fill out the picture. In Daniel the evil powers are beasts, in 4 Ezra a hostile multitude; the Old Testament leads us to expect this equation. The hostility is towards the man figure in 4 Ezra, but towards the Holy Ones in Daniel; the *interpretation* in Daniel links the Holy Ones to the man figure. Both books mention the stone/ mountain, which is a recurring but as yet inexplicable feature of this tradition

117

(4 Ezra 13.6; Daniel 2.45); cf. Zech. 4.6ff, an obscure text and Deut. 32.4ff, also obscure. The rock is a frequent image in the Psalms and Isaiah.

The other major feature of Dan. 7 is the arrival of the Son of Man figure before the throne of the Ancient of Days. Bentzen thought the whole vision an eschatologizing of Ps. 2;[31] but can we know when eschatology in our sense of that word became an appropriate description of this ancient world view? Ps. 2 claims divine sonship for the king, which is hardly an event in the non-eschatological sphere, and several other psalms expect a future judgement such as became the basis of what we recognize as Judaeo-Christian eschatology, e.g. Pss. 58; 73; 82. Since there can be no proof that Daniel 'eschatologized' the ancient imagery, or even that eschatology would have meant anything at all in a system which did not separate earth and heaven, temporal and eternal, the stronger possibility is that Daniel's vision is drawn directly from the tradition of the old Temple, and that the very latest book of the Old Testament represents its oldest ideas, and *therefore testifies to the fact that all the intervening works had a knowledge of these traditions.* Thus Dan. 7 has material in common with Ps. 2 and Ps. 89, the imagery of the royal exaltation, and the picture of judgement simultaneously on earth and in heaven. We must not demand an exact correspondence since both are poetry based upon a common theme, but we cannot fail to note that both these Psalms are royal psalms, and that the Danielic material was therefore messianic from the beginning. It is most unlikely that it 'became' messianic due to later interpretation.

In Dan. 7 the Son of man figure is angelic, but this does not exclude an origin in the ancient cult, since the king was an angel in his heavenly aspect, whilst functioning on earth as the Davidic king. He was a Holy One, a son of God, as was announced in the royal titles (Isa. 9.6). The question we must bring to this chapter is not, 'At what stage did it acquire a messianic significance?' but, 'Was the whole text based upon memories of the older royal cult, which, given the context, must be described as messianic from the beginning?' Dan. 7 had an established messianic interpretation by the end of the first century AD, and there is considerable evidence that the interpretation was well known long before that date. May we assume that interpretation implies an *alteration* of a text's original meaning? A pattern of similar ideas occurs in a play of the second century BC, where Moses, in a dream, plays the same role as Daniel's Son of Man figure and ascends to the great throne.[32] Philo describes Moses as god and king whose ascent of Sinai was an ascent to heaven.[33] Samaritan traditions are similar. These texts do not just refer to a man who became king; they refer to a man who became *divine*. There was therefore a pattern in some traditions, widely attested (and this is important, since it argues against this being a minority or sectarian view) of a divine royal figure who ascended to meet God. In Daniel we find this figure as the Son of Man, the heavenly archetype who *in Daniel's case* was thought to have an earthly referent in the people, but who was more commonly associated with an individual figure.

There are several places in the Psalms where the king is addressed as Son of Man. We do not know the significance of the phrase, but this should not deter us from recognizing that it meant *something* above and beyond what seems to *us* the natural meaning of 'son of man'. The term 'man' also meant more than just a man, as we can see from the Enochic histories, and from the several biblical interpretations where 'man' was understood to mean the Messiah.[34] Ps. 8 is an obscure text dealing with those who sing praises in heaven, but who or what these were is not clear.[35] There is one *crowned* with glory and honour: this at least is clear. He is a little less than the *'elohim*, and set over the creation. This must have been a royal psalm, with the king described both as man and son of man.[36] Ps. 146.3 warns against any noble, or any 'son of man'. Ps. 80.16–18 is a confused text. The MT of 80.16 reads 'The *kannāh* which your right hand has planted, the son which you have made strong for yourself'. The Targum here understands 'son' as the king Messiah, and *kannāh*, although translated 'stock', has a whole web of royal and messianic associations.[37] The LXX has 'son of man' both here and at 80.18, where the MT has, 'Let your hand be on the man of your right hand, and upon the son of man whom you have made strong for yourself'.[38] We have thus the association of *kannāh*, stock, the man at the right hand, the son, and the son of man, in a prayer for national deliverance. The context is similar to that of both Daniel and 4 Ezra, the material is similar, and the understanding of it was messianic as early as the translation of the LXX. Three examples from the Psalms can prove nothing; but the confused state of two of these texts, and the clear associations of one of them at least beg a question.

Finally, the key word in Daniel's vision of the Holy Ones is 'kingdom'. The ancient cult of the king would be a natural place for the origin of the imagery for that reason alone. Dan. 7 promises to Jerusalem what had been promised to the kings. We are perhaps mistaken in looking for a Son of Man figure as such, and then pronouncing that he did not exist. The figure was an aspect of the old monarchy, a way of understanding the king's role in the heavenly order, but a role not confined to the king alone. Others such as prophets and wise men could function in the heavenly realm, and thus be called Son of Man, or simply man. The Son of Man was one of human origin who was a member or observer of the heavenly council. After the Deuteronomists had democratized the old royal theology, the king figure who had once represented the whole people before God, came instead to symbolize them.[39]

Texts dealing with Holy Ones and the Holy One have significant elements in common: theophany, judgement, triumph for Yahweh, triumph for his anointed son, ascent to a throne in heaven, conflict with beasts and with angel princes caught up in the destinies of earthly kingdoms. Many of these texts are corrupted; much of their subject matter is that of the 'lost' tradition thought to underlie the apocalyptic texts.[40] The textual corruption and the lost tradition are aspects of the same question.

119

In view of the subject matter associated with these holy one texts, I suggest that their original context was the royal cult in which the king was a more than human figure. We do not know how he achieved this status, but wisdom was an important factor. He triumphed over the beasts and enemies, ascended the holy mountain to the presence of God, functioned among the Holy Ones and acted as a channel for the right ordering of creation due to the power of his divine wisdom. The king received oracles and acted as the mouthpiece of God.[41] All of these features can be fitted into a framework widely attested in other cultures which confirms that this set of motifs, established simply on the basis of the occurrence of the word 'holy one', forms a workable system.

Trance travellers are a phenomenon known from Siberia to South America, from Australia to South Africa, from Central America and Indonesia. The emperors of ancient China 'flew', as did the god-kings of south-east Asia. The kings of Mesopotamia ascended to receive their kingship, along with the secrets which constituted the divine knowledge and gave them the right to rule. These trance travellers have been described as 'technicians of the sacred'.[42] They are mystical and priestly as well as political figures; they are healers, seers, visionaries, human beings who have mastered death. They communicate with the upper world. They are judges, politicians, repositories of their people's knowledge of cosmic and physical sciences, knowing the secrets of plants, animals and elements.[43] The trance condition can be induced by drugs, by music, by fasting or by sensory deprivation;[44] but the results are remarkably similar, if one makes allowances for variation due to culturally conditioned forms of expression. The magical flight is associated most frequently with the god-kings, but it is not their monopoly. Sages and mystics also travel, once they have achieved the necessary superhuman state. The mythology of the people forms the map of the travels, and the travels in their turn confirm the reality of the myths.

The problems we encounter when we compare these phenomena with Old Testament materials are manifold, since we know neither the rituals of the Temple, nor the mythology of which they were the manifestation. Such fragments as can be retrieved from the holy one texts are, however, *all* compatible with the experiences of the trance travellers. Their initiation was a painful and traumatic affair, which resulted in the conviction that they had overcome death and achieved enlightenment.[45] They had been chosen. The death experience was often that of being attacked by a wild beast, and a terrifying vision of the seer's own bones being reclothed with new flesh.[46] When life returned, the traveller was illuminated, restored to the paradisal state, and given the power to 'see' both at a great distance, and into other dimensions. Restored to the pre-fall state, the seer learned the secrets of creation. Everything seen in the upper world was remembered as bright and clear, enabling him to see through the ordinary material world into its hidden structures. The practical arts of healing were often derived from this trance travel, as was the ability to talk to animals.[47] The travellers also learned to control evil spirits, through the help of their own particular guardian.

When we compare these experiences of trance travel with the many definitions which have been offered of 'apocalyptic' literature, we find that they can all be rooted in this one phenomenon. 'Apocalyptic' has been rooted in wisdom, the disintegrating royal cult, prophecy, the transcendence of death, astrological and esoteric lore, ascents to heaven and mystical experiences, the communication of heavenly secrets and oracles by means of visions, the nationalism of a warrior god mythology. No one of these is satisfactory on its own as a definition, because the actual root of apocalyptic lies further back in a situation which *gave rise naturally to all these various characteristics*. The ultimate origin of apocalyptic must lie in a royal cult which involved the ascent of the king. There is need for much more work to be done in this field.[48]

I began this chapter with the royal titles in Luke and the exorcism titles in Mark, which are the same. Both use 'Holy One', implying that in New Testament times the royal figure was expected to be a Holy One, and a Holy One was expected to join battle with evil spirits. Texts in the Old Testament chosen simply because they mentioned the 'holy ones' show that this association was very ancient, and part of a tradition known elsewhere in the apocalypses, where it has survived in greater detail. Thus the New Testament, Old Testament and extra-canonical materials come together in an extraordinary way *on the basis of material no longer central to the Old Testament or the view of Israel's religion which we are accustomed to draw from it*. The roots lie in the royal cult.[49] Thus the Similitudes of Enoch, with their Son of Man/Elect One figure are important for reconstructing the mythology presupposed by the New Testament writings, even though there is no material evidence that the Similitudes existed in their present form in pre-Christian times. The early Christian tradition of the Son of Man as Messiah is, despite recent arguments to the contrary, not an innovation, or the result of the creative exegesis of Dan. 7. It is the natural use of the most ancient beliefs about the Davidic kings.[50] When we bear in mind the quantity of material at our disposal, the state of its preservation, and the enormous periods of time over which it was handed down, we cannot hope to build a structure which will satisfy the most cautious. But, used with imagination, such evidence as we do have can illuminate much more than it does at present.

NOTES

1 Nineham (1963).
2 1QapGen 2 in Fitzmyer and Harrington (1978); 1 En. 106.
3 Rowland (1982), p. 104; Eichrodt (1961), pp. 193–4: 'If the prophets could appeal to Yahweh Ṣeba'ot as the Judge exalted both over his own nation and over all the nations to support their threats against Israel, then both for themselves and for their hearers this name must have connoted more than simply the national deity ... there is a universalist tendency

in the older Israelite conception of Yahweh ... This still gives no indication of when or under what influences this name expressive of the divine sovereignty came into fashion. It would only be permissible to draw definite conclusions from the fact that it is not found in the Pentateuch or in the books of Joshua and Judges, if there were no reason to suppose that later redaction might have deleted it; but such a possibility cannot be excluded. Furthermore, the question of whether foreign influence has to be taken into account is still very obscure. In any event, the choice of this particular epithet to express the whole essential character of the Yahwist faith remains of the utmost significance.' For more recent discussion see Mettinger (1982). Black (1985), pp. 190ff, argues that the Lord of Hosts was *changed* in the Similitudes to conform to the *changed* beliefs of those who used it. But 1QM12, 8–9 has 'host of angels' (*ṣb' ml'kym*) and 'host of his spirits' (*ṣb' rwhyw*) in parallel clauses, which makes one wonder how great the change can have been from what I am proposing was the original. Black (1985), p. 192, asks: 'Was the interpreted version of the traditional 'Lord of Hosts' the creation of the Ethiopic translator of the Parables, or was it already present in some form in his *Vorlage*?'

4 Hab. 3.13b has '*rwt*, possibly linked to '*yr*, watcher; also '*d*, which elsewhere denotes a heavenly witness figure, e.g. Job 16.19; Ps. 89.37; *sw'r*, for which the apparatus proposes *ṣwr*, a heavenly creature which features in the Third Isaiah. The Greek has δεσμούς, 'bonds, fetters', or ἕως ἀβύσσου τῆς θαλάσσης καταδύσονται, 'they shall sink to the bottom of the sea', both reminiscent of the myth underlying Exod. 15.

5 Rowland (1982), p. 83 and notes.

6 Jer. 51 begins with a destroying spirit sent against Babylon: 'winnowers' (better 'strangers' or even 'loathsome things'). The spirit, singular, of the kings of the Medes is to be roused. Although the text is not entirely clear, we could have here *one* spirit as the patron of the monarchy of the Medes, just as the princes in Daniel seem to be in each case the heavenly archetype of a series of kings. Jer. 51.25 tells of a *destroying mountain* to be burned, and the mountain is Babylon. Clifford (1972), pp. 132ff, has traced a similar pattern in the myths of Canaan. Philo of Byblos links mountains and the sons of God. 'If an old theogony is behind this confused account, then divinised mountains played a role in the Phoenician structure of the cosmos.' cf. 1 En. 18.13. The angelic fall and judgement appear at Jer. 51.53, where Babylon is threatened with destroyers from Yahweh even though she is able to mount up to heaven; cf. Ezek. 28 and Isa. 14. The angel mythology was the natural way to describe the defeat of enemies.

7 Eaton (1976), p. 34. It is difficult to see how a royal interpretation can be avoided. We shall return to this psalm for an explanation of the beasts in Daniel's vision of the Holy Ones, Dan. 7.

8 Weiser (1962), *ad loc.*, says this is a portrait of history 'burdened with unsolved and unsolvable problems'. It could be simply a recital of deep-rooted prejudice within Israel. The tent of Joseph was rejected long before the fall of Samaria. Ephraim, despite its Deuteronomic ideas of election, had also been rejected, and the house of David had been set up instead to care for the chosen people.

9 In 89.38, *wᵉ'ēd baššahaq ne'ᵉmān*, 'and a faithful witness in the sky' (not rendered clearly by RSV and NEB) is at least a personification: can it even imply a person of some sort, like the 'witness' in Job 16.19?

10 Suggestions include: '*eš doleqet*, 'burning fire'; '*ašdod*, 'Ashdod'; '*eš yoqedet* 'burning fire'; '*eš lopedet*, 'burning fire'. Cross and Freedman (1948), p. 198 n8, suggest the preceding line be read, following the Targum, the Vg and in part the LXX, '*itto-m ribᵇbot qᵈdošim*, also '*šr 'lm* representing '*ašru 'elim* (omitting the final waw in accordance with tenth-century orthography), 'proceeded the mighty ones'. Milik (1957) offers '*šrt* for '*šdt* and suggests Ugaritic '*atr ba'l*, 'la suite de baal', giving here 'des myriades de saintes à sa droite la suite des dieux'. Beeston (1951) offers '*sd* from S. Arabic 'warriors', taken up by Miller (1964), who

offers 'the warriors of the gods', like the 'mighty ones of the gods', *gbwry 'lym* in 1QM15, 14; or possibly from *d'h*, 'dart, fly swiftly', which occurs elsewhere in contexts of theophany and judgement, e.g. Deut. 28.29; Jer. 48.40; 49.22; Ps. 18.11.

11 In Matt. 25.31ff the *separation* is a feature of the judgement.

12 See ch. 10.

13 Eaton (1976), p. 106.

14 Gesenius, cited in BDB, p. 891.

15 Rather than *nūs*, 'flee, escape', as rendered by the AV.

16 This name has been linked to Azazel, but the problem of changing Asael to Azazel is greater than that of linking Asael to *'ṣl* and whatever that word once represented. In the LXX sigma is the normal rendering of ṣade; the sigma in Greek Enoch could then represent an assimilation of the two names. See also Hanson (1977). The name Azazel is inexplicable, thought to come from *'zl*, 'remove', an otherwise unknown verb.

17 It is argued that vv. 1–2; 3–8; 9–11 represent units which were not originally combined. Part of vv. 1–2 was the original introduction to vv. 9–11, a separate unit within the Sinai pericope.

18 Nicholson (1974; 1975; 1976), argues that the theophany tradition of Exod. 24.9–11 was older than that of Exod. 19. Moses was added to an established tradition which dealt with a delegation of Israel's ancestors who saw God on the holy mountain. This antedated Moses in Israel's tradition. Vriezen suggested this other tradition originated in the settled life of Canaan, not in the semi-nomadic lifestyle which characterizes the more familiar version, and derived from the cult of El. The deity differs from Yahweh; the covenant, if there was one, was of El of Shechem. Nicholson disagrees on the grounds that there is insufficient evidence to know what El was like. He also rejects the 'banquet of the gods' parallel frequently cited from Ugaritic sources, and emphasizes the idea that no man could see God and live. Significant differences point away from Ugarit as source. Nicholson was right to emphasize the importance of the vision of God. This is the crucial element of the later apocalypses, which have their deepest roots in the early cult exemplified in this theophany *which later writers sought to contradict*, e.g. Deut. 4.12. Moses was indeed a later addition to this tradition.

19 cf. the LXX on the elders at Exod. 24.11, τῶν ἐπιλέκτων. The chosen ones are not hurt, not cast off, the fate of others who had climbed the mountain. The LXX of Isa. 41.9 also hints at the old myth; 'ends of the earth' is ἄκρος, which also means 'aristocrat, man of high rank', and 'farthest corners' is σκοπιά, which has associations with *watching*.

20 Torrey (1928) for discussion; Engnell (1967) on *'iyyim*.

21 See Chapter 1, nn83, 84.

22 W. R. Smith (1914), p. 74; J. Z. Smith (1970), p. 278 for interesting later parallels.

23 J. Z. Smith (1970).

24 Cross (1973), pp. 258ff.

25 Murray (1982a), p. 209.

26 Lacoque (1979), pp. 163ff.

27 It was also insight into these plans which was the concern of the prophets, which may provide us with the real link between prophecy and apocalyptic.

28 Casey (1979) has an excellent summary of Son of Man scholarship, but to say (p. 44) that Dan. 7 has no angels is indeed strange. Also Horbury (1985b).

29 More reasonable, I think, than to search the literature of the ancient world for references to sea monsters. Details of the appearance of the monsters in Daniel may have been influenced by contemporary ideas of the frightful, and by astrological symbolism, see Casey (1979), p. 20 and notes, but our first question must be to ask if there could possibly have been a role for these beasts in the cult of the Temple. See Keel (1978), pp. 78ff.

30 Kraus (1966), p. 187, for discussion and bibliography.

31 Bentzen (1955).

32 Horbury (1985b); Meeks (1970).

33 Meeks (1970), pp. 354ff.

34 Horbury (1985b); also Vermes (1978), but, despite his massive erudition, we all tend to see what we want to see, and if two positions are compatible with the evidence, one cannot automatically be given more weight than another.

35 Are they babes and sucklings? In a heavenly court extolling the power of Yahweh in creation, those who are to be a bulwark against God's enemies are surely more likely to be members of his army. The 'babes and sucklings' could conceal more warlike beings, perhaps *'ōlym w'noq'mym*, 'ascenders and avengers'.

36 This raises the whole question of the date and purpose of the creation narratives in Gen. 1, and the significance of Adam being made in the image of his father, Gen. 5.2 (see Chapter 10). Adam and the old royal figure coalesce at many points. What prompted the Christian association of Ps. 8 and Ps. 110? Were the two already linked?

37 See Chapter 9; *kannāh* is also the name for a branch of the great candlestick which represented the presence of God in the temple.

38 See Horbury (1985b), p. 49 for further discussion.

39 See Chapter 5.

40 As reconstructed by Nickelsburg (1972). Lust (1978) argues for a Hebrew underlying the Aramaic of Daniel 7 that was used by the LXX, which had the older picture of the Son of Man as the Ancient of Days, as in Ezek. 1.26.

41 Lacocque (1979), pp. 37, 50 and notes.

42 Halifax (1979), p. 3.

43 ibid. *passim*; also Harner (1973).

44 That this is not just a remote and exotic phenomenon can be seen from Pinard (1957), a report on the nature, value and effect of spontaneous imagery in 334 subjects invited to look with their 'inner eye' and report their findings. They experienced flying, the sense of chaotic struggle, inundation, death resulting in heightened consciousness followed by a world of light and beauty. Sometimes they saw a figure giving out light whom they recognized as their greater self. The result of these experiences was a sense of inner strength and freedom.

45 Does this underlie the ideas in Isa. 52—3?

46 Is this the experience in Ezek. 37 and Ps. 22?

47 cf. Jub. 3.28.

48 Many books give food for thought. Apart from the obvious ones such as Eliade (1960 and 1964), which strangely neglect the Judaeo-Christian materials, Widengren (1950) and Frankfort (1948), pp. 237ff, there are Halifax (1979); Harner (1973); the writings of A. David-Neel on experiences in Tibet; Castaneda (1970); Leary (1964), and the many texts which accompanied the drug-related experiences of the 1960s. These must be used with care; but they cannot be ignored. Some scholars have already suggested the possibility of links to shamanic experience. Rowland (1982) mentioned the link but did not explore further (pp. 450, 481ff); Perrin (1974) noted the similarity between visions of different peoples even though they were expressed in the terms and symbols characteristic of their own culture; Carley (1975), p. 6.

49 After completing this chapter, I read van Selms (1982), who argues from parallels to *qdš* in Ugaritic, Aramaic and Phoenician that the Holy One of Israel was a heavenly being like the gods of other nations, but recognized as being worshipped by Israel. The frequency of the title in Isaiah indicates a Jerusalem origin, and the name Israel, rather than Judah, shows that it antedates the division of the kingdoms.

50 We must not sit in judgement upon our materials, as this is bound to distort them. Lindars (1983), p. 155, establishes that the title meant no more, initially, than being a member of the human race. The usage of the Fourth Gospel is a problem, however, because 'the son of man sayings never occur during the discussion of the humanness of Jesus. From this point of view it may be considered a rather misleading phrase to use. One might feel that John might have found *a better and more precise expression for the agent of revelation*' (my emphases).

4

ISAIAH OF JERUSALEM

Enoch's angel mythology is complex, as we have seen, and reflects in its various emphases the several situations for which the sections were written. But running through the whole is a temple theme which has no clear link, as yet, to the mythology. There is temple imagery in the description of Enoch's ascent, and temple imagery in the judgement passages. The people who transmitted the Enochic materials thought the *second* Temple impure and apostate, yet regarded a new temple as essential for the messianic age. To find the roots of the angel traditions we have therefore to go back to an earlier period, when these people were attached to both the city of Jerusalem and to its Temple. This must be the period of the monarchy; we must read carefully the First Isaiah, who was the prophet par excellence of Jerusalem and its Temple at this time.

So little is known of the cult and myths of pre-exilic Jerusalem that we have been heavily dependent for our reconstructions upon finding parallels in other cultures. Such a process can be dangerous. Attempts to *establish* the inner nature of Israel's religion by reference to the gods of Canaan, for example, can often cast a shadow over the very texts they seek to illuminate.[1] This operation should be clearly distinguished from attempts to find parallels to known Old Testament texts, e.g. the creation stories, in order to see what is distinctively Israelite.[2] In reconstructing the angel mythology, it would be extremely dangerous to use materials from other cultures to *establish* any point. They can only be used to *confirm*. I therefore restrict myself in the first instance to materials within the same cultural tradition. Although several centuries separate Isaiah from 1 Enoch, any similarities between them are likely to be deep-rooted, and points of contact will be significant.

The texts which mentioned the 'Holy Ones' divided into two groups: those whose context resembled material found in the Qumran Enoch, and those with other elements. In making these comparisons, we must bear in mind that 1 Enoch and Isaiah may have been committed to writing for very different reasons, and each may have used only those parts of a common tradition relevant to its purpose. If we similarly divide up the Isaiah materials, we shall be able to see which elements resemble the Enochic material from Qumran and the 'holy one' texts, and which elements resemble only the 'holy one' texts, and *not* the Enochic material from Qumran. We have the Enochic material in a recognizable corpus (although it has been suggested that it is only a random collection), and we have the 'holy one' texts drawn from several sources. It is just conceivable that both 1 Enoch and the 'holy one' texts represent an amalgam from several sources. Isaiah, however, despite several additions and reworkings, exists as a recognized block of texts for which an underlying consistency of background may reasonably be assumed. If the scheme in the 'holy one' texts is present in all its aspects in Isaiah, the text in which the title 'Holy One' occurs with the greatest frequency within the Old Testament, we have stronger grounds for saying that the angel mythology as thus reconstructed *did* exist in the time of the first Temple, and that the royal element which is so important in Isaiah was an integral part of that mythology. The Similitudes with their Son of Man figure would then be built upon the royal elements of the mythology which have not been used in the Qumran Enoch texts.

The most remarkable feature of the Isaiah texts is that they have no apparent basis in the Moses/Exodus pattern.[3] Perhaps these were not the most significant elements in Jerusalem's cult at that time.[4] I shall examine in detail only five aspects of Isaiah, to illustrate the extent to which I think the Enochic tradition can illuminate the text. This is intended only to establish a case, and in no way pretends to be exhaustive.

(i) The opening oracle is likely to have special significance if placed at the head of the collection. Isa. 1.1–4 sets the scene for the whole work with the words: 'Sons have I reared and brought up, but they have rebelled against me.' The LXX is significantly different; as at Deut. 32.8, the *sons of God* seem to have disappeared from the Hebrew. The Greek has 'Sons have I begotten . . .' Such a change in the Greek would be explicable were this a messianic passage used by the early Church; but it was not. We have here in the Greek a recollection of the original significance of Isaiah's words. The only known 'sons of God' in Jerusalem were the kings. Psalm 2 speaks of the king as 'begotten' by God and exalted to the holy hill. When Isaiah condemns the Lord's 'sons' and accuses them of rebellion, let us try out the possibility that he is referring especially to kings. Isa. 1.3 is a wisdom saying: it laments Israel's lack of understanding and knowledge. In the Psalms rulers, sons of God, are similarly condemned: Ps. 58.1–3, and especially Ps. 82.5. Lack of knowledge is not a sin familiar to us from the laws of Deuteronomy, but it is the key motif in the angel mythology. Isa. 1.4 calls the 'sinful nation' the 'offspring of evildoers', in contrast perhaps to the claim of divine sonship, and referring to the offspring of the angels who corrupted the earth through their progeny.[5]

(ii) The call narrative gives insight into the role of the prophet, and into the world in which he functioned. Isa. 6.1–13 thus gives us important information about the man and his message. His call was 'in the Temple', in the presence of 'the King', the Lord of Hosts'. Of these three we know very little, and, ignorant of their context, we must surely be far from understanding the original import of these prophecies. We know that the historical context was the Assyrian crisis, the threat to Jerusalem and the death of the king. The cultural and cultic context, however, has to be pieced together as best we can.

The Temple was a place of ministering creatures around the throne of God. Other descriptions of the Temple show that it was an Eden-like place – not the Eden of Genesis, but the mountain garden of Ezekiel 28.[6] It was decorated with cherubim and palm trees (1 Kings 6.29; Ezek. 41.17ff) and it was on a hilltop (Ezek. 40.2; Ps. 15). Ezekiel's Eden contained a 'cherub', beings called 'stones of fire', and a godlike figure who vaunted his wisdom against the Lord Yahweh, but who was an earthly king. Such figures formed a heavenly host, the 'princes of the sanctuary' whom we meet in Isa. 43.28, who were punished with political disasters and downfall to the pit (Isa. 14.15; Ezek. 28.16), or with mortality (Ps. 82). In this other Eden there was a heavenly throne, the seat of judgement, and it was this that the prophet saw, as did the later mystics in their ascent.[7] Jubilees shows that this other Eden survived in certain circles long after the Genesis Eden had taken over elsewhere. The expulsion of Adam from Eden was an expulsion from the sanctuary (Jub. 3.27); Enoch's translation to heaven took him to Eden as the heavenly scribe for the great judgement (Jub. 4.23). Noah knew that Eden was the holy of holies, the abode of God (Jub. 8.19). The prophecies of Isaiah, then, could well reflect an Eden setting (cf. 'my holy mountain' in 11.9) and the holy ones who lived there. His view of the politics of his time would have been structured according to his beliefs about the affairs of the heavenly mountain. Like Enoch, Isaiah was commissioned as an envoy of the heavenly world, to bring notice of the judgement.[8]

Isaiah also sees the King, perhaps a vision of the King of Jerusalem whose reality was the counterpart to the succession of earthly kings. The relationship between Yahweh and the king is assumed in many texts, although it is never explained.[9] It is significant that the texts which deal with the kingship of Yahweh are also those which deal with the heavenly hosts and the angel mythology (Exod. 15.18; Num. 23.21; Deut. 33.5). In later texts the king and his Holy Ones appear in 1QapGen 2 and 1 En 9.12; cf. Matt. 25. It is the king and his host of Holy Ones which gives us the title Lord of Hosts, common in Isaiah, but absent from the texts which describe Israel's early histories. If these histories were themselves early texts, this absence would be significant, and it would be possible to conclude that Isaiah had invented the title himself.[10] But since the Deuteronomists have had a hand in the composition of these histories, the absence may be significant for another reason.[11]

A more elaborate version of the call of Isaiah is to be found in the call of Enoch (1 En. 12—14).[12] The similarity could be due to 1 Enoch's dependence on Isaiah, but even were this so, we should have to ask why the Enochic material derives from Isaiah, when it has little contact with any part of the Old Testament as we know it, and gives no special place to Isaiah in its history of Jerusalem. But if Isaiah's call is cast in the imagery of the older cult which the Enochic circle retained during the period they describe as post-exilic deviation, we should have an explanation of the similarities. 1 En. 14 describes the throne surrounded by hosts; Enoch is given power to reprimand the watchers, and the ability to understand the word of wisdom. The angelic wisdom on earth is useless (1 En. 16.5), causing only evil (cf. Ps. 82.5). If we allow the call of Enoch to illuminate Isa. 6, we can begin to understand the role of wisdom in Isaiah. His conflict with the wise men of his day has been much discussed, as has his use of wisdom language, but no satisfactory explanation has been offered.[13] Isaiah said that Israel lacked knowledge and understanding, and his curse was to deprive them of it; in other words, Israel lacked true wisdom, and would be deprived of it as a punishment. The result would be devastation and a desolate land, a sign that the eternal covenant was broken (cf. Jer. 4.22ff; Isa. 33.8).

The strongest argument against Enoch's vision being spun from Isa. 6 is that there is a comparable vision of a throne in 1 Kings 22. Although this is an insertion into the narrative, a general tale about a prophet does not reduce its value as a source of information as to what the prophets *saw* when they *saw* (not *heard*) the word of the Lord. Micaiah saw Yahweh and his throne, surrounded by the hosts who were deeply involved in the politics and wars of the day. Evil spirits could inspire the prophets, and the king of Israel feared a prophet who would speak against him. Here we have the three basic components: the throne, the council and the politics. It supplements the picture in the Psalms, and is exactly like those of Daniel and Enoch. The heavenly beings are involved in the affairs of the nations. There is, however, a completely different picture in the Second Isaiah, where the supremacy of Yahweh is based on the fact that the other beings do not exist, and in Deut. 4.19, where the hosts of heaven are not for the chosen people. We seem to have two strands: the throne and hosts are the basis of the political philosophy of old Jerusalem, as seen in a tradition traced from Isaiah, 1 Kings 22, Daniel and Enoch, and another world view advocated by the Second Isaiah and required by Deuteronomy.[14]

(iii) The sins of Jerusalem and the other nations will show the prophet's ideas of right and wrong, and thus the framework within which he made his judgements. Isaiah's catalogue of sins is so striking that it demands close scrutiny. There are three dominant sins: pride, rebellion, and wisdom, the sins of the angels.

(a) The sin of pride

On the day of the Lord the pride of men will be humbled and Yahweh exalted (Isa. 2.11, 17). Sheol will receive the haughty and humble them (5.15). Ephraim and Samaria are condemned for pride and arrogance (9.8ff; 28.3). Foreign nations are also guilty and pride is the commonest charge against them: Assyria (10.12); Babylon, who had tried to ascend the holy mountain (14.12); Moab (16.6ff); Tyre to be wasted after its exultation (23.9ff); the whole world is proud and heading for destruction (13.10ff); Egypt has false pride in worthless wisdom (19.11ff). Assyria fails against Jerusalem because of her pride (37.23ff). Against whom was this pride? Who took exception to the exaltation of other nations and why was this such a sin? When Amos condemned the surrounding nations, he did not mention pride, but only injustice and crimes of violence. The sin of pride is therefore crucial to our understanding of Isaiah's attitude to the other nations. The taunt against Babylon in Isa. 14 describes the pride of one who would ascend the mountain of God, a component of the angel myth.[15] Isaiah's political prophecies describe the fate of those who came against Jerusalem and its God in pride. Their fate was to be thrown down.

The Psalms are full of references to the king as the one who bore the brunt of all this angelic hostility against Jerusalem and its God. The king, as his earthly representative, saw in his earthly warfare a reflection of the hostilities of heaven. Thus the nations conspire against Yahweh and his anounted (Ps. 2);[16] the king has vast numbers of foes (Ps. 3); the horrifying effects of these adversaries are listed (Ps. 31.11–13); his foes are described as flood waters (Ps. 69.1–4); the nations combine to assault Yahweh's king (Ps. 118.10–12). The Psalms show that the virtue of the king was his humility and dependence upon Yahweh, the very opposite of the sins of the angels.

The thrust of Isaiah's message is that this dangerous pride has penetrated even God's own people. They had assumed knowledge for themselves, and had become a people of unclean lips. They had ceased to trust only in their Holy One (Isa. 7; 31.1ff) and this was a sin. Isaiah's oracles against the nations, and his entire message to Jerusalem, must be read in the light of the Psalms and the expectations we can deduce from them. Although this condemnation of pride is not emphasized in 1 Enoch, it is implicit in the Similitudes, with their emphasis upon the humiliation of the kings and the mighty, and their recognition of the Son of Man.

(b) The sin of rebellion

Yahweh's own sons have become rebels (Isa. 1.23); those who forsake Yahweh are rebels and sinners (1.28);[17] the law of Yahweh is rejected (5.24); the earth is polluted and desolate because the laws are transgressed, statutes and the eternal covenant are broken (24.4ff; 33.7ff).[18] The whole of Chapter 30 deals with rebellion; rebel children who have not asked Yahweh's counsel, who have not trusted his protection, whose condemnation is to be written in a book as a permanent witness against them (Isa. 30.8ff; cf. 1 En. 12; Jub. 4), and who refuse to listen to Yahweh and reject his instruction. The final accusation of revolt is in Isa. 31.6, where the people are exhorted to turn back to him from whom they have revolted.

(c) The sin of knowledge

Isaiah's use of wisdom vocabulary shows that he had much in common with that tradition, even though the exact nature of his relationship to the wise men of the day is still not clear. Lack of wisdom was a sin, and yet Isaiah opposed many of the wise men. Failure to attain wisdom was an important factor of the call narrative; the prologue links lack of wisdom and rebellion. There was foreign wisdom in Jerusalem (Isa. 2.6); the leaders of the people were misleading them (3.12); many were wise in their own eyes (5.21); exile was threatened because the people lacked knowledge

(5.13); there were evil decrees (10.1–2); there was a refuge of lies to be swept away (28.17). In these prophecies knowledge has links with politics, an important link with the angel myth.[19]

Isaiah's emphasis on pride and rebellion, wisdom and knowledge is shown in his use of the myth of the heavenly secrets, abused on earth by evil powers. The political advisers of his time, in so far as they relied upon foreign powers, were relying on evil sources for their wisdom. The cult demanded total trust in the Holy One. We see similar demands in the polytheistic framework of Job, where Yahweh is one god among many. The loyalty of his servant is tested by assaults of another heavenly being, Satan, and eventually is rewarded.

(iv) The punishments Isaiah expected will show us his God at work. It has become the fashion to assume that certain features of the future hope are a late development, and that their presence in Isaiah is proof that the text has been reworked by later hands;[20] but it is more likely that these are very old features, since they are in no way inconsistent with the rest of the book, and that we have assigned them to a later period because we have constructed for ourselves a false picture of the ancient cult. Form- and tradition-criticism can run into great difficulties because there are many units which defy comparison. Sufficient material has not survived.[21] Isaiah expects punishments of fire, enemy attack, desolation, fall from power, desertion by false wisdom, and cosmic catastrophe. There are isolated references to the sea, the sword, the felling of a tree, Sheol, shaving and Leviathan, and one reference to exile.

(a) The punishment of fire

The evil ones who have rejected the Law of the Lord of hosts and despised the Holy One of Israel will be punished in the great fire. The anger of the Lord, which causes the mountains to shake, will burn them like stubble.[22] Evil and its punishment are both likened to fires (Isa. 9.18; cf. Nahum 6); the Holy One is a devouring flame (Isa. 10.16); the Lord burns with anger as he judges the nations (30.27ff – the most Enochic chapter in Isaiah); the evil ones will destroy themselves in their own fires (33.27 – a chapter full of angels).[23] Edom will be burned, her streams turned to pitch (34.9) as part of the universal devastation set out in the Book of Yahweh (34.16).

(b) The punishment of desolation

Desolation is frequently envisaged; it was part of the Holy One's great judgement (Deut. 33.2–3). The structures of society will disappear (Isa. 3.1ff); the Lord's vineyard will be wasted (5.5ff); the prophet is to work towards this desolation (6.11); the land will be overgrown (7.28); Babylon will be haunted by strange creatures (13.19ff); Moab will be parched and its vineyards deserted (15.16ff); the Nile will run dry (19.5ff). The greatest of the desolations is described in 24.1–23; the created order will disintegrate, because the eternal covenant has been broken (24.4–6), the host of heaven and the kings of the earth will be imprisoned in the pit, the Lord will be king in Zion. This chapter has been thought to be the basis of the Similitudes which give a much fuller picture of the devastation of the great judgement. It has also been thought to be a late addition to Isaiah because it resembles the apocalypses which are known to be late. Neither of these suggestions is necessarily correct; the Similitudes are heir to the tradition in which Isaiah also stood, and the elements of this chapter are in no way inconsistent with the rest of Isaiah, so as to appear an obvious addition. It is unwise to be too certain what he could, or could not, have written. There are similar ideas in Jer. 4.23ff, and it is likely that both prophets knew the same expectation of the day of judgement. Isaiah sees an overwhelming scourge coming upon Jerusalem (28.14–22); he sees the city forsaken and used for pasture (32.9–14) until the great outpouring of the spirit; he sees Edom left to the beasts with birds nesting in the strongholds (34.15ff). The pictures are not just of natural disasters; there are supernatural forces at work. The creatures are evil, and the destruction is eerie.[24]

(c) The punishment of the proud

Pride is the dominant sin, to be punished by fall. The day of the Lord is a time of bringing down (2.12ff); the king of Assyria and the king of Babylon will be cast down (10.12; 14.12); Damascus and Ephraim are to be brought low (17.1ff); Tyre and Sidon dishonoured (23.1ff); a lofty city, unnamed, will fall (26.5ff) and its inhabitants will despair.[25] These oracles against foreign nations envisage one structure which embraced both Jerusalem and the other nations, such as is implied in Deut. 32.8; Ps. 2; 82; 89; Daniel and 1 Enoch.

(d) Punishment by alien powers

Isaiah wrote in time of war, but he did not write of earthly warfare. The Assyrians are agents of divine punishment, who must not exceed their charge (7.20; 10.5ff). Babylon is punished by the Medes at Yahweh's command (13.17ff), but the warfare is in heaven as well as on earth.[26] The clearest example of this warfare in two worlds is 22.1–8. Elam and Kir fight against Jerusalem, but are they Elam and Kir? It is not easy to find a date at which these two nations could have fought together.[27] Indeed the whole chapter is so full of problems that an eschatological rather than an historical reference has been suggested; for Isaiah this distinction would not have occurred. The whole chapter demands another translation, not least because textual confusion, as so often, suggests that angels were once present.[28] There is the mysterious Ariel (29.1–4), here a name for Jerusalem, but in other contexts, at least in Talmudic tradition, a name for the angels of the lower world;[29] there are other angel figures in the warfare and desolation of 33.1–9,[30] and various supernatural creatures infesting Edom after the great judgement (34.8–17).[31]

(e) The punishment of imprisonment and the pit

The imprisonment of the evil angels is the dominant theme of most of 1 Enoch. The picture is not entirely clear, but the pit of imprisonment and the final judgement of fire are elements common to all the variations. Isaiah has similar ideas; evil ones brought low into the pit, and a final fiery judgement. The haughty are humbled and the nobles go to the pit (5.14ff); the proud star angel of Babylon is brought to the pit (14.15); there is terror, and the pit for the host of heaven and the kings of the earth (24.21);[32] the inhabitants of the mighty city are brought low, other lords who have ruled Yahweh's people, the *rephaim*, have been destroyed (26.13–14).[33]

There is a covenant with Sheol in 28.8ff, made by the rulers of Jerusalem to protect them in time of danger. Isaiah probably has in mind one of the treaties made during the Assyrian crisis, when Jerusalem was looking for allies. The foreign nations are described as Sheol, which here is not a place for the dead, but a power opposed to Yahweh manifested in foreign rulers. The covenant with Sheol was an attempt to escape from the wrath of Yahweh (28.22). But Isaiah had heard Yahweh's decree of destruction and no alliance with other forces could avert the disaster. The erring rulers are warned not to mock lest they be put in bonds. Covenant imagery was a part of the framework within which Isaiah thought.[34]

Covenant and a fiery judgement appear in 33.14; those who come through this fire are acceptable on the holy hill (cf. Ps. 24). For Isaiah, this is the group who will survive the judgement.[35]

The punishments which Isaiah predicts prompt several questions. Were these all part of one existing scheme of expectation, a concept of the day of judgement current in Isaiah's time which corresponds to a remarkable degree with the expectations of the Enochic tradition, or were the images invented by the prophet and drawn together only by the later writers of the Enochic texts? The former seem more likely, since the Enochic circle despised the post-exilic developments in Jerusalem, and, by implication, kept to the older ways. If the images were original to Isaiah, it is remarkable that he has no place in the writings of those who apparently developed his ideas.

(v) Fertility. In a primitive economy the fertility business is vital, and the relation between religion and fertility is not merely academic. Hosea came to terms with the symbolism of the Baal cult. The Deuteronomists claimed that rain came as the result of keeping the commandments (Deut. 11.13ff), and that disobedience brought desolation. This Deuteronomic stance was probably offered as a replacement for an older view, when the person of the king was bound up with the fertility of the land. It is not clear how the fertility business related to the rituals of the first Temple; a sacred marriage pattern has been suggested, but there is little evidence. The Enochic tradition has, however, a distinctive attitude to fertility which could throw light on the situation in the time of the monarchy. Fertility followed the destruction of the evil angels, and the establishment of the rule of the great Holy One. Perverted knowledge was removed from the earth. The pattern was judgement, true knowledge and then fertility (1 En. 10; 80.2–8). It derived, I believe, from the sequence of the autumn festival, where the renewal of fertility was bound up with the renewal of kingship after the enactment of the great judgement which gave rise to the biblical imagery of judgement as harvest. The psalter pictures fertility in this way; thus the royal marriage psalm (Ps. 45) does not mention fertility, whereas Ps. 72 does link the king to fertility in so far as he is a righteous judge.[36] Were the king the agent of the great judgement, this removal of evil as the precondition of fertility would correspond exactly to the Enochic picture. In every case where Isaiah mentions fertility, it is in such a context of judgement. The people are exiled though lack of knowledge, the nobility go to the pit, Yahweh is exalted and lambs graze in their pasture (5.13–17); the ideal ruler is endowed with wisdom and rules with divine justice, fearing the Lord and bringing harmony to the creation (11.1–9); the wisdom of the wise will perish and the ruthless be destroyed with the advent of justice and fertility (19.13–21); after a period of desolation, the spirit will transform creation with justice and fertility (32.16ff). The most detailed of the judgement-fertility sequences is 34—35. Yahweh's judgement upon the hosts of all nations is a day of great vengeance; the skies are rolled up and the stars fall, Edom is set ablaze and left as the haunt of strange creatures (34.1–17). Then follows the promise of fertility in the desert and safety for the chosen ones. There are significant word patterns in 35.5–6: the blind, the deaf, the lame and the dumb are healed in the renewal of the creation, but the names of these four are also those of four types of angel. The *blind* are the 'watchers', *'wrym*, the *lame* are *pisse\u1e25*. These two occur in 2 Sam. 5.6 as the lame and the blind, but it has been suggested that the words conceal the names of the old guardian deities of Jerusalem, repointed as a gesture of contempt. The Chronicler omits them from his account (1 Chron. 11.4ff).[37] The *dumb* are the gods, *'lm*, as in Ps. 58.1, and the *deaf* are in some way connected with the magic arts, *\u1e25r\u0161m*; cf. *\u1e25km \u1e25r\u0161m* in Isa. 3.3, rendered 'skilful in magic', and the *\u1e25r\u0161ym* in Zech 2.3, who are not 'smiths', but rather enchanters of some sort; *\u1e25r\u0161y m\u0161\u1e25it*, the agents of destruction. How these supernatural beings were connected to these disabilities is not clear, but it is surely no coincidence that Jesus used the curing of these four types as his sign. John the Baptist asked if Jesus was the one expected (Luke 7.20ff), and the reply was an amalgam of these verses and Isa. 61.1. The Servant figure is also described as the only true *blind* and *deaf*, an impossible meaning, despite the patina of pious exposition (Isa. 42.18). Were some supernatural being intended, then the fertility and renewal theme of Isa. 35 would have built into it a reference to the role of the heavenly creatures. In the Gospels, the defeat of what these creatures represented is seen as a sign of the kingdom of God.

Isaiah's frame of reference was clearly that of the Enochic tradition, but there are several more points where elements correspond. The dominant feature of 1 Enoch is the angels, their influence and their fate. Isaiah is also peopled with angels, but a selective reading of the text has distorted the emphases to such a degree that this major feature receives little or no attention. The prophet's call is in the angelic assembly, the taunt against Babylon is the clearest example of the angel mythology in the Old Testament, and the destruction of the Assyrian army is attributed to angelic intervention. We do not know what exactly was meant by the 'sons' at 1.2, but the judgement scene in 3.13ff is very like that of Ps. 82. A heavenly army is on the move in 13.2–6; the envoys of 14.32 could also be read as angels;[38] angel figures assault Jerusalem (22.1–8); there is the angelic judgement in 24.1–3;[39] a whole nest of angel figures appear in 33,[40] but they are concealed by our custom of altering the text in the interest of sense. The angels appear too often for their presence to be unimportant. We have no alternative but to read Isaiah in the light of what we know of the angels from later sources. They were the basis of Isaiah's world view as they were of the Enochic tradition. They shaped the threats against the foreign nations because they were the basis of his political philosophy. All the indications in the Enochic material point to an origin in the royal cult, and the curious patterns in Isaiah confirm that this was indeed the case.

Isaiah has frequent references to a book, as does 1 Enoch.[41] A somewhat confused line tells of the book where people are written down for life, to be called holy (4.2ff); 8.1 is probably not significant, but 8.16–17 suggests that Isaiah sealed up his judgement until the day of Yahweh's intervention, just as did Enoch (Jub. 4.18ff). A sealed book cannot be read (29.11); there is judgement upon the wisdom of the wise, and the deaf (whatever they were) hear the words of a book (29.18). The following chapter deals with the woes and judgements upon rebels, which are to be inscribed in a book as a perpetual witness against the sons who will not hear the instruction of Yahweh (30.8). This is exactly the Enochic picture.

In addition, there are elements in Isaiah which are not explicit in 1 Enoch, but help to explain features in 1 Enoch and fill out some of the gaps in its mythology. Isaiah describes a royal figure, and a holy mountain.

Although 7.14ff; 9.6–7; 11.1–9 have been hallowed by centuries of Christian usage, this must not blind us to the fact that they represent but three per cent of Isaiah, and we cannot assume that these passages carry a weight out of all proportion to their size.[42] Here, as with 1 Enoch, we have a natural tendency to emphasize what is familiar to us and to grasp those parts of this mysterious prophet where we feel we can cope. I have suggested from the Psalms and 1 Enoch that the king may have been regarded as a son of God, an 'unfallen angel'. If the presence of the divine son guaranteed the triumph of Jerusalem over her enemies, then the assurance of a further divine son to perpetuate the dynasty (7.14ff) would be a natural way of assuring the beleaguered city that the invading kings would suffer the fate of all who rebelled against the city and the Holy One. Not only is the continuation of the dynasty promised, but the king is also reminded of the very basis of his rule, the divine sonship and attendant triumph over the fallen sons. It is probably a royal prince who is to be called Immanuel (8.8), his name affirming the divine presence in the king. There is to be a great new beginning (9.1–6) described with pictures of warfare, darkness and light, and the birth of a child. It is fashionable to look for a particular occasion in the Assyrian crisis which could have prompted this oracle;[43] but in view of the mythology underlying the other parts of the prophecy, it is likely that this oracle has similar roots.

> 9.1 describes light coming into darkness, perhaps the old solar imagery. 9.2 describes rejoicing before the Lord, i.e. in the Temple.[44] The joy is that of victors and of harvesters, an association of ideas which points us to the autumn festival, and to the celebration of the triumph of Yahweh,[45] which was enacted in the enthronement of the king. There follow three themes in parallel; each section begins *ki*, 'for': 9.4 describes the end of oppressors, 9.5 the relics of war, and 9.6 the birth of the child.

Several other texts have a similar pattern: Pss. 46 and 76 both describe the defeat of enemies and the exaltation of God in Zion, Isaiah 33 is entirely upon this theme,[46] with enemies scattered, divine judgement, help coming with the new light of dawn, and the vision of the king in his glory. It is possible that all these are based upon memories of the Assyrian crisis, but it is more likely that an underlying mythology structured the perception of historical events, which, in their turn, confirmed the validity of the myths. To whom was the royal child born? If the first person in 9.1ff denotes the speakers, then the son belongs to them, but who were they? The second person is God, and the third, the rejoicing people. For whom did Isaiah speak? An obvious choice would be the heavenly court, by whom he deemed himself commissioned. The angel figures proclaimed the birth of the royal son.[47] The titles for the royal child confirm the supernatural element, and we must accept that these titles, strange though they be to us, reflected beliefs about the monarchy.[48] The royal son had wisdom ('Wonderful Counsellor'), permanence ('Everlasting Father'), brought harmony ('Prince of Peace') and was divine ('Everlasting God').[49] The fact that we are unable to translate any of these titles with confidence shows how little we know of the ancient monarchy and its claims. If the king was addressed as 'mighty God', then our reconstruction of the role of the monarchy must take this seriously, as must our reconstructions of the origin of Christian ideas. The king was probably seen as one of the *'elim* of the heavenly court, as in Ps. 82, obliged to maintain justice on earth, or incur a fearful judgement. We glimpse a similar scene in Zech. 3.1–8, a corrupted text which describes the installation of Joshua as High Priest. He stands in the heavenly court before Yahweh, and is told that if he keeps to the ways of Yahweh he will have rule over the house of Yahweh, and the right to stand among those of Yahweh's presence. The LXX translation of the titles is confused, possibly due to Christian interest and alteration, but the first appears as ἄγγελος, 'angel'.

The third passage, Isa. 11.1–9, says that the spirit of Yahweh will rest on the royal figure to give him wisdom and knowledge, especially *fear of the Lord*. We have encountered this fear in the wisdom literature, where I suggested that it was the acceptable face of the ancient wisdom, distinguishing it from that of the other heavenly creatures who acted in pride. Such a meaning would be quite appropriate here if the royal figure had been seen as an unfallen son of

135

God. The king was to be a just judge, in whose time harmony would return to the natural order and knowledge of Yahweh would fill the earth. Such a conception would explain the Son of Man figure in the Similitudes, and the association there of the judgement of kings and mighty men with the restoration of creation and the revelation of true wisdom to the Elect.

The mountains of the gods played a major role in the mythology of Canaan.[50] In 1 Enoch there are several mountains in the heavenly landscape; there is one whose summit reached to heaven, from which Enoch saw the wonders of the creation;[51] and there were seven mountains which burned at the place of punishment (18.2, 13; 21.3). There is one mountain in the centre of seven on which was the throne of God surrounded by trees, one of which was destined to be transplanted to the Temple (24.1—25.6). Several other mountains appear, possibly inspired by the geography of Palestine (26; 28; 29; 32.1), and there are seven mountains of metal destined to melt before the elect one, a description of the fate of the angels who were depicted as mountains. Thus the triumph of Yahweh and his king could be expressed as the triumph or superiority of his mountain, and in Isaiah the great mountain is part of the picture of the glorious future. Zion is to be the greatest mountain, the source of teaching and judgement for all nations. Zion will be the great holy place, the refuge for all who are written in the book of life (Isa. 2.3; cf. Ps. 87). Weapons have no power before the holy mountain, enemies are defeated (Isa. 33; Pss. 46, 48); cf. 1 En. 8.1ff, where the makers of weapons are destroyed. In the vision of 2.2–4 the weapons became the tools of agriculture. In the underlying mythology, the kings *see* something wonderful (Ps. 46.9; Ps. 48.6, cf. Lam. 4.12; Isa. 33.17; Ps. 2; 4 Ezra. 13). Isa. 2.2–4 envisages the conversion of the nations, as does 1 En. 90.30; but Zech. 14.16 limits the pilgrims to Jerusalem to those who survive the great battle. Jerusalem is to be purified (Isa. 4.4) by spirits of judgement and burning and the whole land will enjoy fertility in the time of the Messiah.[52] Whether these two passages were part of the original text of Isaiah is not relevant. The ideas were certainly not original to him, as can be seen from the number of similar texts in the Old Testament, and the fact that the two passages were incorporated into the book indicates that they were appropriate to how it was understood. Both passages are aspects of the one future hope, linking judgement, fertility, a royal figure, a purified sanctuary and the triumph of Yahweh over defeated/converted enemies.

A thorough study of the whole of Isaiah is imperative before any conclusions can be drawn; but if there are these links to the Enochic material, we cannot assume that the Enochic texts are based upon Isaiah in the sense that they are elaborations upon a selection of texts from that book whose original meaning has been altered in the process. If, as seems likely, the Enochic material derives from the same tradition as Isaiah, we have in 1 Enoch materials whose ultimate origin must be the royal cult, and in Isaiah a remarkably full account of the political philosophy of pre-exilic Jerusalem. Changes apparent in the wisdom literature suggested that it was the Deuteronomists who were responsible for several major shifts in emphasis. They themselves record with approval that there were great upheavals in the time of Josiah, and that they were committed to altering the ancient cult. We are accustomed to call this a *reform*, but 'reform' is a loaded word; 'alteration' is neutral. Exactly what they did is shrouded in propaganda, but even if their sole contribution was the rewriting of history, in an investigation which relies upon written sources, this fact must be of paramount importance in any attempt at a reconstruction. The problems we encounter in reconstructing the ancient cult, and the way we now read the Old Testament, testify to their success. Isaiah's world was one of angels; he saw the heavenly throne, he was commissioned in the heavenly council, he knew of the conflict with corrupted wisdom, of royal star figures climbing the holy mountain. He knew of heavenly armies, and of the angel of Yahweh destroying an army before the walls of Jerusalem; he could assure Hezekiah that any king who came in pride against the Holy One would not succeed.

However we analyse these materials, attributing some to the prophet, some to an Isaianic circle or to later editors, we have to retain the distinction between the framework, i.e. the underlying mythology, and successive reuse of it, either in the form of interpretation, which is the more easily recognized, or in the derived forms and metaphors which we encounter, for example, in Wisdom.[53] I shall show later how those whom we call the Second and Third Isaiahs are each working within a common framework, but with very different results. No one disputes that the prophetic writings were used, reused and modified over the years, but the underlying imagery remained. We can often overlook this simply because it is so familiar to us, and has always been regarded as the usual imagery for such and such an idea. The persistence of the imagery points to very deep roots. Isaiah and Enoch have much in common, not because a small eccentric Enochic group quilted together a marvellous pattern from older texts wrenched from their earlier context, but because the tradition of the older cult and its vivid imagery persisted long after a small group had attempted to reform and eradicate. The old mythology persisted as the immediate source of the Enochic works, but it also underlies the thought forms and metaphors of those who, in various ways, attempted to move beyond it. In the next two chapters I shall offer two examples of this: Deuteronomy, whose metaphors and concerns can be explained as reaction of the older mythology, and the Second Isaiah, whose message was based upon the belief that the older mythology had been fulfilled and therefore superseded.

NOTES

1 Miller (1973), p. 60, is a good example of this. 'The question still remains, however, as to the role El played in the understanding of Yahweh as warrior. That question is emphasized by the strong rejection in normative Yahwism of the worship of Ba'al, whereas from an early

stage on, Yahweh seems to have been strongly related to El, as Cross, Eissfeldt, and others have shown. Part of the answer is to be seen in the fact that Ba'al and El shared certain characteristics which must have been assimilated to the character of Yahweh. Such could be the case with regard to the role of war leader. At Ugarit, however, it is Ba'al, the god rejected by Israel, who is war leader, whereas El, who appears to have borne kinship with Yahweh, is not primarily a warrior or the leader of a military host, although in the preceding pages we have shown some indications of his warlike character even at Ugarit. The assimilation of Ba'al's characteristics by Yahweh could easily have resulted from the frequent tendency to syncretism and apostasy. One would expect, nevertheless, that the El figure would have manifested more influence upon the warrior aspect of Yahweh's role, which was central to Israel's early conception of her god. The Ugaritic texts in themselves do not suggest such influence. Philo, however, paints a very different picture of El and suggests that also in the imagery of divine or cosmic warfare the association of Yahweh and El may have been strong.'

2   Cross (1973), p. 120: 'One of the problems is the confusion of two types of myths, owing to the tendency to approach Canaanite and other Near Eastern myth utilizing the biblical creation story as a yardstick. Often this is an unconscious prejudice. The biblical creation accounts, however, are atypical.'

3   Vriezen (1962), p. 129: 'One of the peculiar things one finds in enquiring into the prophet's relation to the tradition of his people is the scarcity if not total absence of an appeal or reference to the Exodus from Egypt.'

4   There are one or two places where an allusion to these events is possible, but no certain reference and no conscious attempt by the prophet to use these ideas.

5   The point is emphasized by word play: 'corrupted sons' (*mšḥytym*) could suggest 'anointed sons' (*mšyḥym*), by a hidden word play not infrequent in Isaiah; cf. chs 6 and 8.

6   Clifford (1972), p. 103: 'The joining of the theme of the garden of Eden and of the holy mountain in Ezekiel 28 appears to be late and peculiar to the Ezekielian passage', is incorrect.

7   Childs (1960), esp. pp. 83ff; the majority of his pictures of ancient Zion come from the Psalms and Isaiah, but we still have no certain knowledge of how Isaiah and his contemporaries structured their world. To say that Isaiah was familiar with the cultic tradition (Kaiser [1972], p. 72) is to say nothing at all. Our ignorance of the real context means that we, in effect, make our own, and this is bound to distort our views.

8   The work of the Deuteronomists, with their ideal of a formless theophany (Deut. 4.12), has had far-reaching effects. Kaiser (1972), p. 74, says that Isaiah did not actually *see* God. Can we really treat the prophet in that way?

9   Eaton (1979), p. 26: 'It is not clear how these rites of the Davidic office fitted in with other expressions of Yahweh's kingship.'

10   Vriezen (1962), for example, considers that Isaiah invented the title to epitomize his theology.

11   Johnson (1967) thinks the name came from Jebusite Jerusalem; cf. van Selms (1982), who thinks 'Holy One' is similarly early. Eichrodt (1961), vol. i, p. 194: 'It would only be permissible to draw definite conclusions from the fact that it is not found in the Pentateuch or in the books of Joshua and Judges, if there were no reason to suppose that later redaction might have deleted it: but such a possibility cannot be excluded.' Also Mettinger (1982), esp. pp. 25ff; the relationship between Isaiah and the Deuteronomic editors can be clearly seen in the parallel passages Isa. 37.14 and 2 Kings 19.15. The D passage omits the title 'Lord of Hosts'.

12   See Rowland (1982), esp. pp. 191ff, for the roots of this material.

13   McKane (1965, 1983) explores the celebrated conflict between Isaiah and the wise men. This should perhaps be illuminated also by the vision materials, since the visions revealed the content of the wisdom as well as validating the claim of the wise man. Our problems in Isaiah's time may be due to the *removal* of vision elements from the texts.

14 Isaiah's message for Israel is very strange; he was to harden hearts and precipitate judgement. The LXX is different, describing rather the present state of the people, who have heavy ears and closed eyes, which prevent them from seeing the truth. The form of the oracle may have been determined by more word-play, such as occurs in 1.4. The hearts are 'fat', the ears 'heavy', and the eyes 'shut', could be a play upon *šmn* meaning both 'fat' and 'oil for anointing', *kbd* meaning both 'heavy' and 'glory', and *š'* meaning both 'blind, close over' and, in a derived form, an 'object of delight', used to describe Israel and God, wisdom and the creator, e.g. Isa. 5.7; Jer. 31.20; Prov. 8.30.

15 Also 14.21, where the prophet sees the slaughter of the sons of the fallen star lest they fill the world with 'cities'. This should be read as 'Watchers'. In the Enochic myth, the sons of the fallen ones remained on earth to corrupt it.

16 They plan to free themselves of their bonds and yokes; cf. 1 En. 10, where the fallen angels are bound and imprisoned until their final judgement.

17 The people are called *rebels*, not harlots. This is important; the city is the harlot, the sons are the rebels (1.21). In the angel myth, the begetting of evil sons is an important element in the corruption process. Here the city is the mother of the evil ones, the female figure, not the people as a whole, which is the Hosea tradition. cf. Ps. 87, where the sons are written down by the heavenly scribe.

18 When the angels in 1 En. 7—9 revealed the heavenly secrets, *lawlessness* grew which corrupted and destroyed. After the judgement, God removed the lawlessness and restored fertility to creation. If Isaiah's covenant relates to Enoch's, then his laws and statutes were something akin to the natural order. See also Murray (1982a), p. 209.

19 cf. Ps. 73, where the evil ones taunt Elyon about his knowledge.

20 This is a circular argument. Even the cautious Blenkinsopp (1977) has some of these assumptions; e.g. p. 103: 'If it were possible to reconstruct the process [of the expansion and arrangement of the Isaiah oracles] in detail, we should clearly be in a good position ... to answer the question how and why the pre-exilic judgement prophets were progressively *transformed* into witnesses of the millenarian hope which reached its furthest expression in the idiom of apocalyptic.'

21 Eaton (1979), p. 4: 'There are many units which defy full comparison not necessarily because of their originality, but arguably because comparable material has not survived.' This was written of the Second Isaiah, but has wider application.

22 Amos 7.4 is similar.

23 Murray (1982a).

24 The haunting creatures were not simply wild animals. In three passages similar names occur: Isa. 13.21–3; Isa. 34.13–15; Jer. 50.39.

   (i) *'yym*, 'jackals', parallel to *tnnym*, at Isa. 13.22: to *ṣyym* at Isa. 34.14; Jer. 50.39; to gods of the earth at Zeph. 2.11; to adversaries of God at Isa. 59.18. In Isa. 41.5 they wait for the judgement. 'Jackals' is not the most likely translation. Torrey (1928), pp. 290ff thought them demonic. The Greek has ὀνοκένταυροι except at Jer. 50.39 where we find ἐν ταῖς νήσοις. Jerome's Latin has *ululae* at Isa. 13.22; *onocentauri* at Isa. 34.13; *fauni ficarii* at Jer. 50.39. The Syriac at Jer. 50.39 has 'sirens' for both *'yym* and *ṣyym*, and at Isa. 34.14 'demons' for both. The pattern in which the *'yym* occur in the Second Isaiah (see Chapter 6) suggests that they were not 'jackals' or 'coastlands' but supernatural beings of some sort.

   (ii) *ṣyym*, 'wild beasts', parallel to *'yym* at Isa. 34.14 and Jer. 50.39. They occur in Isa. 13.21 and 23.13 also.

   (iii) *s'yrym*, 'satyrs', occur at Isa. 13.21 and 34.14 as haunting creatures, but also at Lev. 17.7 and 2 Chron. 11.15 as objects of forbidden worship.

   (iv) *tynnym*, 'jackals', occur at Isa. 13.22; 34.13; 43.20. They are apparently confused with *tnnym*, 'dragons', at Ezek. 29.2 and 32.2. They occur most often as the companions of

(v) *bnwt y'nh*, 'ostriches' (Mic. 1.8; Job 30.29; Isa. 43.20; Isa. 34.13). The name is thought to derive from *greed*, and both *tnnym* and *bnwt y'nh* came to symbolize desolation and loneliness.

(vi) *'hym* are unique to Isa. 13.21. Usually rendered 'jackals' (as are both *'yym* and *tnnym*, suggesting that we do not really know what they were) there is another root *'hh*, associated with burning, which could indicate that these are fiery creatures, rather than yet more jackals.

If we begin a pattern of association with *'yym*, we find that these could be enemies of God awaiting judgement, other gods; they are parallel to the *syym* and also to the *tnnym*. The *tnnym* in their turn are linked to the *bnwt y'nh*. The *'hym* are unique to one passage, but all the passages where these creatures occur suggest that they were figures of desolation, the sign of judgement. In view of the close association of animals and demon figures, especially with those of the desert (see Keel [1978], pp. 78ff), we cannot read these descriptions of desolation without taking into account the supernatural element in that desolation.

25 Was this lofty city the heavenly dwelling of all the counterparts to the earthly rulers?

26 Yahweh commands the *mqdšm*, 'consecrated ones'; Miller (1973), p. 136, links this to the Holy War idea. The targum has 'my appointed ones'; the LXX omits. This host is also *'allīzē ga'awātī*, 'proudly exulting ones'; cf. Zeph. 3.11 where similar creatures are removed from the holy mountain because of their pride. The *gibbōrīm*, mighty men, are γίγαντες in the LXX; cf. Gen. 4.6 where they are the *n'pilim*. This is supernatural warfare, perhaps the origin of the later ideas of holy war. Stars fade (13.10); the arrogant are humbled (13.11); the heavens tremble at Yahweh's anger (13.13).

27 Kaiser (1972), p. 138.

28 Hebrew has Valley of *vision* (22.1, 5); LXX has *Zion*, making Isa. 22 refer to the Day of the Lord against Jerusalem, as we find elsewhere in Isaiah, e.g. Isa. 3. The host of Elam and Kir might well conceal angels (*'lm* and *'rm*), especially as this is so obscure a text. 22.2, your *slain*, not slain with the sword; *hll* is the key word in Ezek. 28, the oracle against Tyre, which, like Isa. 22, describes the fall of a great city. Ezekiel is clearly dealing with angel figures in that context. 'Slain' is probably not an appropriate translation here in Isa. 22. 22.3 has a chiastic structure. 3a and d read 'your rulers have fled together, they have fled far away' from the LXX of 3d rather than from the Hebrew. 3b the rulers were 'captured', from *'sr*, 'bind', but the targum has 'revolted', from *sūr*, 'revolt', 'turn aside'; 'without a bow' (*mqqšt*), but in the LXX σκληρῶς, reading from *qšh*, 'stubborn'. 3c 'All who were found were captured', perhaps better for the parallelism to read with the LXX ἰσχύοντες, *'mmsyk*, 'your mighty ones revolted'.

22.5 *mqrqr qr*, 'tearing down walls', from *qr* 'wall', and a pilpel of *qrr*, but this is unique to this verse. Read rather in the light of two very similar passages: Num. 24.17, where *qrqr* describes the battle of the star figure against the sons of Seth, and Jer. 48.45, describing the battle against the sons of tumult in the judgement upon Moab. Num. 24.17 is usually altered to agree with Jer. 48.45, which has the very similar *qdqd*.

22.6 has two significant words; bearing in mind that Isaiah's description of the Day of the Lord against Jerusalem involves judgement on those who practise the magic arts, I wonder if there is word-play, or even the need for another translation. Should *nś 'šph*, 'take up the quiver' and *'rh mgn*, 'lay bare the shield', be read *nś 'špm*, 'take away exorcists'; *'rh mgm*, 'destroy the magicians'?

22.8, 'uncover the covering of Judah'; perhaps rather 'remove the sanctuary of Judah', related to *mskh* in Ezek. 28.13, which was the cherub's *sanctuary*, not simply his covering. The word is a technical term for the various curtains of the sanctuary; see BDB *ad loc*.

29 Feigin (1920).

30 Murray (1982a).

31 See note 24.

32 There is a similar picture in 1 Enoch; this passage is thought to be the source of the Similitudes (Suter 1979a). The chapter ends with the confounding of the sun and moon, and with the triumph of Yahweh of hosts in the presence of *his elders*. The Syriac says he triumphs in the presence of his *Holy Ones* (Murray 1982a). Why this reading, unless this chapter had these associations?

33 Gaster (1961) and others hold that the *rephaim* were divine or semi-divine; thus 26.13–14 depict the overthrow of supernatural rulers vanquished by Yahweh.

34 Murray (1982a), pp. 209–10.

35 This is one of the few places where Isaiah gives details of the sins of Jerusalem apart from pride and the failure to trust Yahweh. Such familiar sins remind us that the prophet was working with ideas and standards familiar to us, but in a very unfamiliar context.

36 Keel (1978), p. 285: 'In Ps. 45, however, there is talk neither of servitude on the part of the king, nor the blessing of fertility which the union is supposed to effect. In Ps. 72.16, to be sure, the king appears in connection with the fertility of the land ... However, this fertility is not the result of sacred marriage, but of intercessions made on the king's behalf because of his action in rescuing the innocent from the violent (vv. 14–15). When he stands up for the rights of the weak, he may consider the harvest blessing a part of his blessed rule'.

37 Murray (1982a).

38 The Hebrew can mean 'messengers of angels'; the LXX has 'kings', doubtless by reading *mlky* for *ml'ky*. We should read: 'What will be the reply of the angels of the nations ... that the Lord has founded Zion?'; cf. Lam. 4.12.

39 See also note 34.

40 Murray 1982a: the destroyer, 33.1; *'r'rllm*, 33.7, remembered in Jewish tradition as the angels of death; *ml'ky šlm*, 'angels of peace'; *'rym*, 'watchers', 33.8; the judgement of burning, 33.13, which the upright faces with confidence; cf. Ps. 15, its link to the ethical decalogue, and *its* link to the 'elders' of Exod. 24.9–11. See also Feigin (1920).

41 See ch. 1, p. 54.

42 Von Rad (1965), p. 169, assumes this.

43 See Reventlow (1971), pp. 321ff, for full discussion.

44 ibid., p. 322.

45 The very existence of the festival is disputed, but the constant association of harvest and judgement imagery throughout the OT and the NT is best explained by a festival in the autumn. Thus Isa. 63 stands in a tradition which culminates in Rev. 14.22ff.

46 Murray (1982a).

47 As in the Gospels!

48 It is suggested that they were an adaptation of Egyptian throne names, but their meaning must be established for the context in which they function, and not just from the context whence they were taken.

49 All are debated; but the gist is clear enough.

50 Clifford (1972).

51 Nickelsburg (1972) shows how the high mountain was the place from which the exalted Israel/wise man looked down on his enemies.

52 Not everyone agrees that the Branch in 4.2 is messianic on the grounds of the fertility context; but the king figure *was* closely linked to fertility, and Zech. 3.8 and 6.12 both make the Branch refer to a human figure of some sort. The pattern of judgement and fertility for a messianic figure is quite consistent with the Enochic view of the judgement.

53 For example see Nickelsburg (1972), pp. 48ff.

5

DEUTERONOMY

There has been a tendency in Old Testament scholarship to make Deuteronomy its fulcrum. It has provided a central point for Pentateuchal source criticism, it shaped the final form of the histories which we read as *the* account of Israel's history, and a Deuteronomic circle is thought to have transmitted and edited the prophetic books.[1] Despite the importance of the book, problems surrounding its date, authorship and general pedigree are amongst the most vexed in the field. The whole process is bedevilled by circular arguments, because most of the written evidence at our disposal has passed through the hands of these same Deuteronomists. As a result it is not easy to see the situation from which it came, because its antecedents have disappeared. Why? This is not a question we ask, and yet when we look for the ancient covenant materials which apparently shaped the book we find that the sources are already worked over, and when we try to reconstruct the ideology of the Holy War and the Warrior God we find the same problem. This is serious; if we fail to understand this book, we fail to reach the starting point for many others.[2] The problem of Deuteronomy is many-headed; we have to consider the origin of the book, as well as the role and function of its final form. The intervening history has to be reconstructed, and patterns of influence traced. What I propose is that there was one major and all-embracing factor, perhaps at a fairly late stage in its history, which caused the book to have its present form.

We now approach Deuteronomy in many different ways, and there are dozens of theories and emphases, each with much to commend it, and not all of them mutually interrelated. Instead of examining all these positions, which would be impossible, I shall take some of the major suggestions and show how the one explanation I propose could bear upon each of them. If Deuteronomy was the product of the exile, prompted by the demise of the royal cult, most of the features of the book can be explained in terms of a royal cult based upon an angel mythology, which formed, consciously or otherwise, the framework of our present Deuteronomy.

It has long been fashionable to link Deuteronomy and Josiah's reform, but no easy equation is possible between that Law book and an earlier version of Deuteronomy.[3] The other version of the story in 2 Chron. 34 differs at several points from 2 Kings 22—23, and only the Deuteronomic version invites the association of Deuteronomy and Josiah's reform. This tells us that the historians *wanted* to associate Deuteronomy with cultic reform. If we did not have this directive, the evidence of the book suggests that they were opposed to the ways of *Canaan*, and not to the *older cult*. This is important; much of what they considered to be pagan and Canaanite may not have been seen as such by other worshippers in Jerusalem. Any questions raised by Deuteronomy cannot be answered solely from materials which it has shaped and influenced. Thus the Deuteronomic histories can only be used to show how these people wrote, or rather rewrote, their people's history. They do not tell us how things actually happened. What we should like to know is why they wanted to rewrite everything, why they argued from a pattern in history, and not from a pattern within the cult. Because of the nature of our evidence, any reconstruction of life in pre-monarchical Israel, any speculation as to the origin of Holy War, or any attempt to describe the role of the kings in Jerusalem may involve us in circular arguments.[4] The histories do, however, show that there were certain differences between their ideals and those of the present form of Deuteronomy. These differences are much debated, but they seem to indicate a development, and we must seek reasons for any changes.[5] The last event recorded by the histories is the reference to Jehoiachin in 561, and his being well treated by the king of Babylon. From this we may conclude only that the histories were written or updated *after* this time; that they reflect the views of the early sixth century may perhaps be better deduced from a comparison of 2 Kings 24.3ff and Jer. 31.29 or Ezek. 18. The prophets' protest about inherited guilt must surely be a comment upon the philosophy of the Deuteronomic historians. The histories set out to show that the Deuteronomists had been correct; Jerusalem had fallen because of the evil ways of her kings, and these had been defined as deviation from the Deuteronomists' standards. Notice that the *kings* and their disobedience are deemed responsible for the fate of their people, an echo of the older ways, even though the Deuteronomists have adapted this assumption to their own needs. The histories point to prophecies fulfilled, and to great sin inherited by later generations. The exiles were left to weep by the waters of Babylon. One cannot help feeling that such an interpretation of history, offered to a people in despair, can only have come from a rather vindictive mentality, perhaps from a group whose views were not widely accepted.[6] Deuteronomy itself is different.[7] It sees a new era beginning, and the book is now thought to be a picture of the exiles themselves.[8] Older scholars have read the book as a product of the amphictyony, nationalist, exclusivist and limiting the chosen people to those who had known Egypt, or they have read it as a reform programme for the northern kingdom after the fall of Samaria; but if Deuteronomy is a product of the exile, then the *experience of exile is a possible explanation for the differences between the histories and the book of Deuteronomy itself.*

One of the most frequently recurring conclusions in the study of Deuteronomy is that it represents fusions of various blocks of material separately attested elsewhere.[9] Moses-Sinai traditions, for example, were fused with David-Zion traditions. The extent of the fusion is debated, and given the present uncertainty as to the precise relationship of the Sinai and Jerusalem traditions in the time of the monarchy, the debate cannot reach a conclusion. If, however, a Moses tradition eclipsed a David tradition, this must be established on the basis of non-Deuteronomic materials if it is to be more than a mere retrojection. The situation of the exile could have given rise to such fusions as we find in Deuteronomy; religious establishments and their critics can often find a *modus vivendi* in the common interest of survival. Such a necessity seems to have prompted the compilation of the Pentateuch with its extraordinary fusions of desert and city traditions. We now attempt to disentangle the various strands, but the purpose of the compilation was to fuse them. It is not hard to imagine divisions within Jerusalem in the early sixth century, just before the fall of the city. There were reformers alongside such colourful characters as we meet in Ezekiel, yet all of them found themselves thrown together in the relatively small community of the exile;[10] and all, I have no doubt, were asking the same question. All of them would have known the Second Isaiah, and the interaction between the reforming ways of the Deuteronomists and the inspiration of the prophet account, I believe, for the direction of developments within the exile.[11]

The relationship of the Deuteronomists and the prophets is fraught with problems; the historians, for example, emphasized the role of prophecy, and yet the writing prophets, with the exception of Isaiah, are not mentioned;[12] the historians emphasized prophecy which had been fulfilled and thus shown to be true, whereas the writing prophets were preserved because their words had not yet been fulfilled. This indicates that the Deuteronomists' view of prophecy was different from that of the people who preserved the writing prophets. It could indicate that the Deuteronomic idea of fulfilment in present or past events was something new. Or it could indicate that the criterion for authenticity was not derived from the claim to inspiration in the heavenly council, but from something more easily demonstrable. We cannot tell. Nor can we know the criterion of authenticity adopted by those who kept the writings expecting fulfilment. All we know is that these writings had an established status before the Deuteronomists became influential, because they were *edited* by the Deuteronomists. They were assimilated and redefined.[13] The whole question of the role of the Deuteronomists in the transmission of prophecy is vexed and complex, but this must not distract us from a more fundamental problem: they were transmitting something which they modified and which, in their hands, became something other than it had originally been.

There are several indications in the writing prophets that they were preserved only because they were not heeded in their own time.[14] Like the Deuteronomists, they had had reason to protest, but the fact that the writing prophets were not used by the Deuteronomic historians as part of their case against the establishment in Jerusalem suggests that the protests of the prophets were not those of the Deuteronomists. We shall perhaps do better to avoid too easy an association between the writing prophets and Deuteronomy. Their cause may have been very different, and their similarities due to later editing.

Deuteronomy's view of prophecy and fulfilment is important in the development of exilic thought, because the Second Isaiah took this up and made it central to his prophecy, even though fulfilment had not been a criterion for the earlier prophets. It is interesting that the prophecy which the Second Isaiah saw fulfilled was not a prophecy in our sense of the word, but rather was the myth of the monarchy, as I shall show in the next chapter. This helps us to understand those earlier prophets, and explains both why they are not mentioned in the Deuteronomic histories, and why they were edited in their later transmission. The Deuteronomists sought to eradicate the mythology of the monarchy which was the framework of the prophecies. It has been suggested that in Israel the correspondence pattern of mythology was broken, and that the change may have been slow and gradual.[15] It is my belief that the pattern was broken only by a small group, the Deuteronomists, who have exercised a disproportionate influence upon our reconstruction of Israel's religion. The change was not slow, but was, rather, a violent reaction to the demise of the monarchy.[16]

The Deuteronomic histories therefore give us a picture of the monarchy very different from any we might reconstruct from the Psalms. It is far from flattering, and judges all kings by the one standard of Deuteronomic orthodoxy. At the very end of the histories there is a postscript about the fate of Jehoiachin which some suggest shows a change of attitude towards the kings on the part of the writer. Perhaps, it is said, the exile had altered his view of the monarchy, and led him to see it in a more favourable light.[17] Such slender evidence is little upon which to build such an enormous theory, but there are several other factors which do suggest such a change. In Deuteronomy itself, for example, a considerable amount of the old royal theology has been taken over and democratized as part of its final scheme.[18] Just as the Second Isaiah proclaimed the fulfilment of the royal mythology, so Deuteronomy counterbalanced and reapplied elements and motifs of that mythology. The chosen king became the chosen people (cf. the single and corporate figure of the Servant in the Second Isaiah), the royal son of God became the nation of the sons of God, the royal wisdom became the Torah, and the chosen city of Jerusalem became the basis of the centralization laws.[19] There are several versions of the transformation thesis: one sees the role and function of the king as lawgiver, judge, political and military leader transferred to Moses rather than to the people as a whole.[20] This transformation of the royal theology was prompted by a rejection of its original basis, whereas in the Second Isaiah, as I shall show, the transformation *entailed* the rejection of the basic myth, an important distinction. What is significant is that both prophet and Deuteronomist had the same underlying pattern of ideas, suggesting that there was a certain substructure which the Deuteronomists retained, perhaps because they could not destroy it, or perhaps

145

because it was so natural a way of thinking that they knew no other. If this transformation is a factor in the formation of both books, it should be possible to confirm other elements of the old mythology from the shape of these books, and thus confirm in some way the mythology I have reconstructed from the Enochic writings and elsewhere.

Another characteristic of the Deuteronomic histories is their emphasis upon sin and retribution, which placed a massive burden of guilt upon the exiles[21] and suggested to the poor remnant left in the land that they were the legitimate heirs and the chosen people. Many continued in this belief, despite the preface to Deuteronomy which counteracts the idea, as do Jer. 24 and Ezek. 33.23ff. Moses gives a new explanation of the Law[22] and demonstrates that the older generation who had not believed the promise would not enter to take possession. The next generation would possess the land. Thus the despair of the exiles was met by a modified Deuteronomy, and their Law was reinterpreted by Moses. They were confirmed as the chosen. We read the reaction of the non-exiles in 1 Enoch who considered them an impure and apostate generation.

The form in which Deuteronomy was written also affords clues to its origin or to its purpose, since we do not know if the pattern in which it is presented was determined by the natural style of the writers (in which case it will reveal their origins), or by the needs of those for whom they wrote (in which case it will reveal the expectations of the hearers). If the Deuteronomists saw themselves as reformers in Jerusalem, it is likely that their work shows a similar tendency to reform.[23] Deuteronomy is presented as Moses' address to the tribes at the foot of the mountain. It is as much a pseudepigraphon as 1 Enoch, or its two successors in claiming Mosaic authority, Jubilees and the Temple Scroll – although our conditioning is such that we do not read it in that way. It is cast in the manner of a farewell speech or testament, a great sermon making its points in the manner of the other great pseudepigraphical testimonies. We are left to guess from the emphases what positions were being opposed, and what threats countered. The factors which influenced the real author's choice of his ancient figure are a matter of debate,[24] but the similarity of the situations in Egypt and in Babylon may have been one of them, and the need to claim the authority of an ancient figure another. The Mosaic prohibitions for the new age give a valuable clue as to the situation against which the Deuteronomic pseudepigraphon was composed. Deuteronomy emphasizes, for example, that no form of God was seen; only a voice was heard. This has been interpreted as emphasizing the transcendence of God,[25] but I wonder if the motive was not more polemical. There was considerable debate over the vision of God in the later writings,[26] some claiming that ascent and vision were possible, others denying it. It was the apocalyptic tradition, the one we have reason to believe was excluded by the work and influence of the Deuteronomists, which retained a belief in the vision of God and the possibility of ascent. Now the vision of Isaiah says that God was *seen*; the description of the seventy elders in Exod. 24.9–11 says that

146

God was seen. If this passage was a Sinai before Sinai, an antecedent to the Mosaic covenant,[27] then we have in the vision of God a clear indication of something which the Deuteronomists rejected. They took over and used a great deal of the covenant theology, but they could deny one major aspect of it, namely its *setting*.[28] The most frequent of the prohibitions in Deuteronomy concerns images. As a simple ban upon heathen paraphernalia this would excite no comment, but combined with their emphasis upon formless theophany, I wonder if the prohibition has deeper implications. Visual images shape new ideas; the prophets *saw* the word of the Lord and interpreted it. The older name for the prophets had been *seers* (1 Sam. 9.9). If the Deuteronomists wanted to alter and to control – which clearly they did – they would not tolerate any innovation beyond their own scheme. This is a characteristic trait of totalitarian regimes, and we must not fail to recognize the religious intolerance of the Deuteronomists for what it was. They said: Listen and obey. Their prophets had to conform to the ways of Moses; even the proof of fulfilment was not enough to justify any change.[29] Another prohibition concerns the veneration of the heavenly host, which does not refer to idolatry,[30] but to the older cultic practices in Jerusalem. There is much to suggest that the cult of Yahweh of Hosts had been *replaced* by another system,[31] and the prohibitions of Deuteronomy indicate that the older ways were for those *not chosen* by Yahweh. The newer, better way was for those taken from affliction and chosen by Yahweh.[32] Thus the implications of Deut. 4.19–20 are my thesis in a nutshell. The elect, those who had experienced the exile, were distinguished from all others by their rejection of the heavenly hosts. This massive innovation had not come simply from the Deuteronomists, but from their contact with the Second Isaiah, and his assertion that the ancient host was no more.[33] I have already argued that wisdom was prohibited by the Deuteronomists in so far as the Law was offered as a substitute. Prophecy was also closely defined, and all additions to the revelation on the mountain were forbidden (Deut. 5.22). This prohibition cannot have referred to any further expansion of the Law, since the rest of Deuteronomy is an expansion of the Law. It must have referred to other traditions of mountain-top revelation or to other heavenly tablets.[34] Even within the Old Testament there are other traditions of mountain-top revelation. Exod. 31.18, for example, describes Moses' descent with the decalogue, and, we assume, all the tabernacle specifications. Outside the Old Testament we find that in Jubilees Moses and the angels were engaged upon writing the whole of the future history of Israel as well as the Law and other admonitions, and the whole of 1 Enoch consists of heavenly revelations. Is it possible that these other books retain a memory of a time when more than just the Law was believed to have come from the mountain of God? It would have been this 'other' material which the Deuteronomists sought to exclude. Taken together, these prohibitions are very significant. They indicate opposition to a certain type of theophany, to the heavenly host, to wisdom and to other mountain-top traditions of revelation.

147

These were all elements in the old royal theology, and they survived as elements in 1 Enoch. It is from Deuteronomy that they have been excluded.

Deuteronomy is also based upon a liturgical pattern from the older cult.[35] Here again we find theories of transformation and fusion, and the same uncertainty as to exactly *what* was transformed. Even though the prophecies of the Second Isaiah are thought to have been shaped by the pattern of the pre-exilic festival,[36] and it would not be unreasonable to suppose that a work from the same milieu was similarly influenced, it is not ancient Jerusalem which is most frequently suggested as the source of the cultic elements in Deuteronomy. We are directed rather to the ancient Shechem. The covenant ceremony at Shechem (Josh. 24)[37] and the reading of the Law (Josh. 8) are both Deuteronomic set pieces, and not necessarily good evidence for actual practice. It is difficult to explain the emphases of Deut. 11.30 and 27.1ff except as memories of Shechem, but Deuteronomy in its present form promotes the interests of another shrine. Centralization of worship is another important theme for Deuteronomy, as is the purification of worship, and any Shechem theory has to explain how and why Jerusalem was reformed by an infusion of tradition from elsewhere. On the other hand, most of Deuteronomy's major features can be explained if the roots lay in the Jerusalem cult.[38] A recent analysis of Deuteronomy concluded that covenant thought was not made explicit until the later stages of its formation,[39] implying that covenant thought was taken over by the Deuteronomists, rather than brought with them. Covenant ideas could have been what they sought to reform, rather than the ideal they brought to their reform. The problem of the vision of God in Exod. 24.9–11 suggests something like this; there was an older mythological notion of covenant whose fundamental aspect, the vision of God and the heavenly court, they sought to eliminate. The setting of the covenant in Shechem presents several problems, but these are not greater than the apparent refusal to accept the *setting* of the covenant in the Jerusalem cult. I offer this only as a hypothesis, but I shall show that there are several other indications – the covenant, the treaty form, the '*rib* pattern' – which all came late to Deuteronomy, and all originate in the one setting. It was the mythological framework of the older cult which the Deuteronomists could not reconcile with their own position.

The clearest description of the royal covenant in terms of the angel mythology is in Ps. 89,[40] where the pattern of parallelism indicates that the Davidic covenant stood as the dividing line between the rule of the angels and the current order. Just as Yahweh was supreme amongst the heavenly powers, so his king was supreme among their earthly counterparts. The royal covenant involved the stability of the natural order (cf. Isa. 11), and other texts enable us to see a very different picture from the one drawn by the Deuteronomists in 2 Sam. 7. The ancient king was established on the holy hill in triumph over his enemies, and he spoke as the son and mouthpiece of Yahweh (Ps. 2); he was

the divine son, judge, guarantor of fertility and victor over alien rulers (Ps. 72);
'knowledge' was crucial to his role (Isa. 11.2–9; Jer. 22.15–16). The
Deuteronomic view of the king promised security to the dynasty and victory
over enemies (2 Sam. 7) and enjoined promulgation of the Law (Deut. 17.14ff).
These are not unusual roles for a king, and coincide well with our modern ideas
of monarchy, but their influence upon our ideas of covenant and kingship have
been disproportionate, and have led to a concentration upon political models at
the expense of the cosmic aspects of covenant. The reading of the Law was
associated with the autumn festival (Deut. 31.9ff, cf. Neh. 8), although there is
no mention of the king in this role. Is it possible that the royal function as the
lawgiver (Isa. 11) was once linked to the autumn festival? It was suggested long
ago that the Sinai narratives were based on the autumn festival in Jerusalem,[41]
but the position was criticized for having insufficient basis in known facts. The
problem for anyone working in this area is always the shortage of hard facts,
and the most to which anyone can aspire is the balancing of possibilities.

Another important feature of Deuteronomy's complex structure is the so-
called treaty form, whose origins and significance have been much debated in
recent years. It is now thought that the original Deuteronomy did not have
these treaty elements, just as it did not have covenant ideas.[42] If the treaty
expression of the covenant relationship was taken over by the Deuteronomists,
then that treaty form would have to have been the expression of the older
relationship between Yahweh and the king if Deuteronomy derived its final
form from the Jerusalem cult. This is quite possible, since the evidence shows
that treaties were usually between vassal and overlord, not between subject
people and overlord.[43] There is some memory of this at Deut. 33.5, where
Yahweh becomes king at the time of the giving of the Law. How the earthly
king fitted into this scheme is no longer clear,[44] but hints such as that in
1 Chron. 29.23, where the king is said to have sat upon the *throne of Yahweh*,
remind us that earth and heaven may not have been entirely distinct.

The third element, the recurring pattern of the covenant lawsuit (the *rib*),
also derives from this setting. The passages in Deuteronomy which use this
formula are also deemed to be late additions to the original, suggesting that the
rib, like the covenant idea and the treaty form, was *adopted by* the Deuteronomists.
The polytheistic law court implied by the *rib* formula points to the heavenly
assembly of the royal myth, where the king had right of access as the chosen
one.[45] Even the prophets who do not use the *rib* formula as such use the picture
of the heavenly judgement: Amos 1—2 is set in the heavenly court, Job appeals
to a heavenly court, and the Second Isaiah depicts the end of the other gods not
in battle, but in the court of the divine assembly. Where the formula *is* explicit,
the contexts often have significant features to point to the angel mythology: for
example, Isa. 1.2, rebel sons; Mic. 6.2ff, where mountains are the witnesses;
Mic. 6.9ff has judgement, the assembly and wisdom themes.[46]

A case can be made for seeing the covenant, the treaty and the *rib* as elements taken over from the Jerusalem tradition, where their natural setting was the politics of the holy mountain and its heavenly council. They now appear as fragments with many parallels in the mythology of surrounding cultures, but they were not always so. Their original context has been destroyed, and with it our appreciation of their significance, since we have been conditioned to read the Old Testament as a myth-less text. Any speculation is beset with problems, but confining oneself to one tradition avoids the dangers of fragmentation which beset many reconstructions, and 'what can be inferred about the beliefs of ancient Israelites becomes more significant than plain statements which the Old Testament contains'.[47]

Another hypothesis as to the form of Deuteronomy is that it was the product of the wise men of Judah,[48] and that much of it reflects the ancient wisdom. I have already argued on other grounds that Deuteronomy offered the Law as a substitute for the older wisdom. If Deuteronomy was composed as part of the massive transformation of the royal mythology, the transformation of the king's ancient wisdom would have been a part of this process.

The most striking confirmation of the transformation thesis is to be found in later traditions about Moses. W. A. Meeks has investigated these materials, but could offer no explanation why Moses was linked to the ideal king – why the ideal king was portrayed in a particular way, and why a mystic ascent was *read into* the Sinai episode. It seems as though Moses was made 'God and king' in heaven and on Sinai; he received a crown of light and the robe of light which was reserved for King Messiah. Meeks thought there were elements of syncretism and later Hellenistic motifs in the legends, but no reason was offered for the accretion of these particular ideas to the Moses figure. They have no obvious aetiological function, but they may have served as the basis for an eschatological ideology, and emphasized Moses' role as the guarantor of the traditions. Nevertheless, there is still no reason to link Moses to kingship. This aspect pointed to the legends having been *woven together from earlier separate strands of tradition*. If, however, we read Meeks' conclusions in the light of what I am suggesting about Moses' taking over the role of the king, and in the light of what I think that role to have been, it is clear that many of the later Moses legends correspond exactly to the royal mythology which I have reconstructed from the Enochic writings and from Isaiah.

> We have seen that in very diverse sources there persist the remnants of an elaborate cluster of traditions about Moses' heavenly enthronement at the time of the Sinai theophany ... Central ... is the notion that, when God gave to Moses his own name (*'elohim, theos*), he conveyed to him a divine status and a unique function among men ... Moses' enthronement in heaven, accompanied by his receiving the name 'god' and God's crown of light, meant that the lost glory of Adam, the image of God, was restored to him and that Moses henceforth was to serve on earth as God's representative, both as revealer (prophet) and as vice-regent (king).[49]

Deuteronomy shows us the beginning of this process of transformation. Where there had once been the king figure as the focus of certain roles, and the recipient of certain promises, there were Moses and the chosen people. Some of the royal roles were democratized and given to the people as a whole, some were given to Moses; but without an accurate reconstruction of what the royal mythology entailed, it has not been possible to recognize all these transformations. Thus the people as a whole became the sons of God; they were holy and chosen (Deut. 14.1–2), their obedience led to their exaltation, and they became *Elyon* over the nations (Deut. 26.18–19; 28.1–2); cf. Ps. 89 where this is exactly the covenant promise to the king; they became a kingdom of priests, God's own possession, a holy nation (Exod. 19.6).[50] Moses, who dominates the Deuteronomic tradition – even though he was not a key figure in the earlier writings of the south –[51] inherits the other royal roles. One of the transformation theses[52] suggests that the roles of lawgiver and judge, along with political, military and cultic functions, would naturally have belonged to a royal figure, but in Deuteronomy these are all attributed to Moses. Of these, his most important was the role of lawgiver, a transformation which gives rise to one of the great mysteries of the Old Testament in its present form. Despite four centuries of monarchy, when the king was the lawgiver, there are no royal laws, no royal decrees[53] in the Law. There are a few clues: David gave orders to his fighting men which, we are told, *became* the law of the land (1 Sam. 30.24), whereas almost identical instructions were given by Yahweh to Moses (Num. 31.27). This could be interpreted as the Mosaic tradition having taken over what the kings had enunciated and made into the law of the land. The Mosaic account also says that this law was given by Yahweh, which affords another clue. The king was believed to be the mouthpiece of Yahweh,[54] passing on his decrees to his people. If any of the laws of old Israel have survived in the Pentateuch, then there must be royal laws among them. The Old Testament presents Moses as the Lawgiver, yet the ideal in the prophets is a *king* who gives good law, and he is depicted as the source of the law, not just as its upholder (e.g. Isa. 9.11; 42.4). If Moses did take over the royal laws, this may shed light on another of the problems in this area; the origin of apodictic law form. It is possible that these are the remains of the royal pronouncements. The present context of these laws is a covenant context, but this is not thought to have been the original context because similar forms are found outside the Old Testament,[55] and there is considerable evidence within the Old Testament that the covenant relationship was not the original concern. Apodictic law, it is argued, probably originated with the clan elders, since the greater part of it deals with everyday matters, and even when the subject of the law is theological, there is reference to God in the third person. On the other hand there are some of these laws, e.g. Deut. 5.7, which could only have come from the cult. The conclusion drawn is that Deuteronomy *transformed* the understanding of Israel's law, and made all of it divine, all of it the condition of the covenant. Now if such forms are found outside the Old Testament, and the original concern of this type of law was not the Deuteronomic covenant relationship, its origin could be sought in a non-Deuteronomic covenant context not unique to Israel. There are other possibilities than the clan elders. Alt's original suggestion,[56] though much modified since, was that the authority behind these laws was Yahweh himself, but in pre-exilic times it was not only the prophets who spoke in the name of God. The king also could report the decrees of Yahweh (Ps. 2.7). Bearing in mind the activities of later editors, we should not expect to find overmuch evidence of this aspect of the king's role, but I suggest that Isa. 11.4; 49.2 and 50.4 could bear this interpretation. If the apodictic form has a single point of origin, we have to find a source which could speak directly as God in a cultic context, and yet deal with the everyday concerns of life. The king did deal with the day-to-day problems of his people (2 Sam. 14.4; 15.1–6; 1 Kings 3), and this makes a royal source likely for the apodictic laws. Some of the pronouncements were attributed to Moses; others, about which there was a greater aura of the divine, were returned to the mouth of Yahweh. We should be wary of saying that the original context of these laws *cannot* have been the divine speech of the covenant cult. Deuteronomy was very keen to limit the extent of the divine pronouncements (Deut. 5.22), and it would have been difficult to exclude some traditions of divine speech whilst inventing others. We cannot explain the transformation by saying that Deuteronomy came to see the laws and teachings concerning non-cultic matters as equally part of the covenant demands,[57] when it was Deuteronomy which removed everyday matters such as animal slaughter *from* the cultic sphere (Deut. 12.20ff).

If the transformation theory is correct, it should explain the 'humanism', 'secularization' and 'liberation of religious institutions and practices from primitive magical elements'[58] which characterize the work. All these must be seen as the natural result of their demythologizing programme and their suppression of the ancient wisdom with its magical associations. In the older tradition we find that the gift of rain had been linked to the autumn festival and the person of the king; in the new scheme it was the reward for obedience to the Law (Deut. 11.8).[59] In the old scheme the passover had had an apotropaic character, but in Deuteronomy it became *the* great pilgrim festival, ousting the autumn festival of kingship as the focus of the year. The ark was no longer the throne or the footstool of the Lord; it was the box in which the tables of the Law were stored (Deut. 10.1–5).[60]

The most dramatic of the transformations explains the terminology of the 'Holy War'. Recent study has concluded that the holy war ideology was created by the Deuteronomists who recorded Israel's traditions within that scheme.[61] Israel under Yahweh opposed the foreign nations who threatened her. I think it more likely that the 'Holy War' resulted from the democratization of the older mythology. The wars which had previously included the angelic hosts were, in the newer scheme, to become the wars of the holy people. To argue from the Deuteronomic historians' account of the ancient wars that

Deuteronomy was reviving an ancient tradition of the tribes is a circular argument. These ancient pictures of warfare have recently been put to another use, and employed to create the picture of the 'divine warrior'.[62] This was an ancient concept of Yahweh, revived in times of national stress, which became the basis for 'apocalyptic'. As it stands, this theory is not acceptable, since the Enochic literature does not have any place for this warrior figure, but if the Deuteronomists were responsible not for *creating* the idea of the 'Holy War', but for transforming it into an operation of the holy people, accompanied by the rewriting of ancient materials where necessary, then the apparent resurgence of the warrior figure in apocalyptic writings need not be construed as a revival of the ancient ways, but as a *survival*, something which managed to escape the reformers. The growth of divine warrior motifs in the post-exilic writings, but divorced from their original astral context, suggests that such imagery was all that was tolerated from the older ways. All other aspects of the ancient myth appear outside the canon and are compatible *with* the 'divine warrior', but in no way based upon it. Hence the undoubted truth of the Cross–Miller insights as to the constant association of the 'divine warrior' with apocalyptic themes and contexts is only a half-truth. The warrior was not central, as can be seen from 1 Enoch, but he was an acceptable figure in the newer scheme, and as such was permitted to appear in the books which became canonical. If the Deuteronomists *did* transform the 'Holy War', this would explain the tolerance of certain imagery, and the exclusion of the rest. The older ways did not disappear; some circles must have kept them alive, because the vision of Dan. 7 is a clear and direct piece of evidence for the survival of the royal tradition intact.[63] It appears within a text now canonical because it, too, has been transformed by the insertion of one word, 'people' (Dan. 7.27), which tips the interpretation of the old cult myth in the direction of the Deuteronomists. What had formerly been a vision of the heavenly court and the king figure, became, through this insertion, a vision of the triumphant people. There has as a result been a long tradition of interpreting these Holy Ones as the Jewish people,[64] but we must not forget that this is an interpretation, a transformation. The original pattern was appropriate because the old mythology dealt with the arrogance of divine beings who came in pride to the holy mountain, exactly appropriate to the claims and actions of Antiochus Epiphanes. We do not know who preserved these traditions, but the fact that a tradition from the monarchy, democratized, could appear at an appropriate moment is evidence that the memory was there.[65] The War Scroll may also be explained in this way.[66] The hosts of angels who smite rebels on the earth and do battle with the 'lot of Belial' are not an elaboration upon the Deuteronomic holy war ideals by an age much taken with angels. Rather, we glimpse in this text the heavenly warfare of an earlier time.

None of these suggested transformations brings us any nearer to knowing the ultimate origins of the Deuteronomists, nor are their ultimate origins relevant to my argument. We began with a tentative reconstruction of the royal mythology drawn from non-Deuteronomic materials (an important point, since the evidence of zealous reformers is not always impartial), and have seen that a consistent pattern of transformation from that mythology can explain much of the shape and content of Deuteronomy. This in turn strengthens the possibility that the myth has been correctly reconstructed. Any essay which restricts itself to an analysis of Deuteronomy itself cannot proceed beyond that analysis. It has all the virtues of caution, but none of the requirements for a creative solution to the problem. Any synthesis such as I am proposing involves risk, but without risk there is no possibility of creating a way forward, or of finding an answer to the riddle posed by this book.

For far too long our reading of the Old Testament has been dominated and distorted by Deuteronomy. Theology has been written in its shadow. We need now to listen to other voices, before our attempts at reconstruction lose contact with reality.

> It is high time the salvation-historical perspective so successfully propounded by von Rad, and which has dominated research in recent decades, was complemented by conclusions arising from the study of Hebrew psalmody and wisdom. It seems to me that von Rad carried out his theological enterprise while being all too enthralled by the spell of Deuteronomistic theology. Admittedly, the Deuteronomistic programme was a magnificent attempt to compose a normative theology, but, as is well known, the Deuteronomistic circle of tradition was not the only one in ancient Israel.[67]

It was the Deuteronomists who cut away the context of the ancient myth, and led us to believe that the mythology of ancient Israel was peripheral, because only perceived by us in its surviving fragments. It is for this reason more than any other that Deuteronomy earns its place as the fulcrum of Old Testament study.

NOTES

1 Childs (1979), p. 204: 'The importance of Deuteronomy for the history of critical research can hardly be overestimated'...[It] is further evidenced by the many modern scholars who hold that Deuteronomy constitutes the centre of Old Testament theology.' Also Nicholson (1967); Clements (1975), esp. pp. 55ff; Blenkinsopp (1977), among many others. Canonical criticism highlights this problem; present texts may have been modified by the communities who used them, but what happened to the versions abandoned or outgrown?

2 Mayes (1983), p. 137, questions the assumption that the Deuteronomic school was as central to Israel's tradition as it is to the surviving evidence.

3 I have often wondered if the mysterious book might not have been the *Book of Yahweh* (Isa. 34.16), which threatened evil cities with doom. Isaiah's 'testimony' (Isa. 8.16) is another possibility, since it concerned national independence, and the fearful result of failing to trust the Holy One. Neither book would have been in public use during Manasseh's time, under whom, by tradition, Isaiah is said to have been martyred; see the Martyrdom of Isaiah.

4 Von Rad (1953), pp. 41ff, is a good example of a commentator reading what the authors of

the Deuteronomic histories wanted us to read in them. He emphasizes the pre-monarchical traditions and yet there is no direct deposit of *any* of these traditions in our Deuteronomy.

5   There are two possibilities: Deuteronomy was earlier than the histories, or it was later. It has been suggested that the histories were written by the descendants of the original Deuteronomists who worked in Jerusalem and reinterpreted Jerusalem's traditions in the light of their own (Nicholson 1967). The present form of Deuteronomy and the differences apparent between the histories and the Law book must indicate the direction in which the thought of the Deuteronomists developed.

6   Mayes (1983), see n2. Also W. E. Claburn in an unpublished thesis (*Dissertation Abstracts* 1068, p. 2784), used collective behaviour paradigms to evaluate Deuteronomy and concluded (i) that Deuteronomy was a typical example of 'totalistic movement literature' and (ii) that Deuteronomy was produced rapidly by people under stress.

7   Jer. 31.29ff has a strange succession of ideas which may be fortuitous, or may reflect a similar development. vv. 29–30 declare individual responsibility, counteracting the pessimism of Deuteronomy. The Deuteronomic version of the covenant is rejected in favour of a covenant upon the heart. The passage ends with the assurance that Israel is secure, a part of the fixed order, guaranteed by the power of Yahweh in creation. Does this show a return to the ideas of the older covenant, a reaction against the conditional legalism of Deuteronomy?

8   Clines (1978), pp. 97ff: 'The Pentateuch, even if it was composed after 539, is still an exilic work!... [it] functions as an address to exiles... Wherever exilic Jewry opens the Pentateuch it finds itself' (p. 98) ... 'Deuteronomy was a vehicle of the divine prompting of Israel to set its face towards the land ... The Pentateuchal theme, in its several forms, functioned among the exiles as an interpretation of their history ... Literature arising out of a vast array of historical situations had been welded into a new unity with a definite and effective function' (p. 100).

9   Von Rad (1962), pp. 334ff, said that the Deuteronomic histories fused the formerly separate blocks of Moses/Sinai and David/Zion materials. This was criticized by (e.g.) Nicholson (1967), who saw the process rather as a take-over by the Mosaic tradition. The Moses-dominated Deuteronomists were the ancestors of the Deuteronomic historians.

10 Jeremiah's figure is 4,600 (Jer. 52.30). Even if this represents only the adult men, it is not a large community.

11 Blenkinsopp (1977), p. 103, has a similar point.

12 Blenkinsopp (1977), ch. 5, suggests parallel collections. The Deuteronomic authors put together the prophecies, which gave the prophetic corpus considerable prestige. This theory leaves many loose ends.

13 Carroll (1979) offers an explanation based upon the theory of cognitive dissonance. Blenkinsopp (1977), p. 8: 'Clerical scribalism met the prophetic claim not by confrontation but by assimilation and redefinition, seeking to bring prophecy within its own institutional grid.' This implies a fundamental distinction between prophecy and law, as law was later understood. The unanswered question is whether the Torah scribes and the prophets were originally part of the same tradition. Echoes of conflicts like this can be seen in the Pentateuch; the priests challenge the Mosaic monopoly (Num. 12); the congregation, led by a Levite and men of Reuben, accuse Moses of making himself a prince, when all the congregation are holy (Num. 16.3, 13). Are these aspects of the Deuteronomic development, with its twin concerns of democratizing the older royal theology, and exalting Moses? Ginzberg (1909), vol. vi, p. 298, describes the tradition, based on Num. 16, that the condemned, as they went down into the earth, cried 'Moses is the rightful *king* and true prophet, Aaron the legitimate High Priest, and Torah has been given by God.' One wonders what prompted this confession!

14 Isa. 8.16; Jer. 36.22; Zech. 1.4.

15 Barr (1959), p. 7.

16 The views of prophecy in Deuteronomy itself are more complex than in the histories; they point to a time when prophecy was no longer thought a good thing. The criterion for prophecy became orthodoxy, not fulfilment, suggesting that by the time of Deuteronomy as we know it, the Deuteronomists had changed their status in society. The fulfilment of prophecy has served to establish their case, but when they found themselves the dominant group, and the butt of criticism from such prophets as the Third Isaiah, then prophecy had to be redefined.

17 Rowley (1963), p. 191ff. Such a concern would have been more consistent on the part of those who wrote, e.g., Lam. 4.20.

18 Clements (1965a), p. 309. Instead of proclaiming the sacral foundation of the Israelite state, in terms of the election of its monarchy, the Deuteronomists declared that what Yahweh had elected was the *people* for his own possession.

19 Centralization is a key concept. Some have thought it a late addition to the scheme, e.g. Childs (1979), von Rad (1966b), Welch (1925); others see it as an expression of the desire to purify worship and therefore fundamental (Mayes 1979).

20 Báchli (1962) argued that the Jerusalem monarchy must have been responsible for the functions which Deuteronomy attributes to Moses. He also sees a fusion of Moses/Sinai and David/Zion traditions. Childs (1974) considers Exod. 19.6 a Deuteronomic passage, i.e. more evidence for transformation. The people became a kingdom of priests. This must be read in the light of Isa. 61.15ff, a mutilated text, in which the reward for certain changes of attitude on the part of the accused is that they will be *recognized as priests of the Lord*. We can only assume that the title was claimed by the accused, but not recognized by the aggrieved. The priestly role will have been another of the king's functions transferred to the people, or to the later High Priests; see Mettinger (1982), p. 72 and notes: 'If we find close similarities in the role of the king in the Babylonian Akitu festival and that of the priest on the Day of Atonement, the intermediary is probably to be found in the role of the *king* in the pre-exilic Israelite autumn festival.'

21 2 Kings 24.3; also n5 above.

22 Childs (1979), p. 213: 'The full significance of Moses' "explaining" (*bē'ēr*) the law has been long debated, but it would seem apparent that his task involved more than simply imparting information which had hitherto been only privy to Moses.' This reminds one of the rewriting of history which has occurred so many times in the twentieth century with the advent of new regimes.

23 This is the conclusion we are invited to draw from the histories.

24 The problem of the choice of Moses is complex. He was not a key figure in the pre-exilic south (Widengren 1970). Noth (1960) suggested he was a late arrival in the Pentateuch. The other ancient worthies in Ezek. 14.14 (Noah, Daniel and Job) *do* each have a work ascribed to them.

25 Mayes (1979), p. 58.

26 Rowland (1982), pp. 52ff; 84ff; Chernus 1982. Cf. Asc. Isa. 2.8, 3.9, where the Mosaic tradition is contrasted with the visionary.

27 Nicholson (1973), pp. 67ff, argued for an ancient theophany, but 'there can be no doubt that this passage as we now have it describes a rite of covenant ratification' (p. 67).

28 There are two possible explanations of the stance of the Deuteronomists with regard to Exod. 24.9–11. Either the ancient theophany was a covenant ceremony and the Deuteronomists wanted to extract the covenant idea but not the setting, *or* the ancient theophany was not the description of a covenant ceremony, and someone other than the Deuteronomists has tried to graft covenant ideas onto this ancient ceremony. The former suggests that the Deuteronomists wanted to separate themselves from certain ancient ways, the latter that the ancient ways were joined to the newer scheme. The former is the more likely, given the other evidence at our disposal.

29 The prescriptions in Deut. 13 and Deut. 18 are not easy to reconcile.

30 Von Rad (1966b) is incorrect at this point.

31 Mettinger (1982).

32 The LXX of Hosea 13.4 is longer than the MT. The Greek says that the Lord as the creator formed the host of heaven but did not teach that they were to be followed, and then, with the Hebrew, 'From the land of Egypt you knew no God but me, and besides me there is no saviour.'

33 Clines (1978), p. 100: 'In the speeches of Deuteronomy Israel hears a parenesis without which the permissions of Persian kings may well have been a dead letter.' The same has been said of the Second Isaiah for a long time. The ancient ways of the heavenly hosts survived the exile of Jerusalem, and remained in perpetual conflict with those who developed the legalism of the new community. It was these people who retained the older myth (as I shall suggest in ch. 8) who found their voice in Isa. 63.16, the people whom Israel did not acknowledge.

34 Stone (1976).

35 Nicholson (1967), p. 45: 'It may be concluded that the form in which Deuteronomy is cast derives from the cult, and follows the liturgical pattern of the festival of the renewal of the covenant.'

36 Eaton (1979) argues for a remarkable correspondence between Isa. 40ff and the tradition of the autumn festival in pre-exilic Jerusalem, and 'the coherence of the many units in an interlocking pattern descended from the festival' (p. 121)... 'The relating of the prophecies to a ritual tradition shows up the depth and range in their meaning which is missed by an interpretation restricted to the historical view' (p. 122).

37 Von Rad (1965a), pp. 36ff, favoured a Shechem festival, as did those who followed him, largely on the grounds that there was no cosmological aspect to Sinai, no enthronement of Yahweh. Whence, then, the later traditions about Moses? (see Meeks 1970). De Vaux (1969), p. 290 notes that Shechem is always 'discreetly veiled'.

38 Von Rad (1966a) was firmly convinced otherwise: 'Our contention that the Sinai tradition had its cultic setting in the ancient covenant festival at Shechem is as certain as such matters ever can be' (p. 38). Despite all his arguments, there was at least one tradition in which the Law did go forth from Zion; Isa. 2 says all nations go to Jerusalem to learn the law; Isa. 11 has a similar hope; Isa. 42.4 links the law to the Servant figure.

39 Mayes (1979), p. 64: 'It is not in fact until the stage of deuteronomistic editing of Deuteronomy that covenant thought is made explicit in the book.' For a very different view, Perlitt (1969); covenant theology was created by the Deuteronomists in the seventh and late sixth centuries.

40 The covenant we encounter elsewhere as the eternal covenant: see Murray (1982a).

41 Mowinckel (1927) proposed that the Jerusalem cult lay behind the ceremony. See also von Rad (1966a), pp. 225ff, where he links the 'testimonies' given to the king to the covenant.

42 McCarthy (1965), pp. 144ff; McCarthy (1972); Mayes (1979), pp. 69ff.

43 McCarthy (1972), p. 50.

44 Eaton (1979), p. 26: 'It is not clear just how these rites of the Davidic office fitted in with expressions of Yahweh's kingship.'

45 See Zech. 3.6ff; Job 1; Ps. 82; Isa. 14.

46 The best study of the relevant materials is still Wright (1962), although I cannot agree with his conclusions, namely that the *rib* pattern in Deuteronomy betrays its origin in the Mosaic covenant traditions, as distinct from the Davidic. The problem lies in the appeal to 'heaven and earth' which accompanies the *rib*. Wright accepts Mendenhall's conclusion that behind the Mosaic covenant lay a suzerainty treaty of the Hittite type, and continues: 'The sanctions of the treaties are purely religious, appeal being made to the gods of the contracting parties to serve as witnesses. Following the detailed listing of divine names, there appears the

summarizing formula, "the mountains, the rivers, the springs, the great sea, heaven and earth, the winds (and) clouds – let these be witness to this treaty and to this oath" – or the like. In this context heaven and earth are meant to refer to all the gods who have charge over the universe. When the treaty form was adopted to depict the meaning of God's election of Israel, this element of the treaty for obvious reasons had to be set aside or re-interpreted ... Only in the "later" poetic and hortatory contexts ... does the reference to the natural elements as treaty testators re-appear' (p. 45). 'One could affirm that Israel demythologised the meaning of the term "earth" in the covenant lawsuit to the extent that it no longer conveyed the notion of divine beings in charge of earth, as in the Hittite treaties ...' (p. 49). Quite so. But we have to ask if this was a gradual and natural development, or if it was the deliberate action of a particular group who *reused* the treaty terminology. If we look at the contexts of the various 'witness' passages in the Old Testament, they are significant. Mic. 6.2 has *mountains* (cf. 1 En. 28.6; Jer. 51.25), and foundations of the earth called to witness; Mic. 6.9ff deals with judgement, the assembly and the wisdom of Yahweh. The Hebrew is obscure: the apparatus of BH2 suggested that for *ūmī yᵉʿādāh ʿōd* we should read *ūmōʿēd hāʿīr*, a reconstruction based on the LXX which apparently read *ʿd* as *ʿr*. If this passage describes a *rīb* before the heavenly court, the state of the text would be explicable. Jer. 2.4ff says the heavens witness the apostasy; Ps. 50.4 appeals to heaven and earth before the judgement; Job 20.27 has heaven and earth witness against evil men; Deut. 4.26; 30.19; and 31.28 appeal to heaven and earth. All these are additions to Deuteronomy (Mayes [1979], p. 64). If covenant and *rīb* both appear in the later stages of the editing, may they not have belonged together elsewhere at an earlier stage?

47 McCarthy (1972), p. 5.
48 Weinfeld (1972).
49 Meeks (1970), pp. 370–1. Also Chernus (1982b), p. 10, shows that second–century *midrashim* about giving the Law on Sinai resemble the Merkabah texts. Israel at Sinai received royal crowns and garments. Schultz (1971) suggests that the later royal material and ascent legends associated with Moses derived directly from Mesopotamian royal rituals (p. 295), but I think transmission through the native cult of kingship more likely.
50 Childs (1974), p. 361.
51 Widengren (1970).
52 Bächli (1962).
53 J. A. Sanders (1972) is hardly correct; this cannot be attributed to the fact that the monarchy had detracted from the concept of Yahweh as king. He was very much Israel's king in the time of Isaiah (Isa. 6.5). If the royal decrees were transformed, we must seek another explanation. See Reviv (1982) for material attributed to Moses which reflects conditions under the monarchy; McCarthy (1982) shows that royal decrees in Chronicles had the force of divine law.
54 Blank (1940) argues that 'servant' was a technical term, meaning the spokesman or mouthpiece of his master. Could this be relevant to understanding the origin of apodictic law?
55 Mayes (1979), p. 75: 'The present context of these [apodictic prohibitive] laws is a covenant context, but from two points of view it is clear that this cannot be taken as the context of origin of the type of law which the prohibition represents. On the one hand such forms are to be found outside the Old Testament ... On the other, the Old Testament itself offers enough indication that the original concern of this type of law is not with the covenant relationship between Yahweh and Israel and that its original authority is not that of God. Even in Deuteronomy, apart from the Decalogue, the speaker addressing Israel is not Yahweh but Moses ... The content of this series of direct prohibitions is, however, such as to make it probable that the original context of their use is the extended family and the original authority behind them that of the elders of the semi-nomadic clan. Moreover, even

when the content of the prohibitions is theological, it frequently refers to God in the third person . . . , so presupposing a human authority on the basis of which the prohibition is made. However, as Gerstenberger has shown, the concern of the majority of these forms is with everyday life, and with cultic matters in so far as they impinged upon everyday life.'

56 Alt (1934, 1966).

57 Mayes (1979), p. 76: 'Apodictic law in general (as well as casuistic law) is *now* to be found in this cultic context. No matter what the particular place of origin of such examples of this law may be, it is now all understood to be divine law, the conditions of the covenant between Yahweh and Israel. In this respect Deuteronomy has a view of Israel's law in common with other collections in the Pentateuch. Clearly a transformation in understanding of the law has taken place. Its authority is no longer that of the clan elders, or of the elders sitting in judgement at the city gates; it is the authority of Yahweh declaring this law as the condition of his relationship with Israel.'

58 Mayes (1979), p. 59; also Mettinger (1982), pp. 67ff.

59 Eaton (1976), p. 106: 'The rooting of this Jewish tradition in Old Testament times is proved by the post-exilic Zech. 14.16ff where the theme of Yahweh's kingship, control of the waters and universal dominion are firmly attached to the keeping of the autumn festival in Jerusalem . . . for not only Zech. 14.16ff but also Psalms such as 29, 68, 84, 93 show Yahweh's kingship at Jerusalem as bound up with his mastery of the rain sources.' Also Patai (1939).

60 Mettinger (1982), p. 23; Nicholson (1967), p. 52.

61 Mayes (1979), p. 64: 'More recent study suggests . . . that holy war ideology or theology is a deuteronomic creation, and that this has been responsible for the schematization of older traditions dealing with Israel in the pre-monarchic period . . .; if this is correct the extent to which any background to the deuteronomic spirit of holy war may be found in older martial tradition is doubtful. The essential aspect of the holy war in Deuteronomy is the people Israel united in the camp under Yahweh in opposition to the foreign nations. This finds an adequate explanation against the background of the exclusiveness and intolerance of the Deuteronomic doctrine of Israel the elect people of God.'

62 The work of F. M. Cross, and especially as developed by his pupil P. D. Miller. See Miller (1973) for full text and bibliography.

63 Bentzen (1955) suggested that Dan. 7 was an eschatologizing of Ps. 2. The position is not without problems, but they are not so great as Casey (1979) implies. The issue is as always one of paucity of evidence. Given the lapse between Ps. 2 and Dan. 7, *any* similarity has to be explained, rather than demanding a one-to-one correspondence of the various elements.

64 Casey (1979).

65 The Holy Ones and the Son of Man in Dan. 7 are thought to be parallel to, or even replaced by, the wise and the Prince Michael in Dan. 12. Davies (1980), p. 43, suggested this was due to development within Daniel, and 'the lack of any inherited systematic doctrine of the eschaton'. It could, on the other hand, be two references within an already complex system, in which the Holy Ones were the wise who turn many to righteousness. That the wise are destined to shine like stars is another contact with the angel myth. The whole Danielic scheme *could* be a development in so far as it applies the old myth to a new situation. See also Collins (1977), pp. 136ff, who says of Dan. 12.3 that the righteous were to *become* angels. This may have been true of the individual righteous, but the weight of Old Testament evidence shows that as the *myth* developed, the angels became the righteous, and the righteous inherited the ancient angel imagery. Labuschagne (1974) argued for this development *from* angels to the holy people. The Blessing of Moses was a transformation of older theophany material. Yahweh does not shine forth at Sinai as in a theophany, but departs from Sinai on his way to Canaan. He is not accompanied by angels, but by his *people* who are called Holy Ones. The terms and motifs adapted from the word field of the theophany are given a new function.

66 1QM12 is the outstanding example. Osten–Sacken (1969) suggested that the heavenly warfare pattern may have developed from the 'Holy War' and the Day of Yahweh; Collins (1975b) argues for Iranian influence to explain the dualism. There may have been several influences which assisted with the development of the later ideas; what concerns me is their origin *within* Israel's own traditions.

67 Mettinger (1982), p. 77.

Covenant, the other dominant theme in Old Testament theology, is also *Deuteronomic* in the form in which it is used.

6

THE SECOND ISAIAH

Since Chapters 40—55 of Isaiah follow upon Chapters 1—39 we should expect to find some links between them. If the Second Isaiah was attached to the first by accident, the resulting corpus is no more than random juxtaposition. But the very power and clarity of the latter section, combined with its present anonymity, suggests that factors other than chance caused the works to be joined.

I have long thought that it is the Second Isaiah who holds the key to our understanding of the Old Testament. So much is crammed into these chapters, so many layers are apparent, so many images fused and re-fused that the mind behind them must have been a religious genius. Unfortunately, such genius is as disturbing as it is liberating, and the needs of ordinary mortals, and of the religious institutions which offer them order and security, can only be met by less exotic stuff. They may be influenced by the heady lines of a prophet, but Dostoievsky's Grand Inquisitor spoke for many when he justified the institutional aspects of religion. A nation of prophets all like the Second Isaiah, all going their own way, would have been impossible to order and to govern, let alone train in a particular tradition which was the institution's very *raison d'être*.

The Second Isaiah is the supreme challenge to Old Testament scholarship, standing as he does between the theology of history and the theology of creation, between prophecy and apocalyptic,[1] between the myths of Canaan and the most powerful assertions of monotheism in the Old Testament. We do not even know who wrote these chapters, and yet the vastly inferior contribution of the nearly contemporary Haggai, whose main preoccupation was the fabric fund of the new Temple, has survived complete with the prophet's name and genealogy, date, and the names of his addressees. The chapters of the Second Isaiah stand out like a brilliant flash which illuminates for one frustrating moment and then vanishes, leaving us to grope in the twilight of the restoration period. Occasionally we can make out a form in the shadows cast by the new light of the Law, and occasionally, too, we can make out a scrambled voice which is interpreted for us. Why? The Second Isaiah seems to have been the catalyst of the new age, but to have represented something which could not be absorbed by it.

If it is possible to distinguish several layers of interpretation and insertion in the writings of the First Isaiah,[2] and thus to conclude that these writings grew and flourished after the time of their originator, then a special case has to be made for the presence of the Second Isaiah, which is a major and self-contained

161

addition to the corpus. Perhaps it was the 'next stage' of the First Isaiah's line of thought, rather than an added insight to the original. Perhaps the 'former things' of the Second Isaiah were the prophecies of the First;[3] but if so, why were his hearers told to forget them (Is. 43.18)? Perhaps we must see these chapters as the completion of the First Isaiah's scheme, offering hope and forgiveness in addition to the original threat of judgement.[4] We simply do not know. All we have is the present shape of the book, and what has come to be called its 'canonical context'.[5] This is a factor which cannot be ignored. The suggestion that Chapters 36—39 were used to link the two prophets seems very reasonable,[6] and, if correct, suggests that the present book of Isaiah is a commentary on the death and rebirth of the nation. But we are also told that the loss of the historical context of the Second Isaiah has given the material an almost entirely theological shape,[7] and that 'the message of the Second Isaiah is not an interpretation of history as such'. These two positions demonstrate the impossible tension which exists with regard to the method and message of this prophet. Was the theology derived from history, Isaiah being a comment upon that history, or was the message not an interpretation of history as such? I shall adopt a position which involves an extension of both these to a point of possible convergence. The prophecies of the Second Isaiah were, I believe, an interpretation of the ancient cult myth, and it was the experience of the exile which prompted the reinterpretation in terms of actual historical events.[8] The message of the prophet was that the divine word, as depicted in the myths and rituals of the old cult, had been fulfilled in history. The First Isaiah had interpreted the events of his own time in terms of that myth; the Second Isaiah completed this interpretation by showing that the lesser deities, the sons of the gods and all that they represented, really had been defeated and judged. They had ceased to exist. The timeless quality of the Second Isaiah stems from the fact that his basic theme was a myth which entered the sphere of historical events, and left them again when its work was accomplished. This passage through reality effected a change in the myth itself, and the new insight into the old myth then took on the function of the older myth. It also took on the timeless anonymity which now characterizes these chapters, and enables them to speak to the individual human condition as much as to the wider affairs of nations.

The final defeat and destruction of the old gods, however, left several aspects of the original scheme adrift. The defeated beings had formerly borne the burden of the origin of evil, a necessary function in any theological scheme; they had been the opposing forces in the struggle to establish order in creation, and they had helped to establish Israel's identity vis-à-vis the other nations. All these structures had to be given new foundations. Ezekiel and Jeremiah taught personal responsibility, Gen. 2—3 made human disobedience the sin of Eden, and not an angelic revolt; creation was depicted as the ordered calm of Gen. 1, and not as a struggle against other forces; the chosen were defined as those who had experienced Egypt, those who had been purified by the exile, and certain national customs became important for defining the identity of Israel.

Bearing in mind that the change in historical circumstances will have modified the actual content and conclusions of the message, and that the First Isaiah's prophecy for a city under siege will have differed from that for a group about to repossess its former city (for I assume this to be the setting of the Second Isaiah), if there is any link between the two prophets it should be possible to discern a common ground underlying the actual prophecies. Suggestions that the basis for the Second Isaiah's thought is to be found in the concern for the remnant, or for 'salvation', are inadequate, since these things were his innovations, his own conclusions. Even though they seem prominent to us, they cannot be deemed the thought structure of his hearers. The process of teaching necessitates grafting innovations into the minds of the hearers, building upon what is already there. It is in the minds and expectations of his hearers that we must look for the substructure of the prophecies. The substructure of the First Isaiah was the angel myth, the myth of the royal rites and the psalms. This has to be the most likely background for the Second Isaiah also, and the point of his message might be better grasped if read in this context.

The problem addressed is that of the exiles after the destruction of Jerusalem. The canonical context alone suggests this. The Deuteronomic histories had offered one explanation of the disasters, and if that explanation had been universally accepted, this inquiry could proceed no further. But the Deuteronomic explanation (even assuming that the reform of Josiah was what the Deuteronomic historians imply it was) had not swept the field. Less than a quarter of a century separated that reform and the first disaster for Jerusalem. The flurry of contradictory ideas about the disaster which is apparent even in the surviving texts shows just how small was the effect of the new ideas. Jeremiah's vision of the two baskets of figs shows the first cracks in the scheme. The disaster had turned upon its head the Deuteronomists' view that obedience leads to possession of the land. That view showed that the current possessors of the land were the chosen ones, whereas the exiles wanted to learn that they were still the chosen. Ezekiel 33.23 is addressed to this situation, but in this case the argument concerned descent from Abraham, suggesting that this claim, too, was important to the exiles, but was not one which could be made by the non-exiles left behind (cf. Isa. 63.16).[9] Jer. 44 gives another explanation of the disaster; it had been caused by neglect of the ancient ways. The people left behind in the land were prepared to return to these ways in the hope of regaining prosperity.

There was also the question of personal responsibility, possibly a direct challenge to the Deuteronomists' views on inherited guilt as exemplified in 2 Kings 23.26ff. Both Jer. 31 and Ezek. 18 deal with this problem, and declare responsibility to lie with each individual. The preface to Deuteronomy itself, saying as it does that the generation which sinned would not inherit the land, but only their children, seems to be yet another attempt to answer the question 'Why did Jerusalem fall?' It tried to establish those with whom the future lay. What is conspicuously absent from all these explanations is any one which could have come from the erstwhile establishment in Jerusalem. Did the priesthood and the monarchy, with all their accumulated cultic paraphernalia, produce no explanation, and offer no reassessment of the situation? The clearest description of the disaster in terms of the old mythology is to be found in Lamentations, which describes Jerusalem's condition as rebellion against God (Lam. 1.18, 20; 3.42). The glory of Israel has been *cast down* from heaven to earth (Lam. 2.1) and the Lord has burned Jacob like a fire. The punishment is like living in the realms of the dead, imprisoned in chains (Lam. 3.6–7), two punishments allotted to the fallen angels. The afflicted believe that they have inherited the punishments incurred by their fathers (Lam. 5.7), and they express their hope in Elyon, exactly as Job is exhorted to do. It is interesting that these two attitudes are both challenged elsewhere; inherited guilt was challenged by Jeremiah and Ezekiel, and the declarations of Lam. 3.38–9 are very like the explanations of suffering which Job rejected. The kings of the earth and the inhabitants of the world did not believe it possible even to enter the gates of Jerusalem (Lam. 4.12), implying a pattern of ideas in which there was a role for the kings of the nations, and strict limits set upon their power. These were exemplified in the old myth. The most extraordinary passage of all is Lam. 4.14–15, rendered in the RSV:

> They wandered blind through the streets, so defiled with blood that none could touch their garments.
> 'Away! Unclean!' men cried at them; 'Away! away! Touch not!'
> So they became fugitives and wanderers; men said among the nations, 'They shall stay with us no longer.'

We are not told who were unclean, who were banished from the city and made wanderers, but in the LXX there is a clear indication of how that translator understood the text. The 'blind' ('*wrym*) are rendered ἐγρήγοροι, the word used in 1 Enoch for the Watchers.[10] There are several interesting ambiguities in the text as it stands, which is far too obscure to offer any translation with confidence. But, given the way in which the LXX understood the lines, and the context of the passage, with the Lord pouring out his hot anger and the kings of the earth amazed that a foe could enter Jerusalem, it is possible that we have in Lamentations a glimpse of the old ways. When the city fell, the old guardian deities were finally rejected.

If there is any significance in the canonical context of the Second Isaiah, we should expect to find in this second part of the Isaiah corpus some indications of the troubles which beset the newer theology in the period of transition. These changes must be viewed in the light of the Deuteronomic writings, since both arose in the same milieu and reflected the same crisis in Israel's development. The great difference between them was due to their difference of approach to the common task. The Second Isaiah was a poet and the Deuteronomists were not. Both reused the ancient cult, but, although the two works have much in common, the relationship between them cannot be understood without taking into account the Third Isaiah who uses the same imagery as the Second, but is bitterly opposed to a group who resemble closely the Deuteronomists. The movement which caught up the Second Isaiah and the Deuteronomists was not without its critics even in the time of the restoration, and the Third Isaiah spoke for these critics. Both the Second Isaiah and the Deuteronomists were concerned with the alteration of the old ways, and the writer of Enoch, a work which kept the imagery of the older ways, had bitter words for those who altered things after the exile. If the tradition represented in the Enochic writings traced its troubles to the time of the restoration, and the Deuteronomists, even in their carefully edited lines, have left evidence that their aim was to obliterate the tradition which has survived in the Enochic writings,[11] then the unambiguous statements of this other tradition must be taken into account in any reconstruction of the post-exilic situation. We must not treat it as a hypothesis, or the manifestation of a later prejudice. This other tradition was doing exactly what the Deuteronomists did, but they interpreted history differently. There is no question of right and wrong in interpretation of this kind; we have two points of view, and they must be given equal weight.

A reassessment of the Second Isaiah is no easy task, since all the arguments I wish to bring to the case are closely woven and interdependent. The picture must be built up by isolating several themes, and then reassembling, so that the superimpositions will show up the final pattern within the book. The Second Isaiah is poetry, and cannot be treated to rigorous or over-literal analysis. We must attempt to move with him, not sit in judgement upon the final form of the text.

'The Former Things'

The phrase occurs frequently in the Second Isaiah, and must have been central to his ideas. It has been much debated, and thought to refer to earlier events, or to earlier prophecies,[12] but it also makes excellent sense if we understand 'the former things' as the older mythology. The thrust of the prophet's argument is then that the older ways have fulfilled themselves; the pattern enacted in the older mythology had actually been realized in historical events, and the way forward was to leave the older ways behind. All but one of the references to the former things have a positive attitude towards them, and a distinct pattern of association emerges.

41.21 introduces the former things. The other gods are asked to recount the former things, and to predict the future as proof of their power. The conclusion is that they have no power.

165

42.8–9 says the former things have happened. The power of Yahweh is such that he knows the future and creates a new order.

43.9ff is very illuminating. It challenges other nations to demonstrate their power by showing the former things and bringing their *witnesses*. There is mockery – the blind and the deaf are clearly a reference to the '*rm* and *hršm*, who are heavenly creatures elsewhere [13]– and these other gods are challenged to defend themselves. We also discover that the mythological framework which encompasses these other beings includes Israel (cf. Deut. 32.8). The other nations have witnesses just as Israel does. Who or what these were we do not know, but Ps. 89.37 and Job 16.19 suggest a heavenly being of some sort.[14] The prophet contrasts the witnesses of the other nations and Yahweh's own witnesses who are his people and his Servant. Here we have his first democratizing of the old royal titles.[15] Whatever was meant by a witness/ servant, he/they (the problem of singular and plural servants in the Second Isaiah results from the process of democratizing and extending the royal titles) had a role in Israel which was paralleled in the other nations. The powerlessness of these witnesses is part of a complex declaration of monotheism.[16]

44.6–8 and 45.20–1 have the theme of the former things, but not the actual phrase. Both emphasize that power to know the future is proof of divinity.

46.8–10 demands that transgressors remember the former things. El issues the challenge; El has planned everything and his counsel will prevail.[17]

48.3–5 says the former things were declared by Yahweh long ago, and have happened. No credit can be given to other gods.

There is a pattern in these verses: the claims of the other gods are prominent, and the power of Yahweh is demonstrated both by the former things which actually happened, and by the new things which no one has predicted. The other gods had claimed to know the future but their time of glory had gone. Their role among the nations had a parallel in Israel, although we cannot determine exactly what this was. They had claimed to give salvation, but they were addressed as transgressors, and worshipped as wooden idols without knowledge. None could thwart the counsel of El. The picture we have is of a challenge in the heavenly court. The other beings have no power to oppose the power of El. The climax of two passages (Isa. 43.13; 46.9), and the emphasis elsewhere at Isa. 40.18 and 45.14, shows that the other great shift which formed the theology of the Second Isaiah was that Yahweh the Holy One of Israel was also El. Israel was therefore no longer at the mercy of contending angelic forces, of which her Yahweh was but one.[18] If Yahweh was El, the others were nothing.

In contrast to these passages we find one other, Isa. 43.16–19, which follows upon the court scene where the gods are declared to be nothing. Here, and only here, the prophet exhorts to forget the former things, and a whole new understanding of Yahweh is outlined.[19] Having been introduced as the Holy One, the creator of Israel and the King, he is then identified as the God of the Exodus, who tells his people to forget the former things. Why are the ancient titles from the Jerusalem cult here joined to the Exodus saga? It was a classic observation of Pentateuchal criticism that there were great blocks of tradition seamed together. The Exodus saga is joined to the saga of the patriarchs by the seaming in Exod. 3.13ff, where Yahweh is identified with the God of the patriarchs. The Second Isaiah does something similar here: the titles of the Jerusalem cult are joined to the tradition of the Exodus, and the new action of Yahweh is the new Exodus.[20] Thus the Exodus tradition is here grafted in to Isaiah's own tradition, and the former things, the ways of the old cult, are superseded.

The Names of God

Identifying El and Yahweh was not entailed in the fulfilling of the old myth. It was a simultaneous movement in the prophet's thought, which resulted in monotheism, a word which enjoys several meanings. For our purposes, monotheism means denying that other gods exist, for that is how I read Isa. 41.24. It may have been bound up with excessive patriotism,[21] but must be distinguished from the exclusive worship of one god amongst many, henotheism, which is the picture of Deut. 32.8. The Second Isaiah is always read as the great prophet of monotheism, with Yahweh the only God, and the heathen gods as nothing. Our custom at this point is to trace the effects of this insight into the theology of subsequent centuries, but in order to understand the context of the original insight, we must trace the theology back into the preceding centuries and confront the questions which present themselves. What was Yahweh before he was identified with El? One Holy One amongst many, the Holy One whose special concern was for Israel? What was El? A title, or simply a noun meaning god? In the Second Isaiah it seems to be the title, and therefore the name of the High God of Canaan. It is only in the post-exilic writings that we have an angelology developing, with patron angels for the various nations, but in the Second Isaiah and earlier texts we have assertions of superiority.[22] To what, or to whom? It must have been that Yahweh was deemed superior to other heavenly beings, yet these have been largely obliterated from our texts, and entirely obliterated from our way of reading them. Did the angels of the later apocalypses have their roots in a pre-exilic polytheism within Israel, as the age of the angel lists in the Similitudes would suggest?

The Second Isaiah makes frequent use of the name El. The only other book to do this is Job, and yet Job is a book which fits in to no known pattern of Old Testament ideas; it is prefaced by a dispute in the heavenly council where Yahweh is one amongst equals and accepts a wager, and the dialogues, as I shall show, make frequent and natural reference to the angel mythology. It used to be suggested that the use of El was a conscious archaizing on the part of the prophet, but now that El is no longer considered a sure sign of primitive material,[23] another explanation of the Second Isaiah's usage is demanded. The opening chapter is a complex argument from creation, which culminates in the assertion that Yahweh is El the Creator (Isa. 40.28). This stands as both preface and premise to the prophecies. We must therefore read the theology of creation and the identification of El and Yahweh as keys to understanding the prophet's thought. In our Old Testament there is no hostility to El as there is to Baal. Perhaps this is because Israel had a place for El in her tradition. It has been suggested that Yahweh took over the role of the creator which in the Ugaritic texts belonged to El.[24] If so, and if the fusion was not gradual but was effected by the inspiration of the Second Isaiah, we should expect to find a significant development in creation theology at about this time as a result of the Second Isaiah. There is insufficient material for certainty, but it is quite clear that there are two distinct attitudes to creation in the Old Testament, and that the ordered calm which is characteristic of Gen. 1 could be a late development. In the older view there is conflict with chaos and its dragon (Pss. 29, 74, 89; Isa. 51.10); when the Second Isaiah argues for the redemption of his people, he argues *from* a theology of creation through conflict, and not from any theology of history or from the ordered calm of Gen. 1. Thus this conflict theology was a *premise* upon which the prophecy was based, even though the movement of the prophet's thought led to this premise being abandoned. The picture of creation in Gen. 1 comes from a time after the Second Isaiah, and its form not only reflects his new insights, but also the concerns of the restored community. Thus the emphasis on a seven-day scheme and the sabbath, even though the divine activities are unevenly distributed, could indicate that another scheme was being adapted to a sabbath-centred system; the emphasis on the precise role of the heavenly bodies as the means of reckoning day and night could reflect the concern of Deuteronomy that the heavenly bodies were not to be worshipped; the statement that the sea monsters were created by God shows that they were no longer the symbols of chaos, but were under the power of the creator (cf. Job 40—41); the creation came about through a series of separations, the predominant preoccupation of the restored community. It is quite possible that the role of the supreme creator implicit in Gen. 1 was taken over late by Yahweh. Any speculation in this area must take into account the speeches of Yahweh to Job, where the basis of Yahweh's power over Job, and Job's inability to argue for what *should* have been his lot, both derive from the power of Yahweh as creator. These speeches (as I shall show in the chapter on Job) are offered as the answer to Job's problem which arises from monotheism, and which therefore can hardly have arisen before the time of the Second Isaiah. The problems of the book arise from the new theology, and the answer of Yahweh, significantly, derives from the new insights; this cannot be coincidence. If the older creation-and-conflict pattern was current as late as the exile, and so fundamental that the Second Isaiah could use it as the basis for his message of reconstruction, we have to bring to our reading of these texts the possibility that before this time there was not the monotheism such as we find in Gen. 1, and still tend to read into all the Old Testament texts.

Three very different studies from different eras and exemplifying different approaches all have broadly similar conclusions about the fusion of two divine names. We do not know that these names denoted one and the same deity before the fusion; it is possible that the fusion of names was in fact the fusion of *deities*, and that the compilations of the Pentateuch were more than the collection of various blocks of material from within one tradition. Eissfeldt's study of El and Yahweh[25] divides the various instances of the two names into three groups. There are texts which imply that El and Yahweh are separate gods, El being superior to Yahweh. All these texts are set within the angel mythology, e.g. Deut. 32.8–9; Ps. 82; Isa. 14.13; Ezek. 28. Then there are texts, all in the Second Isaiah, where Yahweh takes over the name of El, and finally there are texts, all of them presenting problems, where El and Yahweh are used as alternatives.[26] Alt's study[27] concluded that Yahweh and an older god were fused in the Pentateuch. The god of the fathers was identified with Yahweh the God of the Exodus at Exod. 3.13. Van Seters investigated the relationship of El and Yahweh,[28] especially the relative dating of the two names, and drew conclusions which, if correct, must radically alter our preception of Israel's development. He found good reasons for seeing the Genesis stories as late compositions in their present form and the use of El in them as reflecting the time and milieu *in which* they were written. The Second Isaiah does not use El as a noun when asserting that Yahweh is El; he identifies Yahweh with El, the Canaanite deity. Similar statements do not occur in earlier prophetic texts, suggesting that this fusion was a 'theological and prophetic concern of the exilic period'. Both the Second Isaiah and the pre-priestly edition of the Pentateuch identified El with Yahweh, and the reform of Deuteronomy is in itself further evidence that 'other' traditions existed even in the later years of the monarchy.[29] We tend to see these other traditions as pagan and quite incompatible with Israel's tradition, but it is not until the post-exilic period that we find a distinctly hostile attitude to a group who must have been indigenous worshippers of Yahweh. In the Ezra–Nehemiah accounts, this intolerance is deliberately based upon the ideals of the Deuteronomists (Ezra 6.21; 9.1). In view of the description of these years in the Enochic tradition, we are bound to ask how alien were the traditions and practices proscribed as Canaanite? The frequent observation that Deuteronomy sought to unify by imposing a common tradition may conceal a whole nest of problems if what they 'reformed' was formerly the legitimate cult of Jerusalem. The fusion of the various fragments was precipitated in the exile as the result of the proclamation that Yahweh was El. It must be relevant to Pentateuchal criticism that the Second Isaiah uses Exodus imagery but grafts it into an *older* scheme of angel mythology; that the traditions of desert and mountain are not joined until the post-exilic prayer of Ezra (Neh. 9.13–14), and that we read this as an *insertion* of the mountain material into the Exodus narrative, rather than, as in the Second Isaiah, a grafting of Exodus onto something older; that the old material used by Eissfeldt as evidence for there being two deities, El and Yahweh, includes Deut. 32.8–9, the only description of election in terms *other* than those of the Exodus. The newer Deuteronomic election theology which came to dominate the Old Testament expressed the fundamental idea in a new way.

The whole field of Pentateuchal study is now in a state of flux, with emphasis being placed more and more upon theological motives behind any changes and developments which can be detected. The tradition complexes were combined only in the exilic period;[30] the theology of the promises to the patriarchs was worked out during the exile,[31] using language reminiscent of the Second Isaiah[32] or language derived from earlier royal forms.[33] The recurring theme is Deuteronomic influence, although there is no agreement on the levels and stages at which this occurred. The pre-priestly edition of the Pentateuch is moving closer to the Deuteronomists;[34] perhaps there *was* no Pentateuch before the Deuteronomists.[35] If we have to find an exilic setting for the Pentateuch, and theological motives for the fusions and developments which occurred, any hypothesis must start from the creative genius of the Second Isaiah, and not from the texts of the Pentateuch themselves. The new ideas put forward by the prophet should become the starting point of Pentateuchal criticism, and effect a control upon otherwise limitless and subjective speculation. A hypothesis derived from the theology of the prophet should be tested against the Pentateuchal texts, even if that hypothesis could not have been derived *from* those texts. The evidence of the Second Isaiah is quite compatible with his having identified El and Yahweh, not only in the commonly accepted sense of having proclaimed monotheism, but also in the sense that he fused the theologies associated with each name. As a poet and prophet it is more likely that he proclaimed the crucial insight, than that he based his poetry and his vision of a new beginning upon an already established position, the theological compilation of the Pentateuch. Our problems arise because we read the Deuteronomic position as the norm; the Exodus saga is the basis *onto* which other traditions were attached, *into* which they were inserted. Salvation history is *the* theology of the Old Testament. But the Second Isaiah shows us another aspect of the movement of fusion. Exodus was grafted onto an older scheme; salvation history was derived from an older cult of royal wisdom. We have to ask how the Second Isaiah's fusion of El and Yahweh related to Deuteronomy's proclamation of Israel's God as One. How does Isaiah's singular and plural Servant figure relate to the democratized royal theology of Deuteronomy? How does his Abraham (Isa. 51.2), who symbolizes the exiles, relate to the Abraham of Genesis who carries the royal promises, and the patriarch who does not recognize the indigenous Yahweh worshippers (Isa. 63.16)? We have to consider the pre-priestly compiler of the Pentateuch, the Deuteronomists and the Second Isaiah as aspects of the one question. All addressed the same exilic situation, with the monarchy, the cult and the land all gone. Massive and simultaneous shifts created a new theology from the older materials. The monarchy was perpetuated in the people as a whole, and the older polytheism was superseded in a monotheism which met the needs of the heightened nationalism of the restored community.

The opening chapter reaches its climax at 40.27–8. The structure and movement of the passage show clearly how the fusion of the two deities was expressed and applied. Israel fears that its fate is hidden from Yahweh, but Yahweh, says the prophet, is the everlasting God, creator of the ends of the earth. This is the grounds for the people's hope. Was he reminding them of something they already knew, or was this identification of Yahweh and El the basis upon which the prophecy grows?

If we bear this in mind, the preceding verses can be read with a different emphasis, and with fewer problems. Verses 40.12–17 are a series of questions which have been variously analysed and labelled,[36] but an examination of the form of the questions shows that this in itself offers no solution to the problem of their intention and meaning. These verses do make excellent sense if they are read as a hymn of praise to the High God who rules the heavenly council and instructs the heavenly beings as the Great Holy One does in 1 Enoch. The series of questions is usually read as rhetorical: Who directed the spirit of Yahweh? Whom did he consult? and so forth. The answer, we assume, is that he consulted nobody. All the questions, however, are not similar. 40.12 asks who created the world. 40.15–17 declare that the nations are as nothing before him. 40.18 asks who is like *El*? If the answer to the questions of 40.12, 15–17 is also *El*, then we have here a series of questions about the power and role of El. Perhaps we should read 40.13–14 differently, assuming that the answer to these questions also is *El*. We should then have: 40.13, Who directed the spirit of Yahweh (perhaps the angel of Yahweh)? 40.14, Who taught him his knowledge, enlightened him and showed him the ways of justice? The answer to both these questions could also be *El*, giving us in these verses a picture of the old high God, distinguished from, and superior to, the Holy One of Israel. The second part of the chapter repeats the themes of power and might, and concludes, 'To whom will you compare me, that I should be like him?' (40.25). This verse is usually read as a challenge by the Holy One, asserting his incomparability, but the context invites another reading. Yahweh is being likened to El. 40.26 is in the third person and not the first, as we should expect if these were the words of the Holy One describing his own power. The verse actually describes El, the one to whom the Holy One cannot be compared. In this part of the poem, El and Yahweh are still distinct beings; El is the great creator and disposer of nations (40.23–4). The climax of the chapter comes in 40.27–8, where El is identified with Yahweh. This statement becomes the premise of the prophecies, and stands here as the high point of the first chapter.

In isolation, such a reading of this chapter would demand far more evidence to become acceptable. But we do not read this or any other text in isolation.[37] In the context of the prophecy it makes admirable sense, and in the context of the exile it also fits well with other developments which we know to have taken place.

Knowledge and Wisdom

If the theology of the Second Isaiah is a reworking of the older myth in the aftermath of the fall of Jerusalem, we should expect to find in it a significant place for knowledge and wisdom, which were major components of the older myth. A distinct pattern does emerge: the possession of wisdom was a criterion of divinity which manifested itself in the powers of creation and prediction; lack of wisdom was contrasted to the uniqueness of El/Yahweh; the wisdom of El was closely bound up with the role and definition of his Servant/witness; the doomed, Babylon and the transgressors had claimed wisdom; wisdom gave power over other rulers.

The first challenge to the other gods declares the scale of the creator's works and the insignificance of all else, and asks the source of wisdom which can topple the princes of the earth, predict the future and safeguard Israel (40.12ff). The thrust of this argument is the same as that of Job 38—9. The power of prediction is stressed, and the other gods are challenged, but they have no knowledge and are a delusion (41.26ff). The power over creation is linked to the power over future events, i.e. creation theology is the basis for the theology of history (42.5ff). The climax of the challenge to the nations and peoples is that Israel will be the witness and Servant to know and understand that 'I am he'. This enigmatic line seems to mean that Israel, as Servant and witness, will have knowledge of the true nature of its God, namely that Yahweh is El (43.10ff). Idolaters can have neither knowledge nor discernment (44.19). Power in creation is also power over wise men, and the ability to direct the course of earthly rulers. There is a similar association at 45.1–7, 12–23, where power in creation, power to create the host, and power over earthly rulers are linked. In the angel mythology, this was a natural association, since the earthly rulers and their heavenly counterparts were not distinguished. The diviners will be shown to be fools, and the wise men foolish, but the word of the Servant and the counsel of Yahweh's angels will prevail.[38] Yahweh did not create the earth a chaos; this implies that at this stage in his thought, the prophet no longer bases himself upon the struggle theology of creation. This stands in sharp contrast to 51.9, where the triumph over Rahab is a mighty act. We find a context for these challenges and polemics in 46.8ff. Counsel is again linked to prediction, and those challenged are the transgressors who, we may assume, have challenged the purposes of El. This is a passage which calls to mind the 'former things' and then declares that none can resist the plans of El. Babylon fell on account of her perverted wisdom and knowledge, because she thought that through them she could resist the counsel of God; her wisdom was sorcery, enchantment and astrology (47.10ff). A crucial passage is 53.11. Despite learned arguments to the contrary,[39] this passage deals with the *knowledge* of the servant figure. In

43.10, as in 9.6 and 11.2ff, knowledge was part of both the purpose and definition of servanthood. Why not here also? The righteous Servant would offer knowledge such as would contrast with the perverted and corrupted counsel of the fallen ones. A later development of this same idea underlies the Son of Man passages in the Similitudes (1 En. 49.1ff; 51.3ff; cf. Dan. 12.3).

The integration of creation, wisdom, knowledge, earthly rulers and heavenly hosts points to the angel mythology; but what is not clear is the exact role of creation theology in this scheme, since the Enochic literature does not deal with this aspect. There may well be allusions in the prophecies which we cannot appreciate because of this, just as, without the pattern of association derived from the Enochic literature, the scheme underlying Isaiah could not have been reconstructed even in part.

Since the Second Isaiah worked from the framework of the old mythology, we are able to place his references to wisdom and knowledge in some sort of context, albeit one not entirely known. The possession of knowledge was a sign of divinity even in the later Enochic material, and the sharing and perverting of this knowledge deemed to be revolt. The giving of knowledge to the servant figure shows that he was cast in the role of an unfallen son of God.[40] The wisdom which came through him was the source of life and renewal for the people and for the creation.

Words

There are several passages where a pattern of words suggests that another translation is possible. None of these examples is conclusive, but the pattern calls for comment, as it is unlikely to be coincidence. The coastlands (*'yym*) and 'peoples' (*l'mmym*) at Isa. 41.1 appear in the LXX as 'coastlands' and 'rulers'. The coastlands are commanded to be dumb, from *ḥrš*, a root with magical and wisdom associations (Isa. 3.3) and elsewhere used in word-play (Isa. 35.5–6). The people/rulers are told to 'change', but *ḥlp* can also mean renew or vanish. Since the coastlands are already suspected of being heavenly creatures,[41] and the 'peoples' were understood by the LXX as rulers, we have two significant groups being given commands as the preliminary to the judgement. The 'coastlands' tremble at the coming judgement, and are associated with idolatry (41.5); in parallel are the 'ends of the earth' (*qṣwt h'rṣ*), which will also bear other translations. The 'ends of the earth' are linked to the 'farthest corners' (41.9), apparently the same word (*'ṣyl*) which elsewhere denotes the elders and rulers of Israel (Exod. 24.9–11) who stood before the throne of God. This sequence of equivalents is startling. 'Peoples' (LXX 'rulers') are linked to 'coastlands', which are linked to the 'ends of the earth', which are linked to the 'farthest corners', which in Exod. 24.9 are the 'rulers' of Israel. Such dovetailing demands explanation. The simplest would be that all these words had another meaning, which must be deduced from their having parallels in the 'enemies of God' (Isa. 58.19) and the 'gods of the earth' (Zeph. 2.11), and from their being rendered in the old translations as 'demons'. If these words represent heavenly and hostile figures of some sort, Isa. 41.8–9 takes on a very different aspect. Israel, the Servant, is taken from the power of these beings, chosen, and not cast off, clear parallels to the fragments we have of the old mythology in Deut. 32.8 and Exod. 24.9–11. Israel was secure on the holy mountain; the Servant would not be cast off (cf. Isa. 14, Ezek. 28). The whole of Isa. 41 is based upon these themes, with the old gods judged, and Israel reassured. We find echoes of the old triumph songs such as Ps. 46 in Isa. 41.11, 13, as the pagan gods tremble at the foot of the holy mountain. The 'coastlands' wait for the Servant's Law (Isa. 42.4) and the Servant addresses the coastlands (Isa. 49.1). What could this mean if the word really was the 'coastlands'? Is it not more likely that we have here an antecedent of the Son-of-Man-in-judgement passages in the Similitudes?

The 'blind', the 'lame', the 'deaf' and the 'dumb' are another cluster of words which invite investigation. They have already been noted in the context of Isa. 35,[42] where the prophet uses the names of the gods as satire upon them. In Isa. 42.18ff we find the 'deaf' and the 'blind' as part of the description of the Servant. Although these passages have been dignified by centuries of exposition, as 'blind and deaf' the words make no sense. If, however, the 'blind' are the 'watchers' and the 'deaf' those with supernatural or magical power of some sort, Isa. 42.18ff is addressed to the discredited and defeated heavenly creatures who are shown the superiority of the son/servant figure – another element of the Similitudes, where the defeated have to acknowledge the Son of Man (1 En. 62). The passage then reads, 'Hear, you *deaf*, look, you *blind*, there is no one *blind* but my Servant, none *deaf* like the angel I send'; where 'deaf' and 'blind' each refer to a heavenly being whose nature we can no longer determine. 'There is no *heavenly figure* like Meshullam (another unknown word), there is no heavenly figure like the Servant of Yahweh'. This is a triumph passage, exactly similar to 42.8ff, where, again, it is the 'blind' and the 'deaf' who have to recognize the Servant.[43]

The Heavenly Court

There are several trial scenes set in the heavenly court on the holy mountain (Isa. 41.21ff; 43.8ff). Nations have brought their witnesses, Israel is Yahweh's witness and Servant, royal titles here applied to the people as a whole, showing that the prophet like the Deuteronomists democratized the royal theology. The people also had the royal gift of wisdom which enabled them to discern that there was no other El but Yahweh. Two major shifts occur simultaneously in a way that is possible in poetry, but not so neatly possible in the more stately progress of theological explanations. The people assume the royal role, and Yahweh is identified with El so that the other deities, amongst whom Yahweh had previously been *primus inter pares* (Ps. 89.7; Job 1.6), could be declared non-existent. This double shift answered the two questions raised by the triumph of

Babylon over Jerusalem and the demise of the monarchy, in the minds of those whose cult myth knew a divine king and a Holy One who triumphed over the kings and angels of other nations. When the role of the monarch was transferred to the people, and the defeat of Jerusalem had been seen as the fulfilment of the ancient royal rites, the defeat of the alien powers followed in history as it had done in the myth. The guarantee of this was the fusion of Yahweh, the Holy One of Israel, with El, the High God, and it was the gift of wisdom which enabled the people to see this new truth. The changes, however, were only achieved at considerable cost to the system, for the prophet cast his theology in the form of a trial of gods who were shown to be non-existent. This shows that the inner movement of his thought was such that it outgrew its own mould. In order to understand him, we must look for a conclusion which grows from the earlier premises, but moves beyond them. Once the ancient gods were declared not to exist, their role as the source of evil was gone, and the foundation of the dependent theological system was destroyed. The prophet was aware of this problem; he portrayed Yahweh as the source of both light and darkness, weal and woe (Isa. 45.7). The vacuum was filled by a new teaching that sin was the transgression of the Law, and the breaking of any one of the elaborate commandments which undergirded the rituals of the second Temple. The influence and role of the ancient angels survived in the doctrine of the two 'yetzers', a relic of the rival influences of good and evil angels.[44] It also appears in the demon-possession depicted so often in Mark's Gospel. Isaiah made a leap of faith, and left to others the problems of detail. To the priests he bequeathed a heap of cultic rubble, and to the scribes the task of rewriting, in which they were almost completely successful.

If, as Eaton has suggested, the whole of the prophecy is based upon the pattern of the old cult,[45] we should perhaps read the opening verses differently. Jerusalem is told that her ṣb' is over (Isa. 40.2). This word can mean 'army', 'warfare', or the 'host' of heaven (1 Kings 22.19; Isa. 24.21; Ps. 103.21; 148.2). Here it is usually read as 'hard service, bondage' (cf. LXX ταπείνωσις, 'humiliation'); but perhaps these opening lines describe the end of the heavenly host, which is the theme of the prophecy. The host has been defeated because the punishment of Israel has been accepted (nrṣh 'wnh). The sequence reflects the royal rites; in the fourth Servant Song it is the suffering and humiliation of the figure that leads to his triumph which his enemies had not expected (Isa. 52.14; 53.12). There is a similar pattern in Isa. 45.20ff. Those without knowledge are invited to present their case, and to see that there is no God but El;[46] but the relevance of this to the royal pattern does not become clear until we see the way in which this passage was used by the early Christians. Isa. 45.23 is quoted in Rom. 14.11, but also in Phil. 2.10–11, where it is the climax of a triumph hymn, thought to be pre-Pauline. The servant figure humiliates himself to the point of death, and *therefore* is exalted to receive universal homage. The Christology of the hymn is popularly explained as derived from Gen. 2—3, but a simpler explanation is to seek its roots in the royal myth, where the king did not grasp at equality with God (cf. Isa. 14), was a servant, was humbled, and then exalted.[47] Those who acknowledged the exalted Jesus were more than human, as the triumph over the 'ends of the earth' in Isa. 45.22 would also suggest. This suggests that those who used this passage in Isaiah as part of an early Christian hymn must have known of *this meaning* in Isaiah's prophecy. These were the people *to whose faith Paul was converted*, and they were in all probability not Jews in the strict sense of that word, but rather the heirs to the older tradition, with roots in the royal cult, and a deep hostility to post-exilic innovations.[48]

Creation and Exodus themes

Throughout the Second Isaiah there is great emphasis on divine power in creation. It is a premise on which the prophet builds; there are no arguments to demonstrate that God is the creator, in the way that there are arguments to demonstrate the powerlessness of the other gods. Von Rad has argued that this is because creation theology was not important to the prophet; all his references were subordinate to his theology of redemption. He found it astonishing to see the powerful effect of harmonizing soteriology and creation theology. The reference to Rahab in Isa. 51.9 was evidence that this doctrine of creation was fully absorbed into soteriology, and so on.[49] Now these are valid observations within a certain view of the development of Old Testament thought, but outside that scheme and its presuppositions they are less convincing. If the redemption theme was only expressed by means of the Exodus stories, then the Second Isaiah could have been the one who brought together the themes of redemption and creation. But redemption had been depicted in other ways too, for example in the royal theology (Lam. 4.20; Pss. 18; 72; 118; 132; 144), where it is inextricably bound up with a creation theology. There was a similar creation theology assumed by the prophet, but he accepted it as a premise, and built upon it without comment. Power in creation is the basis for the redemption hope (Isa. 40.27); power in creation is the basis for confounding the wise men and restoring Jerusalem (Isa. 44.24); power in creation is the basis of the Holy One's ability to use Cyrus (?) for freeing the exiles and rebuilding the city (Isa. 45.12).

Conspicuously absent from the Second Isaiah is any idea of the Deuteronomic theology of history, or of Yahweh having acted in the past for the benefit of the elect by intervening in the affairs of kings and nations.[50] Much emphasis has been placed on his use of Exodus typology, which, it is argued, he eschatologized: 'It is clear that Second Isaiah's eschatological perspective is profoundly shaped by the main outline of Israel's *Heilsgeschichte* ... The Second Isaiah knew a historical tradition which reached back before the patriarchal period to the Creation.'[51] If this is so, it is remarkable that he has no evaluation of the period of the monarchy, no theology derived from the immediate past. He shows no knowledge of the theology of the Deuteronomic historians. Granted that their pessimism was inappropriate to his theme, what evidence is there that he used the fundamental theme of release from Egypt?

The Exodus theme does occur throughout, but always transformed, always 'eschatologized'. Such a description is misleading, because it is the manner and direction of the transformation which gives the clearest indication of its purpose. To say that a theme was eschatologized describes a process, but does not explain it. Here again, a certain pattern emerges. The way in the wilderness is formed by an upheaval in creation (Isa. 40.3–5); the desert will become fertile and give water to the thirsty (Isa. 41.17–20); the blind will be led in a new way (Isa. 42.14–16); Israel is created, named and redeemed, passing through waters and rivers, but also through 'fires' (Isa. 43.1–3); Babylon will not hold the chosen, whose Holy One will make a way in the sea and defeat chariots and warriors, making the desert fertile and receiving homage from the mysterious creatures which were probably demon figures (Isa. 43.14–21); Israel is redeemed and released from Babylon, but there is a warning of *judgement* on the wicked (Isa. 48.20–2); the exodus is fused with release from prison and darkness (Isa. 49.8–12). The defeat of Rahab the ancient chaos dragon is linked to the Exodus release (Isa. 51.9–10); the people will depart bearing the holy vessels, but not in haste as in the Exodus from Egypt (Isa. 52.11–12); creation will once again flourish after the release of God's people (Isa. 55.12–13). In most of these passages, the Exodus theme is joined to pictures of a transformed creation which is not part of the Pentateuchal accounts. Was this eschatologizing, or was the Exodus theme being joined to another pattern of ideas which described a release? The first Isaiah gives ample evidence for a belief in judgement followed by fertility and the renewal of creation, possibly derived from the autumn festival whose themes also shaped Zech. 14 and 1 En. 10. The Second Isaiah describes the release from angelic bondage in the older mythology *in terms of the Exodus*. Hence the eschatological aspects, and the fertility and judgement passages. Thus the prophet is not fusing creation and Exodus theologies, nor is he absorbing creation theology in his soteriology. He is showing how the cult myth was fulfilled in historical events. The final outcome of the old myth was the basis for his predicting release, but it was described as a new Exodus embellished with the eschatological motifs of the older myth. In Ps. 89 the quelling of the waters and the smiting of Rahab are joined by a process of simultaneous symbolism to the superiority of Yahweh over the heavenly beings and the forces of nature. The structure of the Psalm shows that the heavenly triumph was the counterpart, and therefore the guarantee, of the supremacy and power of the Davidic king. In other words, the imagery of triumph over waters and victory over enemies belongs to the royal cult. This can be seen most clearly in the use and reuse of old material in Exod. 15, the Song of the Sea.

Exod. 15.1–18 is a complex and obscure piece of poetry, about which scholars have not even begun to agree. The following points from the debate do, however, seem relevant to my arguments for the shape of the Second Isaiah. The poem is a triumph song, singing of the power of Yahweh who has no equal among the gods (Exod. 15.11). The MT and the LXX differ: the Greek has gods and holy ones, the Hebrew has only the gods. The discrepancy between Greek and Hebrew over this significant word gives a possible context for the poem immediately. Form critics have reached no agreement about the passage,[52] since the criterion for placing Hebrew poetry is its form and function within the tradition, and with this passage that question is wide open.[53] The sea triumph is here used to describe the fate of Pharaoh, but the triumph ends upon the holy mountain (Exod. 15.17), presupposing the Jerusalem tradition of the kingship of Yahweh.[54] Despite its present context, neither Moses nor his feats are mentioned, Israel is passive, and the perspective of the poem is cosmic, with events of earth and heaven seen in parallel. Although now attributed to Moses, one wonders if this might not once have been a song of the king, given to Moses as were the royal laws. The earth swallows the enemies, Yahweh consumes the enemies like stubble, foreign rulers watch the triumph in terror. It is possible that we have in Exod. 15 another example of Exodus imagery being grafted onto that of the older cult, just as the Second Isaiah fused water, dragon and Exodus at Isa. 51.9–10.

Conclusions

If the Second Isaiah's vision was based upon this massive transformation and fusion, it will never be possible to penetrate his inspiration with certainty. Nor must we presume to say which motifs dominated his thought. The frequency with which he refers to particular ideas may indicate that these were his points of growth, not that these were the dominant features of his prophecy. Thus my emphasis upon the angel figures is to be taken as showing that this was a major point of growth within the ancient tradition. His use of the Exodus pattern may be another such innovation, frequently used because it was a point of growth. We cannot therefore conclude that creation theology was not important for the prophet because it is *mentioned* less frequently than redemption.

After his time there was a parting of the ways; his final message was based on the supreme power of the creator which could not be challenged. The gods and powers who had been the basis of the older cult were declared to be non-existent. Thus the momentum of his thought carried him beyond his own basic mythology, and the supreme power of El/Yahweh became the basis of the future hope. The writers who stood in the tradition of the restored community altered and re-expressed in the light of the new insights. Thus Genesis does not allow the political significance of the host, and the stars become only timekeepers. The dragons become a part of the created order, not its opponents; thus the whole process of creation was expressed as a projection of the world-view of the new community.

But the prophet's judgement upon the angels has left its mark not only on the text of the Old Testament, but also on the way that we read it. K. I. Johannesen, for example, writing upon myth, is quoted as saying:

> The presuppositions of mythopoesis were not really present within the framework of Israelite Yahwism ... Moreover, the belief in Yahweh as the only real God in Israel was a factor most unfavourable to the assimilation or the fresh production of myths. Myths prefer to involve several gods ... Myths lack their essential framework in Israel.[55]

Again, H. Ringgren says:

> But even if the existence of demons is never denied in principle, they are still basically alien to genuine Yahwism ... The conviction that everything, both good and bad, comes from Yahweh actually made belief in demons superfluous.[56]

Both these writers (and they are but two of many) illustrate how the exact opposite of what I am proposing has been the accepted position of Old Testament interpretation for a long time. The belief in demons was not Yahwism; the production of myths was not Yahwism. An exactly opposite construction is possible upon the materials at our disposal. There *was* a mythology in which heavenly beings were held responsible for the origin of evil. A movement which sought to remove these beings also lost the benefit of their mythology and its explanation of evil. The accounts of the creation in Genesis lead several scholars to a similar conclusion.[57] They suggest that the first stage of the story is missing.

Deuteronomy has shown one aspect of the transformation, the Second Isaiah has shown another; but the case for this comprehensive reworking of the older traditions is considerably strengthened by the form of Job. The book deals with suffering, almost certainly the suffering of the exile, and with the destruction of the city. The name Yahweh is not in the poetry which forms the bulk of the book, but it occurs in the framework, and in the introduction to the speeches from the whirlwind which are thought to be a later addition to the book. Now the general tendency in the use of the divine name is in the opposite direction; the earlier writings use the name Yahweh, and the later ones drop it in favour of more general designations.[58] Job's question arises from the new problems of monotheism and the individual responsibility for evil which came in its wake. The answer given to Job is based on the power of Yahweh in creation, and yet the questions of Job had used other names for God. Could this indicate the date of the work? It suggests that creation theology had recently been recognized as an answer to the problem of suffering, an application of the insight of the Second Isaiah. Job had questioned suffering, the three friends had given answers, all of which he had rejected, and the whole of this stage of the discussion takes place in a world replete with angels. The balance of the book alters with the speeches from the whirlwind. The three friends are condemned, and Job's claim to wisdom, to know what *ought to have happened*, is rejected. He prospers when he accepts the explanation based upon the power of Yahweh in creation, a power expressed in terms of his knowledge. This is exactly the situation of the Second Isaiah. Job presents his case as a lawsuit, and, like Isaiah's defeated angels, he has to accept defeat because his wisdom is not capable of predicting what will happen, he cannot alter the course of the new creation.

The effects of the Second Isaiah's innovations were far-reaching: the Deuteronomists democratized the royal theology, and worked to its logical conclusion his insight that the suffering of the whole people had been but one stage in the working out of the royal theology in history. His fusion of Exodus and Zion traditions precipitated the extraordinary patchwork of temple and desert traditions which now characterizes the Pentateuch. When we contemplate all the problems of the Pentateuch and try to explain why it was thus assembled, we have to find a situation which would have compelled the fusion of separate, carefully guarded traditions. What force would have been great enough to exert such pressure on the natural jealousy and conservatism of those who transmit religious traditions? Necessity could have been the answer, but the sheer scale of the vision suggested that it originated with a poet and visionary, rather than with the careful deliberations of the various redactors, or even authors, of the Pentateuch.

Since so many of the prophet's ideas grow from the same complex of mythology, our understanding of his poetry can be greatly enriched by the addition, tentative though the reconstruction must be, of the mythology with which he worked. We can bring to his lines a little of the world in which and for which they were written, and we can appreciate the inexorable logic of his thought, which could realign ideas and create from their destruction.

NOTES

1 Hanson (1975).
2 As suggested by Blenkinsopp (1977); Carroll (1979); Childs (1979) and others.
3 Childs (1979), p. 329.
4 ibid, p. 325.
5 This is the overall theme of Childs (1979).
6 Ackroyd (1974), pp. 329ff.
7 Childs (1979), p. 326.
8 In this I follow Eaton (1979), except that I am prepared to make a reconstruction of the myth being reinterpreted, whereas he confined himself more strictly to the evidence, which in each case is only a secondary source. The Psalms are poetry, which allude to and comment upon the underlying myth, and the Second Isaiah is a reuse of that myth.
9 Theirs, perhaps, were the voices here, which claimed Yahweh as their father, but in this case the argument concerned descent from Abraham. Israel did not acknowledge them, and they bewailed the fact that their adversaries had trodden the sanctuary.
10 The verb *nā'ā*, here rendered 'wander', has a commoner meaning 'tremble, totter', giving a

possible 'The Watchers trembled in the streets, defiled/desecrated with blood so that none could touch their garments.' The second half of the verse is not easy, although the gist is clear enough. There are several problems to v. 15; the apparatus suggests removing a phrase from each of the first two lines, but even the remainder is obscure. If the subject of the passage is the Watchers, why do we find 'Turn aside polluted ones, turn aside and do not touch' (strike?). Why turn aside? Of the two verbs of 15b, *nā'ū* means 'tremble', 'totter', but *nāṣāh* has been variously read. Possibilities are *nāṣāh*, 'struggle', or *nāṣāh*, 'fall in ruins'. Both RSV and NEB read as *nāsū*, 'flee, escape'. If this verse deals with the fallen angels, we have 'Because they have angered/struggled/fallen', and 'because they have tottered/trembled, they shall no longer remain' (or is it 'quarrel' or 'stir up strife' – another possibility for *gūr?*).

11 See ch. 5.
12 See survey in Childs (1979), p. 328.
13 This mockery is a feature of Isaiah, and appears also in the Third Isaiah.
14 cf. also Isa. 33.8, where *'rm* is often emended to *'dm*, witnesses, even though *'rm*, 'watchers', makes better sense.
15 'Servant' was a royal title in the Psalms (Ps. 89.20, 26) with links to the title Son; also Ps. 36.1, David the Servant of Yahweh.
16 Eaton (1979), pp. 25ff.
17 The transgressors are commanded *hit'ōšāšū*, which is unknown, but possibly is changed from *bōš*, 'be shamed', reading *hitbōšāšū*.
18 Compare here the prologue to Job, where there are many sons of God, and Yahweh has no particular pre-eminence.
19 Bentzen (1948), pp. 183ff.
20 For an exactly opposite view, see Anderson (1962), p. 188: 'The "former things" ... are the events of Israel's *Heilsgeschichte*, pre-eminently the old Exodus.'
21 Morton Smith (1952), p. 136.
22 Labuschagne (1966).
23 Van Seters (1980).
24 Eissfeldt (1956).
25 Eissfeldt (1956).
26 Eissfeldt chose three: Josh. 22.22, a Deuteronomic passage, and therefore possibly edited; Ps. 104, which mentions El but once, and Yahweh throughout, and is therefore assumed to refer only to Yahweh; and Job, where El occurs in the dialogues along with Shaddai, Eloah and Elohim, and Yahweh in the rubrics and prose framework, implying that all refer to the same being. The first example is clearly dubious, the second is ambiguous, and the third could be explained as the fusion of deities.
27 Alt (1966).
28 Van Seters (1980).
29 Van Seters notes the anointing of sacred pillars (Gen. 28.18ff; 31.13, and especially the P text 35.14); yet these cultic actions do not come under the ban of the Deuteronomic reform because they are not related to foreign worship (p. 321).
30 Van Seters (1977), p. 18.
31 Van Seters, ibid.
32 Wagner (1977), p. 24.
33 Schmid (1977), p. 36.
34 Rendtorff (1977b) says the larger elements were combined by a final Priestly redactor; but Rendtorff (1977a), pp. 160ff, agrees with Schmid (1976), pp. 167ff, that the larger units were brought together under Deuteronomic influence. Rendtorff (1977c), p. 43, says of Van Seters (1975), Schmid (1976) and Rendtorff (1977): 'All three books have one thing in common: they reject the previous view of the Pentateuchal sources especially in regard to their dating. Van Seters and Schmid wish to move the "Yahwist" into the near vicinity of

the Deuteronomistic tradition, and to date it accordingly in the exilic or post-exilic period. I myself ... [believe] that there never was a "Yahwist" in the sense hitherto intended; ... I cannot assign any comprehensive redaction of the Pentateuch to the pre-Deuteronomic period.'

35 Rendtorff (1977c), p. 43, quoted in the last note.

36 Whybray (1971), pp. 4, 26ff.

37 Of interest here is H. Bloom (1983), p. 106: 'An empirical thinker when confronted by a text seeks a meaning. Something in him says: "If this is a complete and independent text, then it *has* a meaning." It saddens me to say that this apparently commonsense assumption is not true. Texts don't have meanings, except in their relations to other texts, so that there is something uneasily dialectical about literary meaning. A single text has only part of a meaning; it is in itself a synecdoche for a larger whole including other texts.' cf. Schmid (1977), p. 34, criticizing Rendtorff: 'In Rendtorff's statements on the patriarchal narratives virtually no texts from the rest of the O.T. are introduced into the interpretation'.

38 Why not angels? The Hebrew has *mal'ākāyw* and the LXX ἀγγέλων.

39 D. W. Thomas (1968).

40 This assumes that the Servant was originally a royal figure whose role was expanded by this prophet to include the whole people, just as the royal theology was democratized in Deuteronomy. Thus Isa. 51.4 refers to Yahweh, but the very similar Isa. 42.4 and 49.1 refer to the Servant, the old identification of the royal cult.

41 See ch. 4, n24.

42 See ch. 4, p. 133.

43 Nickelsburg (1972), p. 72, traces the later use of this same pattern in the intertestamental texts. 1 En. 62 clearly use this same idea. There are also references to the blind at Isa. 42.7, where they are bound and dwell in darkness, and Isa. 42.16, where they are led in a new way. There could be a reference here to Deuteronomy, *'ēlleh hadd'bārīm*. The LXX of Isa. 42.18ff has a different meaning, since the verse has several plurals, 'Who is blind but my servants ...?' The Targum is similar. Isa. 42.20 becomes, 'you see many things but do not observe them', implying that this is addressed to the blind and deaf of v. 18, a very different emphasis. Another passage relevant here is Isa. 50.4–5, also a Servant Song, impossible to translate from the present Hebrew, and very different in the Targum. The root *'yr* occurs twice, and *y'p*, commonly rendered 'be weary', has a homonym **y'p*, explained from Arabic as 'ascend', connected with which, presumably, is *tō'apōt*, occurring in the Balaam oracles (Num. 23.22; 24.8) to describe the horns of the wild ox, and in Ps. 95.4 as the peaks of the hills in the power of Yahweh, who is king above all the elohim. Since Isa. 50.4 has *l'wt*, also unknown, there is a large measure of obscurity affecting this passage. We do, however, have 'The Lord Yahweh has set me up ... to know ...', which is a recognizable pattern, especially in a mutilated text.

44 Sanders (1977), p. 273ff.

45 Eaton (1979).

46 The 'ends of the earth' can also be translated 'nothingness'.

47 For a typical explanation based on Gen. 2—3 see Dunn (1980), pp. 114ff. For the view sketched here see Murray (1985), pp. 275f. J. A. Sanders (1969) had already suggested that the rebellious angels in 1 Enoch are the best background for the hymn.

48 This anticipates my conclusions.

49 Von Rad (1966), *The theological problem of the doctrine of creation*. For a penetrating criticism of this type of approach, see Schillebeeckx (1980), pp. 516ff.

50 He does of course use the idea of fulfilment, but it is *what* is fulfilled which distinguished the Second Isaiah sharply from the Deuteronomists.

51 Anderson (1962), p. 184.

52 Childs (1974), p. 244.

53 ibid., p. 245: 'The fact that the sea was transmitted in the prose account with the wilderness tradition but in the poetic account with the Exodus, would point to the antiquity of the sea tradition. The common tradition preceded the period in which the prose tradition was transmitted within a larger traditional complex. In sum, Exod. 15 reflects a poetic tradition of the event at the sea, which, although as old as that in the J account, has been transmitted within the larger framework of the Exodus and conquest traditions ... the poetic tradition represents a parallel development with the prose account ...' cf. Clifford (1972), p. 141: 'The Patriarchs seem to be dealing with the Canaanite El, judging by the name of the deities they encounter. By the time of the earliest Israelite poetry ... [e.g. Exod. 15], Yahweh is described in Baal language... Yet the Sinai traditions, in the main, are El traditions.' Perhaps we may conclude that the Song of the Sea belonged to Yahweh's earlier role of creator, before the fusions effected by the Second Isaiah. In Exod. 15 we see Yahweh's triumph over the waters, and the subsequent triumph of his people before the terrified rulers of the nations. This is exactly what we find in Ps. 89, where the triumph of Yahweh over the waters is the counterpart/guarantee of the triumph of the king over his enemies. We have to ask when these two lines, triumph and Exodus, were first merged.

54 Mettinger (1982), pp. 27, 70, 75.

55 Quoted by Otzen (1980), p. 24.

56 Ringgren (1966), p. 103.

57 e.g. Thompson (1971), p. 203: 'The original version, the creation story proper ... must have had a more extended introduction, probably telling of the creation of the gods ...' Also Widengren (1958), p. 200; Cross (1973), p. 306: 'There is no account of primordial human rebellion in the Priestly strata of Gen. 1—11 ... P's summary statement referring to violence and corruption [in the Noah story] must presume a knowledge of concrete and colorful narratives of the corruption of creation.' We might also ask how the serpent came to be the most cunning evil creature assumed by Gen. 3; what type of creature is envisaged as *sin* waiting by the door, Gen. 4.7; what the strange name Yahweh Elohim signified in Gen. 2—3. Was it a construct relationship, Yahweh of the Elohim, or the characteristic name of the Deuteronomic writers, without the personal suffixes? See von Rad (1963 revised), p. 75, also BDB, p. 219: 'either [*Elohim*] inserted by R^P [the Priestly redactor] ... or [*Yahweh*] inserted by J into an older source' – which covers all possibilities without actually telling us anything.

58 BDB, p. 218: '[*Yahweh*] is the common divine name in pre-exilic writers, but in post-exilic writers gradually falls into disuse.'

7

THE ERA OF THE RESTORATION

It is now time to test the hypothesis on the literature of the restoration period. Even though well documented, there is still considerable disagreement and confusion about these years, due to the contradictory nature of the primary sources. Thus Haggai and Zechariah, two carefully dated and therefore contemporary works, give very differing pictures of the expectations of the time. Ezra, Nehemiah and Chronicles give another picture, and the Third Isaiah yet another. The work of those who have edited and compiled accounts of the time have only added to the problem, in so far as they have attempted to present a picture of harmony and consistency. The period was far from being one of harmony.[1] How such a wide variety of points of view was retained within the same body of writings is a question for a later period. At the moment we can only note that the one characteristic which the Third Isaiah, Haggai, Ezra, parts of Ezekiel and Zechariah have in common is a polemical tone. I propose to place a special emphasis on passages where conflict and disagreement are apparent, since only thus can we go behind the work of the editors.

The point of view from which we have become accustomed to study this period is that of those who edited and preserved the Old Testament. This bias has been compounded by the preferences of many modern expositors, especially Protestant, which have led to the work of the Chronicler and the Priestly writer being neglected in favour of the 'prophetic' religion, and the emphasis upon the Deuteronomists' salvation history.[2] Evidence from Elephantine, from the Samaritan tradition, and from the Pseudepigrapha has made it clear that the Old Testament gives but one view of the situation, and our own minds are predisposed in a certain direction from the moment we start to label and define what happened. The Samaritan schism, as we call it, describes a rift between Jerusalem and Samaria. The date is disputed,[3] but even the Jewish records of the restoration period show that it was the Jerusalem people who separated themselves from the people of the land of Palestine. The identity of these people is open to debate, but Josephus believed they were the Samaritans.[4] Whether or not he was correct, he presumably recorded the view held in his own time, which is in itself important evidence for the way the Samaritans were regarded by the people of Jerusalem. It would be fairer to the evidence to speak of a Jewish schism, but we have yet to read an account of the intertestamental period which regards the Jews as schismatics.

Students of the period are often preoccupied with the problems of its

184

chronology, at the expense of the problems which *were* the problems of the period. F. M. Cross said of the period:

> Little progress has been made in solving the hard problems of the history of the restoration since the assimilation of the new evidence of the Elephantine papyri published in 1911 ... the scholarly procedure has been to review the same body of evidence and arguments, and to come down boldly upon one of three dates for Ezra in relation to Nehemiah.[5]

This relationship is indeed a problem, but we also learn a great deal about the problem if we ask why the Samaritans considered Ezra such a great sinner because he altered the Law for polemical purposes;[6] why 1 Enoch 98.72 knows of only three leaders of the restoration, with either Ezra or Nehemiah missing (we cannot determine which with any confidence); why Ben Sira 49.13 mentions Nehemiah as the hero of the return and omits Ezra, or why there is a tradition recorded in 4 Ezra 14 that Ezra dictated all the Old Testament to his scribes, a tradition echoed in the Samaritan accounts of the period.[7] Cross makes an ingenious reconstruction of the High Priest lists for the fifth century, showing how gaps in the biblical evidence and the confusion in Josephus have had 'diabolical results for the history of the restoration', and concludes with a sketch of the period written entirely from the point of view of the Jerusalem community. He makes no mention of the theological and social problems which accompanied whatever did happen at this time. I would not deny that it is of interest to know the relative order of events in this period, but the major question must be how this muddle arose in the first place. Was it, perhaps, deliberate, that there was a period of silence between the time of Zerubbabel and Nehemiah?

This silence cannot be set in a proper context until certain other presuppositions are recognized. On the first page of a volume dealing with the theology of the period,[8] I found the statement that in 587 the *last Judaeans* were rudely expelled from their land. Similar ideas are apparent in many writings on this period; if we accept them, all the references in the intertestamental literature to an exile of several centuries' duration must refer to a group left in Babylon.[9] If, on the other hand, all the people of Judah were not removed, there are other possibilities for talk of exile. Another group might have considered themselves cut off from Jerusalem, equally in exile. The same author continues with a crucial question: How was it that Israel's faith was transformed more dramatically in the twenty years between 600 and 580 than in the two centuries between 1000 and 800? Twenty years is perhaps too short a span, but one or two generations certainly did see an enormous change. The reason for this change was not, I suspect, just the fall of Jerusalem. Yahwism had lost its shrines before. Samaria had gone, and so had Shiloh. In each case there had been others who saw in the disaster the hand of the Lord punishing wickedness in others. The four centuries of Temple and monarchy had seen many disasters in war, and there must have been incredible challenges to the faith of ordinary folk. These are unrecorded, because they did not challenge the position and the security of those whose records we possess. In 597–586 it was different; this time it was the establishment in Jerusalem, those writing the theology, the priests and the princes, who found themselves on the receiving end of a disaster. The poor of the land were left, apparently the rightful heirs to the land, since possession of the land was a sign of the Lord's favour. It was this situation which caused the radical restatement of the theology. The exilic developments were designed to show that those who had been the élite in Jerusalem were still the chosen people. The great unanswered question of both exile and restoration is what all the other people of Palestine thought of the changes.

Two internal developments were responsible for the return to Jerusalem: the vision of the Second Isaiah moved the people to return, and the Deuteronomists provided a blueprint for the new society and the possession of the land. Troubles arose when this new form of Yahwism returned to Yahweh's ancient land. We know that the innovations of the Deuteronomists had not been accepted by those left behind after the deportations.[10] Ordinary folk had returned to the ancient ways and resumed worship of the queen of heaven. The arguments of the reformers were cleverly inverted; it was the changes, said the people left in the land, which had caused the disaster. We have to imagine the impact of a new form of those changes returning from a foreign land, financed by foreign money and brought by those who thought themselves the sole heirs. They had debated who were the chosen ones, those in Babylon or those in Judah. If obedience to the Law was rewarded by possession of the land, then the poor remnant were the chosen. Jeremiah's vision of the two baskets of figs shows that it was necessary to make clear that, despite appearances to the contrary, the good figs were those in exile. What is not recorded, at any rate in the Old Testament, is what the bad figs felt about that judgement. Whoever compiled and edited the prophecies of Jeremiah promised the 'other' people a judgement in Egypt. If Nicholson is correct in seeing these compilers as the Deuteronomists' next of kin,[11] we have a further indication of the nature of the division within the restored community. We do not know the obverse of the idea of the remnant, the chosen few who would form the basis of the great new age. Outsiders might well have thought that it was religious exclusivism masquerading as piety.

There were also the practical problems of the repossession. The history of our own times illustrates vividly what can happen when exiles return, backed by the money of a super-power, to take possession of their holy land.[12] The Samaritan tradition says that people of northern stock moved south after the fall of Jerusalem to occupy the city and the vacant lands. The area around Jerusalem was administered from Samaria, because the returning exiles had to present their letters there. We may also assume that many of the people who had been left in the south were, by the time of the return, oriented towards the north.[13] The area in question is very small;[14] there could have been intermarriage, and, apart from the writers of Kings, nobody seems conscious of a great rift between north and south, and the impurity of the north.[15] Coggins reaches a broadly similar conclusion, but he traces the change in attitude to the time and place of the exile in Babylon:

> Deutero-Isaiah ... knew and alluded to a wide variety of sacral traditions in his people's history ... yet his theological application of them is confined to the community exiled in Babylon ... It is often maintained that Deutero-Isaiah's vision was a larger one than that of Ezekiel, but found little response in post-exilic Judaism; in this respect [i.e. in his use of older traditions] the reverse is true, and it was the more limited view of Deutero-Isaiah, applying the promises to those in Babylon, which came to prevail. The status both of the northerners and of those who had remained in Judah during the exile came thus to be lowered. Indeed, as we shall see, these two groups came to be identified with one another, and both would be dismissed as no part of the true people of God.[16]

When the exiles returned, it was a time of divided loyalties. The new ideas from Babylon found their opponents formed from two strata of tradition. The southern restoration involved the rejection of the people of the north,[17] and the rejection of certain elements in the south who retained links with the temple cult. They kept alive the older myths of Jerusalem. The rejection of both these groups becomes extremely important when we come to try to understand the patterns which emerge in the intertestamental literature. In 1 Enoch and the Testaments of the Twelve Patriarchs there is a curious mixture of pro-northern and old Jerusalem material[18] which cannot be explained with an over-simple opponents-of-the-Jerusalem-Temple theory for the origin of the sectarian groups.

Ezra 2.28 and 2.70 tell of exiles who returned and resettled in the towns of their origin. What happened to those who returned to Bethel, a northern shrine? It is not possible to date this list in Ezra with any certainty, but all this means is that we cannot date the question it poses. The question remains. To which centre would these people have attached themselves? To Jerusalem, or to a northern centre? Were they even aware of a division between north and south? Many exilic writings show that the north and south were regarded as one, with little to choose between them. Both were faithless (Jer. 3.11); Jerusalem was of dubious origin (Ezek. 16.3), exactly what Jerusalem said of Samaria (2 Kings 17.24ff). Pilgrims from the north came to Jerusalem after its fall to mourn in the city (Jer. 41.4) and the later Elephantine letters were written both to Samaria and to Jerusalem. Was it therefore only with the wisdom of hindsight that the divisions became clear-cut?

Another formative factor in the restored community was the experience of the exile itself, and the insularity which had become imperative for maintaining national identity. In such circumstances intermarriage, for example, would have been unthinkable and national customs would have been elevated to a level of great importance. These attitudes caused bitterness when transplanted to Palestine. If the holy people were limited to the exiles and those who joined them, all others being the unclean people of the land from whom a separation had to be made (Ezra 6.16ff), then many indigenous worshippers of Yahweh would have found themselves excluded from the holy people. They would no longer have been recognized by their laws, or protected by them. Thus we find in Deut. 23.19ff the laws of interest and moneylending, which show that only a foreigner could be lent money at interest, and yet in Neh. 5 either the law was disregarded, or the people in question who had been exploited were deemed to be foreign. These poor people made an outcry against their *Jewish brothers* who had lent them money at interest.[19] Josephus tells us (*Ant.*, xi, 173) that *Ioudaioi* was the name for those who came back from Babylon, by which they were subsequently known.

The problem of the redefinition of the chosen people also underlies the scandal of the foreign marriages at this time. Men whose genealogies had been carefully scrutinized before returning to Jerusalem (Ezra 2.59ff) became involved in marriages which are depicted as blatantly illegal. Is it not more likely that the people contracting these unions thought them legal, and that the writers of our histories disagreed? The details of the humbler marriages are lost, but we have, by chance, the details of several high priestly and aristocratic marriages. The law limited the marriage of priests to virgins of Israel and the widows of priests,[20] but if there was dispute as to the extent of the true Israel, those once considered Israel might have found that they were so no longer. If we look at the names of the people involved in these illegal marriages, we find that in every case the 'foreign' spouse, or the family, had Yahwistic names. Eliashib's grandson, for example, married Sanballat's daughter, and was expelled by Nehemiah as a result. His brothers-in-law, as we learn from the Elephantine letters, were Shelem*iah* and Del*iah*.[21] Tob*iah* and *Jeho*hanan both had significant names, yet Nehemiah thought they had neither *right, portion nor memorial* in Jerusalem (Neh. 2.20). As worshippers of Yahweh they had perhaps assumed otherwise. Tobiah was himself near (*qārōb*) to Eliashib the High Priest; perhaps this made him acceptable as the son-in-law of a Judaean aristocrat? Had these people only recently become foreign?[22]

Two further snippets add to this picture; one is from Josephus (*Ant.*, xi, 346) who says that the temple of Mount Gerizim became a haven for people of Jerusalem who did not come up to the standard expected of them in their own city. The people claimed that they had been unjustly expelled. The other is from a later ruling which says that the women of the Samaritans and the Sadducees (the northerners and the priests?) were unclean and unfit for marriage to a Jew (*Niddah* 4, 2). Both these comments are consistent with the picture of the post-exilic situation which I am proposing; the Jerusalem community developed a religious exclusivism which met with opposition on the part of many who were quite competent to question it, for example the priests themselves.

The economic situation exacerbated the religious divisions. When the exiles returned from Babylon with the intention of rebuilding the Temple, the money for this rebuilding came from Persia. The immediate source was the tribute money collected in the Samaritan province, which can only have added insult to injury (*Ant.*, xi, 16). The greatest discrepancies between the contemporary prophets and the later historians can be found in these accounts of the rebuilding. Ezra and Nehemiah seem to have been written with the clarity of hindsight, and there are several points where there is conflict with the picture drawn by Haggai, Zechariah and the Third Isaiah. The Ezra-Nehemiah account may be the only history that we happen to have of these times, but it is not the only possible reconstruction upon the surviving evidence. Much of the picture is contradicted by the prophetic texts, but the overwhelming influence of the Ezra account has tended to obscure this important fact. Ezra–Nehemiah was written long after the events it purports to describe, and was written to demonstrate certain things about the new community, the role and status of her people, her leaders and the great divine plan.[23] The issues are clear even if the facts are not, and the less glorious aspects of the restoration have disappeared. The importance of these accounts is that they testify to a certain view of the return and restoration which was both promulgated and accepted, and became the way in which later generations of Jews in Jerusalem understood the events of these years. We see them in that same way. Ezra gives no account of the famine which prompted the prophecies of Haggai (Hag. 1.10–11), nor of the sloth in rebuilding which he also condemned. Ezra sees the rebuilding as history repeating itself, with timber from Tyre and Sidon (Ezra 3.7), and payment made in food, drink and oil provided by Persian money. Haggai says that the timber was local produce, and that food was very scarce. It would appear that Ezra's sources have been supplemented by the account of Solomon's building programme in 1 Kings 5.10. Ezra says that the people of the land opposed the building of the altar (Ezra 3.3), but offered to help with the Temple. The offer was refused (Ezra 4.2–4). Haggai says the *people of the land* were assured of God's help and support in the matter of rebuilding the Temple (Hag. 2.4). These are striking discrepancies, and the tendency is always in the same direction, that of glorifying a none-too-glorious tale. This is doubly curious when one compares this body of histories with the other extant in the Old Testament, the Deuteronomic corpus. In places this is no more than a catalogue of the follies and failures of Jerusalem. What, then, was the complete change of circumstance which necessitated a new approach, especially when both are retained in the same canon?

The material in Ezra–Nehemiah–Chronicles has survived in several different forms, evidence of a complex process of transmission, but the many theories offered to account for the changes only serve to emphasize the obscurity in which the period still lies. Later additions have been seen as consistent with the original,[24] or as totally different.[25] There may have been as many as three different editions of Chronicles, with Ezra material and then Nehemiah material expanding an original.[26] There may be great differences between Chronicles and Ezra–Nehemiah.[27] The heart of the problem seems to lie in the very early period, immediately after the first return. There is a significant gap during which emphases change; the monarchy ceases to be an important theme and messianic hopes have gone. A hierarchy is established. There have been numerous attempts to find the theology of these writings. They are an attempt to reconcile various groups and interests by excluding all alien influence and building upon priestly and Deuteronomic elements, with emphasis upon the royal theology;[28] or they are a strikingly different theology from that of the Deuteronomic group.[29] Ezra, regarded by the Samaritans as the arch-villain of the schism, is traditionally associated with these books, and yet Chronicles was apparently used by the Samaritans themselves for compiling their own Chronicle.[30] The pieces as we define them do not fit together. The Samaritans are not mentioned in the Old Testament in connection with the schism,[31] yet Josephus identifies them as the enemies,[32] and the Samaritans told tales of an Ezra who falsified the holy books for his own ends. Ezra has been presented from the Old Testament evidence as the great universalist, but after his time many were excluded.[33] The Chronicler is presented as a reconciler, but after his time there was deep division.[34]

The answer to the problem must lie in the type of literature which we have from this period. It is not an objective reporting of history, but a traditional view shaped by a community for whom this period was vital. It was bound up with self-identity, and was thus a necessary presentation for the Jerusalem community. Ezra was the new Moses, his coming the new Exodus with the new law and the new possession of the land.[35] The emphasis was upon continuity with the past, even though the Enochic account of the same events says that they were a deviation. There is emphasis upon legitimacy, even though Zech. 3 and Isa. 61 indicate that the priestly line was not universally acceptable. We find Ezra and Nehemiah linked and made contemporaries as the religious and political founders of Judaism, which means that questions about the relative dating cannot reasonably be asked of this material. What should be asked is how the Chronicler's explanation and justification of the status quo in Jerusalem relates to the condemnation which appears in the Samaritan and Enochic tradition, and even within the Old Testament in the Third Isaiah. Why is there a fusion of theologies? Why is there a different view of prophecy and fulfilment?[36] Why do the ideals of the monarchy fade? The gap in our records between the time of the first return and the time of Ezra is very significant. Several aspects of the silence reward further probing, not least because the way in which this period has been understood by subsequent generations, including our own, has been fixed by the writers of the final edition of the Ezra–Nehemiah corpus. With our minds thus set, it came as a surprise to discover what the actual religion of Palestine was like in the next two centuries.[37] If we take other sources as our primary evidence, e.g. the prophets of the period, the Enochic tradition, the Samaritan tradition, we find a very different picture, and the 'Judaism' of the third century comes as less of a surprise.

The People of the Land

There have been many attempts to define the *'am ha'areṣ*, and these have been clearly summarized elsewhere.[38] One conclusion drawn is that the use of the term varied according to context.[39] Its use as a Rabbinical term of opprobrium for the illiterate and the irreligious seems to have had its roots in the Ezra situation. If the writings of the Chronicler both shaped and reflected the attitudes of the later Jerusalem community, then 'people of the land' as a term of opprobrium arising from the troubles of the restoration period is a distinct possibility. It is quite clear that the Chronicler and the restoration prophets saw these people in different ways. Ezra 4.4 says they were hostile to Zerubbabel, whereas Hag. 2.4 addresses them and Zerubbabel in the same breath as joint recipients of the prophet's word of hope. Zech. 7.5 speaks to the priests and the 'people of the land' on the subject of fasting. What is strange is the silence of Isa. 56—66, which says a great deal about the enemies of the Lord, but does not mention the 'people of the land'. One explanation of the discrepancies could be that the term did not have any fixed meaning in post-exilic times. Another might be that they can be explained by a change of attitude towards the 'people of the land' which occurred during the half-century of silence. A group which is distinct but not hostile in the time of Haggai and Zechariah had become clearly *bad* with the wisdom of hindsight. It was the situation which developed during the years of silence which led to this change of attitude. The Jerusalem group came to see as hostile and impure a group which had not originally been seen in that way. Josephus' account of the events of Ezra 4 says that the hostile 'people of the land' were the Samaritans.[40] This must have been the later view of the events. Ezra 6.21 gives an earlier view, but still not a contemporary one; the 'people of the land' were those from whom the restored community wished to distinguish themselves. 'The people of Israel who had returned from the exile, and also everyone who had joined them, separated himself from the pollutions of the peoples of the land.' It was possible to belong to one group or the other. This was the background of Haggai's pronouncement on uncleanness (Hag. 2.10ff). Holiness was not contagious, but uncleanness was. The people from whom they separated themselves are graphically described in Ezra 9.1 as 'peoples of the lands, Canaanites, Hittites, Perizzites'; in other words, their exclusion was the exclusion of Deuteronomy, a separation from the evil ways of Canaan. Here, as with the reform of the older temple cult, we have a strong indication that what the Deuteronomists opposed was not in fact pagan and alien, but an older tradition of Yahwism. The unflattering picture of the *dalat ha'areṣ* in Jeremiah also came from the hands of the Deuteronomists.[41] For an entirely different picture, we must read the Third Isaiah, who does not mention the evils of the people of the land. *His* enemies, I believe, are the Deuteronomists.[42] A list of their characteristics shows clearly that the evils he condemns are those of the reformers as seen by the indigenous population; in other words this prophet spoke for those who were later called the 'people of the land'. His writings chronicle a growing rift between two groups, which was made absolute by the work of Nehemiah – who, we must not forget, had to *impose* his Judaism upon many of the people (Neh. 13 *passim*), and this is recorded to his credit. He also built the walls of Jerusalem, a phrase destined to become proverbial on both sides. In *Aboth* 1.1 it came to mean the protecting wall about the Law, but in the Damascus Document (CD IV, VIII) it meant something divisive.[43] Zechariah had hoped that only Yahweh would be the wall of Jerusalem (Zech. 2.9). Was this hatred and division linked to Ezra as the first of the men of the Great Synagogue? Legend said that he had dictated all the scriptures, and his successors interpreted them. The Samaritans remember the period with bitterness:

> Ezra the priest assembled his friend Nehemiah and all the princes of his community, and they wrote the book of the Holy Torah in the tongue of the Assyrians and in their letters, and he altered many things in the text of the holy Torah out of hatred for the community of the children of Israel who are Observers of the Truth, that is to say, the children of Joseph the righteous, adding some things and subtracting many others ... many errors were made by him in the book of the Torah, which neither he nor his people perceived or understood. In addition he gathered many sayings and writings composed by former authors and prophets such as suited his aims and desires, and he and his colleague Nehemiah commanded his community to keep them all ... (He did) all these things of his own design.[44]

The source of this is late, almost recent, but presumably it has its roots in something much older, from a time when disputes of this type were a living issue.

Even if we can deduce nothing about the people of the land from the Chronicles–Ezra–Nehemiah account beyond the fact that these writings present them in a poor light, we do have one other possible source of information in the writings of Elephantine which have not been 'edited', and which give us a glimpse of a Jewish community settled in southern Egypt. We know that *a* group of Yahweh worshippers fled to Egypt in Jeremiah's time (Jer. 43), which could mean that the religion of this group was similar to that which the returning exiles encountered in the people of the land two generations later. Now there is nothing to link the group described in Jeremiah and the Elephantine community, but both are evidence of a type of Yahweh worship very different from the Deuteronomic ideal, and from that of the second Temple. It is possible that the group who settled in Elephantine took with them a cult similar to that which the people of the land were still practising at the time of the restoration. In Elephantine several beings were worshipped, all with Semitic names, showing that they were brought from their homeland by the settlers, rather than absorbed from Egyptian polytheism. We find names such as Eshembethel, Anathbethel, Herembethel.[45] There is evidence that the Jews took oaths in the names of other gods. The major study of this community, by B. Porten,[46] seems determined to see it in as pure and orthodox a light as possible, making a careful distinction between all the other deities and Yahweh, and describing them, wherever possible, as 'Aramaean but not Jewish'.[47] This raises again the whole question of names and labels, since according to Josephus' definition the people of the land also were 'not Jewish'. Names such as Anath-Yahu cannot but be linked to Yahweh. If the context was not Jewish, then we have a non-Jewish group worshipping Yahweh, which merely relocates the problem. The list of monies collected by the community shows that they were distributed between Yahweh, Eshembethel and Anathbethel. Porten conceded that there might have been some connection between the female deity at Elephantine and the cult of the queen of heaven which was condemned by Jeremiah and practised by the group who emigrated to Egypt.[48]

It is also noteworthy that there are no names in this community compounded with El, such as were found in names from Judah and Babylon at the time of the restoration.[49] This odd snippet of information is entirely consistent with my suggestion that it was the Second Isaiah in Babylon who first identified El and Yahweh. Only the prophet's community, and those influenced by him, would have used both El and Yahweh in their personal names. It is also surprising, in view of the theory of Van Seters as to the age and purpose of the present form of the Abraham sagas, which only came to prominence with the Deuteronomists and the exile, that at Elephantine none of the 'early Israelite' names which 'reappear' in fifth-century Judah is found.[50] The Elephantine Jews practised papponymy, and thus they perpetuated the names they brought with them from Palestine, but they did not use names from the stories which we have good reason to believe were late. Both of these observations about names are consistent with the possibility that the El and Yahweh traditions were fused during the exile in Babylon. The account of the destruction of the Elephantine temple shows that the leaders in both Jerusalem and Samaria were held in equal esteem; like the prophets of the exile, they did not consider the north impure. This could have been another feature of the people of the land: both the northern ways and the older ways of Jerusalem were condemned together by the reformers, who established their identity over against them.

It is in this context of rejection that we must place the two visions of Zech. 5, which deal with the earlier stages of the economic crisis we find in Neh. 5. The Targum tradition suggests that the visions of the flying scroll and the woman in the ephah concerned trade.[51] The visions came to Zechariah some two months after Haggai finished his recorded prophecies (Hag. 1.1, cf. Zech. 1.1).

The two dealt with the same events, but had very different interpretations. Hag. 2.6ff had inspired the rebuilding of the Temple, in the hope that wealth would flow to it, and make Jerusalem a prosperous city. Haggai supported Zerubbabel (Hag. 2.23). Zechariah had different views; Zerubbabel is obscured in the text of Zechariah, which records a strong criticism of him (Zech. 4.6ff). Haggai also advocated a firm line towards the unclean and undesirable element in the land. If Zechariah is a consistent critic of his contemporary, we should not be surprised to find support for the outcast group in his prophecies.

The first vision in Chapter 5 was of a curse flying over the land, directed against thieves and perjurers. This is not a general outcry against social evils, but a specific condemnation of commercial and legal malpractice. The wasting curse upon thieves was Zechariah's interpretation of the famine recorded by Haggai, and attributed by him to the failure to rebuild the Temple. Isaiah 58.3b, 6–7 shows that there was evil in high places at this time; Zechariah reflects this. The vision of the woman in the ephah is far more complex. There are two crucial words of interpretation offered in the text itself, 'eynam and riš'ah, but both words present problems. I have argued elsewhere[52] that 'ynm probably means hostile attitude, and that rš'h was the particular wickedness of idolatry, in other words, that this vision was making the same point as Isa. 66.1–6. The new cult of the exiles was an evil form of idolatry which had come from Babylon. This idolatry was not the worship of foreign deities, but was associated with trade. The actual form of this vision was determined by Ezekiel's vision of the chariot throne, or by whatever lay beneath that vision, and, like all Zechariah's visions, it was associated with temple imagery. What Zechariah saw was not the law in the ark throne, but *lawlessness* (the LXX translation of wickedness) in an ephah, the symbol of trade. The ephah of lawlessness is carried away not by the fiery creatures of the chariot, but by two *money-lenders*, a word whose consonantal form (*nšym*) is identical with the word for 'women'. The English versions read 'women', but the whole text at this point is full of gender problems, suggesting that these ladies had an interesting past.[53] The whole episode makes admirable sense as a comment upon the commercial crisis in the restored community, with the prophet linking the economic problems to the commercial ones, and looking forward to a time when prosperity and toleration would return.

Priesthood, Temple and Exile

Between the lines of Ezra and Nehemiah we read that the people of the land questioned the rights of the exiles to act as they did. Official documents were needed before they were allowed to rebuild what was, apparently, their own ancient city. The actual course of the events and delays is no longer clear, but the priesthood played an important role. For the Chronicler the validity of the priesthood and the holiness of Jerusalem were of paramount importance. These

194

issues can only have been so much emphasized if there was a dispute in progress concerning the rights and legitimacy of the Jerusalem Temple and priesthood. What we read in the Chronicler is not the first gropings for a new idea; we have a mature system which has developed over a period of time. We must read these accounts in the light of Josephus, *Ant.*, xiii, 74ff, to appreciate the significance of these problems. Josephus says that the continuity and legitimacy of the priestly line were held by the Samaritans to prove their claim to have *the true shrine*. Thus when Ezra is presented he is presented as the legitimate successor to the high priesthood. The unique genealogy at Ezra 7.1ff shows that Ezra is not called the son of his true father, but the son of Seriah, the last officiating priest of the old Temple. He is presented as the legitimate successor to the priestly line.[54] We must read these claims in the light of 1 En. 87.73ff, which describes the restored cult as impure and apostate, with blind shepherds and blinded sheep.

There are several indications that the affairs of the Temple and priesthood were not all that they might have been at this time. Hanson has made a detailed and ingenious attempt to reconstruct the course of the troubles which were exacerbated by deep-rooted divisions.[55] He concluded that the bitter polemic between the priestly factions was over by the time of the Chronicler. This conclusion does not fit with the evidence of the non-biblical sources, because it is based entirely upon the biblical accounts and materials. The divisions in fact remained for a very long time. We see a glimpse of them in their early stages in Zechariah. Zechariah was himself a priest, and his vision in Zech. 3 declares the Jerusalem High Priest to be pure, and promises him rule over the house of God. We may only assume from this that there were some people denying his claim to be the pure and legitimate High Priest. The case against Joshua is dismissed in Deuteronomic style: 'The Lord who has chosen Jerusalem rebukes you.' The Third Isaiah gives the view of those who did not accept the priesthood when he says (Isa. 61.5ff) that if the Jerusalem group were to accept those whom they despised, they would then be called priests of the Lord.[56] There can be no doubt that these texts represent two sides of the same issue. The Jerusalem priesthood was not recognized by those who were in their turn despised.

A challenge to the legitimacy of the priesthood must have come from another priestly group with a rival claim, and this also appears in the visions of Zechariah. By the sides of the lamp in Zech. 4.14 there stand two identical figures, the anointed who stand by the Lord. The context is temple worship; one of the figures was Joshua, but Zerubbabel was not necessarily the other. In Zech. 6.11ff there is the hope of peace between two ruling figures; the man on the throne was Joshua the high priest, who had been designated the 'branch', a messianic title. His task was to build up the Temple, and to live in peace with another person whom we cannot identify. The whole passage is corrupt, suggesting a deliberate attempt to obscure the text.[57]

The concern to be recognized as legitimate also underlies the much reworked Zech. 7—8. The story tells of a group sent to inquire of the Lord, but their question is not clear, nor the direction of their journey, their number or even their leader. The conclusion (Zech. 8.20–3) shows that the embassy went to Jerusalem and that the narrative is about the recognition of Jerusalem as a legitimate shrine. One of the key problems in the passage is the amalgam of names at Zech. 7.2 in which the LXX found 'to Bethel', a translation which has influenced many subsequent attempts at reconstruction. This cannot have been the original sense, since the embassy was going to Jerusalem. *Regem Melek* has been read as the corruption of an official title, *Rab Mag Hammelek*,[58] which then reduces the embassy to one figure, Bethel Sharezer the Rab Mag. Now an official of similar name and title appears in Jer. 39.3, Nergal Sharezer the Rab Mag. This strange similarity could suggest that Nergal and Bethel were both comparable, i.e. theophoric elements in the names. If so, then the occurrence of Bethel as a divine name would place the leader of the embassy among those Yahweh-worshippers whose cult resembled more that of Elephantine than that of Ezra. This embassy was inquiring at Jerusalem, and thus affording it recognition. Emphasis upon the actual question asked is misplaced. Zechariah is never elsewhere concerned with the question of fasting, but he is very much concerned with the status of Jerusalem. Insertions into the chapter show that it was the question of recognition and hostility which the later writer found in the chapter, for he writes of wars and hostilities which were things of the past. Appended to the episode is the hope that one day many peoples and nations would come to Jerusalem to seek the Lord. This is the summary of the prophet's hopes: Jerusalem recognized as a holy city, and in her turn recognizing another group and allowing them access. 'We have heard that the Lord is with you' (Zech. 8.23) would be the recognition that the Lord was, or was again, with his people. Zechariah faced a divided country; he hoped for a time when the only wall would be the wall of the fire of Yahweh (Zech. 2.9), when the glory of the Lord would return. Isa. 58.10 gives another prescription for the return of the glory of the Lord: justice and the recognition of the indigenous worshippers of Yahweh. There was a desperate need on the part of Jerusalem to be recognized as legitimate and a simultaneous movement to exclude all those who did not conform to the new ways. Both Isaiah and Zechariah saw these ways as the very idolatry which the newcomers claimed to despise.

When we read the texts from this period, we cannot read them in isolation, or even devise their setting from the texts themselves, supplemented by the archaeological evidence. We have to read everything with at least one other body of evidence before us, and remember that the imagery of 1 Enoch derives largely from the first Temple, with Enoch himself presented as a priestly figure. The Temple plays a central role in his vision of the new age. The Book of Watchers in its present form is thought to be an attack on the corruptions of the priesthood. The writer of the Apocalypse of Weeks believed that true

196

wisdom had been forsaken at the end of the period of the first Temple, and both that apocalypse and the Book of Dreams describe the generation which returned from Babylon and the Temple which they built as 'impure and apostate'. It is for this reason that the preoccupation of the restoration texts is the legitimacy of the priesthood, the purity and holiness of the new Jerusalem, and the continuity with the past. Only thus could they hope to counter the accusations of the people who had not seen the exile, nor adopted the newer ways.

Those who had not experienced the changes of Babylon came to regard their own ongoing exclusion as in itself an exile; many writings depict Israel thus long after the end of the sixth century. Knibb has examined this subject in detail,[59] and drew most of his evidence from texts we should classify as apocalyptic. God's people were waiting for the time when God would intervene to establish his rule and end their exile. This was exactly the hope of the cult of the first Temple.

Ass. Mos. 4.5–6 says that some portions of the tribes shall go up to their appointed place and surround it again with walls, but that the two tribes shall continue in their prescribed faith, sad and lamenting because they will not be able to offer sacrifices to the God of their fathers. Ten tribes will multiply among the nations. Whatever the date and origin of this passage, it must be relevant to our understanding of Isa. 63.16ff, and the complaints of those who were excluded in his time. We have a picture of two southern tribes excluded from their Temple and keeping to their ancient ways. 1 En. 93.8ff is similar: 'In the sixth week all who live in it shall be blinded and the hearts of all of them shall godlessly forsake wisdom ... an apostate generation shall arise.' Malachi speaks of polluted offerings and of priests whose *torah* caused many to stumble; Dan. 9.25 tells of sixty-two weeks of years of troubles, which suggests turmoil in Jerusalem. The situation of those who retained the older ways was similar to that of the Second Isaiah; they looked forward to a time when evil would finally be defeated and the scattered people brought home, but because their ways had not been influenced by the Second Isaiah, they did not accept the demise of the older cult.

Conclusions

Any picture of the restoration period must take account of the questions raised by the glaring discrepancies between the sources. To harmonize them does no service to the truth. We have to ask why so many of the texts from this period are polemical, confused and at variance with the extra-canonical accounts. We need to know why Jerusalem is condemned in the pre-exilic histories of the Deuteronomists, yet claimed a continuity with that past as proof of legitimacy in the post-exilic period. We need to know why there were accusations of impurity on one side, and apostasy on the other, what groups were involved and what distinguished them. We need to know the impact of the new Judaism on Palestine, and the influence of the Deuteronomists and their heirs. The Chronicler, who is our major source for the period, has been described as the 'first Old Testament theologian',[60] unifying strands and trends which otherwise appear separate. The Second Isaiah was another unifier of older traditions, but both the Chronicler and the prophet applied them to only one group.[61] It is clear that we must go behind and beyond these sources if we are to appreciate what they unified and at what cost to the system.

No exposition of the other major source for the period, the Third Isaiah, can proceed unless these issues are taken into account. None of them is raised by the texts itself, but each was of great importance at the time when the prophecies were made.

I propose the following sketch of the restoration period as the background to the Third Isaiah. The indigenous Judaeans who had not gone into exile kept to the old ways and reacted against the changes of the Deuteronomic reformers. When the exiles returned with their Deuteronomic blueprint for the new community, and the old cult myth transformed by the Second Isaiah, the result was conflict. The exiles, though the smaller group, dominated because they had the backing of Persian money. The other population questioned the legitimacy of the new Temple, the new priesthood and the new city. They resisted the unfavourable position in which they found themselves both cultically and economically through the action of those whom they called the 'Jewish brethren' (Neh. 5.1). As a result they attacked them on their own terms, accusing them of false worship, idolatry, blindness, all those things which they most abhorred. The purity of the new group, and the ghetto mentality born of the need to survive in Babylon, led to exclusions and expulsions.[62] Amongst those excluded were those later called the Samaritans, and the preservers of the Enochic traditions. Thus Ezra was remembered on one side as the great founder of Jewish Tradition, and on the other as the evil destroyer of the ancient ways. The restored community found its sense of identity by looking to the past, but only when that past had been rewritten. The writers of the Enochic literature regarded all the post-exilic cult as defiled. Jerusalem, the restored Jerusalem, was perpetuated in the apocalyptic tradition as Babylon, the place of great evil. The city of Rev. 17 was not always Rome, for Rev. 17.6 says that the ten horns of the beast, i.e. ten Roman rulers, would attack her. The image of the harlot city upon many waters had originally been applied to Jerusalem, drunk with the blood of earlier saints. The city and its cult were despised by those whose traditions have survived, by and large, only outside the canon. The armies surrounding the evil city, and bringing her destruction, were part of the hope of the old tradition, and of its New Testament heirs, as was to be reflected in Mark 13.

NOTES

1 Hanson (1975), p. 43. A similar approach would read the evidence about the Temple very differently, not as in Clements (1965).

2 Ackroyd (1976), p. 146. See also reviews in SOTS Book list (1973), p. 51, and *ExpT* LXXXV (1973–4), pp. 40ff, criticizing recent inadequate treatments.
3 Coggins (1975).
4 ibid., pp. 67, 94.
5 Cross (1975), pp. 4–18.
6 MacDonald (1964), p. 290.
7 Bowman (1977), p. 102.
8 Raitt (1977).
9 Knibb (1976).
10 Jer. 44 shows how ordinary people reacted to the disaster, and returned to their ancient ways.
11 Nicholson (1970).
12 In the time of the Third Isaiah the details were different, but the comparison is still interesting.
13 G. A. Smith (1966), p. 174.
14 The distance between Jerusalem and Samaria is less than forty miles.
15 Macdonald (1964) emphasizes this (pp. 22ff), citing Gaster to the same effect. At the time of Ezekiel there was no idea that the northerners were impure or mongrel.
16 Coggins (1975), p. 37.
17 Although there is considerable doubt about the date of the formal rejection.
18 e.g. The Testaments favour Joseph and depict the sins of the other brothers in most cases as their sins against Joseph. Nickelsburg (1981) considers Enoch to have Galilean links in its present form.
19 There had been a great influx of Persian money; together with poor harvests, this made the economy unstable. Haggai had earlier talked of wages in a bag with holes in it (Hag. 1.6). If the non-exiles were no longer held to be a part of the holy people, they would not have been protected by the interest laws and therefore would have been open to exploitation.
20 Ezek. 44.2; Lev. 21.13ff, both in existence at this time.
21 Cowley (1923), Papyrus 31.
22 It was the priests who retained the wider definition. Ezekiel thought all twelve tribes were the true Israel, and Zechariah was also in favour of a broader definition; cf. Zech. 5.
23 Ezra is presented as the new Moses, the procession from Babylon as the new Exodus: Ackroyd (1976).
24 Ackroyd (1973), p. 20.
25 Freedman (1961).
26 Cross (1975); Japhet (1982).
27 McCarthy (1982).
28 Ackroyd (1977), p. 24.
29 Childs (1979), p. 653.
30 Coggins (1975), p. 125.
31 Rowley (1962), pp. 280ff.
32 Coggins (1975), pp. 67, 95.
33 Koch (1974).
34 Ackroyd (1977).
35 Childs (1979), p. 635; Japhet (1982), esp. pp. 89ff; Ackroyd (1976).
36 Childs (1979), p. 653.
37 Stone (1980a), p. 35.
38 See Ackroyd (1968), p. 150, for an excellent survey and bibliography: a nationalist group has been suggested, or the old country priesthood, or even the ancient Hebrew Parliament! Coggins (1965) opts for local groups rather than northerners.
39 Nicholson (1965), p. 66.
40 Coggins (1975), pp. 94, 96, emphasizes the caution needed for evaluating such statements,

but I find it hard to accept his distinction between local and northern hostility at this point when the distances involved were so small.

41 Nicholson (1970).

42 Smart (1967) also links the people of the land with these chapters; a memory of this period of opposition underlies the Chronicler's tradition that the people of the land, the non-exiles, frustrated the building of the Temple.

43 Charles, *Pseudepigrapha* p. 818, argues for a link with Eph 2.14, the dividing wall. At a much later period we find the people of the land proverbially hostile to scholars, whereas the Pharisees believed the people of the land impure (T. Bab., Pes 49a).

44 Chronicle Adler in Bowman (1977), p. 102.

45 Cowley (1923).

46 Porten (1968).

47 ibid., p. 164.

48 ibid., p. 177.

49 ibid., p. 135; Van Seters (1975).

50 Porten (1968), p. 145.

51 These are the people who were giving and receiving false measure; see Sperber (1962), p. 483.

52 Barker (1978).

53 ibid., p. 25; the consonants here are pointed *nāšīm*, 'women', but in Neh. 5.10 as *nōšīm*, 'moneylenders'. Two of the words associated with the women have masculine forms, usually explained as mistakes; of the five remaining feminine forms, there are problems in four.

54 Koch (1974), p. 190.

55 Hanson (1975).

56 This involves reading the Hebrew as it stands, and not emending the pronominal suffixes as is customary in English translations.

57 Barker (1977). We have also to account for the new imagery in the vision of the two trees. I shall deal later with the symbolism of the Menorah and the tree, but the conclusions of Chapter 9 are also relevant here. In this vision we have the tree-like lamp which represents, as elsewhere, the presence of God. It is separated from two other trees, which are the anointed ones. The Menorah, as I shall show, was a complex tree-symbol of life-monarchy-divinity. In Zechariah's vision the component parts are teased out to cope with the new situation. No longer is there one divine king figure, but only a lamp, representing the presence of God through his seven eyes, and two other tree figures representing rulers who are no longer divine, no longer in themselves the sign of the presence of God.

58 D. Winton Thomas, in The Interpreter's Bible VI (New York 1956), p. 1082.

59 Knibb (1976).

60 Ackroyd (1977), p. 24.

61 Coggins (1975), p. 37.

62 Horbury (1985a), esp. p. 30.

8

THE THIRD ISAIAH

The final chapters of Isaiah raise several questions of date and authorship. There is great variety of tone and material within them, and several parts resemble the Second Isaiah. Visions of a glorious future for Jerusalem are set between chapters promising judgement which reveal disillusionment and bitterness. If these chapters were written by the Second Isaiah, we should have to envisage a situation in which his original message had been accepted and then corrupted to bring disastrous results. If they were written by another, he was a prophet who reused the earlier writings as the basis for his polemic. We know from the dated and parallel prophecies of Haggai and Zechariah that it was possible for one prophet to comment upon another. It is possible that the Third Isaiah was doing this. It is also possible that he spoke for a later generation. If the Second Isaiah had seen the end of the exile, then these final chapters probably came from the period of the return to Jerusalem, and the question which must be answered by anyone attempting to reconstruct the period is: 'How did the bitterness in these prophecies arise from the events of this period?' The earlier prophecies have been reused in an extraordinary way, yet they have survived as an appendix to the Isaiah corpus. I shall examine these chapters to see if their content is compatible with my proposed reconstruction of the tensions of the restoration period. The chapters themselves cannot give a complete picture, but if fragments and allusions within them can be fitted into a picture drawn entirely from other sources, it increases the chances of that picture being correct.

There are two distinct themes in the chapters: salvation for Jerusalem (57.14–20; 60—62; 65.16–25; 66.6–16) and complaints against transgressors. The prophecies cover a period of deteriorating relationships, for in 65.8 there is hope for the condemned group, but in 66.6 we read of the coming judgement upon them. This was the period when the divisions in Judah began, because the context of 66.6 shows that it was 'brothers' who were to be judged as the enemies of God. It is possible that the Third Isaiah illuminates the fifty-year gap in the Chronicler's record, and shows us the stages whereby the initial division hardened into a rift. If we assume that the transgressors were addressed at various stages in a deteriorating relationship, some of the difficulties of the book are eased. One of its most telling silences, as I noted in the previous chapter, is the absence of any reference to the people of the land. These people acquired an increasingly bad name as history was rewritten and attitudes hardened; the Third Isaiah seems to speak for this group, who were tolerated at first, and then rejected by those whom the prophet could call brothers destined for judgement.

The Hope for Reconciliation

Chapters 60—62 and the related materials (57.14–20; 65.16–25; 66.6–16) are often treated separately from the rest of the work because they most resemble the language and ideas of the Second Isaiah. The first problem facing anyone who tries to comment upon the Third Isaiah is how to account for the material in these passages. Chapters 60—62 depict a glorious future for Jerusalem, because both the prophet and his enemies had similar hopes for the eventual glory of their ancient city. The prophet's people had not abandoned their interest in the city, nor their claim to rights within its Temple. It is likely that this assertion of rights within the city was the basis of the dispute with the returned exiles. The prophet offers in these passages a path of reconciliation, but as he does so the hopes and grievances of both sides can be seen.

Chapter 60 is a vision of the sunrise, the end of the night being the end of evil. The messianic prophecy of Isa. 9 uses the same imagery,[1] a sure sign that the Second and Third Isaiahs could have been using the same mythology because they wrote within a common tradition, and not merely because the latter was dependent upon the former, as is often assumed. The holy city will become a place of pilgrimage and receive great wealth. This shows the aspirations of the builders which we have already seen in Hag. 2.17ff, and there was a similar theme in Zechariah, who hoped for the eventual recognition and prosperity of the city, once the exiles had modified their ideas.[2] A time would come when the city gates would be open day and night (60.11), unlike the contemporary situation when they were closed due to threats from enemies, and also closed in the face of many who felt that they belonged there. 60.21 emphasizes the hope to possess the land – an important theme – and to multiply as a great nation. In all, this chapter is relatively straightforward; it is a vision of Jerusalem as it could be, expressed in terms of the older mythology with its solar imagery. The exiles' concerns and aspirations are clear from what the prophet promises to them.

Chapter 61 is more complex. It begins with the passage most commonly read as the prophet's own declaration of his role (61.1–4), and continues with a picture of division within the community (61.5–9). The prophet gives us here a glimpse of his self-awareness: he has been anointed, he has the Spirit of the Lord, as does the royal figure in Isa. 11; his task is to release captives, and to bring the Day of the Lord. It would be easy to find allusions to the Second Isaiah's Servant figure here, but our present passage deals with a *post-exilic though non-exilic* interpretation of the old royal role. Such features as the two have in common derive from their common origin, and not from the later prophet's reuse of the earlier. The Second Isaiah had used the Servant to explain the sufferings of the exile; the Third Isaiah, in a different situation, needed to develop the earlier royal patterns in a different way. Thus we find in this chapter that the expected deliverance was still to come (61.1–3), whereas the Second Isaiah had announced that the deliverance had already come (40.9). The Third Isaiah knew that his people were still in captivity, although exactly what he meant by this is not clear, whereas the Second Isaiah had proclaimed release (42.7; 49.9). It could be that the later prophet was contradicting the earlier, or it could be that both were preaching very differently from the same basis, because they addressed very different situations.

If we examine the Second Isaiah's use of captivity imagery which the Third Isaiah uses at this point, it is at once clear that both used the same pattern. The earlier prophet linked the release of prisoners to the opening of eyes (42.7) and to bringing from gloom. This could be a simple description of release from prison, but since imprisonment was not a common punishment in Israel, the reference could be to a particular imprisonment, that bondage to evil angels from which the Day of the Lord was expected to bring release. 49.9 links release from prison and darkness with the covenant and Exodus theme, the Second Isaiah's characteristic fusion. It is the association of prison and blindness which is curious; it appears also in 1 Enoch, where greater detail is given. In the allegorical history the opening of blind eyes is linked to the overthrow of evil powers (1 En. 90.9). The rulers of this world and those who have fallen under their influence are described as the blind (1 En. 90.23ff), and when their eyes are opened there is no idea of repentance. It is simply a sign of the breaking of the power of evil, of release from bondage. This pattern in 1 Enoch is not only important for our reading of Isaiah; it can also illuminate our reading of the Fourth Gospel, for example at John 9.3ff, where blindness and its cure are a means of *showing the power of God*. Blindness is not a punishment for any sin on the part of the man or his parents. In the case of the Third Isaiah, his commission to release from prison and blindness makes him yet another in the line of those who were called to oppose the evil ones. His was the royal role. The text at 61.1 has problems, with the LXX differing from the MT. The Hebrew means 'to proclaim freedom to the captives, and to the bound *pqh qwh*' – otherwise unknown words in biblical Hebrew. The Greek means 'to proclaim freedom to the captives, and sight to the blind'. This suggests that the second part of the Hebrew might once have read 'blind' instead of 'bound', especially as the difficult words in the Hebrew do have one component, *pqh*, which can mean 'to open eyes'. The text itself is now beyond reconstruction, but that in itself is significant in a passage concerning the blind and their release, an Enochic theme.[3]

The prophet has also to proclaim the year of the Lord's favour and his Day of Vengeance. For the chosen this would be a time of rebuilding and prosperity, but for their enemies (63.4) it would be a time of fearful punishment. In that future time the chosen would be called the 'oaks of righteousness', *'ēlē haṣṣedeq*, which has been read also as 'nobles',[4] but another possibility would be 'gods'.

The fact that they are to be planted is no problem, since trees and their planting were a common angelic/messianic motif in both the Old Testament and the extra-canonical literature.[5] 61.5–9 is the most important evidence in the whole book for division within the post-exilic community.[6] In the Hebrew, the five verses contrast two groups, but this is obscured in the English versions because we alter the pronominal suffixes in the interests of 'sense'. Read without either presuppositions or emendations, a divided society emerges from these lines. The first part deals with the exiles, who are addressed in the second person, and the second part deals with the prophet's own people, referred to in the third person. The aspirations and concerns of each are clear. 61.5 is a vision of prosperity for the city; 61.6 recognizes the exiles as legitimate priests;[7] 61.7a promises a double portion instead of shame. The second section refers to the prophet's people who will no more have dishonour but rejoice in their lot, who will have a double portion in the land with everlasting joy, and Yahweh will make a covenant with them because he hates injustice and robbery, an indication that a covenant claim of some sort lay beneath the troubles (61.8). The descendants of these people will prosper and be recognized as a people blessed by the Lord (61.9). This is the prophet's plea for tolerance and compromise; the exiles would achieve prosperity and recognition as the guardians of a legitimate shrine and the non-exiles would have their inheritance and their ancient right to be recognized as the people of Yahweh. Even if the exiles rejected the prophet's people, Yahweh did not and would not. It is important at this point to look forward again to the New Testament, and compare these aspirations with the terminology of the Beatitudes. The promises made there to the blessed are couched in terms (whether spiritualized or not) which are drawn directly from this situation; kingdom, inheritance, satisfaction, seeing God, and being the sons of God, both the latter being elements of the older mythology. The rejected people of Jesus' time are clearly associated with the ideas and aspirations apparent in the Third Isaiah. By New Testament times, these expressions may have been no more than a metaphor, but metaphor is rooted deep in the culture which uses it.

Chapter 62 is another vision of the glorious possibilities for Jerusalem. The city is the bride and God her husband.[8] The city is to have a new name and never again to fall to her enemies. There are echoes of the Second Isaiah, but again there are significant differences. 40.3 had proclaimed a way for Yahweh himself, but 62.10–12 says that the way is to be prepared for the *people* of God who will be called the people of the Holy One, the redeemed of Yahweh. It is *their* coming which will be the beginning of the glorious future. After their coming, the city will be called 'Sought out, Not Forsaken'. The contrast is clear; God returns to the forsaken city with the return of his people.

57.14ff is linked by subject matter to these chapters and it, too, deals with a way for God's people. The Holy One dwells with those who are crushed and fallen in spirit, in order to bring alive the spirit of the fallen and the heart of the crushed. The anger and the *rib* do not last forever, because God is the creator and the source of life. This evokes not only the vision of Ezekiel in the valley of the dry bones; it recalls the older confidence in the supreme creator as the source of both life and judgement. The Third Isaiah gives these ideas a new application.

65.17–25 echoes the hopes of the old Jerusalem for a future kingdom in the time of the great king. Isa. 11 is the basis for this passage, but there is added to it the hope that the chosen people would prosper. In view of the prophet's condemnation of so much that was happening in Jerusalem, it is significant that he recalls the ancient hope for harmony on the holy mountain. He adds to it, however, something not in the prophecy of Isa. 11. He hopes for a time when the serpent will eat the dust. This is the curse of Eden, and one wonders what it is doing here. Now there is, as I shall show, a strong possibility that the story of the expulsion from Eden was once linked to the exclusion from the sanctuary/holy mountain. The cause of this exclusion, the serpent, was cursed. It is this curse upon the creature responsible for the expulsion which expands the Third Isaiah's picture of future harmony.[9]

66.6–16 is the third detached section usually linked to 60—62. The discrepancy between the vision of happiness in 60—62 and the acrimony elsewhere is often thought to indicate that these chapters are the work of many hands, but the composition of this chapter shows that the two aspects of the prophet's message were inextricably interwoven, and that even if the chapters came from several hands, they addressed a single situation.

From these sections of the work, we may conclude that the prophet had seen the new Jerusalem, but did not like what he had seen. He kept his attachment to Jerusalem as an ideal, but began to project into a new and better future. The present troubles were the birth-pangs of the new age, the preliminary to the great judgement, a pattern which we find also in 1 En. 90.13ff and 91.2ff, where great struggles precede the new age.

The most striking feature of the remainder of the book is its polemical tone, and although the finer tools of criticism subdivide the chapters on various grounds, this overall tendency must be explained for the book as a whole. A relatively uncritical appraisal of the book gives a picture of the enemies whom the prophet attacked, but because the picture is not one for which we have been prepared, I have not found any commentary which actually dwells upon the identity of these enemies, or draws the very obvious conclusion. They were those inspired by the ideals of the Deuteronomists.

Chapter 56 describes the characters in the conflict. Both groups claim to derive their standards from Yahweh, and both claim to be his people, but one group was clearly dominant because it had power to exclude the other. Thus 56.3 says that foreigners were separated and eunuchs despised.[10] The prophet assured them of a place within the community, and a future within the walls of the Lord. Their name would not be cut off, nor would they be separated from the holy people. They would have access to the holy mountain, freedom to offer sacrifices, and a place at the great ingathering of Israel. These must have been the aspirations of the prophet's people. Their enemies must have excluded foreigners and eunuchs, and denied that they had any place within the walls of Yahweh, or any right to stand upon the holy mountain. 56.8 implies that these enemies had themselves only recently been gathered in, and, if we suppose that poetry such as this is more likely to be full of allusions than simple statements, we may also deduce that the enemies put great emphasis upon the Sabbath, upon separation, and upon their posterity who would inherit and perpetuate their name. Such a reading of this chapter fits perfectly with the post-exilic situation in Judah as I have reconstructed it from other sources. If there were these two groups at this time, we should expect to find evidence of one from Babylon, with the ideals of the Second Isaiah and the blueprint of the Deuteronomists. The divisions will not be so clear as we might like them to be, however, because the Second Isaiah is an element common to both groups. He was the catalyst for the Deuteronomic ideas as we know them, and yet he also represented the last link with the older ways which the indigenous people retained. Ideas from this prophet may then be expected to appear on both sides of the division, without this implying the direct dependence of the Third Isaiah upon the Second.

If my proposed reconstruction is correct, the details of Isa. 56 are very significant, for it is Deut. 23 which specifically excludes foreigners and eunuchs from the assembly of the Lord. Neither of these two is condemned as ineligible for approach to the heavenly hill in, e.g., Ps. 15. The prophet opted for these two because they represented the very lowest point of his enemies' ideals. The passage also mentions *separation*, which was one of the key words for the self-identity of the restored community, as can be seen from Ezra 9.1ff, which echoes Deut. 7.1ff. The prophet returns to this taunt in Chapter 59.[11] Both the prophet and his opponents give an important place to Sabbath and covenant; these are not grounds for dispute. The differences arise when it comes to deciding what the two institutions entail. External rituals, divorced from justice and righteousness, are deemed to be perverse interpretations (56.1–8).

The prophet then describes the leaders of his enemies (56.9–12), using many words which have proved elsewhere to be significant indicators of angels.[12] 56.9 summons the 'beasts of the field' and the 'beasts of the forest' to devour. 'Field' and 'forest' are not exactly parallel, since the second is prefixed by *b*; the state of the text may indicate that these creatures were something other than beasts of the field and forest, and that this passage describes the punishment of the leaders of Jerusalem by the avenging angels. *Šāday* is the older and poetic form of *šādeh*, 'field', 'open country'. Now there are several places where the word 'field' seems to be an inappropriate translation, leading to the suspicion that, were the *šāday* of 56.9 read *šadday*, we could recover the original sense. Jer. 4.17 describes the 'guardians of the field' surrounding the rebel city as punishment from Yahweh. Since Jeremiah's characteristic stance was that God was fighting against his people, these creatures were probably not the 'guardians of the field', but the watchmen of Shaddai. Deut. 32.13 describes a time when Israel rode upon something no longer clear,[13] and was fed with three things: the produce of *śāday*, the honey from *sela'* and the oil from *ṣūr*. These three words can mean, respectively, 'field', 'rock' and 'rock', but two are also common as names for God: *sela'* in Ps. 18.2; 31.3; 42.10; 71.3, and *ṣūr* in Deut. 32.4, 18; Hab. 1.12, and frequently in both Isaiah and the Psalms. It seems likely that 'field' here also functions as, or conceals by word-play, another name for God.[14] Job 5.23 has 'stones of the field' and 'beasts of the field' with whom one should be at peace. Later commentators linked this verse to supernatural creatures.[15] It is possible, then, that the 'beasts of the field' conceal the living creatures who accompanied the deity and executed his judgements, such as we also find in Ezek. 1.19. The 'beasts of the forest' may also have been something else[16] and should be understood in the light of the threefold curse upon Jerusalem found in Mic. 3.12 and Jer. 26.18. The three fates of the city are to become a *ruin*, a *field* and a *wooded height*. 'Field' is word-play upon one divine name;[17] 'ruin' is often used as play upon Elyon, as I shall show,[18] and 'wooded height' is the word we have in Isa. 56.9. If it was the old divine names which were being used as the basis of the taunt/curse, to describe the fate of the holy place, or perhaps to bring it about, then *y'r* was one of the names.[19] 56.10 has '*dumb*' (*'ilľmīm*) dogs, unable *to bark* (*nbḥ*). Since *nbḥ* is not known elsewhere in the Old Testament, and the meaning 'unable to bark' depends upon *'lm* being read as 'dumb', we do not have a certain translation. Were *'lm* the *gods*, we should have a reason for the 'dumb' dogs also being 'blind' (56.10), since we should have here an established taunt pattern against the *gods* and the *Watchers*. The leaders are *'azzey nepeš*, another ambiguous phrase, and also they do not know how 'to be satisfied' (*śb'h*).[20] Another possibility would be to read this as *śb'h* oath, or *hšb'*, 'to swear', giving us headstrong shepherds (a possible meaning for *'azzey nepeš*) who do not know the oath and have no understanding (56.11b). Read thus, we have exactly the Enochic picture of the evil rulers: angelic creatures, shepherds under whose rule the people of God suffered. From the Similitudes we know that these creatures lacked knowledge of the oath and the Name, and that their wisdom was worthless. Each had turned to violent gain (Isa. 56.11), and there follows *mqṣhw*, another difficult word which elsewhere in Isaiah, as I have argued, may denote a heavenly creature, e.g. 41.5, *qṣwt h'rṣ*, the 'ends of the earth' awaiting judgement.[21] We are too far removed from these ways of thinking to appreciate the exact thrust of what is being said, but the presence of so many suggestive words indicates that the whole section describes the leaders in Jerusalem as being in league with, and therefore a part of, the evil ones, *exactly as the later leaders are depicted in the Enochic Book of Dreams*.[22]

Chapter 57 tells us more about the prophet's enemies. They are the children of witches and harlots, children of sin, offspring of lies. Allowing a little for rhetoric, we see here too the angel mythology, for it was the children of the fallen angels who ensured the ongoing corruption of the earth. These colourful accusations were particularly apt when the object of the attack was a group who placed great emphasis upon the purity of their descent. The opening verses of the chapter describe the religious relationship in sexual terms, but is this a reference to more than the survival of the old fertility cult? Hanson has suggested that there are several pieces of word-play in this passage, to heighten the bitterness.[23] There are two emphases: the claim to possess the land, and current religious depravity. He cites as examples of this word play (i) *ḥlq*, meaning both 'apportion' and 'slippery'; (ii) *nḥl*, meaning both 'inherit' and 'wadi', and (iii) *grl*, meaning both 'allotment' and 'stony place' (57.6). In addition to Hanson's points, there are *'ēlīm* (57.5) with which the people comfort themselves. The RSV reads this as 'oaks', but the LXX read as τὰ εἴδωλα, 'idols', i.e. the gods. 57.4 is also ambiguous. In the context, a sexual reference would be more fitting than the usual renderings. BDB cites this as the only example of a hithpa'el of *'ng*, with the sense 'to make sport of'. Elsewhere it means 'taking delight'. Here it is followed by 'against whom did you open your mouth and put out your tongue', in the usual rendering, but the LXX's χαλάω means rather 'loosen' than 'put out'. If the sense of the Greek is followed, we find 'Upon whom were you delighted, upon whom did you open your mouth and let loose your tongue'; this is consistent with the overall sense of the chapter, reminding the prophet's enemies that their behaviour betrayed their origins. They were the children of the evil ones. Hanson shows how the attack continues in 57.8 with a description of the new Temple as a harlot's bed, punning upon *miškāb*, 'bed' and *miškān*, 'tabernacle'. Just before there is a 'memorial' (*zikrōnēk*), which is said to refer to a male fertility symbol, but I am not happy with this suggestion, although it is certainly true that this word *zikkārōn* was part of Nehemiah's catch-phrase which was presumably current at the time, *the right, portion and memorial* in Jerusalem for the chosen people (Neh. 2.20).[24]

57.8 reads: 'You have gone into *exile* from me, you have *gone up* and *made wide* your bed.' Now *gālāh*, 'exile', can also mean 'uncover'; '*going up*' to the Temple on the holy mountain was a part of the cult, and 'making wide' was what they had not done to the temple doors. The whole verse is a bitter comment upon a group whose attitudes had exiled them from God, when they were proclaiming that their exile was over. They had welcomed foreign money to build the Temple, but had rejected offers of help from their own kin. Next there is a description of a covenant which is unique in its structure.[25] The covenant is made *from* someone, a clause commonly regarded as corrupt. In fact, the actual word 'covenant' is not in the verse, and, although there are allusions which could be to a covenant, what is actually described is something which 'cuts off' or 'separates.' In H and P this word *kārat* is a technical term for cutting a person off from the community, for an offence such as is described in

Lev. 7, as well as being idiomatic for the making of a covenant. Again we have word-play, comment upon a covenant which divides rather than unites.[26]

57.9 is also opaque. RSV renders, 'You journeyed to Moloch with oil'. NEB has 'You drenched your tresses with oil'. The verb *šūr* is difficult. BDB suggests 'travel', 'journey', and cites Ezek. 27.25, where it is used in the context of ships, and accompanied by another unique word *ma'ᵃrābēk*. In both Isa. and Ezek. the meaning has to be deduced from the context. Wernberg-Møller suggested that the verb was from *šārah*, 'lavish',[27] whence the NEB. G. R. Driver argued for an extension of the meaning 'journey' to include 'go about with malicious gossip', although he opted for 'be resplendent' as appropriate at Isa. 57.9.[28] Instances of the related word *šōrēr* in the Psalter, whether we translate 'speaker of malice', or with BDB, 'insidious watcher', indicate that these were hostile beings who had rebelled against God, had been cast down, were associated with witnesses, with the fallen and with the dreadful, who fought from on high, who were proud and spoke falsely. These are the heavenly figures whom we have met elsewhere. Some word derived from this meaning is what we find in Isa. 57.9, a technical term for a cultic action, even though an exact translation is not possible.[29] The picture we have is of the harlot city sending her envoys to worship the King, an old name for the Jerusalem deity, but here a reference to the new condition of the Jerusalem cult, that there should be prayers for the well-being of another king (Ezra. 6.10). The harlot city sent out her envoys to distant places, but brought them to Sheol. Again we find word-play. The word for envoy is *ṣīr*, but this is a word of many meanings. In the later part of this same chapter it is *idols*, elsewhere it is closely related to *'ir*.[30] In terms of the old myth, the prophet describes the certain fate of the city; her envoys/guardians will be brought down. The climax of this section shows us another of the prophet's concerns: the possession of the land and the inheritance of the holy mountain. His own people had been denied these things. Thus in 57.13b we find, 'He who takes refuge in me shall *possess* the land and shall *inherit* my holy mountain'.

Chapter 58 is closely related to the Second Isaiah,[31] but since many of the themes isolated as characteristic of the Second Isaiah were not his original creation, but the material with which he shaped his message, any similarity between the two prophets does not necessarily indicate dependence of the one upon the other. Working within the same tradition, a degree of similarity is to be expected, and their relationship must be determined by the differences between them rather than by their similarities. Thus 58.8b echoes 52.12, but makes it very clear that the presence of the Lord is dependent upon a certain standard of behaviour on the part of the people. This was not the unconditional promise of the earlier prophet. 58.12 links to 61.4a; the former gives the conditions upon which the ancient ruins would be rebuilt and the latter shows the aspirations of the prophet's enemies, similar to those of the Second Isaiah, but clearly unrealized. The rebuilding was delayed, and the prophet gave the reason for the delay. Hanson again finds word-play in this chapter, and shows how the prophet describes and satirizes the business of cultic observance. The enemies *seek* the Lord, *delight* to *know* his ways, as if they were *doing righteousness*, and as if they had not deserted the Lord's ordinances. They delight to *draw near*. All these are terms from the cult, and are a convincing argument as to the nature of the prophet's attack. In addition to the examples offered by Hanson, there is an extraordinary phrase in 58.3, 'In the day of your fast you seek your own pleasure and *oppress all your workers*.'[32] This is the only place in the Old Testament where *'aṣṣᵉbēkem* is translated 'workers'. Elsewhere it is 'idols': e.g. Isa. 10.11; 46.1; 48.5. 'Oppress' (*ngś*) is very similar to *ngš*, the technical term for the priest's approaching God. Thus we have a double meaning, perhaps another taunt; you oppress your workers, you approach your idols. Here again we have the theme of these writings; the mistreatment of the prophet's people in religious and social matters is an idolatry as great as anything which the purists abhorred.[33] When the walls are rebuilt (58.12), the city will be called *the builder up of the breach, the restorer of the ways which are to remain*. The LXX hints at something not apparent in the Hebrew, with τούς τρί βους σου ἀνὰ μέσον παύσεις, 'You will put an end to the paths in your midst'. What did the translators think was to be ended, and by whom? The prophet's final promise (58.14) comes from the Song of Moses in Deut. 32, and links the passage firmly to the view of Yahweh and the angel mythology characteristic of that chapter. A return to right values and attitudes would be rewarded in the way long expected, as recorded in one of the least well understood poems in the Old Testament.

Chapter 59 divides into three parts: verses 1–8, 9–15a and 15b–20. The relationship between them rewards examination, since it points to the original setting of the passage. It is easiest to start with the final section, which describes the coming of Yahweh against his enemies. They are called 'adversaries' (*ṣrym*), 'enemies' (*'ybym*), 'coastlands' (*'yym*). 'Coastlands', as I have already suggested, conceal the name of supernatural beings,[34] and 'adversaries' can be shown to be a similarly significant word.[35] The great variety of contexts in which this word *ṣrm* occurs in the Third Isaiah, and the variety of English words necessary to translate it, suggest that there may be some underlying meaning in the Hebrew which now escapes us, or some set of associations which could have prompted the prophet's use of the word. 57.9 translates by 'ambassadors' to Sheol, with the LXX similar; 59.19 has the 'rushing' stream of a theophany. 64.1 has 'adversaries', to be judged at the coming of Yahweh; 65.16 has 'troubles' which are to be forgotten.

The most suggestive passage of all is 63.9, where the Hebrew is obscure, and the LXX renders *lō' ṣār ūmal'āk* by οὐ πρέσβυς οὐδὲ ἄγγελος, showing that *ṣar* was read as a parallel to *mal'ak*. This phrase, 'Not by an angel and not by a messenger', occurs frequently in later writings, but *always to deny the activity of such creatures* at vital moments in the history of Israel.[36] One must assume that there was a reason for this polemic, that someone *was* attributing such activities to angels and ṣarim.[37] The word ṣar which we find at Isa. 63.9 and elsewhere must indicate a being whom later commentators sought to deny and exclude. The Third Isaiah knew of ṣārim from Jerusalem who went to Sheol, of ṣārim to be judged at the coming of Yahweh, of ṣārōt to be forgotten. Elsewhere in Isaiah we find them as enemies (9.11) or idols (54.16), where the LXX renders 'opposed to him'.[38] Chapter 29 uses these words, and the fine distinctions drawn between ṣūr and ṣārar must be questioned. It may be that here again in the mysterious Ariel passage, we need distinctions because we are forcing a highly mythological form of expression into our very different understanding of what the Old Testament says. If their whole world was structured in terms of the heavenly powers and their fates, we should expect to find this in other places than just the temple rituals. Did the writer of the Ariel passage distinguish between the siege works and the angelic agents? Did the Second Isaiah distinguish between the idols and the hostile beings? It may well be that to talk of word-play is a serious misunderstanding of the respective sets of meaning, even though this is the only way we have to express it. The most conclusive piece of evidence for the identity of the ṣārim is drawn from a comparison of three readings of Deut. 32.43. The RSV adapts a confused MT and gives, 'Praise his people, O you nations, for he avenges the blood of his servants and takes vengeance on his *adversaries*, and makes expiation for the land of his people.' The LXX is longer, and we must note the differences: *'Rejoice with him heavens, bow down to him sons of God. Rejoice with his people, nations, confirm him all you angels of God*, because he will avenge the blood of *his sons*, he will take vengeance upon his adversaries, he will repay those who hate him, and will purify the land of his people.' The reading of 4QDeut[q] is different again, with 'sons' for the 'servants' of the MT, and, with the LXX, 'bow down to him gods, the sons of El'. It appears that the ṣārim here are the subject of a passage which has been treated in the way we have come to expect for references to the older cult. The MT has changed 'sons of God' to 'servants', and removed all explicit references to the heavenly beings who were to be judged.[39] It is important to remember that the changes in the MT always follow the same pattern, and that this pattern distinguishes it from much at Qumran, and also from much in the New Testament.

If this final section of Isa. 59 looks forward to the judgement of enemies, 'coastlands' and ṣārim, we must look again at the rest of the description of the coming of Yahweh in 59.19. It is to be like a 'rushing' stream (nhr ṣr), driven by the Spirit of the Lord. This translation of ṣr is not needed anywhere else in the Old Testament, and nhr could be translated differently to avoid bringing a stream into a passage describing the sunrise. Apart from stream, nhr can mean 'beam, shine', and were this the meaning here, we should have the description of a theophany like a shining ṣr, driven by the spirit of the Lord (cf. the Enochic Astronomy Book, where the heavenly bodies are driven by the winds). The remainder of the chapter describes the situation which made the intervention necessary. A clear distinction is drawn between two groups, the prophet's enemies and his own people. The enemies are addressed in 59.1–3; they do not know the way of peace, and their road is not straight (cf. Isa. 40.3, 'make *straight* a highway'), nor is there justice in their paths (*ma'g'lōtām*), better rendered by 'circumvallation', 'entrenchment'. This becomes a very pointed remark about the new city. The group addressed is preoccupied with unanswered prayer, and the prophet suggests a reason for this state of affairs. He takes the words from their own mouths, and says that they have *separated* themselves, the Deuteronomic ideal, but separated themselves from God as a result of their evil ways. The presence of God has been hidden, and the prophet's people suffer from the evil in the city. The second group, the prophet's people, had been looking for the sunrise, the old image for the coming of God to his people, but no new era had dawned. 59.12–13 imply that the existence of these people in Jerusalem was deemed by the prophet's people to be a punishment for their own sins. They confess using traditional forms, but their sins are very significant; they have acted deceitfully against God, they have turned away from Yahweh, they have conceived words of oppression and rebellion. None of these is a sin proscribed by the decalogue, but *all* are the sins of the fallen angels. They express their sins in terms of adopting the ways of the evil ones, and as a result, justice and righteousness have left them. The reading of 1QIsa^a is 'I have made them depart', the direct action of Yahweh. Evil is permitted until the time of the judgement, exactly as depicted in the later apocalypses. The sad state of the prophet's people is described in 59.10–11. They stumble and creep and moan in a state of living death. The exact meaning of 'groping like the blind for the wall' is not clear.[40] What is clear is that the prophet's people were still waiting for the intervention of Yahweh against the evil ones who were no longer the foreign rulers, but the new regime in Jerusalem. This adaptation of the old mythology is the form in which it appears in the Book of Dreams. The people of the Third Isaiah were still interpreting their world in terms of angels, but the application of the myth had altered with the changed circumstances.

In Chapter 63 there is another description of the Day of the Lord. Chapter 62 had described the glorious hopes of the returned exiles for the new city; the present arrangement of the writings emphasizes the stark contrast between the two aspects of the prophet's message, because Chapter 63 did not refer originally to Edom at all.[41] It was a description of judgement upon Jerusalem. 'Who is this who comes *in red*, his garments redder *than a vinedresser?*' (*m^e'oddām*, rather than *mē'^edōm*, 'from Edom'). The significance of the passage is that it is a parody of the Second Isaiah's own proclamation to Jerusalem, or perhaps a form based upon the same pattern as the earlier prophet's proclamation. There is a similar pattern in Nahum 2.1. The Second Isaiah had announced the coming of one bringing good tidings (*mbśr*): Isa. 40.9; 41.27;

52.7; cf. 61.1, where the Third Isaiah uses it of the messianic role. The Third Isaiah proclaims *mbśr*, the threat of judgement. The root *bśr* can mean 'cut off, fortify', or 'harvest grapes', whence the rendering 'vinedresser', but both Jeremiah and Obadiah use the word in contexts of judgement (Jer. 6.9; Obad. 5). In Chapter 63 we find that the city which has cut itself off will be cut off, and this will be the judgement, the treading of the grapes which will come on the Day of the Lord. Again we find the coalescing of harvest and judgement imagery, which was the natural result of judgement expectations associated with the old autumn festival of Yahweh's kingship. Lam. 1.15 also has this vintage imagery, showing that it was known and used before the time of the Third Isaiah. Isa. 63.1–6 is a clear picture of judgement yet to come upon Jerusalem, a contradiction of the message of the Second Isaiah, who had assured Jerusalem that its troubles were over, its judgement past. In the Third Isaiah, the exile was not seen as the purification of the remnant, the actualization of the great judgement.[42] 63.7–9 recalls the older account of Israel's election in Deut. 32, with Israel as the faithful sons and Yahweh their protector, but 63.9 is much debated and far from clear. The LXX rendering points to its having links to angel figures.[43] 63.10–14 are also opaque. After rebellion and rejection (63.10), we have in 63.11 the curious *mōšeh 'ammō*, which the Syriac and the Lucianic Greek version must have read as *Mōšeh 'abdō*, 'Moses his servant'. In 63.9b Yahweh 'carried' his people, suggesting that the original here might not have been 'Moses' but *maśśā'*, 'burden'. In other texts it has been shown that *maśśā'* was a key word in the controversies of the restoration period, where the two meanings 'oracle' and 'burden' were used in word-play against the new prophets.[44] Was there a reciprocal bitterness on the part of the prophets against the new Moses tradition? Isa. 63.11 invites speculation. It has a uniquely bitter tone, and the whole section is without precedent in the earlier prophetic materials.[45] The text is confused; while the LXX in 63.11 reads 'shepherd', singular, the MT has the plural: 'Where is he who brought up out of the sea the shepherds of his flock, where is he who put in the midst of them his holy spirit?' To understand this, we have to ask who the shepherds might have been, and from what sea they were brought up. Hanson links the passage to Exod. 15, the royal triumph later adapted for Moses. In the symbolic language of the old cult as reflected in the Psalms, the shepherds brought up from the sea, in whose midst was the holy spirit, were the ancient kings, but how do they fit here? If the Second Isaiah had combined the old sea imagery and the events of the Exodus to fuel enthusiasm for the return from exile, we can be fairly certain that any reference to the events of the sea in the literature of the period is a comment upon the events of the return. It is the bitterness of the passage which raises the questions we cannot answer.[46] Two references to the 'name' theology of the Deuteronomists (63.12, 14) show us one component of the situation, but the exact thrust of the attack is not clear. 63.15–19 is another passage whose bitterness is beyond doubt. Two new elements appear which enable us to define

213

further the beliefs and traditions of the prophet's people. They claim God as their *Father* (63.16, also at 64.12), and Abraham and Israel will have no dealings with them. Commentaries are quick to point out that such a form of address to God is not found elsewhere in pre-exilic literature,[47] even though we know that literature to have been full of the imagery of sonship. Here the Father God stands in contrast to the descendants of *Abraham and Israel*. Is there, we must ask, anything else to suggest that Abraham represented opposition to the older mythology? Chapter 65, a bitter passage contrasting the true servants of God with another group who are promised punishment, culminates with a reference to the blessing to Abraham, 65.16, and an implicit criticism of it. The truly blessed will not bless themselves by Abraham, but by the God of truth. If Abraham was the figurehead of the prophet's enemies, this would be consistent with the conclusions of J. Van Seters,[48] that Abraham achieved importance in the exile as the focus for the new promises to the exiles, promises based upon a democratization of the old royal covenant. Westermann compared this passage with John 8.33,[49] and concluded that it was very different. I disagree. If there had been a division within the Yahweh tradition, one side retaining the imagery of royal sonship and the other emphasizing the traditions which are now in the edited Pentateuch (traditions not emphasized in the Enochic tradition, an important point) we should expect, in view of the Christian terminology of sonship, to find Jesus within the sonship tradition rather than within the Abraham tradition. Both the Fourth Gospel and the source for the teaching of John the Baptist suggest that this was the case: those who prided themselves on being the sons of Abraham appear as a group hostile to the first Christians. Thus Matt. 3.7–9 = Luke 3.7–8 depict the Pharisees as a brood of vipers, claiming great things because they were the children of Abraham. John the Baptist denied that this descent would save them from the coming wrath. John 8 is also full of allusions to the myth of sonship, and contrasts the claims of the one Son with those of the sons of Abraham.

Returning to Isaiah 63, the prophet's people are then described as the servants of God (63.17), the tribes of his heritage; 63.18–19 conceal yet another reference to the judgement of the sons of God. The MT and LXX differ: 18a in the Greek is 'so that we may inherit your holy mountain' and 18b is missing, whereas the MT and the Targum have 'people' in place of 'mountain', giving 'your holy people possessed for a little while . . .', which is less satisfactory, since we do not know what was possessed. If 'mountain' was part of the original, we could have a pair of lines, 'For a while they (LXX 'we') possessed the holy mountain, Our *ṣārīm* have trampled your holy place'. 63.19 is a reference to the older picture of election such as we find in Deut. 32, thus linking together those ruled by Yahweh and called by his name, those who should possess the holy mountain, and the hope of a judgement which would rend the heavens and cause the mountains to quake.

Chapter 64 makes few additions to the picture, except for the plea in 64.8

(English versions, 64.9): 'consider Lord, for we are all your people'. 64.3(4) seems to contradict the Deuteronomic view of theophany; Deut. 4.12 says that only a voice was heard, no form was seen, whereas here we find that nobody has seen or heard any God *but Yahweh*. 64.4(5) is confused; Yahweh's anger in the LXX is 'because we strayed', but in the Hebrew 'in them from of old and we were saved', a colon described by Hanson as 'hopelessly corrupt'. I would hesitate to add to this.

65.1–7 is similar to 57.1–10. Neither is simply a description of Canaanite religious practices, but rather a bitter comment upon the restored cult in Jerusalem. The evil is practised before the face of Yahweh (65.3), i.e. in the cult itself,[50] and the details of necromancy are simply the strongest possible language to express defilement. The people who say 'keep away' are also using the language of the cult, and 65.5 contains three of the cardinal terms used to express the special sanctity of the Zadokite priesthood. Ezek. 44 shows this same vocabulary in a contemporary text. Thus Isa. 65.5a should be read, 'lest I communicate holiness to you', just as in Ezek. 44.19 the word is used to forbid a holy vestment's coming into contact with ordinary folk. The manner of these verses is reminiscent of the Deuteronomists,[51] and the Second Isaiah's assurance that the past was over and done is ignored (65.7). Here the emphasis is upon inherited guilt (cf. 2 Kings 24.3), and here too the most cherished tenets of the reformers are turned against themselves. 65.8–12 returns to the familiar theme of the chosen, the servants inheriting the holy mountain. The threat of judgement is coupled with assurance that the servants would produce children to inherit the 'mountains'. The LXX has a singular, reminiscent of 65.11, where there are others who have forgotten the holy mountain. Important too is the fact that we have here the plurals, 'servants', 'chosen ones'. The Second Isaiah also has assurances that the Servant and Chosen One will not be cast off (41.9), derived from the old belief that the Chosen One would stand with impunity upon the mountain of God. In the Third Isaiah it is given a new and topical twist, with the hope that his people will be allowed, literally, to stand upon the holy mountain. 65.13–16 describes the judgement, and shows clearly that economic factors accompanied the religious divisions. This meshing is important, because it illuminates the prophecies of Zechariah, especially the visions of Zech. 5, and it is consistent with the picture in Neh. 5. In the glorious future, the prophet's people would see their own afflictions heaped upon their enemies: hunger, thirst and anguish would be theirs. Even their name would be a curse, and the prophet's people would be known by a new name. If we but knew these two names, we could write a history of this period with confidence! We do not. All we have is a clear indication that the ways parted at this point, and that the true servants deemed themselves separated from those who claimed the promises to Abraham.[52]

Chapter 66 opens with the much-debated condemnation of temple building. It is true, as Westermann says, that similar statements can be found in the

Psalter, but to say that this similarity rules out any idea that the verses represent a polemic against the building of a particular temple does not follow. Even if the prophet was using a well-known idea, we are bound to assume that it was a *relevant* idea. Haggai had also spoken of the role of the Temple in the restored community (Hag. 2.19). Material blessings were thought to depend upon the existence of the temple, and Haggai was not saying anything new, nor characteristic of his own group. That the Temple and its services ensured and promoted fertility is clear from the Psalter and from 1 En. 80.2–8, where the distortion of the calendar, and therefore of the temple rituals, was linked to rain failure and crop failure. Haggai did not depart from the ancient ways when he promised the imminent overthrow of kingdoms, and the establishment of a new servant and chosen one. There would have been agreement between Haggai and the Third Isaiah on these points. Where they disagreed was over uncleanness; Hag. 2.11–13 must be read in the light of Isa. 65.5, 'Keep away from me lest I communicate holiness to you'. Haggai advocates separation from the peoples of the lands because they could communicate uncleanness. Not even contact with holy things could improve their condition. The Third Isaiah rejects this position completely, and with bitterness. We must note at this point that it is not simply a Deuteronomic group which has the upper hand; Haggai was using the imagery of the old Temple, and he had the hopes of the old monarchy. He had much in common with the Third Isaiah's people, just as both the returned exiles and the indigenous group had much in common with the Second Isaiah, being based within the same tradition. The characteristic thrust of the Third Isaiah at this point is to question whether temple building really can ensure the attention and favour of Yahweh. By way of contrast he offers the man who is humble, who really does tremble at the word of Yahweh. This strange expression is another indication of the object of his anger, since it occurs only in two other places, both describing the very pure who separate themselves in horror from the peoples of the land (Ezra 9.4; 10.3). The oppressed group, the 'humble', is addressed again in 66.5, and assured that the 'brothers' who hate and expel them will themselves be put to shame. The word here translated 'thrust out' became in later times a technical term for excommunication.[53] Westermann says that in this passage 'this is not yet so', but how can we be so sure? The context gives us a group inspired by the ideals of Deuteronomy, engaged in temple building, brothers who expel in the name of the Lord. Excommunication is a very likely meaning for 'thrust out'. If the enemies of 66.6 are the same as the idolaters of 66.3–4, we find that yet again the ways of the enemies are described as pagan (cf. 57.1ff; 65.1ff). The prophet puts the legitimate practices of the cult on the same level as the worst of Canaanite excesses, thus emphasizing that the ways of the new Jerusalem were equally abhorrent. Both were a deviation from the way of the Lord. When Yahweh appeared in his Temple (66.6), perhaps at the time of its consecration (cf. 1 Kings 8), it would be a time of judgement for his own city. This theme reappears in 66.15–16, and between the two pictures of judgement is an explanation of the plight of Jerusalem. The mother city is in travail, about to bear more children.

I began this chapter by asking whether or not my reconstruction of the exilic period could illuminate the work of the Third Isaiah, and I made two assumptions: that the writings actually referred to this period, and that the enemies described in the book were not several groups, but one group at different stages in a deteriorating relationship. The master picture against which I have read these chapters of Isaiah has been drawn entirely from other sources, to avoid the dangers of circular arguments which illuminate the writings by using information drawn from the writings themselves. The reconstruction I offer shows that my thesis is compatible with the evidence in these prophecies. A more detailed investigation is necessary, especially into such areas as the direction of the textual alterations, and the intricacies of the word-play which I suspect have more to reveal. There is nothing to be gained from the debate about composite authorship, if a single *situation* could have accounted for all the materials. All that several authors would prove is that the position was widely held, and not the lone voice of one who was unheeded. Nor is there any need to see the Third Isaiah as a sad decline from the heights of the Second. Both prophets worked within the same mythology, both faced crises, but if the events of the destruction and exile precipitated many movements within the ancient mythology, subsequent developments within the Yahweh tradition can only be appreciated if each of these several movements is viewed as an equal heir. The processes of entrenchment and mutual hostility may have served to harden certain positions within the later situation, and both sides will have drawn further away from their point of division. Nevertheless, the idea of the true interpretation being that of Jerusalem and the exiles, with all falsehood and error lying elsewhere, is no longer tenable. How this diversity of opinion survived within one canon is a question for a later period, as is the question of such selective textual corruption; it cannot be coincidence that such a high proportion of the material dealing with the ancient mythology is now either altered or opaque, and that such a high proportion of *difficult* texts in general are those concerned with this subject. What the Third Isaiah can teach us, if nothing else, is that the Deuteronomic theology and its offspring were neither normative nor universally accepted.[54] Our preoccupation with Deuteronomy is a hindrance to our understanding of both the earlier and later materials in the Yahwistic tradition, and to our reading of these as systems in their own right, rather than as deviations from a norm.

NOTES

1 As do Isa. 33 and Ps. 46. See Murray (1982a).

2 See Chapter 7; cf. P. R. Davies (1983a), who argues for a rather different disillusioned group

at this time, with roots in the exile, but like the people I would regard as the non-exiles, this 'group' (which presupposes a minority) had strong priestly characteristics, a 364-day solar calendar, a sense of exile since the time of Nebuchadnezzar and much in common with 'the Judaism outside it' (p. 202).

3 This association of blindness and bondage is crucial for our understanding of Jesus. Luke 4.18 shows that this passage in the Third Isaiah was used to define the nature and content of Jesus' ministry. He is quoted as using the LXX version, release to captives and sight to the blind, but the particular associations of blindness in the 'apocalyptic' tradition make me wonder whether this reading of Isaiah was confined to the LXX.

4 Hanson (1975).

5 e.g. 2 Bar. 36—40.

6 Hanson does not mention this, even though it adds to the weight of his argument.

7 cf. Zech. 3, where this is disputed, and the whole controversy with the Samaritans.

8 cf. Ps. 87, where the city is the mother, and Elyon the father; see Chapter 11.

9 See Chapter 10 on the Eden stories and their development.

10 I am not entirely convinced by the ingenious suggestion of Morton Smith, 'The attack was personal because Nehemiah was a eunuch' (M. Smith [1971], p. 180).

11 The post-exilic creation story in Gen. 1 also sees the Lord establishing order by means of separations, and crowning his works with the sabbath rest, a projection of the ideals and aspirations of the restored community.

12 56.12 does not appear in the LXX, and may have been an addition to fix a particular reading of the rest of the passage.

13 It now seems to read 'high places', but the LXX has τὴν ἰσχὺν τῆς γῆς, 'the *strength* of the earth'.

14 Wifall (1980a; 1980b) has drawn a similar conclusion from the evidence of Egyptian mythology. El Shaddai was El of the Field, the watery field of reeds which surrounded the abode of God. In 1980b he suggested that the crossing of this reeded area to a place of safety was the origin of the Red Sea story. This might account (although the author does not mention this) for the absence of Sinai from the song of Exod. 15, and also for the eventual fusion of the Sinai story with the existing one of a holy mountain at the end of a journey.

15 'Rashi interpreted the "beasts of the field" as werewolves (*grwsh*, i.e. *garoux*) and on the curious . . . "stones of the field" showed he knew of an old variant . . . referring obscurely to Lev. 17.7, on satyrs' (Murray [1982a], p. 21).

16 The letters *by'r* might have been *bw'r*, 'burning one'.

17 Word-play is not a satisfactory description of something which was far more than just a stylistic matter; satire is also too sophisticated and classical a term.

18 See ch. 11.

19 I suspect that this conceals what we now read as a Watcher, *'yr*.

20 There is the possibility that 1QIsaᵃ reads here *šm'h* ('not knowing how to *listen*') for *šb'h*. The forms for *m* and *b* are very similar.

21 See ch. 3.

22 Commentators, e.g. Westermann (1969) *ad loc.*, point out that these verses resemble the polemics of the pre-exilic prophets, but they have more in common than simply the tradition of attacking evil powers. The choice of words links the Third Isaiah firmly to the thought forms and myth of the pre-exilic prophets such as the First Isaiah.

23 Hanson (1975), p. 198: 'This is no objective description of a cultic practice, but rather a highly sardonical paranomasia used to ridicule the cult of those being attacked.'

24 Hanson does not mention this link.

25 BDB, art. *krt*, p. 504a.

26 The verse ends with two impossible words, a sign that we are dealing with a mutilated text.

These words have been described as 'meaning uncertain, gloss, vestige of disintegrated colon...'

27 Wernberg-Møller (1958), deriving from Vg *ornasti.*

28 G. R. Driver (1934).

29 The contexts of these instances of *šōrēr* are significant; the enemies are to fall by their own counsels, and be cast down because of rebellion against God (Ps. 5.9); the enemies are false witnesses, *'ēdē šeqer*, with *'ēd* known elsewhere as a heavenly being of some sort, and *šwr* meaning 'watch' in a hostile sense, Ps. 27.11; enemies who are *zārīm* (Ps. 54.5 – possibly *zēdīm*, 'insolent', rather than *zārīm*, 'strangers') but see also Ps. 58.3 where the evil ones *zārū*, 'go astray',) and *'ārīṣīm* 'dreadful, awe-inspiring', rather than 'ruthless men' as in RSV (cf. a similar usage in Ps. 86.14, where there are 'proud ones', *zdym*, possibly even 'proud gods', *'lhym zdym*, and an 'assembly of dreadful ones', *'dt 'rysym*, who rise up to seek the psalmist's life and have no regard for Yahweh); enemies who trample and crush and who fight *mārōm*, possibly 'proudly', but LXX 'from on high' (Ps. 56.3); enemies who are dogs (cf. Isa. 56.11), who sinned through pride and false words and will endure the consuming wrath of God (Ps. 59.11); enemies who will fall in contrast to the righteous who will flourish like trees in the house of the Lord (Ps. 92.12).

30 Murray (1984).

31 Hanson makes much of the fact that these verses are imbued with the language and themes of the Second Isaiah.

32 BDB, II *'ṣb*. There are other places where idolatry/painful toil seem indistinguishable, e.g. Ps. 16.4; which contrast the good with those who multiply sorrow/idols, and will not be part of the community; Ps. 139.24 which contrasts the loyal man with those who have defied the Lord, the way of eternity with the way of idols/pain. Both texts are obscure; Ps. 139.20 also mentions *'yr*, and is untranslatable.

33 There are many accusations of idolatry in this period, usually in the context of social injustice, e.g. the visions of Zech. 5. The prophet emphasizes that only when certain conditions and attitudes change will the expected salvation come. *tiṣmaḥ* (58.8) can be linked to *ṣemaḥ*, the 'Branch' of Zechariah's hope, showing how this dawning light and the growing tree were fused as symbols, and how both depended upon a changed attitude on the part of Jerusalem.

34 See ch. 4 n24.

35 Murray (1984).

36 Goldin (1970) collected such instances, and demonstrated the frequency of this set formula. For example, Deut. 11.14, 'then I will give rain', is commented on by the *midrash*: 'then I will give rain, I, not by means of an angel and not by means of a messenger'; Deut. 32.35 is similarly expanded; the Mekilta on Exod. 12.12 emphasizes that it was the Lord who smote the firstborn, not by an angel...; Abot de-Rabbi Natan denies that Moses received the law from an angel or a seraph. Goldin gives many examples. Paul knew another tradition; the law *was* given by angels (Gal. 3.19; cf. Acts 7.53).

37 Murray (1982a).

38 Were the makers of idols in 45.16 once something altogether different? The root *ḥrš* has several meanings: 'to engrave'; 'to have magical skills', as in Isa. 3.3; 'to be silent, dumb'. The people of 45.16 could have been the makers of idols, or the ones who communicated with the *ṣirim/ṣarim*. False gods/dumb ones is common word-play.

39 This indicates that 'Servant' and 'Son' are related terms, important for our reading of the New Testament, and also that there were several forms of this text in existence.

40 The word rendered 'grope' is not found elsewhere in the Hebrew of the OT, and 'blind' is already a suspect word. The Targum here has, 'The world is shut in our faces, as graves are shut in the face of the dead.'

41 For a bibliography of suggestions made for this passage, see Westermann (1969), p. 381.

42 Knibb (1976); Davies (1983a).
43 Murray (1982a).
44 Petersen (1977), esp. pp. 18, 27ff.
45 Hanson (1975); also von Rad (1966a), esp. pp. 1–13: the survey of sacred history in which Moses here appears is in itself unusual.
46 Hanson interprets this as evidence for the claims of a Mushite branch of the priesthood, many of whom were among the Third Isaiah's people.
47 Westermann (1969), *ad loc.*
48 Van Seters (1975).
49 Westermann (1969).
50 Hanson (1975).
51 Westermann (1969), not taken up by Hanson.
52 These verses afford a close parallel to the Beatitudes, especially in the Lucan form which has both blessings and curses (Luke 6.20ff).
53 Horbury (1985a).
54 Mayes (1983), pp. 137ff.

9

TRANSFORMATIONS IN THE POST-EXILIC
PERIOD: (1) THE MENORAH

I had never intended to pursue this topic, but what began as a possible footnote has grown into one of the strongest, if strangest, arguments for the nature of the older mythology. The great variety of symbolism associated with the Menorah may have been due to chance accretions over the centuries, or it may indicate that all the symbolism stems from a common source, and is perceived by us as a variety because we view the Menorah out of its true context. The great lamp is associated with light, life, the homage of the heavenly bodies, the eyes of the Lord, the presence of the Lord, the Tree of Life and the Davidic succession. All these could have had a single point of origin were the Menorah an ancient symbol from the old cult. I offer this as speculation, no more.

In the popular Judaism of Roman times, the Menorah was universally employed as its symbol, and yet the Rabbis forbade its use.[1] It was forbidden to make a menorah like the one in the Temple; lamps with five, six or eight branches were permitted, but a lamp with seven branches was not. The significance therefore lay in the number of the branches, and not just in the form of the lamp. Goodenough summarized the problem thus:

> Only one body of evidence speaks directly for popular Judaism in the Graeco-Roman world, namely the archaeological data. Everything else deriving from the period, conspicuously the talmudic literature, is, in relation to popular Judaism, secondary to that evidence, because the literature comes ... from a group who could not have inspired such productions, and who destroyed this art as soon as they had the power to do so.[2]

Goodenough was writing of a period extending a few centuries after that of the Enochic writings, and yet the pictures are remarkably similar. There was a writing group, whose work survived and came to be accepted as normative, which denied and even destroyed a popular cult which was equally Jewish (for want of a better term). 'In the Talmud', says Goodenough, 'I have been unable to find a single passage which attempts to explain the menorah symbolically' (ibid., p. 88). So far as I can see, there is hardly any direct comment upon the Menorah in either the Mekilta or Exodus Rabbah. Goodenough attributes this silence to the fact that the Menorah had become a symbol for mystics, but I wonder if this is the whole truth. There are several hints in the extant literature which suggest that the prohibition upon the Menorah was rooted in a very ancient feud.

It is not easy to trace the history of the great lamp or its significance. There is much to suggest that there was *no* seven-branched lamp in the first Temple: for example, 1 Kings 7.49 only says that there were ten lamps in Solomon's Temple. Meyers in her detailed study of the Menorah doubts whether there was a menorah in the furnishings of the second Temple at the outset. Zechariah's vision was based upon a memory of the single lampstands of Solomon's Temple, not upon the branched Menorah, and he projected the object of the priestly tradition into an incomplete Temple.[3] Now there is no doubt that Zechariah saw *a* lamp, in a vision which occurred before the building of the second Temple (Zech. 1.1, cf. Ezra 6.15), but the prominence of the seven motif in Zech. 4.2, 10, linking seven lamps to the eyes of the Lord, makes it more reasonable to suppose that the vision was based upon a type of lamp known to him and his hearers, i.e. one from the first Temple. Later traditions certainly associated that vision with the seven-branched lamp, and shared Zechariah's feeling that the presence of the Lord was in the presence of the lamp. Numbers Rabbah 15.10, for example, records the words of R. Jacob son of R. Jose: 'The Holy One, Blessed be he, was constrained to dwell with mortals in the light of a lamp.' Why, then, if the lamp had such great significance, does the description of the Temple in the Deuteronomic history want us to believe that the Menorah did not exist? Mettinger has argued that the crisis of the exile precipitated a change in the theology of the divine presence of Zion.[4] The fate of the Menorah seems to have been a part of this transformation; memories of its ancient significance did survive in shadowy form (Exodus Rabbah 36.16 says that the lamp is God who gives light, and the Torah), as did traditions linking it to the first Temple and the Messiah: Numbers Rabbah says the Menorah was one of the five things which would be restored in the messianic age, along with the fire, the ark, the spirit and the cherubim, all things which were absent from the second Temple.[5] The description of the first Temple in 1 Kings does not only omit the Menorah; it also makes quite clear that the ark, for example, was only a box containing two tablets of stone (1 Kings 8.9) and nothing more. Mettinger's investigation of the exilic transformation concludes:

> This treatment of the Ark and the cherubim in the D-work would seem to be the result of the conscious suppression of the notion of the God who sat enthroned in the temple.[6]

A similar tendency can be seen by comparing Isa. 37.16 and its parallel in 2 Kings 19.15. The Deuteronomic account omits the title Lord of Hosts. Such evidence as we have points to a toning down of the significance of the older cult objects, but to a complete removal not only of the significance of the lamp, but of the lamp itself. One can only assume that this was the cult object par excellence, upon whose significance no compromise was possible.

The prescriptions in Exodus for the construction of the great lamp are so full of detail that it must have been more than just a means of lighting the

Temple,[7] yet the later commentators, who loved to embroider every facet of their texts, are curiously silent. The Chronicler does mention the great lamp (2 Chron. 13.11), but says that there were also the ten lamps made by Solomon (2 Chron. 4.7, 20), which may be a reconciling of traditions in the manner of the later Rabbis,[8] or a memory of an actual situation. Jeremiah mentions lamps among the booty taken to Babylon (Jer. 52.19). Several sources of light in a large Temple would not be an unreasonable hypothesis; what is strange is the omission from 1 Kings of the great lamp. In the account of 1 Kings 7 there are several clues which suggest that the number *ten* for the lamps was a later elaboration. Gray summarizes thus:

> Noth ... emphasizes the singular *peraḥ* ('flower') in v. 49 as the base of a lamp-bowl, which would hardly be a collective singular even if the ten lampstands in v. 49a were original. Ten lampstands before the inmost shrine are peculiar to this passage and are independent also of P. It may fairly be assumed that, on the clue of the singular *peraḥ*, one lampstand was listed in the original source, and that this was subsequently elaborated to ten in the light of a development in the later monarchy.[9]

What necessitated such a elaboration? Such a thing could not have been done during the period of the first Temple, when the actual furnishings were there for all to see. It must have been done after the destruction of the first Temple, during that period when the past was being rewritten, and the lamp being written out.

Apart from the Rabbinic prohibition of the *seven*-branched lamp, there is another indication that it was this *form* of the lamp which was significant. In the second century BC, when Onias fled and built the temple at Leontopolis, he replaced the Menorah with a single gold lamp. Josephus tells us that he designed an altar like that in the home country, and adorned the buildings in a similar way, but the lampstand was different: 'Instead of making a stand, he made a lamp of wrought gold which shed a brilliant light (λύχνον χρυσοῦν ἐπιφαίνοντα σέλας) and was suspended by a golden chain.'[10] Liddell-Scott-Jones shows that ἐπιφαίνω and the related words are frequently associated with manifestations of the divine. If the new cult at Leontopolis represented God by the Lamp, as did the Jerusalem cult, but by a single and not a sevenfold lamp, we have another reason to believe that it was the sevenfold form which was important. The sevenfold lamp was used by the Samaritans,[11] showing that this form antedates the schism, but was forbidden by the Rabbis even though widely used. One possible answer might be that the lamp was linked to a tradition of worship peculiar to Jerusalem. It would have to have come from a period when the Samaritans were not excluded from and hostile to the city, and be associated with a tradition which the writers of the Talmud did not find acceptable. The cult of the first Temple is an obvious choice, bearing in mind that the division between north and south did not play so important a part in the affairs of the time as certain records would have us suppose, and a

'Samaritan' retention of a Jerusalem symbol is not out of the question.[12] The evidence for this possibility is consistent over several centuries. Both the earliest interpretation of the Menorah in Zech. 4, and the later one in Numbers Rabbah, link the lamp to the presence of God on earth, i.e. to that aspect of the cult which was written out after the crisis of the exile; but Zechariah also links the lamp to the role and status of the anointed rulers.[13] Standing by the *lamp*, they are said to be standing by the 'Lord of the whole earth' (Zech. 5.14). In his earlier vision, a passage now full of obscurities, Zechariah had seen the earth patrolled by angelic beings and we have the possibility that there was a link between the angelic agents in this vision, and the patrolling eyes of the Lord in Zech. 4.10, which were explicitly said to be the lamps of the Menorah. These *eyes* appear also in Ps. 87.7, where the princes and eyes of Yahweh are present in Zion as he records his elect.[14] The branches of the lamp thus represent beings other than Yahweh who were his agents on earth. As I shall show later, the king was one of these agents.

Josephus gives us the next materials for our reconstruction. He says two important things about the great lamp.[15] There was, he says, a popular slander which described how the Jews had been deceived by a temple robber. They were told that an epiphany was about to take place, and withdrew reverently to a suitable distance. This 'epiphany' then took the form of the robber wearing a headdress of lights, such that, to those at a distance, it seemed as though the stars were moving upon the earth, in the manner, we may assume, of Zechariah's patrolling eyes. 'Presumably', says Morton Smith, 'Josephus is right in describing the story as a malicious fiction, but presumably also the story reflects what it was the Jews would expect to see if ever a theophany took place'.[16] Josephus also gives a description of the lamp and its meaning. The sanctuary contained three works of art: the lamp, the table and the incense altar. The seven lamps represent the planets; the twelve loaves on the table, the circle of the zodiac and the year, and so on.[17] Philo assumes the planetary symbolism to be common knowledge.[18] In the first century AD, then, the presence of God, the lamp and the planets were associated in popular belief, a pattern not unlike that in the Enochic literature, where the stars and the angels are equated. As early as Zechariah and as late as Josephus, the lamp was linked to the angelic tradition extant now in the extra-canonical apocalypses. Both the lamp and the apocalypses were forbidden.[19]

It is not necessary to look for explanations of the Menorah's symbolism in the cultures of neighbouring peoples. Full investigations have been made of the Greek and Mesopotamian evidence for stars being associated with the presence of deity, and with the interpretation of divine plans.[20] Fascinating though such exercises are, they do not carry so much weight as even the smallest hint which can be gleaned from sources known to be 'Jewish'.

We must now establish the significance of the *seven*-branched form, which was the forbidden form. *Seven* clearly had planetary associations, but since

Uranus, Neptune and Pluto cannot be seen without a telescope,[21] the seven lamps cannot have been the planets as we know them. Very little is known of ancient Hebrew astronomy, apart from a few names in Job 38.32; Amos. 5.8, and the idea that Yahweh determined both the names and the numbers of the stars (Ps. 147.4; Isa. 40.6). We know that there was some distinction between the constellations and the 'host of heaven' (2 Kings 23.25), but whether or not these constellations were a zodiac is not known. It is thought that the zodiac originated in Babylon in the fourth century but no conclusions can be drawn.[22] Both constellations and 'host' had been venerated in Israel, and the personified stars rejoiced at the creation (Job 38.7). The stars in Gen. 1 are defined as no more than lights to rule over the day and night and to determine the seasons, thus reflecting the post-exilic community's attitude to them. The stars were associated with royal figures (Isa. 14.12; Num. 25.17) and, most significant of all, were thought to be *bound* by Yahweh in order to serve him (Job 38.31). Hence the characteristic stance of the later apocalypses, which distinguished them from their Hellenistic counterparts; the stars in no way compelled man to act.[23] The wisdom tradition did concern itself with the stars (Wis. 7.17ff), and the Jews were known as astronomers;[24] our failure to recognize this has led to the Enochic Astronomy Book being hailed as one of the great mysteries of third-century Judaism. What we have in Aramaic is fuller than in the Ethiopic, showing that the tradition was contracting, not expanding, with the transmission of the Enochic material. We can never know what was lost, but the planetary symbolism of the great lamp invites speculation.

There is insufficient evidence to determine which seven bodies were represented by the menorah lamps. Diodorus Siculus (II, 39. 2ff) says the Chaldeans knew of five planets which they called the 'interpreters', and designated by the names of their gods. Since a relationship between Chaldean and Enochic astronomy is possible,[25] we may perhaps assume that the seven represented the five planets, the sun and the moon. If the menorah lamps did symbolize the ancient pattern of belief, we should expect to find evidence for the subordination of the heavenly bodies to the rule of Yahweh, and this evidence is there. Several fragments from various sources confirm the subordination of the heavenly powers to the rule of Yahweh. There are many carvings and pictures of the seven-branched lamp in the Graeco-Roman period.[26] One found in the Nawa synagogue depicts the central lamp as higher than the others, and it is surmounted by a large round object. The obvious explanation is that the round object represented the sun.[27] Several clay lamps have the wick spout forming the central light of the menorah pattern, emphasizing the importance of the central shaft. We also know that in the Temple, the six side lamps were turned in such a way as to point towards the central shaft,[28] an arrangement interpreted by Philo as symbolizing the planetary system shining its light back to God its source, since the whole universe is constantly worshipping its creator. This idea may be late, but it could also be the vestige of an earlier belief that the lesser lights were subordinate to the central deity, a pattern well attested in the Old Testament as the demotion of the angelic powers.

Ginzberg's collection of Jewish legends gives excellent examples of menorah traditions. The ten lamps of Solomon's Temple, for example, were each held to be sevenfold, and the resulting seventy lights represented the seventy nations. Since the seventy nations correspond to the seventy rulers/shepherds of 1 Enoch, and these shepherds were in their turn the angelic rulers of their respective peoples, we have even here a hint that the Menorah was linked to the ancient angels. If we suppose that the central branch with its sun motif represented Yahweh, we should still be well within the Old Testament tradition. Ps. 84.12 describes Yahweh as the sun and the shield of the upright; the LXX version of Solomon's dedication prayer (3 Kms 8.53) begins, 'The Lord has set the sun in the heavens', but the Hebrew (1 Kings 8.12–13) sees fit to omit this line; Hos. 5.9 inveighs against a cult at 'Beth Aven', the latter word perhaps playing on On, the sun shrine; Amos 1.5 knows something similar in Syria; Josiah burned the sun chariots and horses set up in the temple entrance (2 Kings 23.11), but Ezekiel still knew sun worship in Jerusalem, showing that Josiah's reform was not successful (Ezek. 8.16). The extra-canonical texts also know of sun associations: Joseph, the patriarch of the northern tribes, married the daughter of a sun priest;[29] the curious story of Joseph and Asenath (whose date and provenance are still uncertain) has solar imagery as its framework; the Essenes greeted the sunrise with traditional prayers; and several times in Isaiah and the Psalms we find the coming of divine help depicted as the time of sunrise.[30]

We can be fairly certain that the lamp in Jerusalem represented the deity, and that the seven branches of the lamp were its most significant feature. The Leontopolis temple, which had a single lamp, may not have intended that lamp to represent the divine presence, but without doubt it was offered to replace a lamp which did. Is it possible that the significance of the Leontopolis lamp lay in the fact that the temple in the ancient city of sun worship would have depicted Yahweh differently from one in which the planets and the angels played an important role? If so, we are pointed again to a royal cult involving angels and planets as the original setting of the Menorah.

Almost contemporary with the earliest known interpretation of the Menorah in the visions of Zechariah are the two descriptions of the great lamp in Exodus, which were chosen, we assume, from existing material, rather than freely invented by the compilers. Bearing in mind that the Deuteronomists are increasingly being recognized as the shapers of the Pentateuch, it is highly significant that there is no reference or allusion in either account to any planetary symbolism, or association with the presence of the deity. Exod. 25.31–40 and 37.17–24 both describe a golden tree-like object, using terms such as branch, almond-like, and flower. The differences which exist between the two accounts of the Menorah in the MT and the version in the LXX are notorious, a fact which we cannot discuss in detail here, but which does raise the question of how and why such discrepancies arose. There are also discrepancies between the two accounts in Exodus itself, and again we must ask why there are two accounts, when the second is so nearly a duplicate of the first. We cannot assume parallel traditions from different shrines; one must have been offered as a substitute for, or corrective to, the other. The second omits all references to the fact that the tabernacle and its furnishings were formed after the *pattern given on the mountain*. Since the first account of the plans follows directly upon the mysterious description of the seventy elders and their ascent of the mountain to see the God of Israel, and since this is the account which emphasizes the heavenly origin of the tabernacle plans, one cannot help wondering whether the elders, the ascent and the pattern of the tabernacle might not have belonged to the same tradition. The business of the temple plans has passed through several stages of editing and alteration; 1 Chron. 28.19 says that David made the plans clear to Solomon 'from the writing of Yahweh concerning it'. As we should expect from the pattern of changes elsewhere, this receiving of temple plans passed from the king figure to Moses. What we do not know is the fate of the Menorah; the discrepancy between the associations in Zechariah and the descriptions in Exodus can only point us in a particular direction, albeit one that is now familiar.

One possible approach would be to attempt to disentangle the antecedents of the tabernacle specification as a whole, but that would be a gargantuan undertaking. A whole web of hypotheses exists which attempts to explain the origin of, and the distinction between, the ark, the tent and the tabernacle traditions still apparent in the Pentateuch.[31] It was not, however, the intention of the compilers that they should be so distinguished. There was a conscious process of fusion of two tent traditions,[32] but it is only by making comparisons outside the Pentateuch that we can also see the exclusions.

Ezekiel was an older contemporary of the compilers of the Pentateuch; he was a priest, he was in Babylon. He is as near as we can find to a double of the mysterious P, but his information about the affairs of the cult separates him sharply from these contemporaries. His call vision of the divine throne, of which there is only a hint in the Pentateuch at Exod. 24.9–11, was implicitly denied by the Deuteronomists, and the reading of Ezekiel's vivid description was forbidden to later generations.[33] Nevertheless, it is the same tradition as the descriptions in 1 En. 14ff, and these are said to be the earliest evidence for a heavenly ascent. A clear and early link has also been established between these visions of Ezekiel, those of Isaiah, and the later Merkabah hymns, pointing to a source in Palestine.[34] The ascents tradition, represented in so many of the apocalypses, rooted here in Ezekiel, and highly developed by the time of the earliest sections of 1 Enoch,[35] is nowhere depicted in the Pentateuch,[36] yet this reached its final form after the time of Ezekiel, and not too many years before even a conservative estimate of the date of the earliest Enochic material. Our present Pentateuch de-emphasizes the throne tradition,[37] transforms some of the cult into a wilderness fantasy, and leaves us but a shadow of the ancient Temple, clumsily but necessarily fused with the desert tradition. Childs's conclusion is worth pondering:

> The idea of a heavenly vision does not belong to the older tent tradition which concentrated fully on the speaking role of Moses ... there are traces of an ancient tabernacle tradition which legitimated its divine authority through a heavenly vision rather than from instructions on Sinai.[38]

If Childs is correct, and there was such a tradition legitimated by heavenly vision rather than by the possession of Torah, it would have been the ultimate root of what we now call apocalyptic[39] and of what we now call prophecy, since access to the divine council also authenticated the prophets.

Since the description of the tabernacle as a whole has passed through a time of fusion and exclusion, and we can expect on other grounds to find removed or transformed during the exile those parts of the tradition which had royal or angelic associations, we could expect something similar to have happened to the Menorah. The later interpretations are unanimous in linking the lamp to planetary and angelic symbolism, and to the presence of God. This is the reason for the strange silence of the other sources. In 1 Kings we find nothing, and in Exodus simply the description of a tree-like object, with nothing to suggest astral or angelic associations. What is remarkable is that commentaries today have a similar silence. The detailed specification of the lamp must have had some meaning, yet neither Childs nor Noth, in major commentaries, sees fit to deal with the Menorah as a symbol.[40] The former treats the origin and significance of the tabernacle at great length, but makes only passing reference to the lamp. The latter comments upon the opaque and confused description of the lamp, and the discrepancies between the ten lamps of Solomon's Temple and the innovation in Zerubbabel's. Noth concludes that the Temple would have needed lampstands to provide light! Haran's major work notes only that the lamp existed.[41]

Apart from Zechariah's rulers standing by the lamp, the restoration of the lamp being a hope for the messianic age, and the peculiar association of the sevenfold lamp with the royal city of Jerusalem, we have no direct evidence to link the lamp to the king figure. This link must be established if the changes in the Menorah were part of the complex upheaval which followed the demise of the monarchy and the decline of the idea of the heavenly king present in Jerusalem.[42] There are two areas which provide possible evidence.

(i) *Passages which associate the king with a lamp before Yahweh*
1 Kings 11.36 promises a reduced but still surviving kingdom for Solomon, 'so that there may be a lamp for David my servant before me ever in Jerusalem';[43]

2 Sam. 21.17 records how David's men begged him not to venture onto the field of battle 'lest you put out the lamp of Israel'; 2 Kings 8.19 records a promise of security for Judah because of David to whom Yahweh had promised a lamp forever. There was clearly an association of king and lamp, and the security of the dynasty was linked to the presence of the lamp before Yahweh. We do not know for certain that this was *the* lamp before Yahweh.[44]

(ii) *The association of the lamp with the Servant Song in Isa. 42*
The branches of the Menorah are described in Exod. 25.32 as *qānīm*, 'reeds'. This may be a technical term, or it may refer to their being hollow.[45] The Servant of the Lord in Isa. 42 is also described as a 'reed'. Now reeds in the Old Testament frequently stand for unreliable allies, e.g. Isa. 36.6; Ezek. 29.6; but this is an unlikely meaning in Isa. 42. The Servant was a *bruised reed*. In the next line we find a *wick*, suggesting that in this passage the reed should be read as a part of a lamp, as it is in Exodus. A different pointing of 42.3 gives perfect parallelism with 42.4, and a very different meaning to the passage as a whole. In 42.3 *yšbwr* should be read as niph'al, *yiššābēr*; *ykbnh* should be read as qal, *yıkbeh*, giving: 'A bruised reed, he will not be broken,[46] a spluttering wick, he will not be put out; he will bring forth justice . . .',[47] to be read parallel to 42.4, 'He will not burn dimly, he will not be broken, until he has established justice.' If an ancient lamp symbolism underlies this Servant Song, we have a strong link between the Servant and the royal figure, and between the royal figure and the lamp. The Servant, the struggling lamp of his people, would not fail, and would eventually bring forth the justice expected of a royal figure. If the passage is not menorah imagery, the readings are a remarkable coincidence.

The lamp was a tree-like object, decorated on its branches with 'almond work' (Exod. 25.33). We do not know exactly what craftsmanship was involved in this type of work,[48] but almonds do have a peculiar significance in the Old Testament. Apart from the tale of the blossoming priestly rod in Num. 17.8, there is Jeremiah's call vision, Jer. 1.11–12. The prophet saw an almond rod and knew that Yahweh was *watching*. There is the word-play *šāqēd/šōqēd*, but there may have been more significance to the almond rod. It was the almond-like branches of the lamp which were the 'eyes of the Lord' for Zechariah. Perhaps Jeremiah saw in the almond rod something which he already knew to symbolize the watching presence of the deity. The tree symbol, however, was associated with the king.[49] Even without the considerable evidence from the surrounding nations, Jotham's parable (Judg. 9), Isaiah's prophecy (Isa. 11) and the messianic title 'Branch' (Isa. 4.2; Zech. 3.8) would indicate the importance of the royal tree. Having established the link between the king figure and the Menorah, it is very significant indeed that Philo links the Menorah not only to a tree, but to the tree of life,[50] especially since the ancient king was believed to embody the life of his people.[51] The tree of life stood in the garden of Eden; later tradition recalled the divine throne set up for judgement by the tree of life

(Ap. Mos. 22ff). Both Eden (see below) and the divine throne[52] must be memories of the ancient Temple. In Solomon's Temple, an Eden place, the heavenly world was indistinguishable from the world below, and what fragments remain of its cult are embedded like pieces of a mosaic in later constructions.

The ancient cult was the original setting of the Menorah. It was a complex symbol of life, light and the presence of God, embodied in the person of the king whom it also represented. There were other agents of God on earth, just as there were other branches of the lamp; each had/was a star, each was a son of God, with access to the divine council and authority to speak in the name of Yahweh. Once our crippling distinction between heaven and earth is removed, expressions such as 'sitting on the throne of Yahweh as king instead of David' (1 Chron. 29.23) and the messianic titles in Isa. 9 can be read for what they really were. We might also have an explanation for the LXX of Daniel 7.13, ὡς υἱὸς ἀνθρώπου ἤρχετο, καὶ ὡς παλαιὸς ἡμερῶν παρῆν.

These possibilities contribute greatly to our understanding of the New Testament, especially the Fourth Gospel. Bearing in mind that the early Church used several trees to carry the tree of life symbolism,[53] the saying about the vine and the branches (John 15.1ff) can be seen to entail all the *sons of God* theology which is made explicit in Paul, but neither of these was a Christian innovation. Similarly, images of sonship, life, light, kingship, ascent, descent, divine judgement in the presence of Jesus and the prominence of the temple setting can all find a common point of origin in a tradition which remembered the older ways. The collection of titles in the first chapter of the Fourth Gospel was not the result of Christian conflation from several current expectations; the Christian position actualized an existing set of expectations.[54] It is remarkable that so many of the themes and motifs of the Fourth Gospel can be related to the symbolism of the great lamp. Where these older ways of thought were perpetuated we do not know, but the remarks in Josephus and Philo show that they *were* remembered, even if we now have no written deposit upon which to draw.

NOTES

1 T. Bab., *Menaḥot* 28b; *'Aboda Zarah* 43a; *Roš Haššanah* 24ab.
2 Goodenough, vol. 4 (1953), p. 25.
3 Meyers (1976), p. 36. For a very different view, Sperber (1965), pp. 135ff.
4 Mettinger (1982).
5 J. J. Slotkis made this point in the footnote in his translation of the Midrash Rabbah of Numbers.
6 Mettinger (1982), p. 51.
7 Meyers (1976), p. 179: 'This object, while part of a carefully balanced ritual arrangement, must be treated as an artistic motif, rather than as a cult instrument, if its significance is to be determined. Not only do the details of its fabrication and its morphology indicate a status which supersedes the requirements dictated by solely instrumental needs, but even within

the priestly texts which are orientated towards this instrumentality, it exhibits a special position not called for were it an apparatus alone'!

8 ibid., p. 36.
9 Gray (1970), p. 200.
10 *B. J.* VII, 423ff.
11 Materials in Goodenough, vol. 7 (1958).
12 See ch. 7.
13 In this case *two* rulers, which may be the point of the vision. What had formerly been a tree-like object representing both the king figure and the presence of God with his people, was separated by the prophet into its component parts to cope with the new post-exilic situation.
14 The English versions have 'singers' and 'springs' for these two words, which I think are better rendered 'princes' and 'eyes'. See below, ch. 11.
15 *C. Apionem*, 2, 112.
16 Morton Smith (1957), p. 500.
17 *B. J.* V, 217.
18 See Goodenough, vol. 4 (1953), pp. 87ff, for discussion and references.
19 See n1; also *M. Sanh* 10.1, Akiba's prohibition of the 'outside books'.
20 Yarden (1971), pp. 42ff.
21 These three were not known until 1781, 1846 and 1930 respectively.
22 See Hengel (1974), vol. ii, p. 160 n834, for details and bibliography.
23 Hengel (1974), vol. i, pp. 192ff.
24 See ch. 1, n51.
25 Neugebauer (1981).
26 Goodenough, vol. 4 (1953), p. 84.
27 Yarden (1971), plate 69.
28 ibid. p. 47, citing Philo, *Quis Haer.* 226; also Goodenough, vol. 4 (1953), p. 84.
29 Jub. 40.10; Eusebius *Praep. Evang.* ix.23, 1–4, quoting Artapanus.
30 Murray (1982a); Morgenstern (1964); Philonenko (1968). Also ch. 1, n202.
31 See Mettinger (1982), pp. 41ff; Childs (1974), p. 529 for summary and bibliography.
32 Haran (1960), pp. 50–65; (1962), pp. 14–24.
33 *M. Hagigah* 2.1; also *M. Megillah* 4.10, which indicates that certain Rabbis forbade Ezek. 1 as a reading from the prophets in the synagogue.
34 Scholem (1960), p. 27.
35 In the later Jewish mystical writings, which are so notoriously difficult to date, there is evidence of much similarity to the earlier apocalyptic writings. The thread which joins the two is slender, but given the vast stretches of time involved and the sheer accident of any heretical literature having survived at all, the fact of any thread being discernible is quite remarkable. Scholem (1960), p. 63, describes how the mystics saw God as a Holy King descending from the unknown to encounter the mystic at the throne of glory. Was this a later form of the tradition of the tent of meeting? (see Haran 1960, 1962) – or was an even older tradition underlying both reflected in the tent of meeting? cf. Clifford (1972), p. 107, on Gen. 28: 'The Bethel story . . . tells of the origin of an important El shrine in Canaan, and in so doing tells how a Canaanite shrine operates.'
36 Except perhaps at Exod. 24.9–11, which is explicitly denied by Deut. 4.12.
37 Mettinger (1982).
38 Childs (1974), p. 535.
39 Rowlands (1982) argues that the heavenly vision was the determining factor in the apocalyptic tradition, and not its eschatology.
40 Childs (1974); Noth (1962).
41 Haran (1978).
42 Mettinger (1982).

43 The LXX reads θἑσις for *nīr*, lamp.
44 The king is also the breath of his people (Lam. 4.20), and his life inextricably bound up with theirs; see Eaton (1976), pp. 160ff.
45 Meyers (1976), pp. 19–20.
46 Or 'allow himself to be broken', where the niph'al would correspond to the Greek middle.
47 To read the next word, MT *le'emet*, 'in truth', as *l'ummōt*, 'to the peoples', as proposed in Kittel's BH² and followed by NEB, would give a sense as in Isa. 49.6.
48 Meyers (1976).
49 Widengren (1951); Keel (1978); and many more.
50 Goodenough (1940), ch. 2; Philo, *Quaest. in Gen.* 1.10.
51 Eaton (1976).
52 Mettinger (1982).
53 Murray (1975), pp. 113ff.
54 Hengel (1976), p. 2. Was the formation of the doctrine of the early Church essentially the consistent development and completion of what had already been unfolded in the primal event of the first two decades?

10

TRANSFORMATIONS IN THE POST-EXILIC PERIOD: (2) THE EDEN STORIES

If the Menorah had once been the tree of life in the Garden of Eden, we must examine this Eden context to see if it, too, shows signs of having changed in a similar way as a result of the exilic upheaval. The most familiar Eden story is that of Gen. 2—3, yet there is neither reference nor allusion to this passage in any other part of the Old Testament. This suggests that the story of Adam and Eve, even though it stands as part of the preface to our Old Testament, was one of the later additions to it. Had this Genesis tale no contact by way of theme or setting with other parts of the Old Testament, we should accept it as a late, possibly foreign, addition to the corpus, and no more. But it carries a theme fundamental to any theological system, the explanation of man's painful lot in life, and it uses for its setting the Garden of Eden, which is known from Ezek. 28 as a very different place. Such evidence as there is is quite compatible with Gen. 2—3 having been offered as a *substitute for* Ezekiel's Eden, and as a different explanation of man's lot. It is this possibility that I wish to explore.

The Eden tale of Gen. 2—3 traces a fundamental disaster to disobedience, and in this sense it prefigures much of later Judaism, where disobedience and obedience, punishment and rewards, were the natural result of God's election of Israel.[1] The Scrolls retain traces of another view of sin, and although they place great emphasis upon obedience (e.g. CD II, III) and sinners can be described as those who transgress the Law, there are also passages which teach about two spirits, and man doing wrong when he falls under the influence of the hostile or evil spirit (1QS3, 17ff; 1QH14, 11ff). Sin is also thought to be simply a characteristic of humanity.[2] The later sections of 1 Enoch say that sinners are not only those who wrong their fellows, but also those who betray the true faith by adopting gentile ways and deserting the ancient customs. The earliest section of Enoch has yet another picture, and shows evil as something brought into creation as a result of the rebel angels. The great judgement was to free mankind from them and their offspring, because they had wronged mankind.

It is clear that there was a whole spectrum of ideas as to the nature of sin and evil (and it would not be appropriate at this time to dwell upon the distinction between the two). At one end, sin was disobedience, an individual's transgression of one of the laws, and at the other sin was also disobedience, but the disobedience of the angels who misused their divine knowledge and brought calamity to the earth as a result. Somewhere between these two extremes, we

233

can place the two spirits at work to influence man's actions, a position which seems to be a compromise between the 'external influences' view of 1 Enoch, and the 'intentional disobedience' view of later Judaism. Looking at these two extremes, we should expect to find the latter within a system which gave prominence to the role of the heavenly powers. If these two systems both developed from Israel's more ancient religion, it should be possible to find in the Old Testament evidence for the roots of both, or else to find evidence in the 'intertestamental' period for the origin of one or the other. If the post-exilic period was the time when the era of the Law was becoming established, and the era of the angel mythology being eclipsed, it is there that we should expect to find evidence of both, and perhaps some relationship between them, at the time when both systems were current.

When we compare the two Eden passages and the further links which they suggest, we find that the greatest similarity exists not between Ezek. 28 and Gen. 2—3, but between Ezek. 28 and Isa. 14.12ff. Genesis does not deal with the fall of a supernatural figure representing the fall of a great kingdom, but the fall of Tyre in Ezek. 28 and the fall of Babylon in Isa. 14 are clearly related, because they do. The setting of Isa. 14 is not Eden, but the heavenly mountain from which an arrogant star deity is cast down because he has tried to make himself like Elyon. We have therefore a twofold problem: relationship between the two stories which have the same Eden setting, and the relationship between the two prophetic taunts which know of a heavenly mountain and an expulsion. It is possible that the materials of Isa. 14, even though the setting is not said to be Eden, may illuminate Ezek. 28, and this in its turn may throw light on Gen. 2—3.

Isa. 14.4–21 describes the fate of a star deity (14.12) who is symbolically identified with the king of Babylon (14.4). Yahweh is depicted as the disposer of earthly rulers who has brought Babylon low (14.5–11). The offence was attempting to set his throne too high and make himself like Elyon (14.13–14). As a result, he had become an object of scorn; the mighty one had been humbled (14.15–17). The king creature was cast out like a despised *nēṣer*. If we could translate this one word accurately, we should understand this oracle. It can be rendered 'Branch', but the instances in the Old Testament show that this word is always applied to *people*.[3] There may have been a significant nuance which provides the clue to its meaning here. The commonest meaning for *nṣr* is 'guard, keep, watch', and the meaning of the participle may be word-play: a branch in the messianic royal sense, but also a guardian figure. If the king creature was such a guardian figure, perhaps in the manner of the later angels of the nations whom we meet in Daniel, this would explain why his sons are also to be slain lest they fill the world with *'irim* – not cities, but fallen heavenly beings, to whose presence on earth 1 Enoch attributed evil and corruption. Isaiah gives us a star figure cast down from the heavenly mountain, guilty of likening himself to Elyon.

Ezekiel's oracles are clearly in the same setting. The first deals with a fallen god, and the second apparently with the first man in Eden.[4] If we read the two together, in the light of the fallen figure in Isaiah, we see that the two figures are one, and that the problems in reading this text come from our using categories and distinctions quite alien to Ezekiel. The fallen god and the first figure expelled from Eden were one and the same. Thus Ezekiel forms a link between Isa. 14 and Gen. 2—3. Ezekiel's Eden is a strange magical place: I believe that we glimpse here the mythology of the old Temple. It is recorded only in this, one of the most obscure and difficult texts in the Old Testament.[5] It is the garden of the *'elohim* (28.13), a holy mountain (28.14) on which there are stones of fire. One of the inhabitants of the garden is the king of Tyre, the description of whom in 28.12, J. van Dijk has suggested, may be rendered 'serpent of perfection'.[6] He had been created full of wisdom and beauty, but pride, corruption and violence had caused his expulsion. He had claimed the wisdom and status of a god, but would be shown his mortality by death at the hand of strangers. Despite the state of the text, it is possible to glimpse a great deal of the lost Eden. It is possible that the picture which we have here of the angelic counterpart to the king of Tyre at home in the heavenly court is what we should also use to understand the role of the Davidic king. It is unlikely that foreign kings would be deemed worthy of the presence of God, and Israel's not. It becomes clear, as we read this oracle, that the setting was not only the heavenly mountain, but also the Temple, which was its earthly reality. The god-king is expelled from his sanctuary, even though some vital details are obscured. I suggest that 28.14, *'at k^erūb mimšaḥ hassōkēk ūn^etattika*, has dropped a mem and an aleph, and should be read *mimmišḥāh '^asuk^ekā*, 'I anointed you with oil', giving *mšḥ* a meaning attested elsewhere, with prefix *min*, as in Ps. 104.15, 'to make the face shine *with oil*'. A first-person verb, 'I anointed you', is a natural antecedent to 'and I appointed you'. We have reason to believe that the anointing of foreign kings was also the concern of Yahweh (1 Kings 19.15ff; Isa. 45.1), and it is not unreasonable to suppose that the king creature dismissed by Yahweh had also been set up by him. The pointing of *'t* is vital, since it determines whether or not the person addressed (*'at*) *was* the cherub or was *with* the cherub (*'et*). The supernatural figure of Isa. 14 and his similar fate suggest that the creature of Ezek. 28 is also thought to be divine, a cherub. I should read *'at*.[7] If we do not read *k^erūb hassōkēk* as 'guardian cherub', we have to look again at 28.16, where an apparently similar name occurs, for the being who evicted the king. But if the king *was* the cherub, then we have to find another explanation for this verse. The sentence begins, 'I profaned you from the mountain of the gods', implying that the expulsion of this being changed his status from divine to human, and that this Eden was indeed the home of gods. There follows obscurity: the LXX rearranges the line to give 'the cherub led you out', but the Hebrew could suggest that it was Yahweh who expelled the being. *'bdk* could be read as a first-person pi'el, giving two first-person verbs: 'I profaned you, I destroyed you, *krwb hskk*'. The LXX omits *hskk*. This word could mean (see n7 above), 'anointed', 'guardian' or 'overshadowing' cherub, but I wonder whether *hskk* does not conceal the cherub's sanctuary.

The figure who is addressed was in Eden the garden of the gods (28.13), and there follows a description of the gold and precious stones, hinges and sockets (or whatever is meant by *tuppeykā ūnᶜqabeykā*),[8] which were his 'covering' (*mᶜsukāteka*). This word is not known elsewhere in the Old Testament, but there are several similar, whose meanings must be deduced from their contexts. *mūsāk* (or *mysk*) in 2 Kings 16.18 was a part of the structure of the Temple removed during the reform of Ahaz. The whole of the verse is hopelessly corrupt, but we seem to have the '*msk* of the dwelling place' and the entrance of the king, removed from the house of the Lord. A similar word *māsāk* means a covering or division in the Temple, or the screens of the tabernacle (Exod. 26.36; 27.16; 35.12), and another, *sukkāh*, means a booth, but also a 'sanctuary' (Job 36.19; Ps. 18.12; Isa. 4.6) and a 'royal house' (Amos 9.11). Since Ezekiel's heavenly creature had something very similar made of gold and precious stones, I suggest that his 'covering' was some sort of sanctuary which he occupied, which represented his royal house, and which was situated on the holy mountain. In 28.16 we find this person driven *from* the mountain, destroyed as *kᶜrūb hassōkēk from* the midst of the stones of fire. I suggest that *hskk* here be read *mmskk*, 'from your sanctuary' giving the line, 'I profaned you from the mountain of God, I destroyed you, cherub, from your sanctuary, from the midst of the stones of fire.' This would fit well with the idea that the Eden mountain was also the Temple, and that the rituals of the sanctuary reflected the workings of the heavenly council.[9]

The fate of this figure is described in great detail, and there is a pattern in vv. 16, 17, 18. Each has a list of sins, followed by the punishment inflicted. Each has verbs in the first person: I profaned, I destroyed, I cast you out, I exposed you, I brought forth fire, I turned you to ashes. Only in the usual reading of 28.18 is this broken, if we read *ḥillaltā*, 'you profaned'; but if we read *ḥillalti* as did the LXX, we have a complete sequence in the first person. The Hebrew then has a plural form, *mqdšyk*, 'your sanctuaries', although there is support for a singular reading, and we tend to read this as from *mqdš*, 'sanctuary'. But there is a shorter form *qdš* also meaning 'sanctuary', as in Isa. 43.28, where Yahweh profanes the princes of the sanctuary and destroys their people at the same time, a similar theme and possibly a similar setting to Ezekiel's taunt. If 28.18 is also from *qdš*, the form *mqdšk* would be 'from your *sanctuary*', and we should have a passage similar in setting and theme to Dan. 8.10ff, where the stars are cast down, and the place of the sanctuary of the prince of the host is overthrown; only in Daniel it is the sanctuary of Israel's Prince which is overthrown, further indication that Israel viewed herself and foreign nations within the same overall scheme.

Throughout the oracle there are several instances of *ḥll*. Traditional lexicographical analysis finds homonyms here, on the basis of which the exegete and translator will recognize word play. But I wonder whether Ezekiel, who lived in his language as we do not, might be better understood if we tried to envisage a relationship between words closer than word-play.[10] 28.7, 17 use *ḥll* to describe spoiling and defiling the splendour of the prince; splendour, *yip'ah*, is most commonly used of divinity, as in Deut. 33.2; Ps. 50.2; 80.2; 94.1, suggesting that the loss of divine status was entailed in *ḥll*. 28.8 used *ḥll* to describe death in the heart of the sea, being brought to the pit. We are reminded of Exod. 15, where the earth swallows those who are overwhelmed by waters, and the frequent use of this apparently mixed imagery in the Psalms. The fate of Tyre, falling into the sea, was seen by Ezekiel as that fate expected for all evil beings, a death in watery chaos. 28.9 uses *ḥll* for wounding the fallen one, who will no longer be divine; cf. Ps. 82.7, where death like a man is the final punishment of the *'elohim*. 28.13 is word-play; the first state of the doomed creature was *kᵉlīl*, in contrast to the later *ḥll*, profanation, mortality. 28.16 uses *ḥll* for Yahweh removing the creature from the holy mountain, 28.18 uses *ḥll* for what was done by the creature to his sanctuary, or, more likely, what was done to remove him from it. It would appear that *ḥll* indicates whatever was associated with the change of status from divine to human; we have no exact equivalent because we do not think in these terms. The process involved defilement, death, wounding which proved mortality, expulsion from the holy mountain and the sanctuary. It is important to notice that leaving the mountain, losing divinity, incurring death, were interrelated aspects of the one process, possibly the obverse of being permitted to stand on the holy mountain and achieving angelic status. *All this happened to a royal figure.*

Ezekiel's Eden offers other glimpses of a lost world; 28.6 makes it clear that to claim qualities as great as those of the *'elohim* was to court disaster, exactly the situation of Isa. 14. Ezekiel threatens death at the hands of *zarim*, perhaps related to the mysterious *ṣarim* of Isaiah's prophecy of doom in Isa. 59.18.[11]

In this older Eden, the royal figure walks among 'stones of fire', which tempts one to read as 'sons of fire', *bᵉnē 'ēš* for *'abnē 'ēš*, but 'fiery stones' do occur elsewhere and must have been a feature of the mythology, or else a very early corruption of an original reading. The LXX has 'stones', and some later commentators said they were heavenly beings, but the tradition is divided: the Targum of Jonathan paraphrases as 'the holy people', Theodoret says they were angels because men could not be called *fiery* stones, and Jerome also opts for angels. This corresponds to the different readings of Daniel 7: the Jewish tradition which we read in the present text changed references to the Holy Ones and made them apply to the holy people, whereas the Christian tradition kept the angels, as it kept so much else.

Finally, we must note the importance of wisdom in this chapter; it is mentioned in vv. 2, 3, 4, 5, 6, 12, 17. It was the corruption of his wisdom which led to the king figure's expulsion in the second oracle, and the claiming of divine wisdom which led to his downfall in the first. The claim to exaltation and the corruption of the heavenly wisdom were thus both present in the tradition which Ezekiel knew, and he presumably also knew the relationship between them; we do not, and this is why we cannot establish exactly the relationship between what seem to be two streams in the angel mythology. One deals with the corruption of wisdom on earth, as in 1 Enoch, and the other with an assault on the supremacy of Elyon, as in Isa. 14. The oracles on Tyre show that the two belong together.

Genesis 2—3 and Ezekiel 28 are explicitly linked; both are set in the Garden of Eden, and we are accustomed, despite appearances, to assume that the Genesis version is the older. Von Rad's treatment of this comparison is a good example of assumption overruling fact. He says:

> The relation of the material [in Ezekiel 28] to Gen., ch. 3, is apparent ... The Yahwist, who wrote in the period of the Solomonic enlightenment or shortly thereafter ... was the last one to pass on myth with archaic piety. Actually ... [Genesis 3] has very little in common with a real myth. How much richer are the mythological colours even in Ezekiel 28.11ff, and how much 'more modern' does the older Yahwist seem ...
>
> The contents of Gen., ch. 2 and especially ch. 3 are conspicuously isolated in the Old Testament. No prophet, psalm, or narrator makes any recognizable reference to the story of the Fall. One actually does justice to the Yahwist only when one sees him in his isolation, facing the received tradition very freely.[12]

The relationship between the two Edens is in fact the opposite of what von Rad assumed; the tradition freely rearranged, i.e. reformed, was the tradition of Ezek. 28 reworked for the post-exilic era of the Law. In what the writer of Genesis says, and in what he does not say, we can detect the earlier myth, but the whole structure has been brilliantly realigned so as to make human disobedience and the hankering after divine wisdom replace divine disobedience and the corruption of wisdom. This is exactly the theme of Job,[13] where Job is challenged and eventually condemned on the grounds of his claim to *knowledge*. The book is not just about suffering but also about Job's claim to *know*. We can see that the characteristics of the Genesis Eden are exactly those of Deuteronomy (given that the emphases upon Exodus and election would not have been appropriate). The Genesis Eden even uses the Deuteronomic form of the divine name, 'Yahweh Elohim', a form unique to this passage in the Pentateuch.[14] Several explanations have been offered for this untranslatable form,[15] but none is really satisfactory. The characteristic suffixes which give 'the Lord *your* God' in Deuteronomy are all that is missing here; they would have been inappropriate in Eden, hence the simple form.

In Gen. 3 Adam and Eve were in the garden and were forbidden knowledge, because it would have made them like the *elohim*.[16] The Genesis writer knew, then, that the *elohim* had wisdom, and that it was the possession of this wisdom

238

which gave them that status. Yahweh walked in the garden, made the rules, and expelled the disobedient. The Genesis writer also knew of a clever talking serpent, of whose origin he says nothing (and there is another unexplained creature at Gen. 4.7). He also knew of a guardian cherub. Once they had disobeyed over the matter of knowledge, and were to be expelled as a result, Adam and Eve became conscious of their sexuality and thus of their mortality. The Genesis writer also knew the fate of those expelled from the garden, but in the earlier version that garden was the mountain. The two would die 'like any man', as did the condemned sons of Elyon in Ps. 82, and the Prince of Tyre. Having left the garden they reared children to replace themselves after death, and they brought upon themselves the curses of a creation no longer perfect. It is possible to be fairly precise about the origin of Ezekiel's Eden myth, which was not foreign to Israel in any meaningful sense of that word. Isa. 14 and Isa. 43.28 testify to the antiquity of the myth, and Dan. 8 to its survival. Isa. 43 and Dan. 8 also afford the vital clue as to its original setting. The myth of the fall belonged to the old Temple. Our problem is to reconstruct that older Temple so as to see how Ezekiel's figures fitted in their natural setting. Ezekiel himself has left us a picture of *a* temple in his vision, and the detail he gives shows that the future ideal was very similar to the remembered form of Solomon's. It was built upon a high mountain (Ezek. 40.2; 43.12), and its courtyards were decorated with palm trees (40.31, 34). The inner parts were decorated with palm trees and two-headed cherubim (41.5ff), and from the temple there came a river which brought supernatural fertility to the land (47.1–12). Each of Ezekiel's temple features is attested elsewhere in the Old Testament. Isa. 2.2–4//Mic. 4.1–3 looks forward to the day when the *mountain* of the house of the Lord will be raised above all other mountains, when the word of Yahweh from Jerusalem will rule the whole earth. Ps. 48.1–3 praises a holy mountain[17] which is the citadel of the great king. The prophecy of Isaiah looks forward to a day when there will be harmony restored to the creatures who live on the holy mountain. Complex though its antecedents may be, there was also some mountain-top vision which lay behind and gave authority to, the actual form of the Temple and its cult. The vision of the elders in Exod. 24 is a startling fossil from an earlier time, and the pattern for the tabernacle and the cultic accessories described in subsequent chapters suggests that Moses had seen a tabernacle on the mountain which his earthly structure had to resemble in every detail (Exod. 25.9, 40). Ps. 92.12(13) describes the righteous as *trees*, planted in the house of Yahweh. The Menorah, the tree of life, belonged in the Temple. Enoch was assured that the tree of life would be transplanted to the Temple. Zechariah sees *waters* from the Temple on the day when the Lord becomes king over the whole earth (Zech. 14.8). Joel looks forward to a fountain from the house of the Lord on the Day of the Lord (Joel 3.18). Isaiah sees broad streams in Zion (Isa. 33.21), and Ps. 46.4 is similar. Ezekiel envisaged a garden sanctuary on a hilltop,[18] not unlike those known elsewhere in the ancient Near East, and he recalled the actual Temple of Solomon which he had known.

We can deduce more about the older Temple from other texts. Jer. 17.12, Isa. 6 and Ps. 11.4 all link the sanctuary to the glorious throne in heaven. Isa. 6 and Dan. 9 link the sanctuary to the host of heaven, and Daniel, even at that late date, links it specifically to the heavenly power struggle, i.e. to the myth of Isa. 14 and Ezek. 28. In the Temple there was also a bronze serpent (2 Kings 18.4).

It cannot be coincidence that amongst the few scraps of information we can glean about the first Temple, we discover trees, cherubim, the throne of God, a mountain cult, life-giving waters, a serpent, and a blurring of the distinction between earth and heaven in the sacred space of the sanctuary. The picture we draw from the Deuteronomic account alone is very different: there is no emphasis upon the supernatural or Eden motifs. The ark is a mere box, there is no mention of the divine throne, nor of the living waters, the mountain setting nor the role of the cherubim. There is no tree of life, no Menorah. In other words, it is possible to fit Ezekiel's Eden into the Temple we can construct from non-Deuteronomic sources, and it is also clear that the myth in which Ezekiel sets his Eden was the myth of the old cult. The ancient Temple was Eden, the mountain of the gods, in which there was the divine throne, and in which the judgement took place (Ps. 73.17).

There is also much in extra-biblical material which associates Eden and the Temple. The Targum to Ezekiel knew a tradition which linked Adam to the celestial temple, the divine throne and the abode of God.[19] Jub. 4.23ff describes how Enoch was conducted to the Garden of Eden to sit as the heavenly scribe preparing accusations for the great judgement.[20] Adam was not created in the garden, but brought there to till it; Eve was brought in forty days later, linking to the purity laws which governed a woman's entering the Temple. Upon leaving Eden, Adam made an incense offering (Jub. 3.27). All animals were struck dumb, and all flesh expelled from Eden. 1 Enoch links the older Eden to the Temple, and the Temple to the form of the heavens. God sat in the inner house of heaven (1 En. 14.10ff) as in the sanctuary of the Temple, and the sapphire throne of Exod. 24.9–11 and Ezek. 1.26 becomes in 1 En. 18.6ff the sapphire mountain at the centre of the seven mountains. These seven have been linked to the seven planet gods of Babylon, but we need not go so far afield;[21] the menorah symbolism shows that the seven motif was integral to the old myth. The central mountain of sapphire must be linked to the central branch of the Menorah, which represented the deity. The mountains of Enoch are personified; seven evil mountains were evil stars awaiting punishment (cf. Jer. 51.25 where the end of Babylon is described in the same way). In 1 En. 24 the throne on the central mountain is encircled by trees, and the heavenly guide assures him that the tree of life which he has seen will one day be planted by the holy place, the Temple of the Lord the heavenly King. Enoch travels yet further and sees another tree, the tree of knowledge growing in the garden of righteousness (1 En. 32.3). Enoch's exclamation, 'How beautiful is the tree', was condemned by later 'orthodoxy'. Aboth (3.10) warns that anyone saying such a thing would incur 'guilt against the soul'.[22] This condemnation has caused commentators much trouble, but Goodenough suggested that the tree in question must have been Enoch's Tree of Knowledge, rather than just any tree, indicating opposition to those who cherished the vision of that Tree.[23] The Syriac tradition remembers an association of Temple and Eden as church and Eden, and remembers Eden as a mountain.[24] Later myths and legends in Judaism also recall the Garden of Eden as a temple place;[25] I am certain that Ezekiel's mountain Eden *was* the old Temple, and that the old temple myth was the framework of Ezekiel's taunt against Tyre. This myth was transformed to give us the familiar Eden of Genesis.[26]

It is also possible to trace the remains of the older myth in later Adam legends, and to detect changes in the canonical texts exactly as we should expect. The origin of the Adam tale is not to be sought in the myths of primeval man, for which nothing comparable has yet been recovered, but in the king figure of the older cult. Ezekiel's fallen figure was royal. His myth was the myth of the angels, his sin was the abuse of knowledge, and his setting was the Temple from which he was expelled. The Genesis Eden has no clear association with the Temple, but it does have many of the features of the Temple and the older Eden. There are rivers of water, a tree of life, unexplained cherubim, and the fallen Adam, who had once enjoyed the presence of God in the holy garden. Genesis has no reference here to the fallen angels, although the sequence of the Book of Dreams does imply that the fall of Asael was in the time of Adam and Eve, and that it was Asael who tempted with heavenly knowledge. Works such as The Life of Adam and Eve and its near relation the Apocalypse of Moses also piece together the two themes in such an extraordinary patchwork of ideas and traditions that we can only suppose both were drawing upon known peripheral materials, rather than constructing a conflated account of Eden using an originally alien mythology of angels. In the Life, the devil appears as an angel, with his own account of the fall. He had been an angel in heaven (chap. 12ff), but when man was created in the image of God, a Genesis element, the devil was required to worship him, and he refused. Threatened with punishment, the devil retaliated by making a claim to the highest throne and claiming equality with God. The devil and his angels were then banished, and from that time have devoted themselves to their vengeance upon man who caused their downfall. A fusion of themes such as this demands a full analysis, and I do not have space for this. The mixture of themes, however, is immediately obvious. The Apocalypse of Moses tells (chap. 22ff) how God appears in the garden (not called Eden), accompanied by the cherubim. At his coming, all the flowers begin to bloom, and the great throne is set up by the tree of life. Man, woman and serpent are cursed, and the angels ordered to expel Adam and Eve.

After many entreaties, the fallen pair are allowed to take with them the seeds of plants for food, and the seeds of plants for incense. Other traditions also remember that Adam was more than an ordinary mortal before his expulsion. He was created so tall that his head reached the heavens, but the Creator shortened him when the angels declared that there were two lords, one for earth and one for heaven.[27] Nor could anyone ever be quite sure what lay beneath the statement of Gen. 1.26 that man was made in the image of God,[28] a phrase which has exercised the ingenuity of commentators ever since it was written. If Adam was the royal figure, a son of God reduced in post-exilic times to human dimensions, the phrase would be explained. The 'image of God' eventually came to be seen as the guiding principle for human conduct, but it was never explained. By New Testament times, being in the form of God was associated with *not grasping at equality with God*, as the hymn in Phil. 2 makes clear. It entailed acting as the servant of God on earth, and the godlike qualities were seen as perfect obedience, rather than ambition and disobedience. The key word for understanding this early hymn is 'therefore' (Phil. 2.9). Why should voluntary humility *therefore* lead to exaltation, unless the hymn's frame of reference was the myth of the old Temple? The speed with which the heavenly and earthly Adams came into Christian thought,[29] and the way in which all the other New Testament titles for Jesus can be related to the old royal mythology, raise the question of the relevance of Adam's antecedent. If the Adam figure derived from the older royal figure, and ultimately from the divine figure such as we find in Ezek. 28, many of the later Christian developments are easily explicable within the Hebrew tradition.

For many years our reading of the New Testament was influenced by the hypothesis of the 'gnostic redeemer'. This position is now largely discredited, but we have yet to find another within which to locate all the material once explained as gnostic. One answer has been rejected, but the problem remains. There are two systems clearly visible in Paul's thought,[30] and if the second was not derived from gnosticism, what was it? We do not know the second system. Daniélou suggested long ago[31] that gnosis grew from Jewish Christianity, and if we further distinguish, as we must, between Jewish and 'Hebrew' Christianity,[32] it is likely that this second system in Paul's thought had its roots in Hebrew Christianity. It is there that we should expect to find something which gave rise to the complex pattern of titles in the New Testament.

Many early Christian arguments were based upon claims to having fulfilled the Scriptures, but 'fulfilment' is a process which maps one set of ideas onto another. It is a matching process, to be distinguished from the process of establishing a set of ideas in the first place. In other words, the titles applied to Jesus, and the position he was claimed to fulfil, are more likely to have existed as a single system before the time of Jesus, than to have been created as a system and simultaneously applied to him. The proof-texts used by the early Church indicate a set of expectations which antedated Jesus. They do not necessarily indicate creative theologizing based upon previously unrelated texts and ideas.[33] There is a more plausible context for the hymn in Phil. 2 than the Adam version of the Eden story, into which Psalm 8 would naturally fit, and this is the old royal myth known to antedate the Adam story and to have had links with it in the extra-canonical legends and traditions.[34] There was a Hebrew tradition of heavenly ideals and earthly counterparts; we need not argue from the relevance of Philo and Plato to the Adam material of the New Testament. Furthermore, these heavenly counterparts were royal, and the champions of their people against evil forces, i.e. they afforded the basis for both Christology and soteriology.

C. H. Dodd asked long ago whether the meaning which the New Testament writers found in a passage of the Old Testament when they reflected upon it in view of the gospel facts was an organic outgrowth or ripening of the original thought, or whether it amounted to no more than an arbitrary reading into the passage of a meaning essentially foreign to it. He concluded:

> I believe reflection will show that the development of meaning is a living growth within the given environment, and that the doctrines associated with these passages by New Testament writers gain in depth and significance when we have regard to the original, historical intention of the psalms they cite.[35]

Our task is to uncover that original intention as it was understood in New Testament times.

Conclusions

There has to be an explanation for the changes which took place in the menorah symbolism, and in the Eden myths, especially since the direction of the change is in each case similar. The situation is such that we have to work by comparing the canonical material with whatever has survived outside it.[36] When we contemplate the process of redaction, and the whole emerging field of canonical criticism, we have to remember that each of these has an obverse. What was left out, and why? What is the difference between redaction and censorship? How did a canonical tradition define itself, if not over against something which had to be rejected? One only needs to define what is included in order to exclude.

The only firm conclusion to be drawn from this chapter is that there is much work to be done, and even more, both ancient and modern, to be undone, if we are to recover any of the tradition extant in many apocalyptic texts. The freedom and familiarity with which the New Testament writers make use of this imagery from a lost tradition make this study of more than academic interest, since it is clear that until the true conceptual framework of the New Testament is recovered, attempts to understand it could be seriously adrift.

NOTES

1 E. P. Sanders (1977), pp. 107ff.
2 ibid., p. 273.
3 Isa. 11.1; Dan. 11.7.
4 May (1962), p. 167. 'In vss. 12–19 the figure changes, presenting no longer a god fallen from his throne in the recesses of the seas, but First Man in Eden, a perfect and wise mortal, driven from his paradise because of his sin.' See also Job 15.7–8; the first man was wise, because he was in the council of God.
5 Again one asks how this obscurity came about.
6 Van Dijk (1968), p. 115, suggests *ḥawwat-m-toknīt* rather than *ḥōtem toknīt*.
7 *mimšaḥ* could be from *mšḥ*, 'anointed'; *hassōkēk* could be from *sūk*, also 'anointed'; it could be 'guardian', see BDB *ad loc.* (one example at Nah. 2.6); it could be 'extended', 'overshadowing' (1 Kings 8.7; Exod. 25.20), the common description of the cherubim in the sanctuary.
8 NEB 'jingling beads of gold and spangles'; RSV 'settings and engravings'; TEV 'ornaments of gold'; AV 'tabrets and pipes'.
9 For a survey of various suggestions for 'stones of fire' see W. Zimmerli (1969), pp. 685ff.
10 This suggestion may seem unscientific, but it is made seriously: people who speak a language constantly reveal that they connect words with each other by links which linguists would judge strictly illegitimate. For another example I suggest the set of physical afflictions in Isa. 35.5–6 which correspond to a set of names for supernatural beings (see ch. 4, p. 133).
11 Murray (1984) explored the complexities of *'r, ṣr* and others, suggesting a possible relationship between them.
12 Von Rad (1963), pp. 95, 98.
13 Glatzer (1966).
14 With the exception of Exod. 9.30, where the MT has this form, but the Samaritan not.
15 BDB, p. 219, says the combination *yhwh 'lhym* is probably due to editors who either inserted *yhwh* into an *'lhym* passage, or vice versa!
16 Thompson (1971); Cross (1973), p. 306. Why do Adam and Eve become conscious that they are *naked*? Can *'ērōm*, 'naked', involve a word-play upon *'irīm*?
17 Although this mountain is in the north.
18 Barnes (1935), p. 51; but Clifford (1972), p. 103, says the garden/mountain fusion was late and peculiar to Ezekiel. The evidence suggests otherwise.
19 Levey (1975), p. 139: 'The association of Adam with the celestial temple, the divine abode, the throne of the deity, is established in recognised strata from which T. Ezekiel could draw.' Also T. Dan. 5.12 where Eden is parallel to the new Jerusalem, and T. Lev. 5.1 where the gate of heaven opens to reveal the holy temple, the throne of glory and Elyon.
20 The reference is first to a land of Eden destroyed by a great flood, and there follows confused reference to Eden and three mountains of God. Is the implication that Eden was also a mountain?
21 Charles, *Pseudepigrapha, ad loc.*
22 Herford, in Charles, *Pseudepigrapha*, p. 700.
23 Goodenough, (1958), vol. 7, p. 129.
24 Murray (1975), pp. 258, 306ff.
25 Gen Rabbah on Gen. 3.22 links this passage to Dan. 8.13 and Deut. 6.4. It associates the expulsion of Adam from Eden and the expulsion from the sanctuary. Adam was with the angels, and the host of heaven is identified with the seed of Adam. The expulsion from Eden is also linked to the destruction of the Temple. Rapoport, vol. 1, pp. 111ff, gives two pictures found in 'midrashic lore' but without reference to sources. One describes Eden surrounded by three concentric walls of fire, each of which limits the area to which certain classes of the righteous are to be confined; one is reminded of the courts system of Herod's Temple. The other sees Eden as a place of several dwelling houses; the first and second are built of cedar,

the third of precious metals and the fourth of olive wood. In the third house was the tree of life, from which there issued the four rivers of paradise.

26 Keel (1978), p. 119. In Mesopotamian mythology the foundation of the temple replaces the creation of paradise. In Gen. 2 we find the opposite; a garden instead of a temple.

27 There is a vast collection of these Adam legends in Ginzberg (1909). Does the shortening of Adam the lord of the earth reflect the demise of the king? Pss. 8 and 89 make the royal figure just such a lord.

28 Altmann (1968).

29 Dunn (1980), pp. 98ff.

30 E. P. Sanders (1977).

31 Daniélou (1964), vol. i, p. 54.

32 Murray (1982b) – though Murray (1985) abandons this use of 'Hebrew' in favour of 'disaffected Judaism'.

33 Dunn (1980), p. 108.

34 For the Adam view, see Dunn (1980), p. 126: but see J. A. Sanders (1969) and Murray (1980); cf. ch. 6, n47.

35 Dodd (1965), p. 133.

36 After completing this chapter I read Davies (1985), who argues that the Cain story (Gen. 4) contains elements of the Enochic Azael: another example of transformation. cf. Ginzberg (1909), vol. i, p. 105; ii, p. 132, the legend of Cain as the son of Satan.

11

THE NAMES OF GOD: (2) ELYON

Occurrence of the title 'Holy One' (Chapter 3) revealed a significant pattern. 'Elyon' can be similarly treated, and I hope to show in this chapter how the Old Testament texts which use 'Elyon' exhibit a consistency which has much in common with the Enochic tradition. There are two possible explanations for this: either the Enoch material is spun from a choice of Old Testament texts which, by coincidence, favour the title Elyon, or the Enochic material developed from an Elyon tradition. The latter is the more likely.

The problem with the Elyon texts, as with so much of the material relevant to the origins of apocalyptic, is the period which separates the earliest material from the latest. I argued in Chapter 2, on Wisdom, that there was a direct link between the apocalyptists' wisdom and that of the ancient wise men, even though the two are separated by the work of reformers who have given us in the Old Testament a very different impression of the nature of wisdom. There is no evidence to show where or by whom the older wisdom was preserved, but its existence as a recognizable descendant of the earlier wise men is proof that it did survive. The Elyon figure was part of the same tradition, and it, too, is obscured in the middle period. Like wisdom, Elyon has been obscured by the business of Hellenization. Just as we can now root in indigenous Israelite wisdom much of what had been attributed to Greek sources, so too we can see that the assumption that Elyon is to be associated in the second century with the Zeus Hypsistos of the syncretizers does not account for all of the evidence.[1] Thus, when Hasmonean priests took the title Priest of El Elyon, they could have been adopting Greek ways, or they could have been reviving the ancient ways of Jerusalem, and the roles of its ancient kings.[2] Solomon and his successors were priest-kings 'after the order of Melchizedek', even if we do not know what this means. Melchizedek was the priest of El Elyon. The fact that we know nothing of the Elyon priesthood only warns us how little we know about the monarchy and the cult of the first Temple. I believe this is due to the manner in which our materials were transmitted.

The process of transmission involved more than the growth and decay natural in any culture. There was the violent upheaval and realignment in the sixth century which affected every aspect of Israel's life. Fragments of the older Elyon cult are embedded in our present Old Testament, but the methods of identifying and retrieving them must, obviously, be open to debate. The problem is made more complex by the fact that Elyon, properly speaking, is an adjective, and therefore has a tendency to disappear back into the text. In Gen.

246

40.17, the 'top' basket is clearly adjectival, but in Ps. 97.9 the adjective has a particular significance, and should be read as the title Elyon. Ps. 89.28 is very similar, but here it is the king who is the *highest* of the kings of the earth. Now the pattern of Ps. 89 shows that heaven and earth operate as counterparts of each other; Yahweh is supreme in heaven, and his chosen monarch is *Elyon* over the rulers of the earth. This virtual fusion of Yahweh and his monarch is quite clear in 1 Chron. 29.23, where the king ruled from the throne of Yahweh, as Elyon amongst kings.

There are also three descriptions of the Temple where a more than adjectival rendering of '*highest*' might be appropriate: Neh. 3.25; 2 Chron. 23.20; 2 Kings 15.35 describe the upper house, the upper residence, etc, but each could be read otherwise. There may have been a 'house of the High King', a 'place of the Highest, the house of the king', a 'gate of the house of Yahweh the Highest'. Until we know exactly the meaning of Elyon when applied to the king, or to Yahweh, any translation must be tentative.

Deuteronomy also has texts which may indicate that memories of the royal Elyon cult are not far below the surface. Deut. 26.19; 28.1 both use Elyon of the chosen people, entirely consistent with the Deuteronomic democratization of the royal theology. In close association with the notion of exaltation we find *holiness* and *obedience*, as though these were natural concomitants for those who were *highest*. They would only be natural in a system which had grown upon the old mythology of exaltation and obedience to the High God.[3] A certain hostility to Elyon is also to be found in one or two places, where there is play upon the words Elyon and *le'iyyin*, 'ruins', in the manner of the Second Isaiah's mocking of the watching gods, when he called them 'the blind'. 1 Kings 9.8, a Deuteronomic passage, has Elyon in the Hebrew, but the Old Latin and the Syriac presuppose 'ruins':

> This temple will be Elyon...
> This temple will be a ruin...

The parallel in 2 Chron. 7.21 has similar confusion. A possible source of this invective is Micah 3.12 (quoted in Jer. 26.18). The threefold threat against Jerusalem promised that the city would become 'a field, a ruin, and a wooded grove', word-play respectively upon Shaddai, Elyon and '*ir*. It is pointless to attempt a translation. This is the climax of the prophet's curse, contrasting the present state with a future disaster.

We are on firmer ground when we compare Deut. 32.8, Isa. 14.14 and Daniel (*passim*), all Elyon texts beyond dispute, and yielding evidence which is consistent with the title having been rooted in the royal cult. In Deut. 32.8, Elyon allocates the nations to their various gods; Yahweh is given Jacob, but the text is confused, due no doubt to uneasiness about the readings at this point. Our Hebrew has the 'sons of Israel', but the LXX and the Qumran Hebrew both have 'sons of God', implying that Yahweh was one of these sons of God.

Yahweh and Elyon are distinct beings, and Yahweh bears a strong resemblance to the heavenly princes whom we meet later in Daniel, national leaders under the supreme control of Elyon. In Isaiah 14.14 the star figure/patron angel of Babylon attempts to scale the heights and set himself above Elyon. He is thrown down, and his sons destined for slaughter lest they fill the world with evil creatures. This is the second element of the Elyon myth, and the ascent of the heavenly mountain will prove to be a significant feature. Throughout Daniel there is an Elyon figure exactly like that of the Deuteronomy and Isaiah texts. In Chapters 3, 4, and 5 the usage could be explained away as a characteristic of the later period, but in ch. 7, where the vision is to offer comfort and the hope of triumph to a city threatened with paganizing ways, it is not likely that the Elyon here is simply the Zeus Hypsistos of the Hellenizers. Daniel's Elyon rules the kingdoms of the earth by means of his watchers and Holy Ones. He, too, throws down a king of Babylon because of his pride, and he rescues his servants from perils by means of an angel or a son of the gods.[4] The Son of Man vision adds something to the Elyon evidence which is not explicit in the older texts, even though we could deduce that something similar lies beneath them. The chosen figure representing the people of God is allowed to ascend (the holy mountain) to the throne of Elyon, and achieves his dominion after that ascent. The language of ch. 7 is that of the old royal cult, and the similarities with Ps. 2 show that the author of Daniel knew of the old patterns. This royal ascent is the ultimate origin of the later ascents which we find as a characteristic of the earliest apocalypses, and which was developed by the later Jewish mystics.

Thus, when we find Elyon as a name of God within all the sections of 1 Enoch,[5] we are discovering the Elyon of old Jerusalem, complete with the ascents and the angel figures, the secret knowledge, the judgement and the triumph of his favoured ones. When we find Elyon in the Genesis Apocryphon,[6] we are not surprised to find that it, too, is peopled with angels, who, like those in 1 Enoch, are thought to father remarkable children. When we search through the Old Testament, however, we find that the Elyon figure has been fused and confused with Yahweh, especially in the Psalms where we might have hoped to find the best relics of the older ways. Nevertheless, even the scattered references in the Psalms occur only in contexts which are consistent with what we already know of Elyon. It is possible that they contain additional detail to fill out the picture.

The proclamations of the Second Isaiah, which identify Yahweh and El, imply that this was a new insight to enable Israel to cope with the disaster of the exile. This invites us to suppose that despite the fusions which we read in the Psalms,[7] the period of the monarchy distinguished Yahweh and El as separate deities. Where we do find fusions in the texts from this period, it is more likely to be a fusion of Yahweh and the king.

The commonest association of Elyon in the Psalter is with triumph: 7.18; 9.3; 18.14; 21.8; 47.2; 91.9. From these texts we can reconstruct the context of the triumph. There was a divine throne, enemies in the pit, theophany, rescue from waters, which are seen as enemies (cf. Pss. 18,77 which tell of triumph over waters), protection from demonic terrors, helping angels and the associated triumph of an obedient king. There is the closely related theme of judgement in 50.14; 82.6; 83.18; 92.1, which is especially interesting in Ps. 82 where it is the sons of El who are judged.

Elyon is associated with knowledge (Ps.73.11; 92.1; 107.10ff). From these contexts we learn the wicked doubted the *knowledge* of Elyon, that there were arrogant, proud oppressors who defied Elyon and challenged his wisdom, that the psalmist was a son who remained faithful, and that the demise of the enemies could be *perceived* in the Temple. There was knowledge which the wicked could not know concerning the fate of evildoers, exactly as was entrusted to Enoch on his heavenly journeys. The psalmist could contrast such ignorant wickedness with his own *exaltation and anointing*. The Elyon texts also have the theme of rebellion, throughout Ps. 107, and in Ps. 78 where the familiar Exodus theme is related as a tale of rebellion against Elyon and the Holy One, leading to the *rejection of Ephraim*. Unlike the Deuteronomic account, this sees the rejection of Ephraim as the prelude to the choice of Jerusalem and the Davidic line, and not as the result of the idolatry of the kings of the north. The most significant of the Elyon texts associate the name with *divine sonship*. Ps. 73 contrasts arrogant and worthy sons. Ps. 82 describes evil sons thrown down to mortality. Ps. 87, which could tell us a great deal, is so obscure that it needs a detailed study. Given that the text is one of the most defective in the Psalter[8] (which may be significant in itself, in view of what we know about the textual corruption of other passages which deal with the old mythology), I do not presume to offer a translation, but merely to observe certain possibilities.

Psalm 87

87.1 has *b'har'rē qōdeš*, 'on the mountains of the Holy One'. The Syriac has 'on his holy mountain', and the Targum 'the ancient mountain'. Similar consonants at Ps.110.3 (another obscure text of relevance to Elyon) read *b'hadrē qōdeš*, but these are often emended in the light of 87.1, to give 'on the holy mountain'. Other suggestions have been 'when the Holy One appeared', and 'in the beauties of holiness',[9] a reference to the royal robes. The LXX of 110.3 has ἐν τῇ λαμπρότητι τῶν ἁγίων, showing that the translator thought he was dealing with the heavenly host. Behind the confusions, we may with confidence say that the setting is the divine court, whether on earth or in heaven. There follows *y'sūdātō*, 'his founded (city)', where the LXX also has the idea of foundation. Another possibility is that the word derives from *sōd*, 'council', which is closely related to *ysd*, 'found'. (The niph'al of *ysd* means 'to sit in council', Ps. 2.2; 31.14.) Psalm 87, then, takes us to the divine council which inspired the prophets, Amos 3.7, and was the scene of the great judgement (Ps. 89.8; Isa. 43). In 87.6 we find that it is Yahweh who is the heavenly scribe in this council.

THE OLDER TESTAMENT

Later writings assign this function to other beings (e.g. to Enoch, 1 Enoch 12), but the notion of a book of life and judgement is present throughout the Old Testament writings (Isa. 4.3; 65.6; Ps. 69.29; 139.16; 149.9; Exod. 32.33; Mal. 3.16; Dan. 12.1ff). It is even called the 'Book of Yahweh' in Isa. 34.16, and seems to have dealt with the details of the fate of Edom. The main theme of Ps. 87 is what the heavenly scribe recorded but, because we are unfamiliar with the idea of Yahweh as the heavenly scribe, the substance of what was recorded is equally strange.[10] In other words, we cannot even begin to translate this Psalm with confidence.

87.4 reads, 'I shall inscribe Babylon and Rahab as knowers of me', followed by 'Philistia and Tyre with Cush'. If, with the Syriac and LXX we point this differently, and read *ṣūr ʿam kus* for *ṣūr ʿim kus*, we find that we have the *ṣr* of the people of Cush, a recognizable supernatural. Thus Babylon, Rahab, Philistia and the *ṣr* of Cush are recorded as 'knowing'. Hebrew *ydʿ*, most often 'know', has a homonym with other meanings; it can imply recognition of defeat and the anger of Yahweh as in Hos. 9.7; Isa. 9.3; Ezek. 35.14, or it can mean 'humiliate'.[11] The recording of defeated adversaries is more in accord with what we know of the old cult, than their registration as converts, which is implied by the English rendering, 'those who know the Lord'. The heavenly scribe records the defeated enemies. The pointing of *zh yld šm* in v. 4 is not clear, but possibly it means 'this one was born there', not unlike the *yld bh*, 'born in her', of v. 5. The LXX rendered this latter by μήτηρ, 'mother',[12] giving the sense that Zion was the mother of whatever was born there. The city as the mother of the faithful is a common theme,[13] and the rest of the verse implies that Elyon was the father. It is customary at this point to emend Elyon to *lʿōlām*, and to read the verb *yʿkōnʿnehā* as from *kûn*, 'establish'. The family theme of the Psalm favours leaving Elyon where it stands, and looking for another meaning for the verb. There is one such at Ps. 86.16, where, in another obscure context dealing with divine fatherhood, we find *knnh* meaning 'stock' or 'tree'. This text has, 'The son you have made strong for yourself/secured for yourself', *bēn ʾimmaṣtā lāk* (with the Syriac and LXX implying the reading *ben ʾādām*, 'son of man'), meshed with the imagery of a felled vine and this word *knnh*. The context suggests that *knnh* was parallel to 'son', the man of the right hand of the Lord of Hosts. If a word related to *knnh* underlies the verb at 87.5, we should have a glimpse of Elyon the divine father, and the Psalm would be recording a promise to a particular son of Zion and Elyon, possibly the king, recorded by the heavenly scribe. The last verse is also a problem. 'Singers and dancers, all my springs are in you', the usual type of rendering, is hardly sense. Even the earliest translators had trouble with this verse, a sign that the real meaning of the verse was lost long ago. There are three groups mentioned, *šrm, hllm, kl mʿyny*. The first group, the singers, appear in several versions as 'princes', i.e. as *śārīm*, not *šārīm*. The second group, *hllm* could also be singers, pipers, dancers; there are several possible translations. The third group could also be musicians. Kittel's

BH proposed *m'yny* from *'ānah*, 'sing'. The Syriac implies that the meaning was from *'ānah*, 'afflicted', although the LXX has εὐφραινομένων, 'rejoicing', presumably from *'ānah*, 'sing'. If these three are not categories of musicians, there is a strong possibility that they were heavenly beings. The 'princes' in Isa. 43.28 in the sanctuary were more than human. The *ḥllm*, which I would not presume to translate, are related to the key word of Ezekiel's oracle against Tyre, *ḥll*, which has so many meanings in this specialized context that none of them is clear to us. The third group should be read as *klm 'yny*, the beings whom we encounter in Zech. 4.10 as the 'eyes of Yahweh'.[14] Isaiah, Ezekiel and Zechariah all use these related words in the context of the sanctuary; it is not impossible that Psalm 87 also describes those who dwell in the sanctuary, with Yahweh the scribe, and Elyon the father god.

It would be easier to extract information about Elyon if we could translate this Psalm, but we cannot. Many other Psalms which seem to us to be straightforward could have had an entirely different meaning in their original context. With Psalms such as 87, we have at least the obscurities of the text to warn us against assuming that we understand it. It may well be that our very familiarity with the Psalter becomes the greatest barrier to our understanding it.

Despite the great problems of fusion and transmission, the psalm texts which still use the title Elyon exhibit a distinct pattern of association, sufficient to suggest that their contexts are an accurate record of their older place in the Elyon cult. Rebel sons, triumph and judgement, demonic terrors, the anointed one, the book and the theophanies are all parts of the pre-exilic mythology of Jerusalem. Other texts, chosen simply because they retain the title *Elyon*, give a similar result.

Elyon occurs, together with other titles, in Lamentations, where we find significant traces of the angel mythology. An assembly is summoned against Zion (1.15); the sin of Jerusalem is rebellion against Yahweh (1.18); the splendour of Israel is cast down (2.1), and the kings of the earth did not believe that anyone could ever enter Jerusalem (4.12). The unclean depart from Jerusalem defiled with blood. The LXX says that they were the *Watchers*; the Hebrew says they were the 'blind' (*'wrym*).[15] Lamentations seems to link the demise of the old gods to the fall of the city.

The oracles of Balaam in Numbers 24 also use the title Elyon and the old mythology. Balaam hears the words of El, knows the knowledge of Elyon and sees the visions of Shaddai. It follows that the oracle must be one in the manner of El Elyon's cult. It is one of national supremacy, promising the destruction of enemies and a triumph for Jacob. The seer foretells a rising star,[16] to crush the *pa'atē mō'āb*. The normal meaning for this would be 'corners' or 'sides' of Moab (BDB), and by extension, in this context, could mean 'Temple'. The RSV opts for the 'forehead' of Moab, the NEB has 'squadrons'. The ancient translations, however, are very different. The LXX has ἀρχηγούς, 'rulers'. Targums Ps.-Jon. and Onkelos have 'nobles', and Neofiti has 'mighty ones'. This broad measure of agreement indicates that the *pa'ate mo'ab* were a ruling group destined for destruction by Israel's star-ruler. The exact meaning may never be known, but there is a remarkable area of overlap with another word we have had cause to investigate, *'aṣīl*.[17] This word can mean 'side' or 'corner', but also 'chief'. In Exodus, Second Isaiah and Zechariah it also refers to a category of heavenly creatures. If the *pa'ate mo'ab* are known as 'sides' or 'corners', but translated by the ancient versions as 'rulers', it is possible that the original sense in the Balaam oracles referred to a group of heavenly creatures destined for defeat at the hands of Israel's ruler.

This figure then deals with the 'sons of Seth'. The verb here, *qrqr*, is difficult, and usually altered to *qdqd* on the basis of a similar line at Jer. 48.45. But *qrqr* also occurs at Isa. 22.5, where *mqrqr* is rendered 'tearing down walls', from a presumed root (*qrr*) in the pilpel. Since both Isa. 22 and Num. 24 deal with supernatural warfare, one translation probably suffices for both, even though we may no longer be able to say with confidence what that is. The versions of Num. 24 offer 'plunder' (LXX) or 'blot out' (Neofiti), which give nothing precise, but the very fact of a rare word occurring in two exactly similar contexts must not pass unremarked.

In a description of supernatural warfare, we should expect the 'sons of Seth' to be creatures like the 'rulers of Moab'; there are several indications that this is so, although the case has to be established by following paths which are heavily overgrown. Commentators have long felt these words a problem, and other readings have been offered,[18] but the ancient versions clearly opt for *Seth*. The LXX has Σηθ; Ps.-Jon. and Neofiti have 'all the sons of Seth', and only Onkelos has the distinctly, and significantly, different reading 'all men'.[19] Read in the light of other differences between the Targums, this is the first indication that the sons of Seth were supernaturals. P. S. Alexander has compared the various Targum renderings of Gen. 6: Onkelos, he concluded, was in agreement with the view of R. Simeon ben Yoḥai, who cursed all those teaching that the *benē 'elohīm* were the sons of God. They were only the sons of *noblemen*, and Onkelos reflects this teaching. Neofiti as it now stands reflects this view of R. Simeon, but the margin reads 'angels', as does Ps.-Jon., recording another, possibly older, view of their identity. Ps.-Jon. links the *nephilīm* of Gen. 6 with Shamhazai and Azael, the rebel angels of 1 Enoch. 'Sons of noblemen' represents an exegesis which originated with the Rabbis shortly after the Jewish war, when they were trying to wean the Jewish people away from beliefs which were *out of keeping with Torah Judaism*.[20] The 'angel' reading was the older tradition which was replaced, and the *sons of Seth were also removed from Onkelos*. We have to ask if these two alterations were part of the same weaning process.

Some early Christian writers said that the 'sons of God' in Gen. 6 were the sons of Seth.[21] Others that they were angels. The Syriac tradition says that the sons of God were the Sethites, the sons of the Blessed One who lived beside the fence of Paradise. They took wives from the daughters of men, and were clearly linked to the angelic creatures of 1 Enoch.[22] Later Jewish traditions linked the sons of Seth to the angels and to their wisdom. They settled on a mountain near Paradise, and developed the wisdom which concerned the ordering of the heavens. There was a considerable tradition which glorified Seth, of which but a few traces remain; he was translated like Enoch to heaven, where he, too, was instructed about the fall of the angels. Seth was associated with astronomy and with the invention of writing.[23] Some angelic root for the Seth figure is clear; what is not clear is how two very different estimates of the Sethites came about. The Palestinian Targum, the MT and the LXX all agree that the sons of Seth were to be crushed by a messianic figure from Israel, but in Christian and later Jewish tradition, the sons of Seth were the *righteous*, from whom the Messiah would come.[24] At best we can make only shadows. In some quarters Seth shared the fate of the angels. Nothing too great can be built upon such tenuous threads, but a significant question emerges yet again: why is it that whenever one probes beneath the surface of the extra-biblical traditions, the same figures and patterns of thought lie just beneath what we thought we were reading? The oracles of Balaam remain a mystery, but sufficient has survived of their original context to associate them with the Elyon cult. The oldest texts which testify to a conflict in this area are very old; the later ones show that this was a living issue into New Testament times.

The text most frequently cited for evidence of the Elyon cult is Gen. 14.18–20, where Melchizedek is the priest of El Elyon, the creator of heaven and earth.[25] A wide range of scholars agrees that this chapter is a late addition to the Pentateuch, and that the crucial verses are, in their turn, a further addition. The Melchizedek tradition, and by implication that of Elyon, was growing and influencing the formation of the Old Testament as we know it. Genesis 14 describes the meeting of Melchizedek and Abraham, both of whom have important associations elsewhere, and could well be taken as representing the two traditions: the old cult and the post-exilic innovations. Melchizedek and his Salem have been claimed by several shrines,[26] an indication of his importance; but for our purposes the roots lie in Jerusalem. Salem was Zion (Ps. 76.3), and the Melchizedek priesthood was a part of the royal cult (Ps. 110). Melchizedek stands for 'the old ways'. Abraham, the patriarch of Genesis, appears in Isa. 41.8ff as the blueprint and figurehead of the exiles' hope, but in the Third Isaiah (63.16) his children are those who reject legitimate children of Yahweh. Abraham represented the division, the newer post-exilic ways. These two themes were distinct even in New Testament times. The Melchizedek Psalm was an important messianic text for the early Church, and the Fourth Gospel debates sonship and authority by contrasting elements from the two ways. John 8 deals with 'children of Abraham' and 'children of the devil', with the fatherhood of God and with bondage. The recorded teaching of John the Baptist in Matt. 3 and Luke 3 also shows this contrast: the children of Abraham and their claims over against those who will survive the great judgement. The debate about Abraham and Melchizedek was not simply a matter of ancient pro-Jebusite propaganda.[27]   In order to trace the development of the Elyon cult in the post-exilic period, we have to examine both the Abraham and Melchizedek figures in detail. It will become apparent that the angel mythology is newly buried beneath Gen. 14, and is the basis of the other Melchizedek text in the Old Testament, Ps. 110. Van Seters has demonstrated how the Abraham figure in Genesis is the embodiment of the needs and aspirations of the exilic group.[28] The unconditional promise of the land made to Abraham superseded the view in the Deuteronomic histories that tenure was conditional upon observing the Law. This latter had put the exilic group hopelessly in the wrong, and demonstrated that the poor left in Judah were the rightful heirs. The demise of the royal cult had left a great vacuum. Abraham, like Moses, inherited much of the royal role; he was addressed in royal forms, assured of offspring, a land, and a secure future. The covenant with Abraham was the Davidic covenant, applied to the patriarch and thence to the whole people. Isa. 63.16 supports van Seters' thesis; the returned exiles regarded themselves as the sole heirs to the old promises, and Abraham their patriarch came to symbolize the new exclusivism. Gen. 14 shows Abraham at his most regal.[29] It is not important to know whether the battle with the kings was fact or fiction; the significance of the episode lies in the claims made for the patriarch. Abraham repulses kings, and defeats them in the Vale of Siddim, identified with the Dead Sea valley. This identification reveals the author's purpose, for this area was associated with the battle against supernatural forces, and with the great judgement. 2 Chron. 20 records an otherwise unknown battle in which supernatural intervention caused the defeat of the King's enemies at just this spot. Ezek. 39 describes the host of Gog defeated here. Joel 3.2, 12 knows a valley of judgement north east of Jerusalem, and 1 Enoch 53 is similar.[30] Although there are those who deny that any precise location was envisaged for the valley of judgement, much in Enoch does point to the Dead Sea area. The very latest sections of Enoch project the judgement to unearthly regions,[31] but there are also descriptions of a place smelling of sulphur, with hot springs heated by the angels burning beneath.[32] This has been compared to Josephus' description of Machaerus, where there were hot springs and sulphur mines.[33] The writer of Enoch warned the evil rulers that they were seeing their own punishment every day! Thus as late as the parables of Enoch and as early as several Old Testament texts, the rift valley was the place of the last battle and the last judgement. Gen. 14 links Abraham to a victory *in this place*. The ancient kings could summon supernatural help against their enemies. So, too, did Abraham. Ps.-Jon. records that 'Abraham armed his young men ... and the night was divided ... one division fighting the kings ... and the other set aside to smite the firstborn of Egypt'.[34] As with the sons of Seth, it is Ps.-Jon. which has recorded the tradition of the heavenly powers. The insertion of Melchizedek to receive tribute after the battle modifies the claims of the patriarch to be heir to the royal role, and raises the question of why the tribute was due. 11 Q Melch offers a clue. Melchizedek in this text is a powerful heavenly figure who rescues from the powers of Belial.[35] A similar role for him might have been known to the writer of Genesis, which would explain why tribute was due. The supernatural forces depicted in the Targum and the role of the Qumran Melchizedek may both be related fragments of the older scheme.

The only other Melchizedek text in the Old Testament is Ps. 110, a psalm of such complexity and obscurity that it may be immediately suspected of having links to the older cult.

110.1–2 are fairly clear. They are an oracle from Yahweh inviting the king to sit at his right hand until his enemies are subdued. Yahweh of Zion sends out his mighty sceptre.[36] One thinks of Ps. 2, and of the New Testament's emphasis upon the defeat of hostile powers.

110.5–6 describe the shattering of kings on the day of Yahweh's wrath, the judgement of nations, heaps of corpses and the demise of the chiefs of men. All these ideas run together well as a bloody triumph song from the old cult, but vv. 3, 4 and 7 are a strange contrast and, in their present state, full of problems.

110.3 *'amm^eka*, 'your people', is μετὰ σοῦ in the LXX, from *'im* rather than *'am*, 'with you'. *N^edabot* is ἀρχή in the LXX, and should be read as 'princes' rather than 'freely'.[37] The princes in question were probably angelic, or at least beings who functioned in heaven and on earth. Other Old Testament instances of the word give hints of this: Isa. 13.2 has the gates of the *princes* through which the heavenly army enters Babylon; Isa. 32.5 says there will be a final distinction between *prince* and fool(!) in the reign of the righteous king, when the Spirit will bring fertility, justice and peace.

Ps. 51.13, 14 links the presence of God and the Holy Spirit, the joy of salvation and the support of a 'willing spirit' (*ru^ah n^edibah*). Would not a guardian figure be a more appropriate interpretation here? Ps. 146.3 has a 'prince' and a son of man in parallel; we cannot translate either term with confidence, but the son of man does have significant associations elsewhere. Job 12.21; Ps. 83.12; Ps. 107.40 describe colourful judgements upon the 'princes', although Ps. 118.9 says that confidence in Yahweh is better than trust in man or 'princes'. Ps. 47.10, a New Year psalm, sees the 'princes' assembled before the throne of God. *B^eyom heyleka* is also difficult. On the day of your 'host', 'birth', 'power', are but three of the current translations. If we read the word from *hyl*, 'anguish', a familiar context pattern emerges. Other Old Testament instances of the word deal with supernatural warfare.

Exod. 14.15 has the 'anguish' of the Philistine leaders before the incomparable Yahweh leading his people to safety. The ultimate origin of this poem is a mystery, but the royal cult has a strong claim to be the original setting.

Ps. 48.6 has the 'anguish' of the kings before Jerusalem about to encounter the power of Yahweh.

Mic. 4.9, a passage of uncertain meaning, indicates that Jerusalem suffers 'anguish' because her king is useless and her source of wisdom gone. Yahweh himself will eventually rescue his people.

Jer. 6.24 tells of 'anguish' as the Scythians prepare to attack. In Jer. 22.23 anguish is parallel to *ḥᵉbālīm*, 'pangs', but also possibly 'binders', 'destroyers'. This is prophet's word-play, as is Jer. 50.43, where the king of Babylon has 'anguish' and *ṣrh*, another word with supernatural associations. The whole oracle resembles Ezekiel's against Tyre, with the punishment of the proud one, the punishment of the wise and powerful, fire in the cities, and the helplessness of the great before Yahweh. Perhaps we may read *'immekā nᵉdābōt bᵉyōm ḥēylekā* as 'princes are with you on the day of your anguish' (cf. Ps. 91.11, 'He will give his angels charge of you'). If we follow Dahood's suggestion to divide the verses differently at this point, we should read, 'In the midst of your enemies, princes are with you on the day of your anguish.'

vv. 3b, 3c are equally opaque: *bᵉhadrē qōdeš* appears in the LXX as ἐν τῇ λαμπρότητι τῶν ἁγίων, showing that the heavenly host was once found here, and this coincides with a similar reading at Ps. 87.1, where the host is also appropriate. The LXX of 3c reads ἐξεγέννησά σε, 'I have begotten you!' rather than 'of your youth', i.e. reading *yldtyk* as a first-person form (cf. Ps. 2.7). The LXX readings at both these points show that two unacceptable aspects of the old cult, the host and divine fatherhood, are missing from the Hebrew as we now read it. This was also the case with Ps. 87. *Mrḥm* is not 'from the womb', but a pu'al participle from *rḥm*, i.e. one who receives compassion. The themes of this Psalm then correspond to, and doubtless were the basis of, Hosea's choice of names to express an exactly opposite idea, that of *rejection*.[38] The children were 'seed of El' (Jezreel), 'not my people' and 'not compassionated'. Ps. 110 shows the royal claims: to be son of God, and to receive his compassion. *Ṭl* is not from *ṭal*, 'dew', but is from *ṭul*, 'hurl', 'cast down'. This verb occurs in sufficient significant contexts to establish that it was used to describe divine intervention on earth in the manner of the angel mythology. In Isa. 22.17 Yahweh hurls down an evil official, in Jonah 1.4 a great storm of wind. He hurls the people from the land as a punishment for idolatry (Jer. 16.19), he hurls down Pharaoh in the manner of the Day Star of Babylon, or the Prince of Tyre. The sun and stars are involved in the disaster, which is a punishment for pride (Ezek. 32.2–8). Yahweh does not hurl down a good man, even though he fall (Ps. 37.24. If we read *ṭūl* in Ps. 110.3 an excellent sense emerges. Instead of *mšḥr lk ṭl yldtyk* I propose *bšḥr l' 'ṭlk yldtyk*, 'with the Dawn Star I will not cast you off. I have begotten you . . .' (Compare Hos. 10.15b (*bšḥr ndmh ndmh mlk ysr'l*, 'with the Dawn the king of Israel will be destroyed'.) The emendation of the impossible Hebrew is necessary, but it is not a drastic change, and in the light of what is known of the cult from other texts, makes better sense than 'From the womb of the morning your youth will come to you' (RSV), or 'You have shone with the dew of your youth since your mother bore you' (NEB). This could also illuminate the alternative reading at John 12.31, 'Now is the ruler of this world *cast down*'.

I would not press any of these suggestions in isolation. What has to be explained is the remarkable correspondence between these confused lines in a royal Psalm and vocabulary known in other places to be associated with the old cult. The translations currently accepted have nothing to recommend them; what I propose in their place is no more bizarre.

The royal figure is then linked to the Melchizedek priesthood (v. 4), and we return (vv. 5–6) to the shattering of kings and the day of judgement. Dahood's translation of v. 7[39] makes excellent sense: 'The bestower of succession sits upon his throne', linking the whole Psalm to the glimpse of the cult which we have in Deut. 32.8 and in Ps. 2. Here, as there, Elyon bestows kingship, and is the father of sons who rule the earth.

Melchizedek was central to the old royal cult. We do not know what the name means, but it is quite clear that this priesthood operated within the mythology of the sons of Elyon, and the triumph of the royal son of God in Jerusalem. We should expect later references to Melchizedek to retain some memory of the cult of Elyon. The fragmentary text designated as '11QMelch' has been dated between 50 BC and 50 AD, but this is not the same as saying that it is an original composition of this period. The Melchizedek of the fragments *is* divine. Texts which in the Old Testament refer to God are applied to Melchizedek. His is the Day of Favour (cf. Isa. 61.2); he is the agent of judgement (cf. Ps. 82.2). He rescues from the power of Belial, and, on the great day, will be proclaimed as king. The importance of certain texts from Isaiah, Ps. 82 and Dan. 9 in 11QMelch shows that it was not just a random concatenation of ideas which the writer presented as scriptural interpretation. *The texts were part of an association of ideas known to be rooted in the older cult, and they can only be appreciated in their original context.* The Melchizedek figure was the royal figure and vice versa. The role of the ancient kings was that of the Melchizedek figure in 11QMelch. This accounts for the Melchizedek material in Hebrews, and the early Church's association of Melchizedek and the Messiah. The arguments of Hebrews presuppose a knowledge of the angel mythology which we no longer have; that is why they are so complex and impenetrable. The Epistle may not be directly dependent upon 11QMelch, but both belong in the same tradition of Elyon and his sons.[40] The Epistle argues in terms of angel roles and sonship, the children of Abraham, Melchizedek and the heavenly counterpart of the earthly shrine.[41] In the Elyon tradition, Melchizedek was one aspect of the role of the king in his embodiment of the Spirit of Yahweh, the Holy One of Israel. There would have been a whole succession of earthly counterparts to this figure; this could lead us towards an explanation of the extraordinary Christology of Hebrews, which has pre-existence and adoptionism side by side (1.2, cf. 1.5). Melchizedek as an angel figure defending against the assaults of Belial would help to explain the Johannine Paraclete, and even though the notion of the continuing presence of the spirit is not expressly mentioned in the extra-biblical writings, it is a logical development of the idea of a heavenly power existing before and beyond, as well as with, its earthly counterpart. Later Christian writings deemed heretical did, in fact, identify Melchizedek with the Holy Spirit,[42] and he was frequently regarded as part of the system of heavenly powers. It has been suggested that these speculations grew from the tantalizing silence of Scripture,[43] but it seems more likely that they grew from the older cult in which the Melchizedek figure was rooted.

When Abraham the patriarch met Melchizedek the priest of El Elyon, two traditions came together. The full significance of this insertion into Gen. 14 must elude us until we know in detail what these traditions were. The pattern of conflict apparent in the New Testament indicates that the Abraham–Melchizedek problem was even then a living issue. This is further proof that the roots of the Jewish Christian division lie deeper than the phenomenon of Jesus. The few examples offered in this chapter show that the cult of Elyon was a feature both of the earliest tradition in Jerusalem, and of New Testament times. It would be foolish to ignore the vast stretches of time involved, and to make simple comparisons across millennia, but there is a similarity between the oldest and the latest texts, and this has to be explained. If it was due to the conscious revival of the older ways, we have to ask where and by whom these older ways had been preserved awaiting the revival, since the consistency extends to aspects not directly deduced from Old Testament texts, and therefore not explicable simply as constructions upon it. Nothing short of a wholesale loss of past tradition and a dramatic recovery in the manner of the Qumran discoveries is necessary to argue for an absolute hiatus between the old cult and the 'intertestamental' evidence for similar ideas. There must have been a continuity, albeit within a circle of whom we know very little, and the poor condition of the Elyon texts in the Old Testament suggests that the cult was not always viewed with favour by those who transmitted and interpreted the text. If we take Judaism as the norm, scholars find it difficult, if not impossible, to account for the strange world of the apocalyptists, without resorting to hypotheses of extensive Zoroastrian influence and so on; they find it likewise difficult to account for much of the earliest interpretation in the New testament without the hypothesis of extensive Greek influence. But if we take the Elyon cult as the norm for both, we find it easier to achieve a working basis.

Several texts in the New Testament may be seen in a new way. Luke 1.32ff promises a new son of Elyon to be given the throne of his father David. The demoniac recognizes Jesus as the son of Elyon when he has commanded the spirit to leave (Mark 5.7; Luke 8.28). The use of Elyon in these instances is exactly what we should expect.[44] The royal figure was the son of Elyon who had power over evil spirits. If we but knew how the ancient kings were both sons of David and sons of Elyon we should probably know how the early Church understood the Son of God. The notion of obedience and unity of will was clearly a part of the royal cult. Perhaps we should understand the works and obedience of Jesus in this context, especially the arguments in the Fourth Gospel.

Much has been written of the Elyon figure and what it signified in surrounding and related cultures. I have not dealt with this material (even though Jerusalem was influenced by her neighbours in many ways) because my concern has been to show the links which can be established between the Old Testament's usage and later material in apocalyptic texts. The correspondence between the older cult and the later writings has not been demonstrated by a simple retrojection to an assumed original, but by imposing several sets of characteristics apparent in extra-biblical texts, it has been possible to recognize an overall context for apparently random occurrences of Elyon in the Old Testament which also illuminates the New.

NOTES

1. Hengel (1974), vol. 1, pp. 295ff; vol. 2, p. 200.
2. Dan. 7, which uses Elyon, can hardly be used as evidence for syncretism, when it was a vision of triumph for a people enduring religious persecution.
3. Recent work in the fields of language pattern and metaphor has led to the conclusion that earlier thought patterns can lie hidden beneath later usage. 'The concepts which govern our thought are not just matters of intellect. They also govern our everyday functioning down to the most mundane details ... Our conceptual system plays a central role in defining our everyday realities ... but our conceptual system is not something we are normally aware of ... Language is an important source of evidence for what that system is like ... On the basis of linguistic evidence, we have found that most of our ordinary conceptual system is metaphorical in nature': Lakoff and Johnson (1980), pp. 3–4.
4. Dan. 3.25; 6.22.
5. 1 En. 9.5; 10.1; 40.1; 60.1; 62.7. Charles (1912) lists all instances.
6. 'Elyon' at 1QApGen 2, 4; 12, 17; 'Great Holy One' at 2,14; 12,17; 'King' at 2, 7; 2, 14.
7. 'Yahweh' and 'Elyon' at Ps. 9.3; 18.14; 21.8; 47.2; 92.4–5. 'Elohim' and 'Elyon' at Ps. 46.4; 50.14. 'Elohim', 'Yahweh' and 'Elyon' in Ps. 77. 'Rock', 'Redeemer' and 'Elyon' in Ps. 78. 'Shaddai', 'Yahweh' and 'Elyon' in Ps. 91. 'Elyon' and 'El' at Ps. 73.11; 'El Elyon' at Ps. 78.35.
8. The NEB makes major changes before translating. Kittel's apparatus is extensive. Weiser (1962): the text has been disarranged.
9. Ackroyd (1966); Dahood (1968); Mowinckel (1956); Cooke (1961).
10. This seems to be the same picture as in Heb. 12.23.
11. Suggested by Thomas (1968), pp. 79–86.
12. *'ēm 'ōmēr 'iš* is the supposed Hebrew behind the LXX.
13. cf. Isa. 62, also Rev. 21.9, where the heavenly city is the bride of the lamb.
14. Although we render 'eyes', the root may well lie in *'anah* which underlies Hos. 2.23ff, meaning 'impregnate', 'fertilize', and indicate a son of God.
15. See ch. 6.
16. Several versions read *zārah*, 'rise', for *dārak*, 'tread'.
17. See ch. 3.
18. *bᵉnē šē't*, 'sons of *battle din*', assuming Num. 24.11 to be the same as Jer. 48.45, where there are also 'corners of Moab'; *bᵉnē šā'ōn* 'sons of *tumult*'; *bᵉnē š'ēt*, 'sons of *pride*'.

19 The Onkelos reading has been explained as due to Seth being a son of Adam and therefore the ancestor of much of mankind.

20 Alexander (1972).

21 ibid, for full references, p. 66.

22 Murray (1975), p. 221.

23 Ginzberg (1909–38), vol. v, p. 149, n53.

24 Alexander (1972), p. 66.

25 See Chapter 3. The combined form 'El Elyon' occurs only in one other place, Ps. 78.35. 'Creator' of heaven and earth undoubtedly records an ancient title of Elyon: *qnh* can mean both 'procreate' and 'buy/acquire' and there are several places where either is possible. Exod. 15.16: the people are bought/created and planted on the holy mountain. Deut. 32.6: the people are bought/created by their father. Isa. 11.11: the Lord acts to buy/create his people again. Ps. 74.2: the congregation is bought/created to be God's heritage. This double meaning may have been deeply rooted in the Elyon cult, but was separated out in the theology of the Second Isaiah, where we can recognize the twin themes of creation and redemption. The vocabulary is different, but the pattern is the same.

26 Gammie (1971).

27 Emerton (1971ab), p. 437.

28. Van Seters (1975).

29 Later Jewish tradition applied Ps. 110 to Abraham. Ginzberg (1909), vol. v, p. 224. Abraham was viewed as a king figure. Van Seters (1975), p. 303, found Deuteronomic influences in this chapter which gives the royal role to Abraham.

30 The Enochic literature is full of these valleys of judgement. The footnotes to Charles (1912) distinguish at this point between two valleys in the overall scheme: there was Gehenna where the final judgement took place, and another place where the evil was stored awaiting punishment. 'The deep valley here is that of Jehoshaphat where, according to Joel 3.2, 12, God was to assemble and judge the Gentiles. It is rendered in Theodotion by the phrase τὴν χώραν τῆς κρίσεως and in T. Jon. by the *plain of the decision of judgement*. According to the Midrash Mishle 68d God will judge the whole world in this valley.'

31 Charles, *Pseudepigrapha*, notes to 1 En. 10.4.

32 This passage is usually thought to be later than the rest of 1 Enoch.

33 *B.J.*, VII, 186.

34 Translation from Bowker (1969).

35 Kobelski (1981), esp. p. 52.

36 Dahood (1968) renders thus.

37 For a survey of suggestions see Cooke (1961).

38 See chs. 4 and 10.

39 Dahood (1968).

40 This greatly strengthens the case for Dan. 7 having been a similar survival. If it can also be shown that 4Q'Amram depicted Melchizedek as the great Watcher opposed to Melchireša' (Kobelski 1981), and this text, of which there are five at Qumran, was brought to Qumran by its founders, then the lapse of time between the biblical Melchizedek in Gen. 14 and the angelic figure of the Qumran text is very small. This also strengthens the case for the angelic associations of the figure having been known to the writer of Genesis.

41 i.e. it was not a fusion of Platonism and Christianity.

42 Horton (1976), pp. 103ff, for examples of third-century sources, although I am not happy with the conclusions he draws from them.

43 Dunn (1980), p. 20 suggests that the Melchizedek of 11Q Melch had *become* an angel because the short visit in Gen. 14 invited this sort of interpretation. Horton (1976) also roots Melchizedek's exaltation in the silence of the Pentateuch; he was the first priest mentioned, and therefore pre-eminent. In actual fact the silence of the Pentateuch may be *due to* Melchizedek's exalted role, and not the cause of it.

44 Hengel (1974), vol. ii, p. 201, is incorrect in saying that Mark 5.7 and Acts 16.17 are typical and show Elyon on the lips of demon-possessed pagans. What of Luke 1.32, or Luke 6.35?

12

THE BOOK OF JOB

Introduction

Job is a problem. The manner and purpose of its composition have exercised commentators for centuries. The book divides easily into several sections: prologue and epilogue, dialogues, Elihu speeches, and Yahweh speeches. This has tempted many to dismember the text, but the fact that we now have a single though composite work necessitates an approach which gives weight both to the final form and to the component parts.

There is no real agreement as to the question which the book asks. We have, in effect, a debate, but no clear indication of the motion, and we are asked to assess that debate whilst trying to discover what it is about.

To say that Job deals with the problem of suffering is inadequate, because this wrenches suffering from the context in which it was both experienced and explained. The Job of the prologue suffers, but there is no debate about it. He simply accepts what happens to him. The Job of the dialogues speaks out and objects. It would appear from this that Job's rebellion was prompted not by suffering but by the *explanation of suffering*. If we are to avoid distortion, we must do our utmost to distinguish our own views of suffering, and their web of associations, from any which might be discernible in the Book of Job.[1]

To attempt any analysis of this book is to court disaster; so much has been written that it is impossible to cover all the material, or even to recall and acknowledge all the many writings which have influenced my thought. I propose an outline, to see whether or not my theory about exilic developments is compatible with the Book of Job. Such an exercise can *prove* nothing, but the more material which can be illuminated by the hypothesis, the more it deserves consideration. I shall attempt in this chapter to plot the similarities between Job and the exilic situation as I have reconstructed it. In so far as the investigation must be linked to those fragments of evidence which happen to have survived the ravages of time and human prejudice, no dramatic correspondence is to be expected. But as this exploration progressed, I realized that in the Book of Job there is a degree of compatibility with my theory which seems inexplicable as coincidence.

The Prose Framework

The framework of the book is a simple tale, possibly very old, telling of the sufferings of a good man, and of his eventual restoration. The moral of this tale is that God will eventually put things right.

Ezekiel 14.14, 20 also refer to *a* Job, a man who would be delivered from calamity because of his righteousness. The prophet is dealing here with the problem of individual and collective or inherited guilt, and with the responsibility for evil. When Yahweh devastates the land, says Ezekiel, only the righteous individuals will be saved. They cannot save others who are unworthy. From references such as these in Ezekiel it is clear that, in the exile, Job had been used as the example of an upright man who was safe in time of calamity. Ezekiel seems to have known a tale which emphasized the goodness of Job, and he used this tale to demonstrate his thesis of individual responsibility for evil. It is therefore quite extraordinary that the debate in our Book of Job centres around an *exactly* opposite situation: Job's *denial* of individual responsibility for evil. The prose framework of the book is different from the dialogues in this respect, and the position in the framework is compatible with Ezekiel's version of the story. In the prologue and epilogue we find the good man rewarded for his goodness. Job refuses to question the acts of God and this is deemed to be piety. His blind confidence brings reward. If we are to date the prologue, it is important to note that the righteousness of Job is not measured in terms of social sins, but rather in terms of cultic proprieties: he sacrifices and ensures that neither he nor his family curse God and cease to trust him.

The same themes of individual responsibility and faith counted as righteousness are prominent in the Abraham sagas. The debate in Genesis 18, for example, where Abraham challenges God over the destruction of Sodom, has many similarities to the debates of Job, and could well serve as the preface to the debate of the book. Gen. 18.23–7 is very like Job 30.19 or 42.6. Abraham extracts from God the promise that for the sake of ten righteous men Sodom would be saved .. and then the city is destroyed. The implication is that there was none righteous, and had there been but ten, they could have saved the city. Ezekiel's reference to the righteous Job who could save only himself is clearly later than the idea expressed in Gen. 18 because for Ezekiel, the presence of three righteous men would ensure the safety of only the three righteous men. There are many similarities also between the Sodom pericope and the debate in Ezekiel. It has been suggested that the Sodom pericope was a *midrash* on the destruction of that city occasioned by the destruction of Jerusalem in 586.[2] The complaint of Job in the *dialogues* is another such development. The righteous man has not even saved himself.

It seems that righteousness itself was also being re-defined. A comparison of the framework of Job and the dialogues shows two different definitions. The Job of the prologue is rich, blameless and upright. The one example given of his goodness, how he feared God and turned away from evil, is that he offered numerous sacrifices, in case his children had cursed God. His goodness is depicted as a refusal to curse God. In the dialogues, however, Eliphaz describes the good life as caring for widows, orphans and the poor (22.6ff), a very different conception. This difference must not be overlooked in the establishing of their respective origins. The three friends came from a tradition which associated righteousness with a certain standard of social conduct, and associated failure to reach this standard with disaster and suffering. The theme of the three friends is therefore the theme of the prophets as we have them, but the fact of this theme's prominence in the prophets indicates that the ideals were not universally observed. The prophets' scorn for the rituals of Temple and purity do suggest, on the other hand, that these were commonly accepted as ways of honouring God. It is one of the problems which we face in reconstructing the actual religious life of the monarchy that the writings of the prophets are largely protests against current religious practices and not accounts of them. Critics do not always give the full picture. When Job gives his own list of social evils, in Chapter 31, he records the worship of the sun and moon amongst these evils, and does not deny that these should bring some related punishment. He himself denies that he has ever committed any of those sins. Thus both Job and the three friends accept similar standards of conduct, but they disagree as to how this relates to *righteousness*. The Abraham sagas also give a new definition of righteousness, for the patriarch *trusted* God and this was reckoned as righteousness. The writer of this passage would have rejected the views of Job's friends, but would not have been too far away from the definition of righteousness implicit in the prose framework of Job. One cannot but ask if there was some link between all these definitions, as there seems to have been between the various attitudes to responsibility for evil and suffering. Righteousness reckoned as certain deeds, i.e. that of the three friends, suggests legalism, whereas righteousness as blind trust (that of Abraham) or righteousness as loyalty (that of Job) suggest another basis. Abraham's righteousness is also linked to the covenant of Gen. 15, an unconditional covenant promising freely both land and offspring, contrasting strongly with the covenant concept of the legalists, which makes land and posterity dependent upon the keeping of certain rules. Thus this first probe reveals exactly the division we have found elsewhere in the exilic period: there was a division between the religion of law and one which was otherwise based.

The prose of Job is in two sections, separated now by a series of debates, but it is reasonable to assume that the prose was once an independent work, related to that used by Ezekiel in the exile.[3] Many scholars favour the opposite view, that the prose passages were added to the dialogues in order to give them a setting, and to give the tale a suitable ending. As such they are held to be of less significance than the dialogues, and an unacknowledged assumption creeps in. T. K. Cheyne, on the other hand, thought that the latecomer to the book was the dialogue, which replaced an older narrative in which the three friends were God's detractors.[4] Hints of such a position occur in the later Testament of Job, where Elihu is cast as the agent of Satan, an angelic figure who does not appear in our version of the dialogue. The most important consideration for the Book of Job is what the tradition was before it received its present form. If we could but know what had been rejected from the ancient tale, we should be in a better position to describe and assess the contribution of the Old Testament version.[5]

The contrast between the framework and the dialogue is heightened by another difference: the explanations offered for evil are respectively the malice of heavenly beings, and personal transgression of the commandments of God. In the prologue Job lives in the world of the angel mythology, trusting Yahweh, who is challenged by Satan, another heavenly figure. Yahweh accepts the wager, and Job is tested simply to prove Yahweh correct. There is nothing moral in this action, and any tale told within such a framework implies certain things about contemporary beliefs as to the nature of the gods. The listeners would have expected their Yahweh to win, but not without a struggle. They viewed their suffering as part of the divine struggle for supremacy, which means that we are not far away from the view of human life as the sport of the immortals. Job is pious and is rewarded for his loyalty. He refuses to curse God and die. The sport is planned in heaven, when the sons of God are assembled, and the disasters as the tale unfolds have an unmistakably supernatural element. Job 1.16 describes the 'fire of the elohim' falling from heaven and destroying the household and flocks. We are told that this is only a figure of speech, but can we be so sure? The picture we have is of a disputation in heaven, and the divine beings, the sons of God, are very real beings. One aspect of these beings is commonly obscured in the English translations. In 1.6 the sons of God come to 'present themselves before' Yahweh, implying that Yahweh dominated the assembly and that the other creatures were subordinate, but in Ps. 2.2 there is an identical construction which needs a very different translation, the kings of the earth 'set themselves against' Yahweh, and against his anointed:

wayyābō'û bᵉnē hā'ᵉlōhīm lᵉhityaṣṣēb 'al YHWH (Job 1.6).
yityaṣṣᵉbū malkē ereṣ . . . 'al YHWH wᵉ'al mᵉšīḥō (Ps. 2.2).

Yahweh is not the undisputed ruler of Job's heaven. In the angel myth of the monarchy such suffering at the hands of other heavenly beings was part of the accepted order of things, as several Psalms make clear. Pss. 18, 22, 144 all describe the king as assailed by evil represented by waters and beasts. The king is rescued *because he is righteous*. The picture is not of someone suffering *because he is evil*, but because this suffering is a part of the world. Job is a similar figure. He is assailed, he refuses to curse God and die, and eventually, after showing blind confidence, he is rescued and restored. A possible association with the royal mythology surfaces elsewhere. Job 19.19, for example, says that he was stripped of his glory and his crown. In Ps. 2, the sons of God come against Yahweh and his *anointed*. In the Testament of Job, he is a *king* who has lost everything. There are also several places in the dialogue where the suffering of Job is described in the manner of the 'Servant Songs' (16.10, 30.10).

The prose prologue has as its milieu a world in which evil and suffering were explained by the struggles within heaven; the chosen one would eventually triumph if he remained loyal. *The framework of Job does not assume monotheism.*

The Dialogue

When the three friends arrive, they do not come to comfort Job. They explain his suffering, and it is *their explanation* which fuels Job's anger. The friends want to prove Job wrong; they want to deny that he is a good man, and that his wisdom is valid. Thus all the four characters are depicted as wise men, and this places the Old Testament Job within the wisdom tradition, as a debate within that tradition, precipitated by great suffering, and based upon the relative values of two conflicting systems. One system makes man, by his own action, responsible for human suffering; the other attributes it to the movements within heaven. Both were wisdom. Job is challenged but not defeated by the arguments of his friends, who in their turn are denounced by Yahweh. Yahweh, who we can assume represents the author's solution to the problem of the book, discredits the friends, and denies that they have spoken the truth about him. Job is humbled but restored. If we are to find a context for the Old Testament Job, we must identify the types of wisdom represented by the characters in the dispute.

The Wisdom of the Three Wise Men

The wisdom tradition of the friends can be partially reconstructed from clues within their speeches. Despite being wise themselves, they maintain that God thwarts the cunning ('*ᵃrūmīm*, the characteristic of the serpent in Gen. 3.1), and traps the wise in their own wisdom. These wise are mighty (5.15) and oppress the poor. Eliphaz contrasts this arrogant wisdom with the more blessed state of receiving wisdom from Shaddai, an attitude which would lead to release from the scourges of destruction and famine, and to harmony with all creation (chs. 4—5). Bildad appeals to tradition, and concludes that man can know nothing. The experience of past ages is that effects have a cause, that evil brings punishments, and that the Almighty is just (ch. 8). Zophar denies the arguments of Job, and longs for God to teach him the secrets of wisdom. One assumes that this means Zophar's wisdom. These secrets cannot come from observing the natural order, for they are higher than heaven and deeper than Sheol (ch. 11). The wisdom of the three friends is thus one of receiving direct instruction from God, in contrast to one which is associated with cunning and oppression, and the secrets of the natural order.

In their second cycle of speeches, Eliphaz speaks of 'knowledge of wind'[6] and reckons Job amongst those wise men who pervert their wisdom and speak with cunning (15.5). The fact that he claims to have wisdom to challenge the ways of God is testimony against him. Eliphaz denies that Job has the monopoly of wisdom, denies that he has listened in the heavenly council, and emphasizes that Job has used his knowledge to rebel against God. He mentions the Holy Ones of heaven who were also at fault and untrustworthy. Eliphaz, by contrast, offers the wisdom given to their ancestors in the days when the land was pure and free from strangers.[7] He dwells at length on the fate of those who rebel against God (15.23ff). Bildad then asks why Job cannot accept their arguments as wisdom, and he points to the condition of Job, with his hunger, diseases, terrors and childlessness as a sure sign that he is one who does not know God (18.21).[8] Zophar appeals to the ancient knowledge, that even though a wicked man climb to heaven (20.6) he will perish and be forgotten. His prosperity will vanish in the day of God's wrath. The old myth of rebellion was, then, an important element in the friends' case. Knowledge which sets a man up against God is, by definition, perverted and merits punishment. The friends know of the heavenly council, of a claim to true wisdom, and of the attempt to ascend into heaven. The way in which these are used suggests that they were a part of Job's own view, being turned against him. The friends claim for themselves another wisdom, and an ancient tradition, in a manner which shows that Job accepted neither.

The third, apparently incomplete, cycle of speeches begins with Eliphaz. He tells of wicked old ways, when men believed that God was remote, above the stars and shrouded in darkness (22.12ff). These same wicked old ways are denounced by the Second Isaiah (Isa. 40.26–7). There was no truth in the teaching that God was too remote to regard the rights and needs of individuals. A similar picture of God has been reconstructed as a possible background for the earliest stratum of Proverbs.[9] There is therefore a link between the position of the friends and the innovation of the Second Isaiah, and between the position of Job and what is assumed to underlie both the earliest known deposit in Proverbs and the despair of the exiles. Job represents the older ways, and the friends are changing them. The only hope for him, says Eliphaz, is to accept the (presumably new) teaching of the Almighty, and return in humility.

The replies of Job set out his view of knowledge, and show how he disagrees with the three others. He accepts that God should punish evil, but asks how any man can be free of evil in the sight of God. His contemplation of creation has revealed to him a God of power, but not a God of justice (ch. 9). In his next speech, Job's opening remark is quite extraordinary. He seems to be saying that the three friends are claiming a special status for themselves, which results in the end of wisdom.[10] The text is not clear, but if this *is* the meaning of 12.2, then it is the key verse for dating Job: *'attem 'ām wᵉ'immākem tāmūt ḥokmah*.[11] What is meant by 'wisdom will die with you'? If it means that the new scheme will end the older, it is significant how closely the wisdom of Job corresponds to the old wisdom of the era of monarchy and the angel mythology. Job observes the natural order and concludes that suffering is part of the scheme. The might and wisdom of God show themselves in power over waters, over good and evil beings, over kings and counsellors. God rules darkness and light, and brings the chiefs of the earth down into darkness. Job can even mock the wisdom of the friends (17.7ff). *Upright* men he says, are appalled at his condition, yet the righteous holds to his way, and he that has clean hands grows stronger and stronger. Is this a bitter reference to those who have set out to explain his sufferings, with a contrast between the upright and the righteous? Job then denies that the friends are truly wise (17.10). He slips naturally into the imagery of the trial he is expecting on the day of judgement, *in addition to* his present sufferings (cf. 13.15ff). He has confidence in a heavenly advocate (19.26), in a God who will judge even those on high (21.22ff), but he realizes that God's justice is different from man's knowledge of it. A picture of Job's wisdom is emerging.

The friends claim wisdom and equate this with confidence in God's justice. Instruction and reproof are an important part of their case. They need to establish the position that punishment implies wickedness on the part of the sufferer, and not on the part of the afflicter. The three thus represent a position advocating suffering as a punishment for sins, and they want Job to accept this point of view. They want him to accept their view of the origin of evil. They claim an ancient pure tradition, but the difference between their position and Job's, as outlined in the prose framework, shows that this tradition was alien to the milieu which produced the original Job.

The heart of Job's dilemma is that there is only one God. He has been asked by the friends to reconcile the all too obvious evil in creation with his confidence in a God who will punish evil. The Job dialogue thus represents the struggles of a man coming to terms with monotheism, and being deprived of the more ancient polytheistic view. His was the difficulty which came inevitably in the wake of the Second Isaiah, whose prophecies carried Israel's thought far beyond the safe structures of the monarchy. Let us suppose that Job represents the sufferings of Everyman in the trauma of the exile. The pattern of Job shows that there had been a polytheistic explanation of suffering which had been replaced by a new wisdom, teaching that the individual was to blame for his own afflictions. These are the arguments of Jeremiah and Ezekiel, who replaced the Deuteronomists' inherited guilt theory with an emphasis upon individual responsibility. Almost contemporary with this new individualism was the great destruction wrought by the Second Isaiah. Everyman then found that the two prophetic insights offered for his consolation brought their own array of problems. If, as the prophet had proclaimed, there were no longer evil forces in creation working against God, forces from which Everyman's God had afforded protection in return for loyalty and certain observances, whence was evil? One God had taken over the ancient functions of the evil ones, because, even though the prophet had claimed their defeat, there was someone keeping things going in the same evil ways. Thus the prophecies of individual responsibility, and the demise of the heavenly beings, told Everyman that evil was his own fault. *This is the dilemma which is explored in the Book of Job.*

It is possible to fill in several details of this proposed picture. The theodicy thought to characterize the final stage of Proverbs,[12] and therefore to represent postexilic wisdom, is the very one which we find in the arguments of the three friends, the one which Job challenges and cannot accept. Any argument based upon presumed layers in a text must be used with caution, but this lateness, coupled with a claim to ancient purity, points in the direction of those who effected such great changes during the exile. They presented their new wisdom as a *fait accompli* by the time of Ezra. We are told that the God of the earliest stratum of Proverbs is a remote judge who does not interfere in the lives of men, a view from which the three friends differ markedly.[13] Job's view could easily have been that of this earliest layer of the wisdom tradition, involving as it did an element which we must call polytheism. At several points in his outcry he is dashed upon monotheism, yet still expresses his hope in terms of the great judgement, and of other heavenly beings. He challenges the idea that God *can* be both judge and accuser (9.15, 33; 16.18ff; 19.25ff). If the Job of the dialogue had been allowed the polytheism of the prologue he would have had no problem, even though the physical suffering would have been identical. We cannot be certain of this correspondence, but any judgements must be made in the light of the extraordinary gaps in our knowledge of the older wisdom. Everything which seems to have disappeared from the system could well have been the world of Job. He was part of the great exilic debate, and remained upon the side which, broadly, rejected the legalism of the Deuteronomists and their fanatical monotheism. This is a very slender thread, but it is much strengthened by some of the ideas to which Job alludes in the course of his arguments.

He claims to have been treated as an enemy of God (6.4), to have been terrified by his attacks (6.10). The enemies of God are the sea and its monsters (7.12) and Rahab (9.13). God is the 'Watcher of men' (7.20), the mighty creator (9.5ff), who makes men from clay (10.9) and attacks them with witnesses, anger and hosts (10.17; 16.7). Job knows that all creation and its suffering is in the hands of God, who is the arbiter of history (12.17), yet he looks for help to another being (16.18; 19.25). He expects a Day of Judgement (24.1) and the judgement of the heavenly beings (21.22). He knows of people skilled to raise Leviathan, he knows of Sheol and of inhabited subterranean waters. He is besieged by hostile forces who surround his tent, and these are the armies of God who has taken the crown from his head. The friends, too, mention angels and spirits: Eliphaz had his fearful nightmare, when he realized that no man was righteous before God (4.12ff). He knew that even the angels stood condemned, and could not answer the questions of Job. He knew of the great council of God, of the unfaithful Holy Ones, and of the sin of defiance and rebellion (15.7ff). He knew something about the first man in heaven which we cannot reconstruct from the surviving reference. Zophar knew a God who passed through to imprison[14] and to call an assembly for judgement. The man who mounts to heaven is cast down. Bildad (if Chapter 25 is correctly attributed to him) knows of heavenly armies, and heavenly bodies deemed unworthy in the sight of God. *Had we no evidence but the dialogue, we could place Job with confidence in the world of the angel mythology.* The details escape us, and the state of the text puts a veil over everything. Nevertheless, it is imperative that the arguments of Job be viewed in the light of what can be reconstructed of that older system, especially as he seems to be arguing against those who changed it.[15]

The Speeches of Yahweh

There have been various estimates as to the date and significance of these speeches, yet it is rarely suggested that they represent the viewpoint of the author of Job.[16] On the contrary, it has even been argued that the theophany contributes nothing to the problem discussed in the drama.[17] This is unlikely. If we are to formulate the question of Job, we must work back from these Yahweh speeches, since they are offered *in the book* as the answer to the question. When the Lord appears to answer Job, the central motif of the chapters is *knowledge*, and the speech is a series of questions to Job, asking about his knowledge. It seems that it was the claim to knowledge which was at the heart of Job's rebellion.[18]

The speeches distinguish between the wisdom of Yahweh and the wisdom of Job, and the difference is not just one of degree. The poet emphasizes the superior power of Yahweh, but he also emphasizes the uniqueness of Yahweh's wisdom, saying that it is something which men cannot share. Yahweh's wisdom actually *forms* the creation, whereas Job's originates in his observing the creation. Thus, any claim to be able to predict what is to happen, or what ought to happen, is futile. This point is crucial, because this argument is exactly that used by the Second Isaiah to dismiss the claims of the other gods. The prophet argued that the creative power of God made any claims to predict the future invalid; in Job we see the other side of the picture. Confronted with the raw forces of creation, man's wisdom is but a puny thing. There must be some significance in the fact that the prophet bases his confident claims for the future of the exilic community upon just that argument from creative power which is used to dismiss the claims of Job.

An analysis of the materials in these speeches of Yahweh defines even more clearly their original milieu. We are told, for example, to look at the creation when there were present the morning stars and the sons of God, at the imprisoning of the might of the sea and at the recesses of the sea, at the gates of darkness and the dwellings of light, at the storehouses of the snow, at the binding of the constellations and at the rules of the heavens. This is no simple appeal to the power of Yahweh as the creator, or the benign figure of Genesis 1. What we have in these speeches is something darker, the echoes of that more turbulent creation whose strange imagery we find in the heavenly journeys of 1 Enoch. The seer there is taken to see the treasure of the stars, the storehouses of the winds, the foundation of the earth, the paths of the angels and the way of the stars (1 En. 10—36). The Book of Astronomy, the third section of 1 Enoch as we know it, has more of these sections of creation, with details of wind and weather (1 En. 76—77) and of the duties and routes of the stars (1 En. 82). Evidence from Qumran shows that this section once existed in a longer form, proof that the secrets of creation were a major component of that wisdom tradition which Enoch represents. The description in the Wisdom of Solomon (7.17) also gives prominence to this knowledge of creation. It may be that the Enochic material is only an embroidery upon the speeches in Job, just as the story of the fallen angels has been explained as a development of Genesis 6, or the Parables as a growth upon Isaiah 24—27;[19] but it is more likely that all these are integral parts of a tradition which we have lost.[20] The form of the Yahweh speeches indicates that Job had claimed a knowledge of these secrets, but that he was mistaken in thinking that his knowledge of them in any way affected or altered the creation in the way that Yahweh's creative knowledge did.

The second section of the first speech deals with a similar subject on a different level. Lions and mountain goats (38.39; 39.1) are more easily perceived than the foundations of the earth or the gates of death, yet even at this level, we are told, Job's knowledge is inadequate. He has no power over these things for good or ill, because his wisdom is too small, and it cannot create. In 40.1–5 Job acknowledges this, and is unable to find fault with the creator. Yahweh then demonstrates his power as judge and conqueror.

There has been much discussion of the *two* speeches of Yahweh, especially when both are so similar, but there does seem, upon a close inspection, to be a difference of emphasis. The first deals with the creative quality of Yahweh's wisdom, albeit a creativity based upon the restraining and ordering of mighty forces; the second deals with judgement and conquest, but not with a view to creativity. Thus 40. 7–9 is a crude statement of power, and 40. 10–14 challenges Job to abase the power of the proud and bring the wicked down to the dust. This alone would prove Job to be Yahweh's equal. Chapter 41 shows Yahweh conquering a monster, something else which is beyond Job. The speeches therefore give us a Yahweh who has superior creative wisdom and superior strength, showing themselves in his bringing down the proud, and overcoming monsters.

Compare this with the arguments and imagery of the Second Isaiah, and the question of Job comes into focus. The overall theme of his prophecies is the creative power of the exiles' God, strengthened by triumphant monotheism.

The other heavenly powers are defeated; they no longer exist. They have been summoned to a trial, and their knowledge has been dismissed as nothing before the superior creative wisdom of the exiles' God. The premise of the Second Isaiah's prophecies is the fusion of El and Yahweh; the framework is the arbitrary election of the exiles as the heirs to the promises given to the ancient kings. From the Yahweh speeches we can deduce that Job was questioning these new ways. He picks up the question which the prophet left unanswered. If there is only one God, whence is evil? Isaiah 45 must be read as the preface to Job:

> I am Yahweh, there is no other, beside me there is no God.
> I form light and create darkness, I make weal and create woe.
> Woe to him who strives with his creator . . .
> Will you ask of me things to come concerning my sons . . . ?
> I made the earth and created it; it was my hands that stretched out the heavens
> And I commanded all their host.
> Will you question me about my children?

Job represents the people who did question the justice of the new ways. Without the monotheism of the Second Isaiah, Job could have explained his sufferings, and he would have had no question. It was not the suffering that caused his problems, but the *explanation* of it which caused him to rebel. Without the creative power arguments of the Second Isaiah, there would have been no answer to Job from the whirlwind.

The Wisdom Poem in Job 28

If Job is a reflection upon the theological movements of the exile, we should expect to find in it some reference to the altered meaning of wisdom. I have already argued in the chapter on Wisdom that the ancient wisdom dealing with the secrets of creation and the practical business of employing these to order the environment was subsumed under the Law, and the older ways were buried in its foundations. The key phrase in the new wisdom was, 'The fear of the Lord is the beginning of wisdom', and this referred not only to the new association of wisdom and Law, but also to the older myth in which the wisdom of the angels had been corrupted through rebellion and *failure to fear God*. Job 28 depicts this transformed wisdom. Its presence in Job at this point is thus entirely appropriate, since the poem makes the same point as the speeches of Yahweh. It denies certain things about wisdom, and this in its turn implies that they had been believed. We may therefore assume that the writer of the poem knew of a wisdom linked to the practical skills of mining and engineering, as well as to the esoteric arts. He knew that men had paid large sums to acquire

271

this wisdom, but the poet is adamant that such knowledge is not wisdom. Man, for his part, finds wisdom only in the fear of God.

In the Yahweh speeches there is the distinction between God's wisdom which creates, and man's which merely observes and predicts. The wisdom poem contrasts man's applied wisdom with true wisdom, the fear of the Lord. Both indicate a period when the concept of wisdom was changing, and its practical element, i.e. the esoteric and scientific lore, was being replaced by an overtly theological system.[21] If the exilic upheavals *were* the background to Job, then the inclusion of this poem is in keeping with the other movements discernible in the work.

The Elihu Speeches

After the words of Job have ended (31.40), a fourth character appears and adds four speeches to strengthen the arguments of the three friends. He then disappears. Since there is no reference to him in the Yahweh speeches, or in the epilogue, the majority of modern scholars agree that Elihu was a later addition to the book of Job. There have been several detailed and elaborate analyses of the language of the speeches, but no firm conclusions have been drawn. Two further lines of inquiry might be later tradition and interpretation, or the content of the speeches themselves, to see if there is any evidence for the origin and significance of the Elihu figure in the present shape of the book.

(i) Later tradition and interpretation
Many commentators hold Elihu in high esteem,[22] but Job himself and later traditions both suggest that he is not a character we are to admire. The three friends do not speak what is right about God (42.7), and Elihu is presented as one who is angered by the failure of the friends to establish their case. He speaks to reinforce the position of those with whom God is not pleased. Elihu needs to prove Job wrong, as did the three friends, but we do not know from the book why it was so necessary for them to establish their position at the expense of Job's peace of mind. If all four stand for a group whose legitimacy is based upon their viewpoint about suffering, the fervour of their arguments is explicable. The three friends needed to establish that suffering was the result of actions committed by the victim. Elihu reinforces this view, and develops it. If the three are typical of exilic teaching, then perhaps Elihu represents a later development upon it.

Later tradition showed Elihu as an evil character. In the Testament of Job[23] the hero appears as a suffering saint, who hopes for a throne in the upper world, and for everlasting splendour, but Elihu is inspired by Satan and is the only one of Job's four visitors not eventually pardoned by God. Thus Job is the man of perfect piety, and Elihu is the agent of evil. This same tradition of Job's patience was maintained by the early Church.[24]

Although we cannot prove that the Elihu character in the Testament is true to the character in the canonical Job, the names given to him in the latter do suggest that he was not a pleasant man. Remembering that Job is a work of fiction, and that the characters could have been named in any way, to find together 'Son of One whom God has blessed, from the Land of Contempt, of Exalted family' among the names of Elihu indicates that the character in the Testament was nearer to the intention of the original author than the modern interpretations who see him in a good light. Whatever the Elihu character typified was condemned both within and beyond the Book of Job.

(ii) *The content of Elihu's speeches*

Elihu represents new ideas. He is young and impetuous, believing himself to be directly inspired, and not the heir to ancient wisdom (32.6–7). He says that wise men should determine amongst themselves what is right (34.2ff), and that God is, by definition, just. He even begins the fourth speech by claiming to speak on God's behalf! He is the spectacle of the man who claims perfect knowledge, yet he condemns Job for a similar claim (37.24), when he ends his speech by saying that God has no regard for anyone who claims wisdom for himself. Elihu also claims to justify God before man, an interesting twist to Job's dilemma of how man could be righteous before God.

There are four speeches from Elihu, each closely linked to the arguments of Job, and presupposing a knowledge of the dialogues. Thus 39.9–11 is parallel to 13.24, 27; 34.5–6 to 27.2; 35.6–7 to 22.2ff, etc. This has led to the suggestion (of which there are several forms) that these speeches are an addition to the original work, intended for insertion at four points in the dialogues, to strengthen the case of the friends against Job.[25] Others think that the Elihu speeches were intended as a preface to the speeches of Yahweh.[26] There are many theories, but no general agreement as to why these speeches have been added so clumsily with no mention of Elihu in any other part of the book, especially as the overall context of the book shows Elihu as a figure intended to add weight to the case *against* Job's friends.

The arguments in the speeches are not clear, but three bases can be extracted.

(a) Punishment is intended to educate and to improve those whom God chooses to treat in this way. God brings man back even from the brink of death (33.12–33). When he returns to God he returns to life. This is different from the psalmist's view of rescue from dire straits, for the Psalms indicate that it was enemies of some sort from which the plaintiff had to be rescued, and not from punishments inflicted by God himself. The afflicted one in the Psalms returns to life because he has not turned away from trust in God. Here, in the Elihu speeches, the afflicted man returns to life when he repents, which is a very different point of view. It neatly avoids the question of Job, as to why man was brought so low in the first place. Elihu thus argues from a position which has no real explanation for suffering, only a theory as to its purpose. This

273

important distinction must be borne in mind when identifying the tradition in which Elihu stands.

(b) The second basis of Elihu's argument is in ch. 36, an enigmatic text whose problems may well arise from our having no real context in which to read it. 36.5–12, for example, contrast two groups of afflicted. There are kings set up by God for ever, exalted, then bound in fetters. They are told that they have been proud. If they accept instruction, they will return to prosperity. If not, they will perish. This is the myth of judgement, but it has a new ending. Even the fallen ones, says Elihu, can be restored if they accept instruction from God (36.11). Those afflicted can be delivered in, or by, their afflictions, and they learn of God in, or by, their distress (v. 15). The sin is pride. By way of contrast, there are other sufferers who do not cry for help when they are punished, whose anger leads them to scorn. They are *turned away by the size of the ransom* (36.18). There have been many attempts to make sense of these extraordinary words, but all the interpretations are strained. If we focus upon the word 'ransom', and read the text in the light of what this had come to mean in the time of the exile, we then have Job refusing to accept the new ideas of a group whose great ransom Job found so scandalous that it reduced him to scorn and anger. This is Job's comment upon the great redemption and ransom themes of the exilic preachers. He was confronted with a statement that God's power was great and could not be questioned. All that he could do was accept a *fait accompli*. To fail to accept would render Job guilty before God. The words of Elihu then became very apt: 'Beware lest the greatness of the ransom turn you aside ... Will your cry avail to keep you from distress ...? Behold, God is exalted in his power. Who is a teacher like Him? Who has prescribed for him his way or who can say, "Thou hast done wrong"?' These verses do read very much as though Elihu was taking up the objections of the non-exilic group who had been ousted by the group from Babylon, claiming that they had been ransomed by God, and set up for a new beginning. At this point in his speech, Elihu begins to describe the power of God in creation, *which is exactly the theme which the Second Isaiah takes up at an identical point in his arguments for the new creation of the people of God.* God redeems as an act of creative power, and none, not even the heavenly beings, can question what he does. Thus this appeal to creation becomes the second basis of Elihu's arguments. At several points in ch. 37 he comes very close to the thought and language of the Second Isaiah. He too, knows that no being can draw up a case before God. Therefore men fear him, and those who believe themselves wise meet an unhappy end (37.24).

(c) The third basis is related to the second. Elihu denies the idea of a last judgement at a future date, and opts rather for a present judgement, with God overthrowing the mighty and setting up others in their places (34.23ff).

These ideas in the Elihu speeches are similar to those in other sources, but not in exactly the same proportions as we find them here. His appeal to the power of the creator is similar to that of the Second Isaiah, but the prophet combined his theology with a very different explanation of suffering. His belief that suffering was educational is similar to that in Deut. 8.5ff, explaining the wilderness, or Deut. 4.30 and 1 Kings 8.46ff, explaining the exile. Elihu would thus seem to be related to both the Second Isaiah and one of the stages of Deuteronomy. If he represents a particular group or viewpoint, we should expect this to be located towards the end of the exile.

The blows inflicted upon its traditions by the reformers and thinkers of the exile were more effective than the armies of Babylon in their destruction of old Jerusalem. It is because we have always read our history differently that the Book of Job has been an enigma. Those aspects of the book which have been fertile ground for exotic growths only emphasize the fact that this text is really a mystery to *us*, even though it cannot have been so opaque to its original hearers. We may try to avoid the issue by assigning Job to a foreign tradition or by acknowledging with reverence the inscrutability of the ancient orient, but Job remains as a major text in the Old Testament, and what it says must be a part of our overall picture. The ever-present experience of human suffering has led to this book's being used in many contexts; it has become a piece of universal application, but I doubt that it was written as such. The references are specific. The points of contact with other Old Testament writings are numerous. The book is clearly a debate, but from a standpoint of which we know very little, and about matters which we thought not to exist. To construct anything from within a given text is a dangerous procedure, but to construct in the light of considerable evidence from elsewhere justifies using these texts in a new way.

The Book of Job does not debate suffering; it debates the *explanations* of suffering, which is a very different matter. The book also questions the definition of righteousness, the role and limitations of 'knowledge' and the implications of monotheism. In each of these areas it is difficult to assess the position and contribution of Job because the definition of these terms in pre-exilic Israel is not entirely clear. We do not know how widely it was believed that cultic sacrifice put one in good standing with God. The prophets fulminated against such ideas, but the people who went to such expense and trouble must have believed that they were acting well, as did Job in the prologue. They were not all wicked men, but their writings and their points of view have not survived. We do not know what was meant by wisdom and knowledge before the exile. A great deal of the material in this area is conspicuously absent, and one must ask the reason for this. Nor do we know the number and nature of Israel's Gods. If we read many Old Testament texts at face value, we find that Israel recognized the power of several heavenly beings, and this is not monotheism, or even henotheism, yet we are not accustomed to read the Old Testament as the literature of a polytheistic people. What we have in Job is a comment upon change. We know the latter state, but the former we can only begin to reconstruct. This is why Job seems so strange.

The prose framework of the book puts Job in the world of the old mythology which can be reconstructed from other texts. The presence of Satan is not, therefore, a sign of lateness. We must note rather the sons of God setting themselves against Yahweh, the malicious angels testing humankind, endurance and loyalty as virtues bringing triumph, and cultic observance. This is the world of the kings and the world of the Psalter. It is the world which cannot accept that the three friends have spoken correctly about the ways of God. It is also the world of the apocalyptists, where, even though cultic observance is no longer prominent, endurance and loyalty are the answer to suffering, and heavenly beings its cause.

The dialogues bring us into another world. The debate is between wise men; three of them teach that sufferings are the result of personal transgression, and Job cannot accept this, even though he is also a wise man. This emphasis upon personal responsibility puts the three friends later than the time of Ezekiel and Jeremiah, and the divisive development within the wisdom tradition could well point to that period of which we know nothing, from which wisdom emerged as the Law. Such a transformation will not have happened overnight, or without enormous debate and resistance on the part of the many varieties of tradition represented in the exilic community. The three friends represent one stage in this process. They can still use the imagery of the angel mythology, and they know of myths which have not survived in any text known to us. They also know the fate of those proud enough to challenge the ways of God. On the other hand, their wisdom is well on the way to becoming the instruction in right conduct which we should think to be the sole concern of wise men were it not for the evidence of 1 Enoch or the Wisdom of Solomon. Like the Second Isaiah, these wise men deny that God is too remote to care about human affairs. Their arguments also use his monotheism, but Job cannot accept the justice of this monotheism. The friends then claim to be the authoritative voice of God, and to be true to the ancient traditions – yet Job is clearly rooted in something else, and has very different expectations of the same God. These traits would link the friends to the Deuteronomic position, and Job to the Third Isaiah's people who also faced a crisis of expectation within the one tradition. Job argues from his own tradition of wisdom. If the enigmatic 12.2 really does mean, 'Wisdom will die with you', then it could be the most crucial verse in the book for identifying its context. There is an equally bitter note in Isa. 65.15, 'You shall leave your name to my people for a curse'.[27] For Job the last judgement was very real. The heavenly court and the trial were a part of his expectation, as were a variety of heavenly beings, none of whom we can identify. The Second Isaiah had also used the trial imagery, but only to highlight the folly of such expectations when confronted with the creative power of Israel's God. The speeches of Yahweh imply that Job had claimed esoteric knowledge such as we find in 1 Enoch, and they deny that this wisdom is either possible or effective. The ways of God cannot be predicted – yet another component of the Second Isaiah's arguments against the lesser gods. Elihu offers another exilic viewpoint. Suffering is educative, and the creative power of Yahweh is the basis of his people's hope.

We know too little of the exile to place these characteristics with certainty, but it is clear that the three friends and Elihu represent ideas attested elsewhere as developing within and characteristic of, the exiled group. It is also clear that Yahweh in the Book of Job *rejects* these ideas.

At the end we find Job humbled by God, but back within his own mythology. His encounter with Yahweh had dealt with his claim to knowledge, and not with any sins he might have committed. He accepts the chastening on these terms, but never accepts the explanations of the friends. He accepts the fact of the power of God, and repents in dust and ashes.

We shall probably never know what stood between the two ends of the Job tradition before it received its present form. We can only read it as and where it now stands, in the Old Testament, as a comment upon the fate of the ancient wisdom, which found itself condemned on its own terms. Job, a wise man, had tried to challenge the hard facts of history. Job, like other misguided beings, had challenged the ways of God, and had been cast down. The Book of Job is proof that the angel mythology survived into the exile as a living tradition, capable of re-interpretation, and forming the framework which was used to explain its own demise.

NOTES

1 Cox (1978) is a good example of what can happen when Job is interpreted using modern criteria.
2 Blenkinsopp (1982). He also observes that later Jewish commentators linked the Sodom pericope to Job (p. 127).
3 Ezekiel's Job is more like the Job of the prose prologue than the Job of the dialogues.
4 Cheyne (1887).
5 Zerafa (1978), p. 39, asked: 'What stood between the two ends of the tradition before it was received by our author?' and, criticizing Rowley (1958), added; 'We should be better qualified to evaluate the message of Job if we knew exactly what the author rejected from the ancient tale, and what he added of his own accord to express his personal opinion about Job's problems.' No text which can be called a pre-Hebrew Job has ever been found, although works with a similar approach are known elsewhere, e.g. the so-called *Babylonian Theodicy*: see Lambert (1960).
6 Or is this *rūᵃḥ*, to be rendered 'spirit'?
7 *zar*, 'stranger', is a word which rewards further investigation; see Murray (1984); Snijders (1954).
8 Job's condition bears comparison with that threatened in Deut. 28, although the similarity may be due to a general expectation for anyone who incurred the wrath of the Lord.
9 Whybray (1965), pp. 24ff.
10 Driver and Gray (1921).

11 *hayyōdǝ'īm* 'those who know', and *hā'ām*, 'the people', are suggested as alternatives to 'a people', but there is no explanation for the extraordinary 'wisdom will die with you'.

12 McKane (1970), p. 421.

13 Whybray (1965).

14 There is debate about this translation; if it does mean 'imprison' it is a very significant reference.

15 Several of the names in Job may be significant, and although it is possible in many cases to find parallels for them in ancient place-names, I wonder whether they might not have been chosen by the author of Job in much the same way as Bunyan chose the names for *The Pilgrim's Progress*. The three friends who are not speaking what is right come from *Teman*, a name associated with good fortune, from *Suḥi* a word for 'smooth easy places', but also for 'treacherous pits', and from *Naamah*, a land of pleasant things, even though these can also be the titbits offered by evil men (Ps. 141.4). Elihu comes from *Buz*, meaning 'contempt'; Job lives in *'uṣ*, related to *'eṣah*, 'good counsel'. Although the meaning of the names cannot be established with uncertainty, Job has often been linked to *'ōyēb*, 'enemy' (see Dhorme 1967) and Elihu comes from a 'high family', the son of 'one whom God has blessed'. All these must be read in the light of the condemnation of the three friends. The LXX says that all three friends were kings and rulers.

16 Driver and Gray (1921).

17 Zerafa (1978), p. 57: 'The theophany does not contribute anything towards the problem discussed in the drama.'

18 Glatzer (1966). This article also shows the association of Job and Adam motifs by later commentators, suggesting that both figures arose from a similar situation (p. 79).

19 Charles *Pseudepigrapha*, *ad loc*; Suter (1979a).

20 See Stone (1976) for details.

21 What are we to make of Ben Sir. 39.1–11, the portrait of the later wise man? The traditional picture has been supplemented by a new fact, that of competence in the Law. See von Rad (1965), p. 23. Why, too, is he one who 'gleans the field after the gatherers' (33.16)? Does this show something of the fate and status of wisdom at this time?

22 e.g. Dhorme (1967), p. lvii.

23 The Testament of Job has inspired no agreement as to its date or origin. The recent trend is to link it to the Therapeutae, and to Qumran. A Hebrew or Aramaic original has been favoured for some time: Kohler (1898), followed by Philonenko (1968), and now many more. It was written in the first century BC or AD, has been linked to Merkabah texts, and may have Christian reworkings. For full bibliography see Kraft (1974): Charlesworth (1981), pp. 134–6.

24 e.g. James 5.2; 1 Clement 17.

25 Freedman (1968), pp. 51ff.

26 Childs (1979), p. 541.

27 And an equally strange sentiment in 1 En. 94.5 about those who make wisdom evil.

CONCLUSION

The monarchy in Jerusalem was built upon an elaborate mythology. The High God had a retinue of heavenly creatures whose natures and roles were as complex as anything we find in the angelologies of the later texts. This world was the counterpart to the physical world, but its powers could only be experienced within the limitations of the physical world. Hence the problems of time and location which are apparent throughout the apocalyptic texts. The powers were outside time, yet governed history; they were spiritual, yet governed the processes of the natural order. Their power was based upon, or consisted of, *wisdom*, by which was meant an all-encompassing knowledge of all things such that they could be controlled, or even created. It was insight into this wisdom which gave the wise men their powers as magicians and healers, and it was disputes about the possession of this creative wisdom which underlay the speeches of Yahweh in the Book of Job. Some believed that man could not attain this wisdom; others knew that he could. The heavenly powers were perceived in the stars and their ordering, and in the great mountains which gave the earth its structure. When the stars and the ends of the earth were numbered and summoned by the High God, it was in their aspect as heavenly powers. These powers were held in check by the High God and his servants. The powers were in themselves neutral, but by an act of will could be used for good or evil. Unchecked by the High God, or released from their bonds of service, the powers distorted, corrupted and destroyed the processes of nature and the patterns of history. Used in the service of the High God, these same powers worked for good in maintaining the natural order.

The High God and his retinue had a mountain garden where there was fabulous vegetation, the tree of life, the waters of life and the great throne. The events in this heavenly place were the counterparts of what happened on earth. Some angels rebelled against the High God by attempting to claim his throne, or by using their wisdom for evil ends. Others marred their angelic state by cohabiting with human kind and producing half-breed offspring who, though angelic, were tied to the physical state.

Some angels had special charge of individual nations. The successive kings of these nations were the earthly manifestation of the heavenly patron, and their roles in earth and heaven were reflected in their titles: the earthly king in his heavenly aspect was a Son of Man, the angel in his human aspect was a Son of God. Wars in heaven were wars on earth; expulsion from heaven meant the end of a nation, for its prince became human and died. Obedient servants, both angelic and human, acted as agents of the High God whose name had the power to effect changes in nature and in history. Knowledge of this Name, and knowledge of the names of the lesser angels, was crucial. It was a sin to utter the Name in vain; it was a disaster if the power of the name fell into the wrong hands, but a cause of great rejoicing when the name of the great Son of Man was finally revealed and restored to the true servants as part of the wisdom of the last times. Certain people had access to this other world. They were the key figures, for they provided the link between heaven and earth, and were in themselves a channel of great power. The king was one who functioned in both worlds. He was a humble servant of the High God, and entitled as a result to stand with impunity upon the holy mountain. He took his place in the heavenly council, and was endowed with great wisdom, which enabled him to rule his people and to control the natural order. The king was thus the key to his country's fertility, and his keeping of the divine law the secret of its prosperity. He had powers to heal and to cure, and his throne was that of his patron angel. He achieved his place in the heavenly council by an ascent, an experience common to many cultures, and triggered by various means. How the experience was induced we do not know, but the reality of the heavenly ascent is older than the Mosaic tradition and the present form of the Pentateuch. The emblem of the royal figure was, as a result, a flying circle. The trauma of the ascent is also widely attested, and it was Israel's own interpretation of this experience which gave rise to the pictures of danger and suffering which were a servant's lot before he reached the exaltation of the presence of the High God.

The Temple was the key place in this cult. It represented the heavenly place. Its Eden setting, with throne, cherubim, menorah and great sea, was the place where the movements of heaven were enacted on earth, and its rituals, which derived their authority from the upper world, were assured of effectiveness on earth. Thus the power of the High God to restrain hostile forces was the power of the king over his enemies and over the forces of nature. The Law of the High God was given by the mouth of the king. A great judgement upon evil forces was expected, and made present in the liturgy of the Temple. Successive royal figures were one unchanging ideal, and when the royal house was no more, the ideal remained as the messianic hope. The king figure was more than human; he had angelic knowledge, but it is not clear whether the angel status gave him this knowledge, or the possession of knowledge effected the transformation. The association of knowledge and the angelic state survived in the extra-biblical tradition as the hope of a transforming wisdom to be revealed to the righteous in the last days before their own exaltation. The suffering which preceded the acquisition of the wisdom and the angelic state was understood as the experience of death, thus giving rise to the belief that the wise ones in their angelic state had passed to a new form of life.

It was the simultaneous occurrence of two great events which ensured the loss of this ancient cult and its mythology. The first was the advent of a group of unknown origin, whom we have labelled the Deuteronomists, who placed themselves at the centre of affairs in Josiah's time and claimed for themselves great reforms. Such was their success that we do not know what they reformed, but there are indications in texts both biblical and extra-biblical that what they labelled and condemned as Canaanite was in fact the indigenous cult of Jerusalem. Their writings show fanatical opposition to many aspects of the cult, and yet, as so often happens, they absorbed much of what they set out to reform. The second event was the destruction of Jerusalem and the eventual demise of the royal house. After Temple and king had been wrenched away, the system was left without a centre.

When the fragments eventually settled and the dust had cleared, several new positions had emerged. One was that of the Deuteronomists, increasingly being recognized as the dominant influence in the Old Testament as we have it, but not necessarily the dominant influence for all the heirs to ancient Jerusalem. Recent scholarship has shown the complexity of their writings, and the several stages of development through which they passed. At one stage they acquired the notion of covenant law, but nobody knows whence it came. The post-Deuteronomistic material in several instances indicates a priestly origin, but again the exact circumstances of the development are not known. A sequence of events such as I have proposed could provide an outline of these stages, with the covenant grafted in from the royal cult, and the priestly material stemming from the exilic fusions necessary for survival. The most vexing of all questions is the relationship between the Deuteronomists and the mainstream of Israel's religious tradition.

> Whatever precise understanding has been projected it is usually taken for granted that the work has an official stance, that it represents a proclamation within the mainstream of the ongoing life of the people ... Some such public and official context is normally accepted for the setting of the work of the deuteronomistic school. *It is perhaps here, however, that the first questions should be raised.*[1]

It is of great interest for my hypothesis that a very different work, namely a redactional study of the Deuteronomistic history, can reach a conclusion so similar to mine. One of the unrecognized heirs to the older tradition (there may have been many others) was the Enochic circle; time and again we find that studies of this, and related materials, produce hypotheses of a 'lost' tradition, because there is a consistent pattern which emerges from the extra-biblical texts. The sealing of the forces of creation, the angelic life for the righteous, the great judgement, and many more, form a coherent pattern which cannot be attributed to alien influences, or deviations from the Deuteronomic norm. The whole myth of the fallen angels which is already highly developed in the earliest pseudepigrapha and continues in the Christian literature is nowhere spelled out in the biblical writings. It was ancient. It was fundamental. But where did it originate? These strange elements of the non-canonical writings were indigenous to Israel, but we have failed to recognize them as such because a major channel of that tradition has been dammed and diverted, and because the non-canonical writings have themselves picked up a quantity of débris along their way. It is not possible to follow them all to their source, but the similarities between the opacities of the Old Testament and the patterns of the non-canonical literature make a common origin likely. The apocalyptic elements of the Old Testament are not insertions, but fossils.

It has proved possible to isolate recurring patterns in the extra-biblical texts and assemble them into a viable whole. It may be objected that the process has been based upon the hypothesis of an early original constructed simply by retrojection. True, but the pattern thus formed and its relevance to so many of the problems of the Old Testament invites consideration. We must not forget that the orthodoxies of Old Testament scholarship are now widely challenged, and that we cannot claim in any way to have understood these writings or the manner of their composition. What I have proposed is also fraught with problems, and it leaves unanswered questions. It should not be dismissed for this reason. I do not claim to understand these texts, but base my case on the fact that they are far less comprehensible than we often so fondly suppose. Nor do I claim to have understood their bizarre mythology. I have recognized that it is pervasively and impenetrably there, covered by an equally pervasive and impenetrable layer of tradition and scholarship, both ancient and modern.

In conclusion I return to my first observations. Our own approach to this material may be the greatest barrier to our understanding. Those competent to handle the ancient texts do not always fully appreciate what they are saying. Their magical and mysterious elements are not attractive to rationalists, and the irrational is not attractive to scholarship. If we are to proceed, we must read these texts on their own terms not ours. We must recognize that their writers knew and experienced things of which we are ignorant. The heavenly ascent was a real experience, not a literary device or a pious fiction, even if in some writings it came to be used as such. The power of the human mind in certain states was known to effect changes in the physical world, or in the perception of the physical world. Increasingly this power of magic (miracle, or whatever term we currently favour), is being rediscovered and recognized by a generation which thought it had outgrown such things. I do not know what we shall eventually learn about the cult of Jerusalem, about Christian origins, about angels, or about the mysteries of the human state which these apocalypses explore. But I am sure that a post-pan-Deuteronomistic era of Old Testament study will be very different from anything we know at present, and that the Older Testament will emerge as the more immediate backcloth to the New.

NOTE

1 Mayes (1983), pp. 137–8 (italics mine).

BIBLIOGRAPHY

Achtemeier, P. J., ed., [1978] *Society of Biblical Literature 1978 Seminar Papers*, vol. 1 (SBL Seminar Papers, 13). Chico, Ca. 1978.

Ackroyd, P. R., [1966] 'Some Notes on the Psalms', *JTS*, NS 17 (1966), 392–9.

— [1968] *Exile and Restoration*. London 1968.

— [1973] *I and II Chronicles, Ezra, Nehemiah*. London 1973.

— [1974] 'An Interpretation of the Babylonian Exile: A Study of 2 Kings 20, Isaiah 38–39', *SJT* 27 (1974), 329–52.

— [1976] 'God and People in the Chronicler's Presentation of Ezra', in *La Notion biblique de Dieu*, ed. Coppens, J., BETL 41 (1976), 145–62.

— [1977] 'The Chronicler as Exegete', *JSOT* 2 (1977), 2–32.

Alexander, P. S., [1972] 'The Targumim and Early Exegesis of the Sons of God in Gen 6', *JJS* 23 (1972), 60–71.

— [1977] 'The Historical Setting of the Hebrew Book of Enoch', *JJS* 28 (1977), 156–80.

— [1983] 'Rabbinic Judaism and the New Testament', *ZNW* 74 (1983), 237–46.

— [1984] 'Comparing Merkabah Mysticism and Gnosticism: An Essay in Method', *JJS* 46 (1984), 1–17.

Alt, A., [1966] 'The Origins of Israelite Law' (1934), in Alt, A., *Essays on Old Testament History and Religion* (ET Oxford 1966), pp. 79–132.

Altmann, A., [1968] 'Homo Imago Dei in Jewish and Early Christian Theology', *JR* 48 (1968), 235–59.

Anderson, B. W. and Harrelson, W., [1962] *Israel's Prophetic Heritage: Essays in Honour of James Muilenburg*. London 1962.

Ashton, J., [1986] 'The Transformation of Wisdom: A Study of the Prologue of John's Gospel', *NTS* 32 (1986), 161–86.

Bächli, O., [1962] *Israel und die Völker*. Zürich 1962.

Bampfylde, G., [1984] 'The Similitudes of Enoch. Historical Allusions', *JSJ* 15 (1984), 9–31.

Barker, M., [1977] 'The Two Figures in Zechariah', *HeyJ* 18 (1977), 38–46.

— [1978] 'The Evil in Zechariah', *HeyJ* 19 (1978), 12–27.

Barnes, W. E., [1934] 'Ezekiel's Denunciation of Tyre (Ez 26–28)', *JTS* 35 (1934), 50–2.

Barr, J., [1959] 'The Meaning of "Mythology" in Relation to the Old Testament', *VT* 9 (1959), 1–10.

— [1968] *Comparative Philology and the Text of the Old Testament*. Oxford 1968.

— [1975] 'Jewish Apocalyptic in Recent Scholarly Study', *BJRL* 58 (1975), 9–35.

Bartelmus, R., [1979] *Heroentum in Israel und seiner Umwelt* (ATANT 65). Zürich 1979.

Beckwith, R. T., [1981] 'The Earliest Enoch Literature and its Calendar', *RQ* 10 (1981), 365–403.

Beeston, A. F. L., [1951] 'Angels in Deut 33.2', *JTS*, NS 2 (1951), 30–1.

Bentzen, A., [1948] 'On the Ideas of "the Old" and "the New" in Deutero-Isaiah', *Studia Theologica* 1 (1948–9), 27–43.

— [1955] *King and Messiah.* ET London 1955.

Betz, H.-D., [1969] 'On the Problem of the Religio-Historical Understanding of Apocalyptic', *JTC* 6 (1969), 134–56.

— [1986] *The Greek Magical Papyri in Translation.* Chicago 1986.

Black, M., [1970] *Apocalypsis Henochii Graece.* Leiden 1970.

— [1976] 'The Parables of Enoch and the Son of Man', *ExpT* 88 (1976), 5–8.

— [1978] 'The Apocalypse of Weeks in the Light of 4QEn⁸', *VT* 28 (1978), 464–9.

— [1982] 'All Powers will be subject to Him' in Hooker, M. D., and Wilson, S. G., eds., *Paul and Paulinism.* London 1982.

— [1985] (with VanderKam, J. and Neugebauer, O.), *The Book of Enoch or 1 Enoch: A New English Edition with Commentary and Textual Notes.* Leiden 1985.

Blank, S. H., [1940], 'Studies, in Deutero-Isaiah', *HUCA* 15(1940), 1–46.

Bleeker, C. J., [1967] *Egyptian Festivals: Enactments of Religious Renewal.* Leiden 1967.

Blenkinsopp, J., [1977] *Prophecy and Canon.* Notre Dame, Ind. 1977.

— [1982] 'Abraham and the Righteous of Sodom', *JJS* 33 (1982), 119–32.

Bloom, H., [1983] *Kabbalah and Criticism.* New York 1983.

Bousset, W., [1903] *Die Religion des Judentums im neutestamentlichen Zeitalter* (1903). 3rd edn by H. Gressmann, Tübingen 1926.

Bowker, J., [1969] *The Targums and Rabbinic Literature.* Cambridge 1969.

Bowman, J., [1977] *Samaritan Documents Relating to their History, Religion, and Life.* Pittsburgh 1977.

Braun, M., [1938] *History and Romance in Graeco-Oriental Literature.* Oxford 1938.

Broadie, A. and MacDonald, J., [1978] 'The Concept of Cosmic Order in Ancient Egypt in Dynastic and Roman Times', *L'Antiquité Classique* 47 (1978), 106–28.

Cameron, R. and Dewey, A. J., ed., [1979] *The Cologne Mani Codex.* Missoula, Mon., 1979.

Caquot, A., [1978] 'Le Rouleau du Temple de Qoumran', *ETR* 53 (1978), 443–500.

Carley, K. W., [1975] *Ezekiel Among the Prophets: A Study of Ezekiel's Place in the Prophetic Tradition.* London 1975.

Carroll, R. P., [1979] *When Prophecy Failed.* London 1979.

Casey, M., [1979] *The Son of Man.* London 1979.

Castaneda, C., [1970] *The Teachings of Don Juan: A Yaqui Way of Knowledge.* Harmondsworth 1970.

Charles, R. H., [1912] *The Book of Enoch or 1 Enoch.* Oxford 1912².

— [1913] *The Apocrypha and Pseudepigrapha of the Old Testament in English* (Oxford 1913), vol. 2, *Pseudepigrapha.*

Charlesworth, J. H., [1980] 'The Portrayal of the Righteous as an Angel', in Collins and Nickelsburg, ed., *Ideal Figures...* (1980) (q.v.), 135–51.

Chernus, I., [1982a] 'Visions of God in Merkabah Mysticism', *JSJ* 13 (1982), 123–46.

— [1982b] *Mysticism in Rabbinic Judaism.* Berlin 1982.

Chevalier, G., [1976] *The Sacred Magician.* London 1976.

Cheyne, T. K., [1887] *Job and Solomon*. London 1887.

Childs, B. S., [1960] *Myth and Reality in the Old Testament*. London 1960.

— [1974] *Exodus*. London 1974.

— [1979] *Introduction to the Old Testament as Scripture*. London 1979.

Clements, R. E., [1965a] 'Deuteronomy and the Jerusalem Cult Tradition', *VT* 15 (1965), 300–12.

— [1965b] *God and Temple*. Oxford 1965.

— [1975] *Prophecy and Tradition*. Oxford 1975.

Clifford, R. J., [1972] *The Cosmic Mountain in Canaan and the Old Testament*. Cambridge, Mass., 1972.

Clines, D. J. A., [1978] *The Theme of the Pentateuch*. Sheffield 1978.

Coggins, R. J., [1965] 'The Interpretation of Ezra IV 4', *JTS*, NS 16 (1965), 124–7.

— [1975] *Samaritans and Jews*. Oxford 1975.

Collins, J. J., [1974] 'Apocalyptic Eschatology as the Transcendence of Death', *CBQ* 36 (1974), 21–43.

— [1975a] 'Jewish Apocalyptic against its Hellenistic Near Eastern Environment', *BASOR* 220 (1975), 27–36.

— [1975b] 'The Mythology of Holy War in Daniel and the Qumran War Scroll: A Point of Transition in Jewish Apocalyptic', *VT* 25 (1975), 596–612.

— [1977] *The Apocalyptic Vision of the Book of Daniel*. Missoula, Mon., 1977.

— [1978] 'Methodological Issues in the Study of 1 Enoch', in Achtemeier, P. J., ed., *SBL 1978 Seminar Papers*, vol. 1 (q.v.), 315–22.

— [1979] 'The Jewish Apocalypses', in Collins, J. J., ed., *Apocalypse: The Morphology of a Genre*, *Semeia* 14 (1979), 21–59.

— [1980] and Nickelsburg, G. W. E., ed., *Ideal Figures in Ancient Judaism*. Chico, Ca., 1980.

— [1980] 'The Heavenly Representative: the "Son of Man" in the Similitudes of Enoch', in Collins, ed., *Ideal Figures ...* (1980), 111–33.

— [1981] 'Apocalyptic Genre and Mythic Allusions in Daniel', *JSOT* 21 (1981), 83–100.

— [1984] *The Apocalypic Imagination*. New York 1984.

Cooke, G., [1961] 'The Israelite King as the Son of God', *ZAW* 32 (1961), 202–5.

Cowley, A. E., [1923] *Aramaic Papyri of the Fifth Century B.C.* Oxford 1923.

Cox, D., [1978] *The Triumph of Impotence. Job and the Tradition of the Absurd*. Rome 1978.

Cross, F. M., [1973] *Canaanite Myth and Hebrew Epic*. Cambridge, Mass., and London 1973.

— [1975] 'A Reconstruction of the Judaean Restoration', *JBL* 94 (1975).

— [1948] and Freedman, D. N., 'The Blessing of Moses', *JBL* 67 (1948), 191–210.

Dahood, M. J., [1966, 1968, 1970] *Psalms*, vols. 1–3. Garden City, New York 1966–70.

Daniélou, J., [1964] *A History of Early Christian Doctrine Before the Council of Nicaea, I: The Theology of Jewish Christianity* (1958). ET London 1964.

David-Neel, A., [1984] *Magic and Mystery in Tibet*. London 1984.

Davies, P. R., [1980] 'Eschatology in the Book of Daniel', *JSOT* 17 (1980), 33–53.

— [1983a] *The Damascus Covenant*. Sheffield 1983.

— [1983b] 'Calendrical Change and Qumran Origins. An Assessment of VanderKam's Theory', *CBQ* 45 (1983), 80–9.

— [1985] 'Sons of Cain', in Martin, J. D. and Davies, P. R., ed., *A Word in Season. Essays in Honour of William McKane*. Sheffield 1985.

Deissman, A., [1927] *Light from the Ancient East*. New York 1927².

Dhorme, E., [1967] *Job*. ET London 1967.

Dimant, D., [1978] '1 Enoch 6–11: A Methodological Perspective', in Achtemeier, P. J., ed., *SBL 1978 Seminar Papers*, vol. 1 (q.v.), 323–39.

— [1983] 'The Biography of Enoch and the Books of Enoch', *VT* 33 (1983), 14–29.

Dodd, C. H., [1965] *According to the Scriptures*. London 1952, 1965.

Driver, G. R., [1934] 'Studies in the Vocabulary of the Old Testament, VII', *JTS* 35 (1934), 380–93.

— [1965] *The Judaean Scrolls*. Oxford 1965.

Driver, S. R. and Gray, G. B., [1921] *Job* (ICC), Edinburgh 1921.

Dunn, J. D. G., [1977] *Unity and Diversity in the New Testament*. London 1977.

— [1980] *Christology in the Making*. London 1980.

Eaton, J. H., [1970] 'The King as God's Witness', *ASTI* 7 (1970), 25–40.

— [1976] *Kingship and the Psalms*. London 1976.

— [1979] *Festal Drama in Deutero-Isaiah*. London 1979.

Eichrodt, W., [1961, 1967] *Theology of the Old Testament*. 2 vols. London 1961, 1967.

Eissfeldt, O., [1956] 'El and Yahweh', *JSS* 1 (1956), 25–37.

Eliade, M., [1960] *Myths, Dreams and Mysteries*. London 1960.

— [1970] *Shamanism: Archaic Techniques of Ecstasy*. Princeton 1970.

Emerton, J., [1962] 'Binding and Loosing — Forgiving and Retaining', *JTS*, NS 13 (1962), 325–31.

— [1971a] 'Some False Clues in the Study of Gen XIV', *VT* 21 (1971), 24–47.

— [1971b] 'The Riddle of Gen XIV', *VT* 21 (1971), 403–39.

Engnell, I., *Studies in Divine Kingship in the Ancient Near East*. Oxford 1967².

Feigin, S., [1920] 'The Meaning of Ariel', *JBL* 39 (1920), 131–7.

Fitzmyer, J. A., [1965] 'The Aramaic "Elect of God" text from Qumran Cave 4', *CBQ* 27 (1965), 348–72, reprinted in Fitzmyer, *Essays on the Semitic Background of the New Testament* (London 1971), 127–60.

— [1971] *The Genesis Apocryphon of Qumran Cave 1*. Rome 1971².

— [1978] and Harrington, D. J., *A Manual of Palestinian Aramaic Texts*. Rome 1978.

Fohrer, G., [1970] *Introduction to the Old Testament* (1965 revision of Sellin, E., 1910). ET London 1970.

Frankfort, H., [1948] *Kingship and the Gods*. Chicago 1948.

Freedman, D. N., [1961] 'The Chronicler's Purpose', *CBQ* 23 (1961), 436–42.

— [1968] 'The Elihu Speeches and the Book of Job', *HTR* 61 (1968), 51–9.

French, P. J., [1972] *John Dee: The World of an Elizabethan Magus*. London 1972.

Gammie, J. G., [1971] 'Loci of the Melchizedek Tradition of Gen 14:18–20', *JBL* 90 (1971), 385–96.

Gaster, M. H., [1901] 'The Logos Ebraikos in the Magical Papyrus of Paris and the Book of Enoch', *JRAS*, 3rd Series 33 (1901), 109–17.

Gaster, T. H., [1961] *Thespis*. New York 1961.

Gilchrist, C., [1984] *Alchemy: the Great Work. A History and Evaluation of the Western Hermetic Tradition.* Wellingborough 1984.

Ginzberg, L., [1909–38] *Legends of the Jews,* 7 vols. Philadelphia 1909–38.

Glasson, T. F., [1961] *Greek Influences on Jewish Eschatology.* London 1961.

Glatzer, N. N., [1966] '"Knowest Thou . . .?" Notes on the Book of Job', in Loewe, R., ed., *Studies in Rationalism, Judaism and Universalism in Memory of Leon Roth* (London 1966), 75–86.

Goldin, J., [1970] 'Not by means of an Angel and not by means of a Messenger', in Neusner, J., ed., *Religions in Antiquity* (1970) (q.v.), 412–24.

Goodenough, E. R., [1940] *Introduction to Philo Judaeus.* New Haven, Conn., 1940.

— [1953–65] *Jewish Symbols in the Greco-Roman Period,* 11 vols. New York 1953–65.

Gray, J. G., [1957] *The Legacy of Canaan,* SVT 5. Leiden 1957.

— [1970] *I & II Kings.* London 1970[1].

Greenfield, J. C. and Stone, M. E., [1977] 'The Enochic Pentateuch and the Date of the Similitudes', *HTR* 70 (1977), 51–65.

— [1979] 'The Books of Enoch and the Traditions of Enoch', *Numen* 26 (1979), 89–103.

Grelot, P., [1958a] 'La géographie mythique d'Hénoch et ses sources orientales', *RB* 65 (1958), 33–69.

— [1958b] 'La légende d'Hénoch dans les apocryphes et dans la Bible: origine et signification', *RSR* 46 (1958), 5–26, 181–210.

— [1958c] 'L'eschatologie des Esséniens et le livre d'Hénoch', *RQ* 1 (1958), 113–31.

Gross, J., [1938] *La divinisation du chrétien d'après les pères grecs.* Paris 1938.

Gruenwald, I., [1979] *Apocalyptic and Merkavah Mysticism.* Leiden 1979.

Halifax, J., [1979] *Shamanic Voices: a Survey of Visionary Narratives.* New York 1979.

Hanson, P., [1975] *The Dawn of Apocalyptic.* Philadelphia 1975.

— [1977] 'Rebellion in Heaven, Azazel, and Euhemeristic Heroes in 1 Enoch 6–11', *JBL* 96[1977], 197–233.

— ed., [1983] *Visionaries and their Apocalypses.* London and Philadelphia 1983.

Haran, M., [1960] 'The Nature of the "'Ohel Mo'edh" in Pentateuchal Sources', *JSS* 5 (1960), 50–65.

— [1962] 'Shiloh and Jerusalem: the Origin of the Priestly Tradition in the Pentateuch', *JBL* 81 (1962), 14–24.

— [1978] *Temples and Temple Service in Ancient Israel.* Oxford 1978.

Harner, M. J., ed., [1973] *Hallucinogens and Shamanism.* New York 1973.

Hartmann, L., [1966] *Prophecy Interpreted: The Formation of Some Jewish Apocalyptic Texts and of the Eschatological Discourse Mark 13 Par.* Lund 1966.

Hasel, G., [1979] 'The Four World Empires of Daniel 2 against its Near Eastern Environment', *JSOT* 12 (1979), 17–30.

Hengel, M., *Judaism and Hellenism.* ET London 1974.

— [1976] *The Son of God.* ET London 1976.

Hennecke, E., [1963, 1965] *New Testament Apocrypha,* ET and ed. Wilson, R. McL., 2 vols. London 1963, 1965.

Hindley, J. C., [1967] 'Towards a Date for the Similitudes of Enoch. A Historical Approach', *NTS* 14 (1967), 551–65.

Hooker, M. D., [1967] *The Son of Man in Mark.* Montreal 1967.

— [1982] and Wilson, S. G., eds., *Paul and Paulinism*. London 1982.

Horbury, W., [1985a] 'Extirpation and Excommunication', *VT* 35 (1985), 13–38.

— [1985b] 'The Messianic Associations of the "Son of Man"', *JTS*, NS 36 (1985), 34–55.

Horton, F. L., [1976] *The Melchizedek Tradition*. Cambridge 1976.

Hull, J. M., [1974] *Hellenistic Magic and the Synoptic Tradition*. London 1974.

Jansen, H. L., [1939] *Die Henochgestalt: eine vergleichende religionsgeschichtliche Untersuchung*. Oslo 1939.

Japhet, S., [1982] 'Sheshbazzar and Zerubbabel', *ZAW* 94 (1982), 66–98.

Jaubert, A., [1953] 'Le calendrier des Jubilés et de la secte de Qumran: ses origines bibliques', *VT* 3 (1953), 250–64.

— [1957] 'Le calendrier des Jubilés et les jours liturgiques de la semaine', *VT* 7 (1957), 35–61.

Johnson, A. R., [1967] *Sacral Kingship in Ancient Israel*. Cardiff 1967.

Jung, C. G., [1972] *Psychology and Religion East and West* (*Collected Works of C. G. Jung*, vol. 11). ET London 1972.

Käsemann, E., [1969] 'The Beginnings of Christian Theology', ET in Funk, R. W., ed., *Apocalypticism, JTC* 6 (1969), 17–46.

Kaiser, O., [1972] *Isaiah 1–12: A Commentary*. London 1972, 1981².

Kaufmann, S. A., [1985] 'On Methodology in the Study of the Targums and their Chronology', *JSNT* 23 (1985), 117–24.

Keel, O., [1978] *The Symbolism of the Biblical World*. ET London 1978.

King, F., and Skinner, S., [1976] *Techniques of High Magic*. London 1976.

Knibb, M. A., [1976] 'The Exile in the Literature of the Intertestamental Period', *HeyJ* 17 (1976), 253–72.

— [1978] *The Ethiopic Book of Enoch: A New Edition in the Light of the Aramaic Dead Sea Fragments*. Oxford 1978.

— [1979] 'The Date of the Parables of Enoch', *NTS* 25 (1979), 345–59.

Kobelski, P. J., [1981] *Melchizedek and Melchireša'*. Washington, D.C., 1981.

Koch, K., [1972] *The Rediscovery of Apocalyptic* (1970). London 1972.

— [1974] 'Ezra and the Origins of Judaism', *JSS* 19 (1974).

Kraft, R. A., ed., [1974] *The Testament of Job*. Missoula, Mon., 1974.

Kraus, H. J., [1966] *Worship in Israel* (1962). ET Oxford 1966.

Labuschagne, C. J., [1966] *The Incomparability of Yahweh in the Old Testament*. Leiden 1966.

— [1974] 'The Tribes in the Blessing of Moses', *OTStudien* 19 (1974), 97–112.

Lacocque, A., [1979] *The Book of Daniel* (1976). ET London 1979.

Lakoff, G. and Johnson, M., [1980] *Metaphors we live by*. Chicago 1980.

Lambert, W. G., [1960] *Babylonian Wisdom Literature*. Oxford 1960.

Laycock, D. C., ed., [1979] *The Complete Enochian Dictionary*. London 1979.

Leary, T., [1964] *Psychedelic Experiences*. New York 1964.

Levey, S. H., [1983] 'The Targum to Ezekiel', *HUCA* 46 (1975), 139–58.

Lindars, B., [1983] *Jesus, Son of Man*. London 1983.

Longenecker, R. N., [1970] *The Christology of Early Jewish Christianity*. London 1970.

Lust, J., [1978] 'Daniel 7, 13 and the Septuagint', *ETL* 54 (1978), 62–9.

McCarthy, D. J., [1965] 'Notes on the Love of God and the Father-Son Relationship between Yahweh and Israel', *CBQ* 27 (1965), 144–7.

— [1972] *Old Testament Covenant. A Survey of Current Opinions.* Oxford 1972.

— [1982] 'Covenant and Law in Chronicles-Nehemiah', *CBQ* 44 (1982), 25–44.

MacDonald, J., [1964] *The Theology of the Samaritans.* London 1964.

McKane, W., [1965] *Prophets and Wise Men.* London 1965, 1983².

— [1970] *Proverbs.* London 1970.

MacLaurin, E. C. B., [1975] 'Joseph and Asaph', *VT* 25 (1975), 27–45.

May, H. G., [1962] 'The King in the Garden of Eden', in Anderson and Harrelson, eds., *Israel's Prophetic Heritage* (1962) (q.v.), 166–76.

Mayes, A. D. H., [1979] *Deuteronomy.* London 1979.

— [1983] *The Story of Israel between Settlement and Exile.* London 1983.

Mearns, C. L., [1979] 'Dating the Similitudes of Enoch', *NTS* 25 (1979), 360–9.

Meeks, W. A., [1970] 'Moses as God and King', in Neusner, J., ed., *Religions in Antiquity* (1970) (q.v.), 354–71.

Mettinger, T. N. D., [1982] *The Dethronement of Sabaoth.* Lund 1982.

Metzger, B. M., [1977] *The Earliest Versions of the New Testament.* Oxford 1977.

Meyers, C., [1976] *The Tabernacle Menorah.* Missoula, Mon., 1976.

Milik, J. T., [1956] '"Prière de Nabonide" et autres écrits d'un cycle de Daniel', *RB* 63 (1956), 407–15.

— [1957] 'Deux documents inédites du désert de Juda', *Biblica* 38 (1957), 245–68.

— [1971] 'Problèmes de la littérature hénochique à la lumière des fragments araméens de Qumran', *HTR* 64 (1971), 333–78.

— [1976] *The Books of Enoch: Aramaic Fragments of Qumran, Cave 4.* Oxford 1976.

Miller, P. D., Jr, [1964] 'Two Critical Notes on Psalm 68 and Deuteronomy 33', *HTR* 57 (1964), 240–3.

— [1973] *The Divine Warrior in Early Israel.* Cambridge, Mass., 1973.

Moltmann, J., [1967] *The Theology of Hope* (1966). ET London 1967.

— [1974] *Man. Christian Anthropology on the Conflict of the Present* (1971). ET London 1974.

Morgenstern, J., [1939] 'The Mythological Background of Psalm 82', *HUCA* 14 (1939), 29–136.

— [1955] 'The Calendar of the Book of Jubilees', *VT* 5 (1955), 34–76.

— [1964] 'The Cultic Setting of the Enthronement Psalms', *HUCA* 35 (1964), 1–42.

Mowinckel, S., [1927] *Le Décalogue.* Paris 1927.

— [1956] *He that Cometh.* ET Oxford 1956.

Mowry, L., [1962] 'Parable', IDB 3 (Nashville 1962), 649–55.

Müller, H. P., [1972] 'Mantische Weisheit und Apocalyptik', *VTS* 22 (1972). 268–83.

Murray, R., [1975] *Symbols of Church and Kingdom.* Cambridge 1975.

— [1982a] 'Prophecy and the Cult', in Coggins, R., Knibb, M. and Phillips, A., eds., *Israel's Prophetic Tradition: Essays in Honour of Peter Ackroyd* (London 1982), 200–16.

— [1982b] 'Jews, Hebrews and Christians: some needed distinctions', *NT* 24 (1982), 194–208.

— [1984] 'The Origin of Aramaic 'Ir, Angel', *Orientalia* 53 (1984), 303–17.

— [1985] '"Disaffected Judaism" and Early Christianity: Some Predisposing Factors', in Neusner, J. and Frerichs, E. S., ed., *"To See Ourselves as Others See Us": Christians, Jews, "Others" in Late Antiquity* (Chico, Ca., 1985), 263–81.

Nardi, S. S., [1960] *The Seven Scrolls.* Jerusalem 1960.

Neugebauer, O., [1957] *The Exact Sciences in Antiquity.* Providence 1957².

— [1964] 'Notes on Ethiopic Astronomy', *Orientalia* 33 (1964), 49–71.

— [1981] *The Astronomical Chapters of the Ethiopic Book of Enoch (72–82): Translation and Commentary.* Copenhagen 1981.

Neusner, J., [1966] *The History of the Jews in Babylonia*, 5 vols. (Leiden 1965–70); vol. 2, 1966.

— ed., [1970] *Religions in Antiquity. Essays in Memory of E. R. Goodenough.* Leiden 1970.

Nicholson, E. W., [1965] 'The Meaning of the Expression '*am ha'ares* in the Old Testament', *JSS* 10 (1965), 59–66.

— [1967] *Deuteronomy and Tradition.* Oxford 1967.

— [1970] *Preaching to the Exiles.* Oxford 1970.

— [1973] *Exodus and Sinai in History and Tradition.* Oxford 1973.

— [1974] 'The Interpretation of Ex xxiv 9–11', *VT* 24 (1974), 77–97.

— [1975] 'The Antiquity of the Tradition in Ex xxiv 9–11', *VT* 25 (1975), 69–79.

— [1976] 'The Origin of the Tradition in Ex xxiv 9–11', *VT* 26 (1976), 148–60.

Nickelsburg, G. W. E., [1972] *Resurrection, Immortality and Eternal Life in Intertestamental Judaism.* Cambridge, Mass., 1972.

— [1977a] 'The Apocalyptic Message of 1 Enoch 92–105', *CBQ* 39 (1977), 309–28.

— [1977b] 'Apocalyptic and Myth in 1 Enoch 6–11', *JBL* 96 (1977), 383–405.

— [1978] 'Reflections upon Reflections: A Response to John Collins' "Methodological Issues in the Study of 1 Enoch"', in Achtemeier, P. J., ed., *SBL Seminar Papers*, vol. 1 (1978) (q.v.).

— [1981] 'Enoch, Levi and Peter: Recipients of Revelation in Upper Galilee', *JBL* 100 (1981), 575–600.

— [1982] 'The Epistle of Enoch and the Qumran Literature', *JJS* 33 (1982), 333–48.

Niditch, S., [1980] 'The Visionary', in Collins, J. J., and Nickelsburg, G. W. E., *Ideal Figures . . .* (1980) (q.v.), 153–79.

Nineham, D. E., [1963] *The Gospel of St Mark.* Harmondsworth 1963.

Noth, M., [1960] *The History of Israel* (1958). ET London 1960².

— [1962] *Exodus* (1959). ET London 1962.

Odeberg, H., [1928] *3 Enoch, or The Hebrew Book of Enoch.* Cambridge 1928; reprint New York 1973.

Otzen, B., [1980] 'The Use of Myth in Genesis', in Otzen, B., and Others, *Myths in the Old Testament* (1976). ET London, 1980.

Parunak, H. van D., [1980] 'The Literary Architecture of Ezekiel's *Mar'ot 'Elohim*', *JBL* 99 (1980), 61–74.

Patai, R., [1939] 'The Control of Rain in Ancient Palestine', *HUCA* 14 (1939), 251–86.

Perlitt, L., [1969] *Bundestheologie im Alten Testament*, WMANT 26. Neukirchen-Vluyn 1969.

Perrin, N., [1974] *The New Testament: An Introduction.* New York 1974.

Petersen, D. L., [1977] *Late Israelite Prophecy: Studies in Deutero-Prophetic Literature and in Chronicles* (SBL Monograph Series 23). Missoula, Mon. 1977.

Philonenko, M., [1968] *Joseph et Aséneth. Introduction, texte critique, traduction et notes* (SPB 13). Leiden 1968.

Pinard, W. J., [1957] 'Spontaneous Imagery: its nature, therapeutic value and effect on personality structure', in *Boston University Graduate Journal* 5 (1957), 150–3.

Porta, G. B., [1957] *Natural Magick*. ET 1658 from the Italian 1589; reproduction, New York 1957.

Porten, B., [1968] *Archives from Elephantine*. Berkeley 1968.

Raitt, T. M., [1977] *The Theology of the Exile*. Philadelphia 1977.

Rapoport, S., [1928] *Myths and Legends of Ancient Israel*. London 1928.

Rendtorff, R., [1977a] *Das überlieferungsgeschichtliche Problem des Pentateuch*, BZAW 147, 1977.

— [1977b] 'The "Yahwist" as Theologian? The Dilemma of Pentateuchal Criticism', *JSOT* 3 (1977), 2–10.

— [1977c] 'Pentateuchal Studies on the Move', *JSOT* 3 (1977), 43–5.

Reventlow, H. Graf, [1971] 'A Syncretistic Enthronement Hymn in Is 9, 1–6', *Ugarit-Forschungen* 3 (1971), 321–5.

Reviv, H., [1982] 'The Traditions Concerning the Inception of the Legal System in Israel: Significance and Dating', *ZAW* 94 (1982), 566–75.

Riesenfeld, H., [1947] *Jésus transfiguré*. Copenhagen 1947.

Ringgren, H., [1966] *Israelite Religion* (1963). ET London 1966.

Robinson, J. A. T., [1976] *Re-dating the New Testament*. London 1976.

Robinson, J. M. and Koester, H., [1971] *Trajectories through Early Christianity*. Philadelphia 1971.

Rössler, D., [1960] *Gesetz und Geschichte. Untersuchungen zur Theologie der jüdischen Apokalyptik und der pharisäischen Orthodoxie* (WMANT 3). Neukirchen-Vluyn 1960.

Rowland, C., [1979] 'The Visions of God in Apocalyptic Literature', *JSJ* 10 (1979), 137–54.

— [1982] *The Open Heaven*: A Study of Apocalyptic in Judaism and Christianity. London 1982.

Rowley, H. H., [1958] 'The Book of Job and its Meaning', *BJRL* 41 (1958), 167–207.

— [1962] 'The Samaritan Schism in Legend and History', in Anderson, B. W., and Harrelson, W., *Israel's Prophetic Heritage* (1962) (q.v.), 208–22.

— [1963] *From Moses to Qumran*. London 1963.

Rowston, D. J., [1975] 'The Most Neglected Book in the New Testament', *NTS* 21 (1975), 554–63.

Sanders, E. P., [1977] *Paul and Palestinian Judaism*. London 1977.

— [1985] *Jesus and Judaism*. London 1985.

Sanders, J. A., [1969] 'Dissenting Deities and Philippians 2.1–11', *JBL* 88 (1969), 279–90.

— [1972] *Torah and Canon*. Philadelphia 1972.

Sandmel, S., [1962] 'Parallelomania', *JBL* 81(1962), 1–13.

Schechter, S., [1910] *Documents of the Jewish Sectaries, I*. Cambridge 1910.

Schillebeeckx, E., [1980] *Christ: The Christian Experience in the Modern World* (1977). ET London 1980.

Schmid, H. H., [1976] *Der sogenannte Jahwist*. Zürich 1976.

— [1977] 'In Search of New Approaches in Pentateuchal Research', *JSOT* 3 (1977), 33–42.

Schmithals, W., [1975] *The Apocalyptic Movement* (1973). ET Nashville 1975.

Scholem, G., [1960] *Jewish Gnosticism, Merkabah Mysticism and the Talmudic Tradition.* New York 1960.

— [1965] *Major Trends in Jewish Mysticism.* New York 1965.

Schultz, D. R., [1978] 'The Origin of Sin in Irenaeus and in Jewish Pseudepigraphical Literature', *VigChr* 32 (1972), 161–90.

Schultz, J. P., [1971] 'Angelic Opposition to the Ascension of Moses and the Revelation of the Law', *JQR* 61 (1971), 282–307.

Segal, A. F., [1978] *Two Powers in Heaven.* Leiden 1978.

Skehan, P. S., [1954] 'A Fragment of the "Song of Moses" (Deut 32) from Qumran', *BASOR* 136 (1954), 12–15.

Smart, J. D., [1967] *History and Theology in the Second Isaiah,* London 1967.

Smith, G. A., [1966] *The Historical Geography of the Holy Land.* 25th edn (1931), reprinted London 1966.

Smith, J. Z., [1970] 'The Prayer of Joseph', in Neusner, J., ed., *Religions in Antiquity* (1970) (q.v.), 253–94.

— [1975] 'Wisdom and Apocalyptic', in Pearson, B. A., ed., *Religious Syncretism in Antiquity: Essays in Conversation with Geo Widengren* (Missoula, Mon., 1975), reprinted in Hanson, P., ed. (1983) (q.v.).

Smith, Morton, [1952] 'The Common Theology of the Ancient Near East', *JBL* 71 (1952), 135–47.

— [1957] 'The Image of God', *BJRL* 40 (1957), 473–512.

— [1971] *Palestinian Parties and Politics that shaped the Old Testament.* London 1971.

— [1978] *Jesus the Magician.* London 1978.

Smith, W. Robertson, [1914] *The Religion of the Semites.* Oxford 1914.

Snijders, L. A., [1954] 'The Meaning of *zar* in the Old Testament', OTStudien 10 (1954], 1–154.

Sperber, A., [1962] *The Bible in Aramaic,* III. Leiden 1962.

Sperber, D., [1965] 'The History of the Menorah', *JJS* 16 (1965), 135–59.

— [1966] 'On Sealing the Abysses', *JSS* 11 (1966), 168–74.

Stanton, G. N., [1974] *Jesus of Nazareth in New Testament Preaching.* Cambridge 1974.

Steiner, G., [1961] *The Death of Tragedy.* London 1961.

Stern, M., [1976] *Greek and Latin Authors on Jews and Judaism,* I. Jerusalem 1976.

Stone, M. E., [1970] 'The Concept of the Messiah in IV Ezra', in Neusner, J., ed., *Religions in Antiquity* (1970) (q.v.), 295–312.

— [1976] 'Lists of Revealed Things in Apocalyptic Literature', in Cross, F. M., Lemke, W. E. and Miller, P. D., Jr, ed., *Magnalia Dei: The Mighty Acts of God. Essays . . . in Memory of G. E. Wright* (Garden City, New York, 1976), 414–52.

— [1977, 1979] and Greenfield, J. C. (q.v.).

— [1980] *Scriptures, Sects and Visions.* Philadelphia 1980.

— [1980a] 'New Light on the Third Century' (ch. 4 of the above).

— [1980b] 'Enoch and Apocalyptic Origins' (ch. 5 of the above). (These are also included in Hanson, P., ed. [1983].)

Suter, D. W., [1978] 'Apocalyptic Patterns in the Similitudes of Enoch', in Achtemeier, P. J. ed., *SBL 1978 Seminar Papers*, vol. 1 (q.v.), 1–11.

— [1979a] *Tradition and Composition in the Parables of Enoch* (SBL Dissertation Series 47), Missoula, Mon., 1979.

— [1979b] 'Fallen Angel, Fallen Priest. The Problem of Family Purity in 1 Enoch 6–16', *HUCA* 50 (1979), 115–35.

— [1981a] 'Weighed in the Balance: The Similitudes of Enoch in Recent Research', *RelStRev* 7 (1981), 217–21.

— [1981b] '*Mašal* in the Similitudes of Enoch', *JBL* 100 (1981), 191–212.

Theisohn, J., [1975] *Der auserwählter Richter. Untersuchungen zum traditionsgeschichtlichen Ort der Menschensohngestalt der Bilderreden des äthiopischen Henoch* (Studien zur Umwelt des NT, 12). Göttingen 1975.

Thomas, D. W., [1956] 'Zechariah', in *Interpreter's Bible*, vol. 6. Nashville – New York, 1956.

— [1968] 'A Consideration of Isaiah LIII in the Light of Recent Textual and Philological Study', *ETL* 44 (1968), 79–86.

Thompson, P. E. S., [1971] 'The Yahwist Creation Story', *VT* 21 (1971), 147–208.

Thorndike, J. P., [1961] 'The Apocalypse of Weeks and the Qumran Sect', *RQ* 10 (1961), 163–84.

Torrey, C. C., [1928] *The Second Isaiah*. Edinburgh 1928.

VanderKam, J. C., [1979] 'The Origin, Character, and Early History of the 364-Day Calendar: A Reassessment of Jaubert's Hypotheses', *CBQ* 41 (1979), 390–411.

— [1983] '1 Enoch 77, 3 and a Babylonian Map of the World', *RQ* 11 (1983), 271–78.

— [1984a] *Enoch and the Growth of an Apocalyptic Tradition* (*CBQ* Monograph Series 16). Washington, D.C., 1984.

— [1984b] 'Studies in the Apocalypse of Weeks', *CBQ* 64 (1984), 571–23.

van Dijk, H. J., [1968] *Ezekiel's Prophecy on Tyre (Ez 26.1–28.19)* (Biblica et Orientalia 20). Rome 1968.

van Selms, A., [1982] 'The Expression "The Holy One of Israel"', in Delsman, W. C. and Others, ed., *Von Kanaan bis Kerala: Festschrift für J. P. M. van der Ploeg* (Alter Orient und Altes Testament 211) (Neukirchen-Vluyn 1982), 257–69.

Van Seters, J., [1975] *Abraham in History and Tradition*. Yale 1975.

— [1977] 'The Yahwist as Theologian? A Response', *JSOT* 3 (1977), 15–19.

— [1980] 'The Religion of the Patriarchs in Genesis', *Biblica* 61 (1980), 220–3.

von der Osten-Sacken, P., [1969] *Gott und Belial*. Göttingen 1969.

von Rad, G., [1953] *Studies in Deuteronomy*. ET London 1953.

— [1961] *Genesis*. ET London 1961.

— [1962, 1965] *Old Testament Theology*, 2 vols. Edinburgh 1962, 1965.

— [1966a] *The Problem of the Hexateuch and other Essays*. ET Edinburgh 1966.

— [1966b] *Deuteronomy*. ET London 1966.

— [1972] *Wisdom in Israel*. ET London 1972.

De Vaux, R., [1965] *Ancient Israel*. ET London 1965.

Vermes, G., [1978] 'The Present State of the "Son of Man" Debate', *JJS* 29 (1978), 123–34.

Vriezen, T. C., [1962] 'Essentials of the Theology of Isaiah', in Anderson, B. W., and Harrelson, W., *Israel's Prophetic Heritage* [1962] (q.v.), 128–46.

293

Wagner, N. E., [1977] 'A Response to Professor Rolf Rendtorff', *JSOT* 3 (1977), 20–7.

Weinfeld, M., [1972] *Deuteronomy and the Deuteronomic School*. Oxford 1972.

Weiser, A., [1962] *The Psalms*. ET London 1962.

Weiss, G., [1973] 'Shamanism and Priesthood in the Light of the Campa Ayahuasca Ceremony', in Harner, M. J., ed., *Hallucinogens and Shamanism* (1973) (q.v.).

Welch, A. C., [1925] 'When was the Worship of Israel Centralised at the Temple?', *ZAW* 43 (1925), 250–3.

Wernberg-Møller, P., [1958] 'Two Notes', *VT* 8 (1958), 305–8.

Westermann, C., [1969] *Isaiah 40-66*. ET London 1969.

Whybray, R. N., [1965] *Wisdom in Proverbs*. London 1965.

— [1971] *The Heavenly Counsellor in Isaiah 40*. Cambridge 1971.

— [1974] *The Intellectual Tradition in the Old Testament*, BZAW 135 (1974).

Widengren, G., [1950] *The Ascension of the Apostle and the Heavenly Book*. Uppsala 1950.

— [1951] *The King and the Tree of Life in Ancient Near Eastern Religion*, Uppsala 1951.

— [1958] 'Hebrew Myths and their Interpretation', in Hooke, S. H., ed., *Myth, Ritual and Kingship*, Oxford 1958.

— [1970] 'What do we know about Moses?', in Durham, J. I. and Porter, J. R., ed., *Proclamation and Presence. Essays in Honour of G. Henton Davies*. London 1970.

Wifall, W., [1980a] 'El Shaddai or El of the Fields', *ZAW* 92 (1980), 24–32.

— [1980b] 'The Sea of Reeds as Sheol', *ZAW* 92 (1980), 325–32.

Wilson, C., [1978] *Mysteries*. London 1978.

Wright, G. E., [1962] 'The Lawsuit of God: A Form-Critical Study of Deuteronomy 32', in Anderson, B. W., and Harrelson, W., *Israel's Prophetic Heritage* (1962) (q.v.), 26–67.

Yadin, Y., [1985] *The Temple Scroll: The Hidden Law of the Dead Sea Sect*. London 1985.

Yarden, L., [1971] *The Tree of Light*. London 1971.

York, A. D., [1984] 'The Dating of Targumic Literature', *JSJ* 15 (1984), 49–62.

Zerafa, P. P., [1978] *The Wisdom of God in the Book of Job*. Rome 1978.

Zimmerli, W., [1969] *Ezechiel*. Neukirchen-Vluyn 1969.

INDEX OF PRIMARY SOURCES

DEUTEROCANONICAL BOOKS

NEW TESTAMENT

OTHER WRITINGS

INDEX OF SUBJECTS

INDEX OF MODERN AUTHORS

313

Printed in the United Kingdom
by Lightning Source UK Ltd.
105326UKS00001B/31-66